Dissertation

A Functional, Comprehensive and Extensible Multi-Platform Querying and Transformation Approach

Tassilo Horn

horn@uni-koblenz.de

tsdh80@gmail.com

January 15, 2016

UNIVERSITÄT
KOBLENZ · LANDAU
Faculty 4: Computer Science

Cover background designed by Freepik

Bibliografische Information der Deutschen Nationalbibliothek

Die Deutsche Nationalbibliothek verzeichnet diese Publikation in der Deutschen Nationalbibliografie; detaillierte bibliografische Daten sind im Internet über http://dnb.d-nb.de abrufbar.

ISBN 978-3-8325-4291-7

Logos Verlag Berlin GmbH
Comeniushof, Gubener Str. 47,
10243 Berlin
Tel.: +49 (0)30 42 85 10 90
Fax: +49 (0)30 42 85 10 92
INTERNET: http://www.logos-verlag.de

Thesis approved by the doctoral committee of the Faculty 4: Computer Science at the University Koblenz-Landau in fulfillment with the requirements for obtaining the degree *Doktor der Naturwissenschaften (Dr. rer. nat.).*

Date of defense: June 1, 2016

Chair (doctoral comm.):	J.-Prof. Dr. Kai Lawonn (University of Koblenz-Landau)
First referee:	Prof. Dr. Jürgen Ebert (University of Koblenz-Landau)
Second referee:	Prof. Dr. Albert Zündorf (University of Kassel)

Abstract

Nowadays, models have become central artifacts in several application areas such as software development, reverse and re-engineering, simulation and verification, and optimization. Their benefits are that they are precisely defined in terms of metamodels and that they can be processed by generic tools.

In whichever application area models are used, there is the need for analyzing and extracting information from them using querying tools and for manipulating models or generating new models from given models using transformations.

This thesis is about a new model querying and transformation approach called *FunnyQT* which is realized as a set of APIs and embedded domain-specific languages (DSLs) in the JVM-based functional Lisp-dialect Clojure.

Founded on a powerful model management and manipulation API, FunnyQT provides querying services such as comprehensions, quantified expressions, regular path expressions, logic-based, relational model querying, and pattern matching.

On the transformation side, it supports the definition of typical unidirectional model-to-model transformations, of complex in-place transformations based on rules using pattern matching for identifying structures of interest and rewriting them, it supports defining bidirectional transformations that built upon its relational querying capabilities in order to synchronize information back and forth between two models, and it supports a new kind of co-evolution transformations that allow for evolving a model together with its metamodel simultaneously.

Next to the querying and transformation services, several auxiliary services such as polymorphic functions, model visualization, and XML processing are supported, too.

There are several properties which make FunnyQT unique. First of all, it is just a Clojure library. Thus, a FunnyQT query or a transformation is essentially a Clojure program. However, most higher-level querying and transformation services are provided as task-oriented embedded DSLs which use Clojure's powerful macro-system to support the users with tailor-made language constructs important for the task at hand.

Since queries and transformations are essentially just Clojure programs, they may use any Clojure or Java library for their own purpose. For example, FunnyQT has no service dedicated to model-to-text transformations because users can just use some existing JVM-based templating tool together with FunnyQT's querying service for this purpose.

Conversely, just like every Clojure program, FunnyQT queries and transformations compile to normal JVM byte-code and can easily be called from other JVM languages such as Java.

Furthermore, FunnyQT is platform-independent and designed with extensibility in mind. By default, it supports the Eclipse Modeling Framework and JGraLab, and support for other modeling frameworks can be added with minimal effort and without having to modify the respective framework's classes or FunnyQT itself.

Lastly, because FunnyQT is embedded in a functional language, it has a functional emphasis itself. Every query and every transformation compiles to a function which can be passed around, given to higher-order functions, or be parametrized with other functions itself.

Zusammenfassung

In vielen Anwendungsgebieten wie Software-Entwicklung, Reverse- und Re-Engineering, Simulation und Verifikation und Optimierung spielen Modelle heute eine zentrale Rolle. Zu ihren Vorteilen gehört, dass sie durch ihr Metamodell präzise definiert sind und von generischen Tools verarbeitet werden können.

Zu den wichtigsten Tools im Umgang mit Modellen gehören Anfragesprachen, mit denen sich Modelle analysieren und Informationen extrahieren lassen. Weiterhin spielen Transformationen eine wichtige Rolle, welche Modelle manipulieren oder neue Modelle aus vorhandenen Modellen generieren.

Das Thema dieser Arbeit ist ein neuer Modellanfrage- und Transformationsansatz namens *FunnyQT*, der als Menge von APIs und domänenspezifischen Sprachen (DSLs) in den funktionalen Lisp-Dialekt Clojure eingebettet ist.

Basierend auf einer leistungsstarken API zur Verwaltung und Manipulation von Modellen bietet FunnyQT Anfragekonstrukte wie Comprehensions, quantifizierte Ausdrücke, reguläre Pfadausdrücke, relationale Anfragen und Pattern Matching.

Auf Seite der Transformationen unterstützt es die Definition typischer unidirektionaler Modell-zu-Modell-Transformationen, und es unterstützt die Definition komplexer In-Place-Transformationen basierend auf Regeln, die mittels Pattern Matching Strukturen im Modell finden und manipulieren. Zudem können bidirektionale Transformationen definiert werden, welche Informationen zwischen zwei Modellen in jedwede Richtung synchronisieren können. Weiterhin wird eine neue Art von Co-Evolutions-Transformationen ermöglicht, welche ein Metamodell evolvieren und dabei gleichzeitig ein Instanzmodell anpassen.

Neben den Anfrage- und Tranformationsdiensten werden auch noch einige weitere Hilfsdienste bereitgestellt. Dazu gehören polymorphe Funktionen, Modell-Visualisierung und XML-Verarbeitung.

FunnyQT besitzt einige Eigenschaften, die es einzigartig machen. Zunächst ist FunnyQT nur eine gewöhnliche Clojure-Bibliothek. Anfragen und Transformationen sind also gewöhnliche Clojure-Programme. Allerdings benutzt FunnyQT Clojures leistungsfähiges Makro-System, um die meisten seiner höherwertigen Dienste als eingebettete, domänenspezifische Sprachen mit speziell für die jeweilige Aufgabe maßgeschneiderten Sprachkonstrukten anzubieten.

Da Anfragen und Transformationen gewöhnliche Clojure-Programme sind, können sie selbst auch beliebige Clojure- und Java-Bibliotheken verwenden. Beispielsweise bietet FunnyQT keine spezialisierte API oder DSL zur Definition von Modell-zu-Text-Transformationen weil diese ebensogut mittels FunnyQTs Anfrage-API und einem beliebigen existierenden Templating-Tool definiert werden können.

Umgekehrt kompilieren FunnyQT-Anfragen und Transformationen wie alle Clojure-Programme zu gewöhnlichem JVM-Bytecode und können somit leicht aus anderen JVM-Sprachen wie Java aufgerufen werden.

Eine weitere Besonderheit ist FunnyQTs Plattformunabhängigkeit. Es unterstützt Modelle vom Eclipse Modeling Framework und von JGraLab, und Unterstützung für weitere Modellierungs-Frameworks kann mit minimalem Aufwand und ohne Änderungen an ebendiesen oder FunnyQT hinzugefügt werden.

viii

Da FunnyQT in eine funktionale Sprache eingebettet ist, hat es selbst eine überwiegend funktionale Ausrichtung. Jede Anfrage und jede Transformation ist eine Funktion, welche an Funktionen höherer Ordnung übergeben oder selbst mit anderen Funktionen parametrisiert werden kann.

Acknowledgements

First and foremost, my biggest thanks goes to my doctoral adviser Jürgen Ebert for supporting my ideas and shaping my works through constructive critics and hours of fruitful discussions.

The work on this thesis and the implementation wouldn't have been possible without a joyful working environment which has been guaranteed by my awesome colleagues Volker, Daniel, Hannes, Mahdi, and Andi. Thanks for that!

I'm also very grateful to Albert Zündorf for being my second referee. He has also been my hardest competitor at several editions of the Transformation Tool Contest. As a reward, I'll leave all TTC awards in 2016 to you!

Also a big thanks to my wife Nicole for all her love and support. And to our son Quentin for just being the sunshine he is.

Finally, a big thank you to my parents and parents in law for their support. Without you, organizing our life would hardly be possible.

Oh, and Leines, thanks for being a good dog!

Contents

Part I

Introduction

Chapter 1

Context and Motivation

With the advent of *model-driven engineering* (*MDE*, [Ken02; Sch06; BCW12]), models have become central artifacts in software engineering nowadays which provide a more abstract view on the system under development. Different models concentrate on different aspects and together provide a complete view on the system. They provide a powerful means for managing complexity by allowing to separate concerns and describe complex systems from different points of view and using different levels of abstraction.

Models facilitate communication among developers and all other stakeholders. Whereas code is understandable only for IT experts, especially the rather abstract models developed in the early phases of a project can be understood and validated by domain experts reducing the risk of design errors which are hard to fix later on.

Another strength of models is that they are defined using modeling languages such as the UML [OMG15c], SysML [OMG15b], or BPMN [OMG11a] which are precisely defined by a metamodel and possibly further constraints expressed, e.g., using OCL [OMG14b]. Therefore, they cannot be structurally incorrect and they can be queried for extracting information.

Transformations play a key role in MDE. The idea is that large parts of the final system can be generated by a chain of model transformations. Starting with very abstract models, these are refined incrementally and the final model is essentially the code realizing the envisioned system using concrete technologies.

For example, OMG's *model-driven architecture* (*MDA*, [OMG14a]) categorizes models into three different architectural layers. Business and domain models (also called computation independent models, CIMs) describe the business domain of a system and its requirements, i.e., they describe the actual domain and not how that domain is to be represented within the system. Logical system models (also called platform independent models, PIMs) describe the components which constitute the system and their interactions without respect to concrete technologies like programming languages, frameworks, or libraries. Finally, implementation models (also called platform specific models, PSMs) enrich the logical system models with knowledge about concrete platforms and technologies.

3

In the MDA vision, model transformations are used in order to come from more abstract to more concrete models. From the CIM models, initial PIMs can be generated which are then extended incrementally until the complete system structure and application logic is defined by them. Thereafter, these PIMs are transformed to PSMs where the transformations add platform specifics. E.g., there might be two different transformations which take a PIM and generate a PSM where one transformation targets the Java EE platform and the other transformation targets the .NET platform.

With MDE and MDA, the most important kind of transformations are out-place or model-to-model transformations that generate new target models from given source models, the final model being the actual source code of the runnable system for a concrete platform and technology. However, this process is usually not linear. Oftentimes, different models are developed separately and need to be synchronized later on. This is a use-case for bidirectional transformations which are able to propagate changes between two models back and forth.

Modeling, querying, and transformation are not limited to software development but many other application areas exist, too.

For example, *executable models* are a further trend nowadays. Here, a system is fully specified by a model which is not eventually transformed to code in some programming language. Instead, the model itself is interpreted in order to execute the system. Such a model interpreter obviously relies heavily on querying and it can be implemented as an in-place transformation which changes the system's model in place. There is a subset of the UML called foundational UML (fUML, [OMG13]) with a precisely specified behavioral semantics and a generic model execution environment for modeling languages whose behavioral semantics is defined using fUML has been developed already in [May14].

Alternatively, [Der14] introduces a realization concept for systems where code and models co-exist. In such a system, performance-critical parts may be realized by code whereas other parts may be realized by models which are interpreted at runtime. Having models at runtime allows for more flexibility because models can be modified so that the system's behavior can be adapted (e.g., by transformations) while it is running.

Models also play an important role in *reverse engineering* [Ebe+02; Bru+14] where different artifacts of legacy systems, e.g., its documentation and source code, are parsed into models which are then analyzed by model queries in order to regain an understanding of the system. For the same purpose, model transformations can be used for generating more abstract models from the overly detailed source code models.

With *re-engineering* and *software migration* [FHR11; Wag14], the reverse engineering activities are followed by forward engineering activities which refactor the legacy system to re-establish its maintainability or to port its functionality to different architectures or to different platforms. These forward engineering activities can be supported by transformations, e.g., refactorings are usually implemented as in-place transformations and migrations are frequently realized as out-place transformations.

Yet another application field is *simulation and verification* [Lar03; ZR11] where the state of a system is represented by a model and the behavior of the system is defined in terms of transformations which transition the system from one state into another state. Thereby, different properties can be checked through queries, e.g., invariants which must be satisfied in all states.

In recent years, there is a trend away from general modeling languages like the UML towards *domain-specific modeling languages* (DSML, e.g., in [BOM15; TFW14; KAL14]) which allow for raising the abstraction level even further by providing custom-tailored constructs for modeling the aspects relevant in a concrete domain. Such DSMLs can be specific to one single company or even project and therefore they can evolve rapidly in order to keep up with the needs of the domain. However, when a modeling language evolves, there is a chance that old models conforming to an earlier version of the language don't conform to the new version anymore. Thus, there is a need for co-evolution transformations which support upgrading models conforming to old metamodel versions to the new metamodel version.

So to summarize, different modeling application areas require different querying and transformation capabilities. Whereas there is no clear categorization for different kinds of queries[1], there are four somewhat distinct kinds of transformations:

1. *Out-place transformations* (also called *model-to-model transformations*) create new target models for given source models. Usually, the modeling languages (metamodels) of the source and target models are different, thus, out-place transformations are translators from one modeling language to another modeling language.
2. *In-place transformations* change a given model in place. Usually, they consist of rules that define which parts of the model have to be changed in which way. A typical use-case for in-place transformations are refactorings.
3. *Bidirectional transformations* are out-place transformations where there is no strict distinction of which model is the source model and which model is the target model. Given one model, the transformation can generate the respective other model. And given two existing models, it can check whether the two models are consistent with respect to the transformation rules. If they are not, it can modify one of the two models in order to regain consistency again.
4. *Co-evolution transformations* are transformations which update models conforming to version i of a modeling language so that the updated models conform to version j of that language. How this is achieved technically, e.g., in-place or out-place, is not important here. The main motivation is to reduce the effort needed. That is, the developer should not need to specify a full transformation from models conforming to version i models conforming to version j but he should only need to deal with the parts of the language which actually changed.

From a very high-level point of view, all four above mentioned transformation kinds are well-supported by the querying and transformation languages and tools which exist today. However, there are certain issues with the current state of the art which are to be addressed by this thesis.

---

[1]One could say there are SQL-like comprehensions, constraints (e.g., quantified expressions), pattern matching, logic-based querying, ...

Most querying and transformation tools target just one kind of models, i.e., they are specifically designed for one single model representation. Usually, this model representation is the one provided by the Eclipse Modeling Framework (EMF, [Ste+09]) which is not overly astonishing given that this framework is the de-facto standard nowadays. But still there are other modeling frameworks around (some are even specific to a concrete transformation tool) which have qualities that might make them a better fit in concrete scenarios. Ideally, the choice of a modeling framework and the choice of querying and transformation tools should be orthogonal issues which don't influence each other. This implies that querying and transformation tools should be generic, i.e., they should be able to work with any model representation.

Model management is concerned with loading and storing of models and query results and with defining algorithms working on models and their elements. Right now, querying and transformation approaches usually don't support model management at all. Therefore, scripting queries and transformations and defining algorithms on models has to be done in a general purpose programming language such as Java using the respective modeling framework's API. This is inconvenient and obviously not generic at all. Model management is the foundation of querying and transformation and as such it should be provided as a first-class service.

Furthermore, current querying approaches are rather inflexible and limited. Usually, they provide only few querying concepts, e.g., one or two out of SQL-like comprehensions, powerful path expressions, logic-based querying, or pattern matching. Each one has its use-cases but ideally one should be able to mix them arbitrarily.

The same situation applies to transformation languages. Most current approaches implement just one single kind of transformations, may it be in-place, out-place, or bidirectional transformations. Thus, when really living the model-driven idea, one needs to use more than one language and tool which requires more learning effort and there is a risk of running into interoperability problems. What is needed is a comprehensive approach where all common querying and transformation services are provided in a seamless manner.

With respect to expressiveness and reusability, there is a lot to be learned from functional languages. Queries and transformations should be represented using proper abstractions. They should be first-class objects that can be passed around, be composed using higher-order functions and be parametrized with other queries and transformations themselves.

Concerning interoperability, queries and functions should be equally accessible and callable from general purpose programming languages like Java. Many current approaches provide APIs which can be used to load queries or transformations from files and then execute them but this is usually not very intuitive. It would be better if queries and transformations were compiled directly to classes which can be instantiated and executed immediately. This would provide a seamless experience when using queries and transformations as integral parts of applications.

In the opposite direction, right now queries and transformations are usually isolated from their surrounding, i.e., they cannot access information which is not represented by models. Ideally, queries and transformations defined using a dedicated approach should be as flexible in this respect as queries and transformations being defined using a general purpose programming language. For example, it is easy to conceive transformations which query a relational database in addition to models, or queries which communicate with remote services over a network.

Last but not least, the usability of most current approaches when defining queries and transformations is far from perfect at least when being compared with the way how programs in many modern languages can be developed today. With the former, changing a query or transformation usually entails editing the definition followed by re-executing it against some test models. The latter step requires the start of a new execution environment, loading the models (which is very time-consuming at least with large models), executing the query or transformation, and inspecting its result. Many modern programming languages provide support for interactive development where editors and IDEs are connected to a life execution environment at all times. After changing some definition in the code, only this single definition is transferred to the execution environment and replaces its former version. Therefore, changes can be re-tested instantly without the need to restart the execution environment and setup the test context anew. This capability provides a much shorter feedback loop and allows for developing complex queries and transformations incrementally.

In the following, the requirements of the envisioned model querying and transformation approach which is going to be to conceptualized and realized in this thesis are defined.

The major goal of the approach is its comprehensiveness, i.e., it should provide the right building blocks for dealing with all model querying and transformation tasks in any of the application areas introduced in the beginning of this chapter. This leads to the functional requirements, i.e., the concrete querying and transformation services it needs to provide. These are introduced in chapter 2 starting on page 9.

Thereafter, chapter 3 starting on page 13 introduces the non-functional requirements that are to be consider during the design of the approach.

Chapter 4 starting on page 17 then sketches a solution concept which provides some insights on how the functional and non-functional requirements are to be fulfilled.

Lastly, chapter 5 starting on page 21 gives an overview of the structure of this thesis.

Chapter 2

Targeted Services

As already mentioned, the primary goal of the envisioned model querying and transformation approach is its comprehensiveness. The set of services it provides should support all common querying and transformation tasks in the different application areas using adequate constructs. In this chapter, these required services are briefly introduced.

Model management. Model management is concerned with all the low-level functionality required in order to handle models. This includes loading and persisting of models, retrieving elements from models, creating and deleting elements, accessing and setting property values of elements, and accessing a model's metamodel. It might also contain auxiliary functionality such as model visualization and persisting of model-related data, e.g., results from queries. Furthermore, a model management language should also provide control flow structures which let users define algorithms on models.

The general model management facilities are already provided by every modeling framework in terms of their application programming interfaces (APIs). However, the envisioned approach should be platform-independent, so its model management functionality has to provide a uniform interface which abstracts away from the APIs of concrete model representations.

Model querying. Model querying means extraction of arbitrary information stored in models. In essence, a query is a function that receives a model and returns some usually simpler structured value, e.g., a scalar value or lists or sets of values.

Queries are typically used for calculating metrics on models, for checking constraints that add further restrictions (invariants) to models in addition to the structural constraints imposed by their metamodel and queries are also at the heart of model transformations where transformations combine querying a source model with creating elements in a target model.

Typical querying concepts include quantified expressions and comprehensions which must obviously be supported by the envisioned approach. Another very expressive concept for querying complex, non-local relationships between elements are regular path expressions which should be supported, too.

Pattern matching. Pattern matching is a special kind of querying. While queries usually encode a concrete algorithm using adequate querying constructs, pattern matching allows for a more declarative and expressive form of querying abstracting away from any concrete algorithm for finding solutions to the query.

With pattern matching, a pattern mimics a structure in the model in terms of nodes and edges connecting these nodes. These nodes and edges include identifiers and typing information and patterns may also include further constraints, e.g., on attribute values.

The matching process then deals with finding occurrences of the pattern in a concrete model. An occurrence in a model is a substructure of the model consisting of elements which correspond to the nodes in the pattern. I.e., every element has to be an instance of the type declared for the corresponding node in the pattern and the elements have to be linked with each other exactly as specified by the pattern's edges[1]. Furthermore, all additional constraints specified in the pattern have to hold.

Pattern matching is a very concise concept especially suited if the structure of the substructures to be matched is local and fixed. It is also at the heart of in-place transformations, thus, the envisioned approach should provide powerful pattern matching capabilities.

In-place transformations. In-place transformations deal with the modification of a given model. The usual concept for in-place transformations is to have rules which use pattern matching in order to find structures of interest in a model and then act on them in arbitrary ways. For example, optimization tasks such as constant folding or refactoring tasks like extract superclass are typical in-place transformation problems where the transformation changes a given abstract syntax graph in-place.

In-place transformations are also used in simulation scenarios where the model under transformation represents the state of a system. Each transformation rule defines a transition from one system state to another system state. Here, important questions are if there is a sequence of rule applications which would transition the system into some erroneous state, e.g., a deadlock, or if all possible rule application sequences lead to one well-defined terminal state.

The envisioned approach should provide means for defining in-place transformations and it should also provide a some kind of state space analysis framework for answering questions like the ones stated in the simulation case above.

Out-place transformations. Out-place or model-to-model transformations are unidirectional transformations which create new target models given a set of source models. Usually, the metamodels of the source models are different from the metamodels of the target models. Therefore, such transformations provide means

---

[1]That is, the mapping from elements in the pattern to elements in the model has to be an isomorphism or at least a homomorphism.

to translate from the abstract syntax of a source language to the abstract syntax of the target language.

The most common way to define out-place transformations is to do it in a rule-based manner where each rule is responsible for creating one kind of target elements for a given kind of source elements. But other approaches are conceivable, too.

Out-place transformations play a very important role in model-driven engineering, thus, they have to be supported by the envisioned approach.

Bidirectional transformations. Whereas in-place transformations deal with the modification of a given model and out-place transformations deal with the generation of new target models given a set of source models, a bidirectional transformation specifies correspondences between a left and a right model without respect to any direction. E.g., a bidirectional transformation between class diagram and database schema models might specify that a class in the left model corresponds to a table in the right model in case they have the same name.

Such bidirectional transformations can be used for creating a new right model for a given left model or vice versa. But bidirectional transformations are more than two out-place transformations integrated into one specification. If they are run on an existing left model and an existing right model, they can check if both models are consistent with respect to the transformation and they can modify the chosen target model in order to achieve consistency again. Therefore, they are important in cases where pairs of models evolve separately and changes in one model should be propagated to the other model.

Therefore, The specification of bidirectional transformations is also to be supported by the envisioned approach.

Co-Evolution transformations. Co-evolution of metamodels and models deals with problems that occur when evolving metamodels. When a metamodel is evolved, models which conform to the previous metamodel version might not be valid instances of the new version. Therefore, they have to be adapted.

Co-evolution of metamodels and models is usually seen as a two-step process. First, the metamodel is evolved resulting in a new version and then all instance models conforming to the previous version have to be adapted in order to conform to the new metamodel version. Several tools have been developed in order to perform the co-adaption step at least semi-automatically.

The envisioned transformation approach should also target co-evolution but using a radically new approach. Instead of considering co-evolution as a two-step process, it should enable evolving the metamodel of a loaded model in-place while keeping the model in conformance simultaneously.

Chapter 3

Design Goals

In this chapter, the general quality goals to be considered during the design of the envisioned approach are introduced. Some are general software quality goals as defined by standards such as ISO/IEC 9126 [ISO01] while others are more specific to programming languages because the envisioned approach is no software tool for end-users but a querying and transformation language.

Usability. Usability is a key factor for the success of a tool or language and there are several aspects influencing it.

One aspect is *commonality*. A user who is already fluent in one querying or transformation language will easily be able to learn another language which provides similar concepts and/or a similar syntax. Therefore, the envisioned approach should borrow well-understood and useful concepts from existing popular languages whenever that makes sense.

Another aspect of usability is *tool support*. A computer language intended to be written by humans is only as good as the tools supporting its use. It is good when a user has a choice in which tools she might use and ideally she can stick to the tools she already uses. This is the usual situation with established general purpose programming languages such as Java where a wide range of excellent editors and IDEs exist, however, for niche languages with restricted scope, the situation is usually less than ideal.

Yet another usability aspect is support for *rapid* and *interactive development* where changes applied to some part of a (query or transformation) specification can instantly be tested and complete solutions can be built in an incremental fashion without going through repeated time-consuming compilation cycles.

Documentation is also an important aspect of usability. Every construct provided to the user should be properly documented and documentation should be a first-class citizen instead of being a kind of secondary appendix which usually becomes outdated rather sooner than later.

Platform Independence and Extensibility.   Nowadays, the Eclipse Modeling Framework [Ste+09] is by far the most widespread modeling framework and most querying and transformation tools are specifically built to handle its models. But there are also some others like JGraLab[1] which is being developed at our institute, or the .NET Modeling Framework[2].

In the end, users should be free to use a model representation which fits their needs best. In other situations, there might be no choice but the kind of models to be used is fixed by someone else. And of course, new modeling frameworks might be developed in the future. Therefore, the envisioned model querying and transformation approach should be as platform independent as possible. It should even allow handling models of different modeling frameworks simultaneously. For example, it should be possible to define model-to-model transformations crossing the boundaries of frameworks, e.g., transformations which query an EMF model in order to create a JGraLab model.

Obviously, it is not feasible to support each and every modeling framework natively, thus the envisioned approach should be extensible by defining some abstract view on models which can be extended upon concrete model representations. This extension mechanism should be applicable by users and it should not induce too much overhead.

Reusability, Flexibility, and Openness.   Reusability is a major concern in software development and there's no doubt that reusability should also be addressed by querying and transformation approaches.

For example, it is reasonable to aggregate queries extracting information from models conforming to a certain metamodel into one metamodel specific querying library. Every transformation that uses this metamodel as its source metamodel should be able to reuse those queries instead of having to define its own versions. The same applies to transformation building blocks such as rules for which sharing between several transformations should be possible, too. On a higher level, also composing queries and transformations from other queries and transformations, or parameterizing queries or transformations with other queries and transformations should be feasible.

Furthermore, the envisioned approach should be flexible and open enough in order to reuse functionality which is not provided by itself. For example, if a transformation needs to query a database in addition to some source models, this should be doable by reusing some external database querying functionality instead of having to support databases directly. Likewise, for model-to-text transformations it would be much better to be able to utilize existing templating languages instead of providing yet another tool-specific solution.

Expressiveness and Conciseness.   Expressiveness in programming languages means that the language allows for notating ideas and algorithms using intuitive concepts without accidental complexity induced by infrastructural code (boilerplate). Conciseness means that this notation is also short.

---

[1]http://jgralab.github.io/ (last visited: 2015-10-31)
[2]https://nmf.codeplex.com/ (last visited: 2015-10-31)

For example, when the task is to invoke a function on every element in a collection and collect the results, a foreach loop is more expressive than a loop with a counter variable because the length of the collection and element access by indices has nothing to do with the actual task. In turn, the higher-order function map: (a -> b) -> [a] -> [b] found in functional languages which receives a function transforming an a to a b and a collection of a elements and which returns a collection of b elements is even more expressive than a foreach loop because it already entails collecting the results of applying the function.

The envisioned approach should provide expressive and concise constructs supporting the concrete querying or transformation task at hand. Especially, it should allow the query or transformation writer to concentrate on the actual problem and the logic required for solving it without blurring the solution with boilerplate code.

For example, important declarative querying concepts such as regular path expressions and pattern matching facilitate expressiveness and conciseness and so do proper abstraction concepts supporting reuse.

Efficiency and Scalability. Efficiency and scalability are further properties required for a comprehensive and generally applicable approach. Both queries and transformations should be evaluated as fast as possible and with larger model sizes their runtime and memory requirements shouldn't increase more than proportionally. In essence, the main influence factor with respect to performance should be the underlying model representation. There should be no significant overhead inherent to the envisioned approach, neither with respect to runtime nor memory requirements.

Whenever possible, techniques for improving the performance, e.g., parallelization, should be supported.

Chapter 4

Solution Concept

As outlined in the previous chapters, the envisioned model querying and transformation approach should be comprehensive providing services for

(1) model management,
(2) model querying including pattern matching,
(3) in-place transformations,
(4) out-place transformations,
(5) bidirectional transformations, and
(6) co-evolution transformations.

Next to the comprehensive set of provided services, it should be *expressive* and *concise*, it should be *generic* and *extensible* with respect to model representations, it should provide *flexible reuse mechanisms*, and it should be *efficient* and *scale well* also for large models. And most importantly, it should be practically *usable* for solving actual querying and transformation tasks.

In order to achieve the above mentioned goals and provide the envisioned services, the implementation of the envisioned approach called *FunnyQT*[1] is realized as an API and a set of *embedded domain-specific languages* (embedded DSLs, [Fow11]) for the JVM-based functional Lisp-dialect Clojure[2]. In the remainder of this chapter, a justification for this design decision is given.

Domain-specific languages are a current trend in software engineering. In contrast to a general-purpose programming language (GPL) such as Java, their aim is to focus on exactly one application domain and provide users with tailor-made constructs for accomplishing the tasks relevant there. In fact, most model querying and transformation languages are DSLs, too[3].

One major advantage of DSLs is that they provide users with expressive, concise, and convenient constructs with an appropriate abstraction level for realizing the tasks relevant in a concrete domain, i.e., they are optimized for usability. For

---

[1]http://funnyqt.org (last visited: 2015-10-26)

[2]http://clojure.org/ (last visited: 2015-10-26)

[3]As notable exceptions, there are some querying and transformation approaches which are realized as APIs in some programming language, e.g., GReTL [EH14] or NMF [HH15]

example, quantified expressions, comprehensions, and role name navigation are concepts one expects from a model querying language and mapping rules implying some kind of traceability relationships are a concept one expects from a typical model-to-model transformation language. Of course, all this can be realized using a GPL and the APIs provided by modeling frameworks. However, a single statement written in a DSL or a simple diagram in a visual DSL might be equivalent to dozens of lines of complex code in a GPL where the actual query or transformation logic realized by the code is blurred by infrastructural aspects (*boilerplate code*).

Because DSLs are limited to a specific purpose by design and have a high abstraction level, they are also easier to learn and provide less possibilities for introducing bugs.

A disadvantage of DSLs is that they are complete computer languages on their own. Each DSL requires its own toolset consisting at least of a parser or a graphical editor in case of a visual DSL and an interpreter or compiler. Given the aspired comprehensiveness of the envisioned approach it becomes apparent that such a DSL would not be very small and every functionality would need to be implemented from scratch. Therefore, the effort would be unacceptably high.

Embedded or *internal* DSLs are a special kind of DSLs. An embedded DSL is usually provided just as a library and enhances a GPL, called its *host language* in this context, with domain-specific constructs. For this purpose, it uses only features provided by its host language itself, i.e., code written in an embedded DSL is also valid code in the host language. The syntactic and semantic autonomy of the embedded DSL depends largely on the features provided by the underlying host language. Languages with *metaprogramming capabilities*, i.e., the ability of a language to treat a program in that language as data which can be manipulated (at compile-time or even runtime), enable further possibilities with respect to development of embedded DSLs.

Embedded DSLs combine the advantages of their general-purpose host languages, e.g., maturity, flexibility, generality, and tool support, with the advantages of DSLs, e.g., expressiveness and ease-of-use in clean-cut domains. They don't require custom tools like parsers and editors but instead rely on the tooling available to their host language. And whenever the constructs provided by an embedded DSL don't suffice in a certain scenario, users can always retract to the host language to fill in the missing pieces.

It should not be neglected that embedded DSLs also have some disadvantages. Whereas a normal, external DSL is limited on purpose, an embedded DSL is open by design and builds upon its host language. Therefore, external DSLs can potentially be much easier to learn, to analyze, and they can have better, domain-specific tool support. In contrast, an embedded DSL requires knowledge of its host language and analyzing an artifact written in an embedded DSL essentially means analyzing a program in the host language.

However, with the goals of the envisioned querying and transformation approach in mind, the benefits of embedded DSLs outweigh their drawbacks. Therefore, the decision has been made to realize the envisioned approach as a set of embedded DSLs, one embedded DSL per targeted service.

Today, the Eclipse Modeling Framework (EMF, [Ste+09]) is by far the most wide-spread modeling framework around. Next to that, there are only few alternatives. Two of them are JGraLab[4] and the .NET Modeling Framework[5]. In addition, some model transformation tools have their own custom model representations.

FunnyQT should be able to handle different model representations and certainly it must support EMF in order to be practically relevant at all. As will be shown later in chapter 8, an approach on genericity which is not founded on conversion or wrapping is highly favored. I.e., the approach should handle all different kinds of models natively by providing some generic view on models which in turn uses the application programming interfaces of the respective frameworks.

Both EMF and JGraLab are implemented in Java which restricts the possibilities of host language choices for FunnyQT to JVM-based languages which are able to call Java APIs, e.g., Java itself, Scala, Clojure, Groovy, JRuby, and Jython[6].

Functional languages provide expressive and concise concepts and abstractions like functions as first-class objects including lexical closures, higher-order functions, and lazy evaluation. Such features can also be used beneficially in the course of model querying and transformation, so the decision has been made to use a JVM-based functional language as the host language of the envisioned approach. From the cited six languages, Clojure is predominantly functional (although not pure). Both Scala and Groovy are multi-paradigm languages which are mainly object-oriented but support many functional concepts, too.

Scala is a statically typed language with strong type inference capabilities whereas Clojure and Groovy are dynamically typed. With Groovy, types may be declared for variables, however, this only leads to Groovy generating appropriate type checks in the relevant byte-code, i.e., typing errors are caught but only at runtime.

In general, all these three languages are viable alternatives for implementing the envisioned approach. For extending existing classes with a generic interface, Clojure provides protocols, Scala provides traits, and Groovy provides mixins. For development of embedded DSLs, Clojure has a powerful macro system, Scala has its implicits, operator overloading, and an experimental macro system, and Groovy also supports operator overloading, is very flexible in its syntax, and also provides a macro system which allows defining transformations on the program's abstract syntax graph at compile time.

In the end, the decision to base the envisioned approach on Clojure is mostly a matter of the author's personal preferences who already had long-term experiences with languages in the Lisp-family in general and Clojure in particular.

To summarize, FunnyQT is a library for the functional Lisp-dialect Clojure which provides a comprehensive set of APIs and embedded DSLs for realizing tasks in various model querying and transformation domains. Concretely, it provides the services enumerated in fig. 4.1 on the following page.

---

[4]http://jgralab.github.io (last visited: 2015-10-26)

[5]https://nmf.codeplex.com/ (last visited: 2015-10-26)

[6]There are several more JVM-based languages but the cited six are the most prominent ones which can be assumed to be mature enough and actively maintained and developed also in the future.

(1) Generic Model Management API
(2) Querying Services
    (a) Functional Querying API
    (b) Embedded Pattern Matching DSL
    (c) Embedded Relational Model Querying DSL
(3) Transformation Services
    (a) Embedded In-Place Transformation DSL
    (b) Out-Place Transformation Services
        (i) Embedded Rule-Based Out-Place Transformation DSL
        (ii) Extensional Out-Place Transformation API
    (c) Embedded Bidirectional Transformation DSL
    (d) Co-Evolution Transformation API

Figure 4.1: FunnyQT Services

The generic model management API provides the ground layer of the approach providing functionality for loading and storing models and accessing model elements and their properties. All other querying and transformation services use this API as their foundation.

FunnyQT provides three kinds of querying services. Firstly, there is a rich functional querying API providing comprehensions, quantified expressions, and regular path expressions. Secondly, there is an embedded pattern matching DSL allowing for defining complex patterns with many advanced features. Lastly, there is a logic-based relational model querying DSL.

Four kinds of transformation services are provided. There is an embedded in-place transformation DSL which allows for defining rules which use pattern matching for finding subgraphs of interest and act on them. There are two different approaches for realizing out-place transformations: one embedded rule-based transformation DSL, and one operational transformation API which defines a transformation's target model in terms of the extensions of its metamodel's constituents. Furthermore, there is support for defining bidirectional transformations, again provided as an embedded DSL. Lastly, FunnyQT also allows to specify co-evolution transformations which operationally evolve a model's metamodel simultaneously with the model itself.

Chapter 5

Structure of this Thesis

Part II: Foundations starting on page 25 introduces the basics required for using FunnyQT and for understanding this thesis. Chapter 6 gives an introduction into the Clojure programming language, and chapter 7 introduces and compares the two directly supported modeling frameworks JGraLab and EMF.

Part III: The FunnyQT Approach starting on page 81 gives a high-level overview. Chapter 8 discusses FunnyQT's approach for achieving genericity. Chapter 9 describes the terminology and conventions which are used and followed both in this thesis and in the implementation. Then, chapter 10 depicts the general architecture of FunnyQT by detailing how it is decomposed into namespaces, each namespace being dedicated to one concrete querying or transformation service, and the dependencies between those namespaces. At last, chapter 11 compares FunnyQT to the Epsilon framework which is similar to FunnyQT because it is also a comprehensive approach.

Part IV: On Model Management and Querying starting on page 105 is devoted to FunnyQT's model management and querying services. First, chapter 12 describes the heart of FunnyQT, the generic model management API upon which all higher-level querying and transformation services are built. Chapter 13 and chapter 14 then introduce the framework-specific core APIs for JGraLab and EMF models, respectively. These are used internally for implementing the generic view on models but they are also provided to users. They also support some details of the respective modeling frameworks which are not exposed through the generic core API. Furthermore, they use the native terminology of the frameworks so some users may prefer them in case they are dealing with just one kind of models anyway. Chapter 15 introduces some more generic model management, querying, and utility services such as regular path expressions, polymorphic functions, persistence of model-related data, XML processing, and model visualization. Finally, chapter 16 discusses related model querying approaches.

Part V: On Pattern Matching starting on page 181 first gives an introduction into this concept by describing the pattern matching features found in many functional languages as well as graph pattern matching services. Chapter 18 then depicts FunnyQT's embedded pattern matching DSL in all its details. Chapter 19 closes this part with a discussion of related approaches.

Part VI: On In-Place Transformations starts on page 221 and is dedicated to transformations which change a model in place. Again, the part starts with an introduction in chapter 20 after which chapter 21 discusses FunnyQT's embedded DSL for defining in-place transformation rules. Thereafter, chapter 22 explains how such transformation rules can be composed using higher-order rule combinators and how their behavior can be modified using rule application modifiers. Chapter 23 describes FunnyQT's state space exploration capabilities which can be used for analyzing in-place transformations. Finally, chapter 24 gives an overview of related approaches and compares them with FunnyQT.

Part VII: On Out-Place Transformation starting on page 259 again gives an introduction into this concept in chapter 25. Thereafter, FunnyQT's two different approaches for defining model-to-model transformations are described: chapter 26 explains a rule-based embedded DSL for doing so, and chapter 27 explains an API which allows to define a target model in terms of the extensions of its metamodel's constituents. The use of both approaches is illustrated using an example. Eventually, chapter 28 discusses related transformation approaches.

Part VIII: On Relational Model Querying is concerned with relational, logic-based model querying and starts on page 311. First, chapter 29 gives an introduction to relational querying in general and then chapter 30 describes FunnyQT's embedded relational model querying DSL. Chapter 31 illustrates the use of this DSL using some examples before chapter 32 discusses related logic-based querying languages.

Part IX: On Bidirectional Transformations starting on page 339 begins with an introduction in chapter 33, and then chapter 34 describes FunnyQT's embedded bidirectional transformation DSL. Chapter 35 classifies the approach according to several characteristics found in the literature. Thereafter, chapter 36 illustrates the use of the embedded bidirectional transformation DSL with a non-trivial example. Finally, chapter 37 discusses related approaches.

Part X: On Co-Evolution Transformations is about FunnyQT's approach to co-evolution transformations, that is, transformations that modify a metamodel in-place and adapt a conforming instance model at the same time. The part starts at page 375 and begins with an introduction in chapter 38 followed by a detailed description of FunnyQT's co-evolution API in chapter 39. Chapter 40 exemplifies the API's usage and chapter 41 discusses the related work in the context of co-evolution of metamodels and models.

Part XI: Finale starting on page 403 concludes this thesis with an evaluation of the approach in chapter 42 and a conclusion and outlook in chapter 43.

Part II

Foundations

Summary

FunnyQT is intended as a comprehensive model querying and transformation approach realized and providing APIs and embedded domain-specific languages in the Clojure programming language. For this reason, some foundational knowledge of the latter is required in order to define queries and transformations using it. Consequently, chapter 6 starting on page 27 gives a brief overview of the Clojure language and discusses the most important concepts and abstractions provided by it which are relevant in the rest of this writing.

FunnyQT is also intended to work with arbitrary model representations. It comes with builtin support for the model representations of JGraLab and the Eclipse Modeling Framework, and support for other model representations can be added without touching FunnyQT's internals. Chapter 7 starting on page 69 gives short overviews of the two directly supported modeling frameworks and compares them briefly.

Chapter 6

The Clojure Programming Language

Clojure is a dynamically typed, general-purpose programming language targeting the Java Virtual Machine[1] (JVM), i.e. Clojure code is directly compiled to JVM bytecode. This implies that Clojure provides wrapper-free access to any existing Java library, which is a very important fact considering that most modeling frameworks such as JGraLab and EMF are implemented in Java.

Clojure is predominantly a functional language, i.e., it has first-class functions including lexical closures, it emphasizes higher-order functions, and it ships with a rich set of immutable, persistent data structures.

In contrast to functional languages like Haskell, Clojure is not purely functional but a slim set of so-called reference types with accompanying functions allow for maintaining mutable state in a clean and consistent manner even in multithreaded systems using a system of software transactional memory and a reactive agent system. These reference types provide mutable references to immutable data structures. However, models are highly mutable data structures, so this important Clojure concept is not relevant for FunnyQT and thus not included in the introduction.

In the remainder of this section, a brief overview of the central Clojure concepts needed for understanding the rest of this work is given. As a convention, whenever a code example is given, the code itself is printed top-level, and the value resulting from evaluating the code is shown in a comment introduced with ;=>. Sometimes, if the code prints to standard out/error, then the output is added as comment between the code and the result.

```
(time (+ 1 2))                    ;; The code
; "Elapsed time: 0.037436 msecs"  ;; Its output
;=> 3                             ;; Its result
```

---

[1]There are also Clojure ports to the CLR, JavaScript, and Python.

6.1   Evaluation Cycle

Clojure facilitates an interactive style of development in that it provides a *read-eval-print-loop* (REPL). The Clojure expressions given in the remainder of this section can be typed in at the REPL. They are read in (R), compiled and evaluated (E), and the results are printed (P) immediately. Thereafter, the REPL accepts further input which makes the loop (L) in REPL.

As already said, Clojure is a Lisp dialect. As such, Clojure source code is represented using the language's own data structures. This property is usually referred to as *homoiconicity*, and it entails very useful metaprogramming capabilities. In contrast to traditional Lisp dialects like Common Lisp [IC96] and Scheme [Spe+10], Clojure not only uses lists but also vectors for representing code, and it reduces the number of parentheses where possible. In any case, humans are encouraged to read the code by its indentation instead of counting parentheses. The Clojure evaluation cycle is illustrated in fig. 6.1.

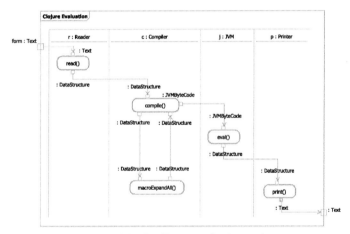

Figure 6.1: The Clojure evaluation cycle

First, the *Reader* parses the source code from a file or the user input given at the REPL. It translates the textual representation into an abstract syntax tree (AST) represented in Clojure's own data structures (e.g., lists, vectors, numbers, symbols, etc.). This data structure is then fed into the *Compiler* which gives a meaning to the elements of the AST, e.g., which symbols denote functions, and then emits JVM byte-code. The byte-code generation is preceded by the *macro-expansion step* allowing for applying user-defined functions, so-called *macros* (see section 6.12 on page 60, to the AST. The byte-code is then evaluated on the JVM delivering the result as some data structure. If the original code was given at the REPL, this result is then translated to a textual representation again by the *Printer*.

6.2 Syntax

The syntax of Clojure and all other Lisp dialects is extremely simple. In contrast to imperative languages, there are no statements but everything is an expression, i.e., its evaluation returns some value. Everything that can be evaluated is called a *form*. If a form is a list, i.e., enclosed in parentheses, it is a function application in prefix notation[2]. Every other form is either a literal or a variable.

```
17                        ;; (1) A literal
;=> 17
*ns*                      ;; (2) A variable
;=> #<Namespace user>
(+ 1 (- 1 2) (*))         ;; (3) A (nested) function call
;=> 1
(println "Hello World!")  ;; (4) Another function call
; Hello World!
;=> nil
```

Literals such as the number 17 evaluate to themselves. The evaluation of a variable results in the value bound to the variable. *ns* is a special variable that is always bound to the current namespace. In (3), there is a nested function call. In each list, the first element is (or refers to) a function (+, -, and * in the example), and all following elements are the arguments passed to the function. A function is evaluated by evaluating all arguments from left to right first, and then calling the function itself. All arithmetic functions are defined for any number of arguments, so the application of + sums up three numbers, the application of - substracts 2 from 1, and the application of * returns the identity element of the multiplication, i.e., 1. As already said, there are no statements but every form is an expression. In (4), the println function is used to print the string "Hello World!" to standard output. This function is useful only for its side-effects, so it always returns nil which is identical to Java's null.

Single-line comments are prefixed with ;. The number of semicolons is not important. A single form, possibly spanning several lines, can be commented by prefixing it with #_.

6.3 Basic Types

As a language running on the JVM, Clojure uses all the basic Java types, e.g., Boolean, Double, Long, Character, and String. Note that integral literals are read as long rather than integer values. Additionally, Clojure has a class for rational numbers. A division between two integral values results in a ratio. In Java, a division between integers results in an integer again and the remainder of the division is disregarded.

```
(class true)
;=> java.lang.Boolean
```

---

[2]It might also be an application of a *special form* (section 6.5 on page 33) or *macro* (section 6.12 on page 60).

```
(class 17)
;=> java.lang.Long
(class 17.3)
;=> java.lang.Double
(class 17/4)
;=> clojure.lang.Ratio
(class \newline)
;=> java.lang.Character
(class "Hello")
;=> java.lang.String
```

Beside those common types, it has two more basic types: keywords and symbols. Keywords are symbolic identifiers that always evaluate to themselves. They are written with a leading colon although that does not belong to their name. They are primarily used as keys of maps.

```
:a-keyword
;=> :a-keyword
(name :a-keyword)
;=> "a-keyword"
```

Symbols are also symbolic identifiers. In contrast to keywords, they don't evaluate to themselves but they refer to something else, e.g., + is a symbol that refers to the addition function, or *ns* is a symbol referring to the variable holding the current namespace. This mapping from symbols to variables is of dynamic nature and managed by namespaces (see section 6.10 on page 55).

Clojure supports regular expressions with a literal syntax which is exactly the one documented in the java.util.regex.Pattern class[3]. In contrast to Java, where regular expressions are specified as strings in order to be passed to the Pattern.compile() method, in Clojure no additional escaping of backslashes is needed.

```
(re-matches #"(\w+)@(\w+)[.](de|com|org|net)" "user@host.com")
;=> ["user@host.com" "user" "host" "com"]
```

6.4 Collection Types

Clojure offers four core collection types: lists, vectors, hash-maps, and hash-sets. They are all *immutable* and *persistent*. Immutability means that the contents of the data structures cannot change. Adding an item to a collection creates a new, updated version of it. Persistency means that all previous versions are still accessible because the new version shares large parts of its structure. Furthermore, the performance of accessing items or "updating" any version of the structure-sharing collections is guaranteed to happen in some strict bounds. For example, retrieving a value for some key in a map is guaranteed to happen in $O(log_{32}(n))$ for n being the number of entries in the map.

---

[3]http://docs.oracle.com/javase/8/docs/api/java/util/regex/Pattern.html (last visited: 2015-01-19)

The simplest collection type are singly-linked *lists*. They are created using the `list` function that receives arbitrary elements as its arguments. Alternatively, the literal form of lists can be used by enclosing the elements in parentheses[4].

```
(list 1 2 "three")
;=> (1 2 "three")
'(1 2 "three")
;=> (1 2 "three")
```

Vectors are the other ordered collection type. In contrast to lists, they provide efficient random access via indices (starting with 0). Vectors are created using the `vector` function or using their literal representation where the elements are enclosed in brackets.

```
(vector 1 2 "three")
;=> [1 2 "three"]
[1 2 "three"]
;=> [1 2 "three"]
```

Vectors are also functions of their indices, i.e., a vector can be applied as a function that receives an index and returns the value at position. If there is no such index, an `IndexOutOfBoundsException` is thrown.

```
([1 2 "three"] 2)
;=> "three"
([1 2 "three"] 3)
; No message.
;    [Thrown class java.lang.IndexOutOfBoundsException]
```

Hash-maps associate arbitrary keys with values without implying any order. They are created with the `hash-map` function receiving arbitrary many key-value pairs (*entries*), or using their literal representation `{...}`. If a key is given multiple times, an `IllegalArgumentException` is thrown.

```
(hash-map :first-name "Jon" :last-name "Doe")
;=> {:last-name "Doe", :first-name "Jon"}
{:first-name "Jon" :last-name "Doe"}
;=> {:last-name "Doe", :first-name "Jon"}
{:first-name "Jon" :last-name "Doe" :first-name "Jack"}
; Duplicate key: :first-name
;    [Thrown class java.lang.IllegalArgumentException]
```

Maps are functions of their keys receiving a key and an optional default value. If the given key is associated with a value, then the value is returned. If not, the optional default value or `nil` is returned.

---

[4]In order to distinguish function calls from literal lists, the latter have to be quoted. Quoting is discussed in section 6.5 on page 33.

```
({:first-name "Jon" :last-name "Doe"} :first-name)
;=> "Jon"
({:first-name "Jon" :last-name "Doe"} :address)
;=> nil
({:first-name "Jon" :last-name "Doe"} :address :not-found)
;=> :not-found
```

The value of the last form could mean two different things. Either the map
contains no :address key (which is clearly the case here), or it contains an entry
where the key :address maps to the value :not-found. To cope with this issue, there
is the function find which given a map and a key returns the complete entry of that
key represented as vector, or nil if the map contains no such key.

```
(find {:first-name "Jon" :last-name "Doe"} :first-name)
;=> [:first-name "Jon"]
(find {:first-name "Jon" :last-name "Doe"} :address)
;=> nil
```

For the sake of completeness, there is also a sorted flavour of maps created with
the functions sorted-map (natural ordering of keys) or sorted-map-by (user-defined
comparator).

While lists and vectors are ordered collections, *hash-sets* obey the usual mathematical set semantics, i.e., the ordering of their elements is unspecified and there
are no duplicates. Sets are created with the hash-set function or by using their
literal syntax where elements are enclosed by #{...}. Essentially, a set is a map
accociating keys with themselves. Thus, if an element (key) is given multiple times,
an IllegalArgumentException is thrown.

```
(hash-set 1 2 "three")
;=> #{1 2 "three"}
#{1 2 "three"}
;=> #{1 2 "three"}
#{1 2 "three" 1}
; Duplicate key: 1
;   [Thrown class java.lang.IllegalArgumentException]
```

Sets are functions of their keys. They receive a key and return it in case it is
contained in the set. If not, nil is returned.

```
(#{1 2 "three"} "three")
;=> "three"
(#{1 2 "three"} 3)
;=> nil
(#{1 2 nil} nil)
;=> nil
```

The last form in the example illustrates that using sets as functions is not suited
for testing if some key is contained in a set in cases where the set may also contain
nil or false. The proper predicate contains? is depicted in the next section.

In analogy to maps, there is a sorted flavor of sets created with the functions `sorted-set` (natural ordering) or `sorted-set-by` (user-defined comparator).

All collection types implement the Java interface java.util.Collection to ease interoperability. Clojure lists and vectors also implement java.util.List, vectors also implement java.util.RandomAccess, sets implement java.util.Set, and maps implement java.util.Map. Since the Clojure collections are immutable, all modification methods specified by the Java interfaces simply throw an UnsupportedOperationException on invocation.

This section only discussed the literal representations and creation functions for the different collection types, and how some of them can be applied as functions. All functions that operate on collections, e.g., access elements or update collections with new elements, are defined upon abstractions instead of concrete types. They are going to be discussed in section 6.6 on page 39 on section 6.6 on page 39.

6.5 Special Forms

In section 6.2 on page 29, it was said that every list-form was a function application. This statement is not completely true: it could also be the application of a special form or macro.

Special forms are forms for which the usual evaluation semantics for function calls depicted above do not apply. They are necessary as primitives responsible for defining functions, scopes, or modeling control flow.

The first special form going to be introduced here is the conditional form `if`. It receives a test-form, a then-form, and an optional else-form. In contrast to a function application for which all arguments are evaluated first, the then- and else-forms given to `if` are only evaluated depending on the result of the test-form.

```
(if (= (+ 1 1) 2)
  :math-works
  :math-is-broken)
;=> :math-works
```

Expressions used as conditionals don't need to evaluate to a boolean value to be valid because Clojure has a more general rule of truthyness:

Everything is logically true except for `false` and `nil`.

`false` and `nil` are said to be falsy or logical false, everything else is said to be truthy or logical true.

The `when` macro[5] is similar to the `if` special form with omitted else-clause. In contrast to `if`, arbitrary many expressions may be given as its body, and the last expression's value is the result of the `when` form.

---

[5]Macros are discussed in section 6.12 on page 60.

```
(when true
  (println "True")
  17)
; True
;=> 17
```

Another special form is `do`. It wraps arbitrarily many other forms in order to create a new compound form. When evaluating a `do`-form, all included forms are evaluated one after the other, and `do`'s value is the value of its last form. It follows that all but the last form are evaluated for side-effects only.

```
(do
  (println "Been here")
  17)
; Been here
;=> 17
```

The special form `quote` suppresses the evaluation of the form given to it, i.e., the form is just read as raw data (symbols, literals, lists, vectors), but neither symbol resolution or evaluation is performed.

```
(quote *ns*)
;=> *ns*
(class (quote *ns*))
;=> clojure.lang.Symbol
```

Additionally, a form can be quoted by prefixing it with a ' (a quote character). This is a shorthand supported by the Clojure reader. By quoting a form twice, it is possible to check what is literally read by the reader.

```
'*ns*
;=> *ns*
(class '*ns*)
;=> clojure.lang.Symbol
''*ns*
;=> (quote *ns*)
(quote (quote *ns*))
;=> (quote *ns*)
```

The last two form shows that `'form` and `(quote form)` are exactly equivalent.

The special form `let`[6] introduces a new lexical scope. It receives a vector of bindings given as symbol-value pairs followed by arbitrary many expressions as its body, which are wrapped in an implicit `do`. Later bindings may refer to earlier bindings. Inside the body, all symbols are bound to the values as specified by the bindings vector.

---

[6]Actually, `let` is not a special form but a macro that expands into the special form `let*`. The same applies to some other forms that are introduced as special form here (e.g., `fn` vs. `fn*`, `loop` vs. `loop*`), but the distinction is of no importance because the latter are never used directly.

```
(let [a 2, b (* a a)]
  (println "a is" a "and b is" b)
  (+ a b))
; a is 2 and b is 4
;=> 6
```

In contrast to the local scopes created with let, the special form def defines a new namespace-global *var* with an optional docstring and an optional initial value called the var's *root binding*. A var is the simplest Clojure reference types and merely encapsulates a storage location holding some value. Evaluating a var returns the value it is bound to.

```
(def answer                                ;; The var's name
  "The meaning of life and everything."    ;; Its optional docstring
  42)                                      ;; Its initial value (root binding)
;=> #'user/answer
answer
;=> 42
(def unbound-var)
;=> #'user/unbound-var
unbound-var
;=> #<Unbound Unbound: #'user/unbound·var>
```

The vars created in the example above are essentially constants. While it is possible to change a var's root binding either by def-ing it again or using the function alter-var-root, those are only meant to be used during interactive development.

As mentioned above, evaluating a var results in the value it is bound to. To retrieve the var object itself, there is the special form var. The reader supports a special literal var syntax: #' followed by the var's name.

```
(var answer)
;=> #'user/answer
#'answer
;=> #'user/answer
```

Retrieving vars instead of the var's value is almost always done for accessing a var's metadata which is discussed in section 6.9 on page 53.

```
(meta #'user/answer)
;=> {:ns #<Namespace user>,
;     :name answer,
;     :doc "The meaning of life and everything.",
;     :line 1,
;     :file "NO_SOURCE_FILE"}
```

Anonymous functions are created using the fn special form. It receives a vector of the function's arguments and arbitrary many expressions as its body which are wrapped in an implicit do, thus the value of the last body form is the value of applying the function.

```
(let [incrementor (fn [i]
                        (fn [n]
                          (+ n i)))
      inc10 (incrementor 10)
      inc20 (incrementor 20)]
  (inc20 (inc10 0)))
;=> 30
```

In the example, `incrementor` is a function that receives one parameter `i`. It returns another function that receives one parameter `n` and adds to that the number `i` given to `incrementor`. Thus, `inc10` is a function of arity one that increments a given number by 10, and `inc20` is a function that increments by 20.

The feature of capturing the definition location's lexical context (e.g., `i`) and making it available in the function's body is usually referred to as *lexical closures*.

Anonymous functions can also be defined using an even shorter notation. A list preceded with a hash is also a function consisting only of the body where the parameters are notated as `%i`, where the highest *i* declares the number of parameters. `%1` may be abbreviated with `%`.

```
(#(+ 1 %1 %2) 2 3)
;=> 6
(#(* % %) 3)
;=> 9
```

This notation is almost only used for very short and simple functions that are passed to higher-order functions (see section 6.8 on page 50).

Functions can be overloaded with multiple arities. The following listing defines a addition function that accepts any number of arguments.

```
(let [add (fn this
            ([] 0)
            ([a] a)
            ([a b] (+ a b))
            ([a b & more] (apply this (this a b) more)))]
  (add 1 2 3 4 5))
;=> 15
```

The first thing to note is the `this` following the `fn`. It is an optional, local function name bound to the function only inside the function itself to allow for recursion. Thereafter, the definitions for each arity are specified as lists where the first element is always an argument vector.

The zero-arity version of the `add` function returns the identity element of the addition. The version with one argument simply returns the given argument. The version with arity two delegates to `+`. The last version is the most interesting one. It receives two arguments `a` and `b` plus arbitrary many other arguments indicated by `&`. All additional arguments, are conflated in a sequence bound to the parameter `more`. In the call to `add` above, `more` will be bound to `(3 4 5)`. The definition then applies the very same function to the result of adding the arguments `a` and `b`. Thus, with every recursion the number of arguments shrinks by one so that eventually, the version with arity two terminates the recursion.

`apply` is a higher-order function (HOF). Several others are going to be discussed in section 6.8 on page 50. It receives a function and any number of arguments. The last argument must be a sequence. It then calls the given function with all arguments where the elements of the sequence are provided as individual arguments. Thus, the following holds.

```
(= (- 1 2 3)
   (apply - 1 2 [3])
   (apply - 1 [2 3])
   (apply - [1 2 3]))
;=> true
```

For conveniently defining namespace-global functions, there is the `defn` macro which is a shorthand combining `def` and `fn`. The following two definitions are equivalent[7].

```
(def fact (fn fact [i]
             (if (zero? i)
                 1
                 (*' i (fact (dec i))))))
;=> #'user/fact
(defn fact [i]
  (if (zero? i)
    1
    (*' i (fact (dec i)))))
;=> #'user/fact
```

The special form `letfn` allows for defining named, local functions that are available only in its lexical scope. It is similar to `let` in combination with `fn`, but all functions defined in a `letfn` may refer to any other function defined in the same `letfn`, thus allowing for mutual recursive functions.

```
(letfn [(even? [n]
           (or (zero? n) (odd? (dec n))))
        (odd? [n]
           (if (zero? n) false (even? (dec n))))]
  [(even? 100) (odd? 100)])
;=> [true false]
```

One issue with recursive functions is that they consume stack space which limits the maximum recursion depth. Considering the `fact` function above, for every level of recursion the current value of `i`, the function to be applied to `i`, and the result of the recursive call has to be remembered in a stack frame.

```
(fact 20000)
; No message.
;    [Thrown class java.lang.StackOverflowError]
```

---

[7]The arithmetic functions +, -, and * throw exceptions if an integer overflow occurs. The variants suffixed with ' automatically promote to bigints instead.

However, every self-recursive function can be formulated in a way where the recursive call is the last expression to be evaluated by using an additional accumulator to pass intermediate results as parameters through the recursion. The recursive call is said to be in *tail-position*.

```
(defn fact
  ([i] (fact 1 i))
  ([acc i]
    (if (zero? i)
      acc
      (fact (*' acc i) (dec i)))))
;=> #'user/fact
```

The version of arity one simply delegates to the version of arity two where `acc` is set to 1 initially. In the aritiy-2 version, the final result is calculated when building up the recursion instead of deferring the computation to when the recursive calls return. Because every application of `fact` depends only on its own arguments, there is no need to remember the current lexical extent in a new stack frame but the same stack frame can be reused over and over again just by rebinding the values of `acc` and `i`. This technique is known as *tail-call optimization* (TCO) or *tail-call elimination*. While some functional language specifications, e.g., Scheme [Spe+10], mandate automatic TCO wherever possible, neither Clojure nor the JVM perform TCO at all. Thus, trying to calculate the factorial of a larger integer with the last definition still results in a `StackOverflowError`. However, Clojure provides the special form `recur` as a form of explicit TCO. It restarts the current function with the parameters rebound to the values given to it. Any occurrence of `recur` other than in tail-position is a compile-time error.

```
(defn fact
  ([i] (fact 1 i))
  ([acc i]
    (if (zero? i)
      acc
      (recur (*' acc i) (dec i)))))
;=> #'user/fact
(count (str (fact 50000)))  ;; no of digits of 50000!
;=> 213237
```

`loop` is similar to `let` except that it also creates a `recur` target. Using `loop` and `recur`, the last definition can be written more consisely.

```
(defn fact [i]
  (loop [acc 1, i i]
    (if (zero? i)
      acc
      (recur (*' acc i) (dec i)))))
;=> #'user/fact
```

The major advantage is that the synthetic accumulator doesn't shine through in the function's signature.

Vars may be defined to have a dynamic scope by adding `^:dynamic` metadata to the var in its definition form. By convention, dynamic vars are often prefixed and suffixed with an asterisk (*, frequently referred to as *earmuffs*). Existing dynamic vars can be rebound using the `binding` special form which is similar to `let` except that the bindings are established thread-local for the whole dynamic scope of its body instead of the lexical scope. Another difference is that the bindings are established in parallel, thus later bindings cannot refer to the new values of earlier bindings. After the evaluation of `binding`'s body, the vars are set back to their previous value, i.e., either the values bound by another `binding` form in whose dynamic scope the execution takes place or their root bindings.

```
(def ^:dynamic *foo* 1)
;=> #'user/*foo*
(defn get-foo [] *foo*)
;=> #'user/get-foo
*foo*
;=> 1
(get-foo)
;=> 1
(binding [*foo* 2]
  (get-foo))
;=> 2
```

There are several predefined dynamic vars. For example `*ns*` holding the current namespace, or `*out*`, `*err*`, and `*in*` bound to standard output/error, and standard input. Since the function `println` always prints to the value of `*out*` (which must be a `java.io.Writer`), `binding` can be used to redirect output to arbitrary other writers on strings, files, or sockets.

```
(binding [*out* *err*]
  (println "Written to standard error."))
; Written to standard error.
;=> nil
```

Dynamic vars are usually used for allowing the user of a library to customize internal behavior. For example, a CSV-reading library might define a variable `*on-invalid-line-fn*` with a root binding to a function that receives the invalid line and throws an exception. An invalid line in a CSV file could be a line with the wrong number of entries, or a line containing a string entry where a number was expected. Then, the user can rebind that dynamic var to an own function in order to treat invalid lines specifically, or to simply ignore them.

6.6 Abstractions

Section 6.4 on page 30 only covered the creation of collections of the four concrete collection types and their usage as functions. The reason is that Clojure's core functions for updating or retrieving elements from collections are defined upon abstractions that are usually implemented by more than one concrete type. Those abstractions and their corresponding functions are explained in this section.

6.6.1   The Collection Abstraction

Lists, vectors, maps, and sets all participate in the *collection* abstraction which has
five associated functions.

The function `conj` (for conjoin) receives a collection and a value and returns a
new version of the collection including the new value.

```
(conj '(1 2) 3)
;=> (3 1 2)
(conj [1 2] 3)
;=> [1 2 3]
(conj #{1 2} 3)
;=> #{1 2 3}
(conj {:a 1, :b 2} [:c 3])
;=> {:c 3, :a 1, :b 2}
```

For ordered collections (lists and vectors) `conj` adds where it is most efficient,
i.e., conjoining to a list prepends and conjoining to a vector appends.

The function `count` returns the number of elements contained in some collection.
For maps, this is the number of entries.

The function `seq` returns a *sequence* view of the given collection's values or `nil`
for empty collections. Sequences, usually called "seqs", are the most pervasive
abstraction in Clojure going to be discussed in the next section. For now, a sequence
is very similar to a list in almost all respects[8].

```
(seq [1 2 3])          ;; non-empty collection
;=> (1 2 3)
(seq '())              ;; empty collection
;=> nil
(seq {:a 1, :b 2})     ;; map
;=> ([:a 1] [:b 2])
```

Since `seq` returns `nil` for empty collections, it is also the canonical non-emptiness
test.

The equality predicate `=` is defined for arbitrary many arguments of abitrary types.
Equality is usually determined intuitively by a type-sensitive, deep comparison. For
example, the character `\x` is not equal to the string `"c"` because their types differ.
However, for collections the type-sensitivity is relaxed. With respect to equality,
there are three categories: *sequential collections* (lists, vectors, sequences), *sets*
(hash-sets and sorted sets), and *maps* (hash-sets and sorted maps). In every category,
two collections are equal if they have the same length, they contain equal elements,
and for sequential collections the order has to match as well. Collections of different
category are never equal.

```
(= '(1 2) [1 2] (seq [1 2]))          ;; list vs. vector vs. sequence
;=> true
```

---

[8]In fact, lists participate in the sequence abstraction directly, e.g., calling `seq` on a non-empty list
simply returns the list again.

```
(= #{1 2} (sorted-set-by > 1 2))        ;; hash-set vs. descendingly ordered set
;=> true
(= {1 "ONE", 2 "TWO"}                   ;; hash-map vs. descendingly ordered map
   (sorted-map-by > 1 "ONE" 2 "TWO"))
;=> true
(= [1 2] #{1 2})                        ;; vector vs. hash-set
;=> false
```

The last function defined for the collection abstraction is `empty`. It receives a collection and returns a new, empty collection of the same type. For sorted sets and maps, the new collection also uses the same comparator on its elements.

6.6.2 The Sequence Abstraction

The sequence abstraction provides a uniform way of traversing different sources of values, i.e., it provides a sequential view on composite data structures. In the previous section, it was shown that the function `seq` produces a seq for a given Clojure collection. But `seq` also works for arrays, Java collections, Java maps (maps are no collections there), all `java.lang.CharSequence` derivates including `String` where `seq` returns a sequence of characters, and all types implementing the `java.lang.Iterable` interface. All types supporting `seq` are said to be *seqable*. In the following, whenever a function is said to receive a sequence, it will always mean the function accepts any seqable object as well.

The sequences abstraction defines three functions for traversing seqs: `first`, `rest`, and `next`.

`first` obtains the first value of a given sequence. Implicitly, it calls `seq` on its argument, so it can be called directly on any seqable object.

```
(first (seq [1 2 3]))
;=> 1
(first [1 2 3])
;=> 1
(first {:a 1, :b 2})
;=> [:a 1]
```

The functions `rest` returns the seq of all elements of its argument except for its first one.

```
(rest [1 2 3])
;=> (2 3)
(rest [1])
;=> ()
(rest [])
;=> ()
```

`next` is almost identical to `rest` except that it calls `seq` on its result. As a consequence, `next` returns `nil` for seqs of length one and empty seqs.

```
(next [1 2 3])
;=> (2 3)
(next [1])
;=> nil
(next [])
;=> nil
```

This slight difference is of importance when working with lazy, possibly infinite
sequences which are going to be discussed in the next paragraph.

Before, the two functions cons and list* for creating new seqs are introduced.
cons prepends a new value to a seq, and list* prepends arbitrarily many new values
to a seq.   Finally, reverse reverses a seq (or any seqable object).

```
(let [xs [4 5 6]]
  [(cons 1 (cons 2 xs)), (list* 1 2 xs), (reverse xs)])
[(1 2 4 5 6) (1 2 4 5 6) (6 5 4)]
```

Lazy Sequences

As stated above, various composite data structures beyond collections may be used
as the source of a sequence. Lazy seqs are sequences whose source is a computation
being able to produce the desired values stepwise. The computation is delayed until
elements are consumed (in terms of first, next, or rest). The process of accessing
elements in a lazy seq is call *realization*.

For creating a lazy seq, there is the macro lazy-seq. It simply wraps a body
of arbitrary many expressions that would produce the desired sequence (usually
recursively). This is best explained using an example. The following function returns
the lazy seq of Fibonacci numbers.

```
(defn fibonacci-seq
  ([]
     (fibonacci-seq 0 1))
  ([a b]
     (lazy-seq #_(println "Realized" a)      ;; for visualizing realization
       (cons a (fibonacci-seq b (+' a b)))))))
;=> #'user/fibonacci-seq
```

The variant for arity zero just delegates to the version with arity two providing
the first two Fibonacci numbers. The second variant returns the seq of Fibonacci
numbers starting with a and b. If a and b are consecutive Fibonacci numbers, then
the seq is a prepended to the Fibonacci sequence starting with b and the sum of a
and b.

When ignoring the lazy-seq, the code clearly looks like a non-terminating recursion. The trick here is that lazy-seq creates a clojure.lang.LazySeq data structure
that receives the expressions wrapped in an anonymous function of arity zero (a
so-called *thunk*) which closes over the arguments a and b. When seq is invoked on
the lazy seq (usually implicitly by first, rest, or next) this anonymous function is

called for realization. Its value is the seq where the first element is the value of a and the rest is the unrealized lazy seq of Fibonacci numbers starting with 1 and 1.

The already realized elements are cached. Therefore, lazy sequences are almost always defined in terms of functions returning them instead of being bound to some global var directly, because the latter would not allow for reclaiming memory.

The realization process can be visualized by uncommenting the `println` form in the example above. In the following listing, the forms evaluating to a lazy seq are wrapped in a `(do ... nil)` in order to suppress printing them which would force their full realization and thus never terminate.

```
(do (fibonacci-seq) nil)               ;; (1)
;=> nil
(first (fibonacci-seq))                 ;; (2)
; Realizing 0
;=> nil
(do (rest (fibonacci-seq)) nil)         ;; (3)
; Realizing 0
;=> nil
(do (next (fibonacci-seq)) nil)         ;; (4)
; Realizing 0
; Realizing 1
;=> nil
```

(1) Creating the lazy seq of Fibonacci numbers realizes nothing at all.
(2) Taking the first element only realizes that.
(3) Taking the rest of the Fibonacci seq returns its tail blindly and so needs only to realize its head.
(4) In contrast, `next` calls `seq` on its result (and thus would return `nil` if the tail was empty) which forces the realization of one more element. Thus, `rest` is a bit more lazy than `next`.

There are many functions that take or return lazy sequences, the most important being discussed here.

`take` gets a number n and a (possibly lazy) seq and returns a lazy seq of the n first values of the seq.   `drop` has the same signature and returns the lazy seq of values after the first n.   `concat` returns the lazy seq that is the concatenation of an arbitrary number of given seqs.

```
(take 10 (fibonacci-seq))
;=> (0 1 1 2 3 5 8 13 21 34)
(take 10 (drop 10 (fibonacci-seq)))
;=> (55 89 144 233 377 610 987 1597 2584 4181)
(let [head (take 20 (fibonacci-seq))
      tail (drop 10 head)]
  (concat (take 10 head) tail))
;=> (0 1 1 2 3 5 8 13 21 34 55 89 144 233 377 610 987 1597 2584 4181)
```

The function `range` returns a lazy seq of numbers with an optional end value defaulting to infinity, an optional start value defaulting to 0, and an optional step value defaulting to 1.

```
(take 10 (range))
;=> (0 1 2 3 4 5 6 7 8 9)
(range 10)
;=> (0 1 2 3 4 5 6 7 8 9)
(range 10 20)
;=> (10 11 12 13 14 15 16 17 18 19)
(range 0 100 10)
;=> (0 10 20 30 40 50 60 70 80 90)
```

The repeat function gets a value and returns an infinite lazy seq of the given value. It also has a variant of arity two that gets the desired number of repetitions and the value and returns a finity lazy seq.

```
(take 10 (repeat 0))
;=> (0 0 0 0 0 0 0 0 0 0)
(repeat 10 0)
;=> (0 0 0 0 0 0 0 0 0 0)
```

To force the complete realization of finite lazy seqs, there are the functions doall and dorun. The former realizes and returns the lazy seq again so that it resides completely in memory. The latter walks through the lazy seq's elements without retaining the head of the sequence and eventually returns nil. Therefore, the sequence doesn't need to fit into memory. Forcing the realization of lazy seqs is only useful if the function computing the values has side-effects.

There are many more functions for working with or creating lazy sequences. Especially, core higher-order functions like map and filter all produce lazy sequences. Those are going to be discussed in section 6.8 on page 50.

6.6.3   The Associative Abstraction

All collection types that somehow link keys with values participate in the *associative* abstraction defining the functions get, contains?, assoc, and dissoc. Maps are the primary example here, but also vectors are associatives where the keys are the indices, and sets are associatives where the keys and values are identical.

The get function looks up the value of a given key in some associative data structure and returns nil if there is no such key. An optional default value may be specified for the latter case.

```
(get {:a 1, :b 2} :b)
;=> 2
(get [1 2 3 4] 3)
;=> 4
(get [1 2 3 4] 4)
;=> nil
(get [1 2 3 4] 4 :not-found)
;=> :not-found
```

One crucial difference between using vectors as functions of their indices and using get on vectors is that the former throws an IndexOutOfBoundsException if there is no such index whereas get just returns nil or the default value.

The second function defined for associatives is `contains?` which checks for the presence of a key in a data structure.

```
(contains? {:a 1, :b 2} :b)
;=> true
(contains? #{1 2 3} 4)
;=> false
(contains? [1 2 3] 0)
;=> true
```

The last form is true because vectors are associatives where the keys are the vector's indices.

For creating changed versions of associatives, there are the functions `assoc` and `dissoc`. `assoc` adds one or many new associations or changes existing associations. It is supported only for maps and vectors.

```
(assoc {:a 1, :b 2} :c 3 :a 4)
;=> {:c 3, :a 4, :b 2}
(assoc [1 2] 2 3)
;=> [1 2 3]
```

The function `dissoc` removes an association. It is only supported by maps since it makes no sense to remove an index from a vector. A vector cannot have gaps.

```
(dissoc {:a 1, :b 2, :c 3} :a :c)
;=> {:b 2}
```

6.6.4 The Indexed Abstraction

The *indexed* abstraction is defined for many data structures that can be numerically indexed. Foremost, these are vectors and Java arrays, but also lists, sequences, strings, and regular expression matchers[9].

The indexed abstraction consists of only one function: `nth`. `nth` takes an object participating in the indexed abstraction, a numerical index, and an optional default value, and it returns the element at the given index. For vectors, `nth` is very similar to `get` except that it throws an `IndexOutOfBoundsException` if the given index does not exist.

```
(nth [1 2 3] 2)
;=> 3
(nth [1 2 3] 3)
; No message.
;    [Thrown class java.lang.IndexOutOfBoundsException]
(nth (list 1 2 3) 1)
;=> 2
(nth (list 1 2 3) 3 :no-such-index)
;=> :no-such-index
```

---

[9]http://docs.oracle.com/javase/8/docs/api/index.html?java/util/regex/Pattern.html (last visited: 2015-01-19)

6.6.5   The Stack Abstraction

The *stack* abstraction enables the usage of lists and vectors with last-in, first-out semantics. It consists of three functions: `conj`, `pop`, and `peek`.

`conj`, which was already discussed in the paragraph of the collection abstraction, adds an item to the stack. `peek` returns the top-most item of the stack, and `pop` returns a new version of the stack with the top-most item removed. Calling `pop` on an empty stack throws an `IllegalStateException`.

When vectors are used as stacks, elements are conjoined to the end, and popping the stack drops the last element.

```
(conj (conj [] 1) 2)              ;; a vector as stack
;=> [1 2]
(peek (conj (conj [] 1) 2))
;=> 2
(pop (conj (conj [] 1) 2))
;=> [1]
(pop [])
; Can't pop empty vector
;   [Thrown class java.lang.IllegalStateException]
```

When lists are used as stacks, elements are prepended to the list, and popping the stack returns the rest of the list.

```
(conj (conj '() 1) 2)             ;; a list as stack
;=> (2 1)
(peek (conj (conj '() 1) 2))
;=> 2
(pop (conj (conj '() 1) 2))
;=> (1)
(pop '())
; Can't pop empty list
;   [Thrown class java.lang.IllegalStateException]
```

6.6.6   The Set Abstraction

The *set* abstraction, only applicable for hash-sets and sorted sets, defines only the single function `disj` (for disjoin) that returns a new version of the set with a given value removed.

```
(disj #{1 2 3} 2)
;=> #{1 3}
```

The namespace `clojure.set` defines many more functions on sets like `superset?`, `subset?`, `union`, `intersection`, and `difference`. For sets of maps which can be seen as a kind of database table, there also exist typical relational algebra functions such as `select`, `project`, `join`, and `index`.

6.6.7   The Sorted Abstraction

The *sorted* abstraction guarantees a stable ordering upon all values of participating collections, namely sorted sets and maps. The functions `sorted-map` and `sorted-set` create maps and sets sorted according natural ordering.

The sorting order can be customized using a comparator or predicate when creating sorted collections with `sorted-map-by` and `sorted-set-by`. A comparator (`java.util.Comparator`) has a method `int compare(T a, T b)` which returns a negative integer if a is smaller than b, a positive integer if b is smaller than a, and zero if both are equal.

If a predicate is given to `sorted-map-by` or `sorted-set-by`, a comparator is created implicitly[10] which applies the predicate to the values to compare, and if this comparison results in a truthy value, -1 is returned. If the comparison is false, then the values are compared in the reverse order given to the comparator. If this is truthy, 1 is returned. If both comparisons are false, the values are considered equal and 0 is returned.

```
(let [s (sorted-set-by > 1 2 3 4 5 6 7 8 9 0)
      m1 (sorted-map-by compare :c 1, :b 2, :a 3)
      m2 (sorted-map :c 1, :b 2, :a 3)]
  [s m1 m2])
[#{9 8 7 6 5 4 3 2 1 0} {:a 3, :b 2, :c 1} {:a 3, :b 2, :c 1}]
```

The function `compare` is a default comparator function working with every object implementing `Comparable` but also for `nil`. It is used by the functions `sorted-map` and `sorted-set`, so the first and the second sorted map creation are identical.

The sorted abstraction specifies the three functions `rseq`, `subseq`, and `rsubseq`.

The `rseq` function is similar to `seq` except that it returns a reversed sequence of the sorted collection's (or a vector's) values.

```
(let [s (sorted-set-by > 1 2 3 4 5 6 7 8 9 0)
      m (sorted-map :c 1, :b 2, :a 3)]
  [(rseq s) (rseq m)])
[(0 1 2 3 4 5 6 7 8 9) ([:c 1] [:b 2] [:a 3])]
```

The `subseq` function receives a sorted collection, a test predicate (one of <, <=, =>, or >) and a key, and it returns a seq of elements whose keys are sorted before, before-or-equal, after-or-equal, or after the given key. The function is overloaded with a variant that receives a second test predicate and key which allows for selecting a range from within the sorted collection.

```
(let [s (sorted-set-by > 1 2 3 4 5 6 7 8 9 0)]
  [(subseq s > 5) (subseq s > 7 < 3)])
[(4 3 2 1 0) (6 5 4)]
```

---

[10] This functionality is also exposed to the user by the `comparator` function. A comparator is a function receiving two objects and returning a negative value if the first object is less than the second object, a positive value if the first element is greater than the second object, or zero otherwise.

The first subseq call results in the sequence of elements that are sorted after the key 5, and the second call returns the sequence of elements that are sorted after 7 but before 3.

Finally, the last function provided by the sorted abstraction is rsubseq. It is signature and semantics is the same as subseq except that rsubseq returns a reversed sequence of the selected range.

6.7   Destructuring

Destructuring is a notion for concisely selecting values inside seqable objects and maps by mirroring their structure. It is supported for let and loop bindings and function parameters.

6.7.1   Sequential Destructuring

All objects participating in the *indexed* abstraction can be destructured by providing a vector of symbols in place of a symbol in a binding form. This includes all sequential collections, sequences, strings, Java collections, regular expression matchers, and arrays. The i-th symbol is bound to the i-th element in the indexed object given as expression. If the indexed object contains more or fewer elements than are destructured, those are dismissed or filled with nil.

```
(let [[a b c] (range)]
  [a b c])
;=> [0 1 2]
(let [[a b c] [1]]
  [a b c])
;=> [1 nil nil]
```

The first form is entirely equivalent to the following listing[11] except that the latter introduces an additional variable r which the former doesn't.

```
(let [r (range)
      a (nth r 0 nil)
      b (nth r 1 nil)
      c (nth r 2 nil)]
  [a b c])
```

Furthermore, the varargs syntax & may be used to bind the tail (next) of the seqable object that is not captured by preceding symbols to another symbol.

```
(let [[a b c & more] (range 10)]
  [a b c more])
;=> [0 1 2 (3 4 5 6 7 8 9)]
```

---

[11]In fact, let is a macro whose expansion replaces the destructuring binding form with exactly this binding form in a let* which is the primitive special form for introducing a new lexical scope.

```
(let [[a b c & more] (range 3)]
  [a b c more])
;=> [0 1 2 nil]
```

Destructuring forms can also be composed arbitrarily deeply to capture elements inside seqables that are contained in other seqables.

```
(let [[a b [c d & e] & more] [1 2 [3 4 5 6] 7]]
  [a b c d e more])
;=> [1 2 3 4 (5 6) (7)]
```

Finally, sequential destructuring allows for a final symbol preceded by the keyword :as for retaining the seqable object being destructured as a whole.

```
(let [[a b [c d & e] & more :as v] [1 2 [3 4 5 6] 7]]
  [a b c d e more v])
;=> [1 2 3 4 (5 6) (7) [1 2 [3 4 5 6] 7]]
```

6.7.2 Map Destructuring

Whereas sequential destructuring is available for every object participating in the *indexed* abstraction, map destructuring is available for every object participating in the *associative* abstraction. Here, a map of symbol-key pairs is used in place of only a symbol, and the symbols are bound to `(get aobj key)` where `aobj` is the associative object being destructured.

The following listing demonstrates how maps and vectors, the latter being associatives of their indices, can be destructured.

```
(let [{a :a, b :b, c :c, d :d} {:a 1, :b 2, :c 3}
      {u 0, v 1, w 2} [10 11]]
  [a b c d u v w])
;=> [1 2 3 nil 10 11 nil]
```

Because maps with keywords as keys are extremely common in Clojure, there is a special :keys notion for this case. A vector of symbols is provided, and those symbols are bound to the values of looking up the keyword with the same name in the associative object. Using that, the first binding form of the last example can be written more concise like so.

```
(let [{:keys [a b c d]} {:a 1, :b 2, :c 3}]
  [a b c d])
;=> [1 2 3 nil]
```

A map from symbols to default values may be specified using an :or clause. In this case, the value is looked up using `(get aobj key default)`.

```
(let [{:keys [a b c d] :or {a 1, d 4}} {:a nil, :b 2, :c 3}]
  [a b c d])
;=> [nil 2 3 4]
```

Just like with sequential destructuring, an :as clause may be used to capture the complete object.

```
(let [{:keys [a b c d] :as m} {:a 1, :b 2, :c 3}]
  [a b c d m])
;=> [1 2 3 nil {:a 1, :c 3, :b 2}]
```

Of course, sequential and map destructuring forms can be combined arbitrarily.

```
(let [[a {:keys [b c]} d & more] (list 1 {:b 2, :c 3} 4 5 6)]
  [a b c d more])
;=> [1 2 3 4 (5 6)]
```

A common idiom is to use map destructuring for function parameters where multiple parameters are optional and have default values.

```
(defn open-socket [host port & {:keys [protocol bindiface bindport]
                                :or {protocol :tcp}}]
  ...)
```

The function receives a mandatory host and a port, and optionally the used protocol (defaulting to TCP), and the locally bound interface and port may be specified. An example call might look like the following.

```
(open-socket "host.domain.com" 1234 :protocol :udp :bindport 4321)
```

6.8   Higher-Order Functions

Higher-order functions (HOFs) are one of the most prominent functional programming constructs. It is enabled by the fact that functions are values themselves and thus can be passed around like any other value. Therefore, a higher-order function is a function that receives another function as argument or returns a function as its value. In this section, the most prominent Clojure higher-order functions are discussed. In most cases, the use of low-level constructs such as recursion can be avoided by the use of high-level HOFs.

The higher-order function apply has already been discussed briefly when introducing variadic functions in section 6.5 on page 33. apply receives a function as its first argument, possibly further arguments, and a sequence as its last argument. It then applies the given function to the argument list formed by prepending all intervening arguments to the sequence given as last argument. For example, the following two function calls are equivalent to (* 1 2 3).

```
(apply * 1 [2 3])
;=> 6
(apply * [1 2 3])
;=> 6
```

In combination with the function range, this allows for defining the factorial function in a concise manner without the need of explicit recursion or loops. The factorial of an integer n is the product of the numbers in the range from 1 to n, inclusive.

```
(defn fact [n]
  (apply *' (range 1 (inc n))))
;=> #'user/fact
(fact 30)
;=> 265252859812191058636308480000000N
(fact 0)
;=> 1
```

It also works for 0, because (range 1 1) is the empty sequence resulting to a call to the *' variant of arity zero that simply returns the identity element of the multiplication.

The function reduce is the core aggregation function. It receives a function of arity two and some sequence. First, it calls the given function with the first two elements of the seq. Thereafter, the function is called repeatedly with the intermediate result and the successive next elements. reduce also has a variant that receives a function, a start value, and a sequence. Here, the the given function is called with the start value and the first element of the sequence[12].

For example, the following function counts the number of even numbers in the given sequence. The reduction function receives two parameters where the first parameter %1 is the intermediate number of evens, and the second parameter %2 is the next number to test.

```
(defn count-even [coll]
  (reduce #(if (even? %2) (inc %1) %1)  ;; reduction function
          0 coll))                      ;; start value & seq
;=> #'user/count-even
(count-even (range 1000))
;=> 500
```

The filter function receives a predicate and a sequence and returns a lazy sequence of the given seq's elements that satisfy the predicate. remove is just the opposite of filter. It results in a lazy seq of the given sequence's elements for which the predicate does not hold.

```
(let [r (range 15)]
  [(filter even? r) (remove even? r)])
;=> [(0 2 4 6 8 10 12 14) (1 3 5 7 9 11 13)]
```

The map function receives a function of arity one and a sequence, and it returns the lazy sequence of applying the given function to every element. map can also be called with a function of arity n and n sequences. In that case, it returns the lazy

---

[12]In that sense, the reduce version with arity two is equivalent to Haskell's foldl1, and the version with arity three is equivalent to foldl.

seq of the results of applying the given function to the respective i-th elements of the given sequences. The shortest sequence determines the length of the result, so mapping with a mix of finite and infinite seqs is finite again.

```
(map + [0 5 10 15 20 25]
       (range))
;=> (0 6 12 18 24 30)
```

The mapcat function has the same signatures as map. It maps the given function through the elements and concatenates the results which implies that the individual function calls must result in collections.

```
(mapcat #(list % (* % %)) (range 5))
;=> (0 0 1 1 2 4 3 9 4 16)
```

The iterate function gets a function f and a value x and returns the lazy sequence x, (f x), (f (f x)), and so forth.

```
(take 10 (iterate #(*' 2 %) 1))
;=> (1 2 4 8 16 32 64 128 256 512)
```

The function partial receives a function f and arbitrary many values. It returns a new function of variadic arity that applies f with the arguments given to partial and any additional arguments appended, i.e., a version of f where the first few parameters are fixed to concrete values. Thus, the last example can be written equivalently like so.

```
(take 10 (iterate (partial *' 2) 1))
;=> (1 2 4 8 16 32 64 128 256 512)
```

comp is the (right-to-left) function composition, i.e., (comp g f) is $g \circ f$ with $(g \circ f)(x) = g(f(x))$. It is defined for arbitrary many function arguments.

```
(def count-evens (comp count (partial filter even?)))
;=> #'user/count-evens
(count-evens (range 1000))
;=> 500
```

The complement function takes a function and returns a new function that calls the given function but returns its logically inverse result.

```
(filter (complement even?) [1 2 3 4])
;=> (1 3)
(map (complement identity) [1 true :foo nil false])
;=> (false false false true true)
```

juxt receives one or many functions and returns the juxtaposition of these functions, i.e., ((juxt a b c) x) is equivalent to [(a x) (b x) (c x)].

```
((juxt + - * /) 2 3)
;=> [5 -1 6 2/3]
```

Functions that are defined entirely in terms of function composition, partial application, or other combinators are said to follow the *point-free* or *tactic programming style*, because they are completely missing explicit parameters and intermediate variables (*points*). While many favor point-free style for its conciseness and proximity to maths, others discourage it for being less comprehensible than explicit functions with sensibly named parameters. E.g., to determine valid parameters for the count-evens function, the right-most function in the composition has to be inspected. In turn, that is a partial function of filter, where filter receives a predicate and a sequence, and the predicate is already preset to even?. Since even? is defined only for integer numbers, count-evens must be a function that receives a seq of integers and returns an integer because count does so.

Concludingly, point-free style is desirable if it's complemented with good documentation. Here, metadata plays an important role.

6.9 Metadata

Metadata is data about other data. In Clojure, metadata takes the form of hash-maps. Every Clojure object can be annotated with metadata. This includes collections, vars, symbols, and functions but excludes Java objects like numbers or strings. Metadata does not contribute to the value of an object, i.e., it does not affect equality or hash codes. If two objects differ only in their metadata, they are equal (but not identical).

The with-meta function receives an arbitrary Clojure object and an arbitrary metadata map. It returns a new version of the object that is associated with the given metadata. While with-meta replaces the object's metadata map, the function vary-meta applies a given function to the current metadata of the object and returns the object with the resulting new version of metadata.

The function meta gets an arbitrary Clojure object and returns its metadata map or nil if it has no associated metadata.

```
(let [v [1 2 3]
      v1 (with-meta v {:k1 true})
      v2 (vary-meta v1 assoc :k2 17 )]
  {:all-equal? (= v v1 v2)
   :hash-codes (map hash [v v1 v2])
   :identical? (identical? v v1)
   :meta-v     (meta v)
   :meta-v1    (meta v1)
   :meta-v2    (meta v2)})
;=> {:all-equal? true, :hash-codes (30817 30817 30817), :identical? false,
;    :meta-v nil, :meta-v1 {:k1 true}, :meta-v2 {:k2 17, :k1 true}}
```

Clojure uses metadate extensively for documentation purposes and for providing information to the compiler using a pre-defined set of keywords with special meaning.

The metadata maps are written as map literal prefixed with ^, and they preced the thing they apply to.

Vars defined with `def` (or `defn`) may have the following metadata.

```
(def ^{:private false,
       :doc "The maximum depth.",
       :tag java.lang.Long,
       :dynamic true}
     *max-depth* 17)
;=> #'user/*max-depth*
```

The value of `:private` determines if var is private to the defining namespace. `:doc` is a documentation string. `:tag` is a type hint used by the compiler to avoid reflective method calls (see section 6.11 on page 57). The value of `:dynamic` specifies if a var is dynamically scoped and thus may be rebound using `binding`.

Every metadata key whose value is a boolean may be abbreviated to `^:key` with the meaning that this key is set to `true`.

```
(def ^:private ^:dynamic *private-and-dynamic*)
;=> #'user/*private-and-dynamic*
(meta #'*private-and-dynamic*)
;=> {:ns #<Namespace user>, :name *private-and-dynamic*,
;    :dynamic true, :private true, :line 1, :file "NO_SOURCE_FILE"}
```

As can be seen, the Clojure compiler automatically adds some more metadata to vars. `:ns` is the defining namespace, `:name` is a symbol denoting the simple name of the var, and `:file` and `:line` provide information about where the var is defined. The value `NO_SOURCE_FILE` indicates that the var was defined interactively at the REPL. For functions, there is also a `:arglists` entry where the value is a list of the function's argument vectors.

```
(:arglists (meta #'map))
;=> ([f coll] [f c1 c2] [f c1 c2 c3] [f c1 c2 c3 & colls])
```

Usually, `:arglists` is automatically constructed from the function definition with `defn` but it can also be specified directly, e.g., for properly documenting functions defined in point-free style.

```
(def ^{:doc "Returns the number of even numbers in coll."
       :arglists '([coll])}
     count-evens (comp count (partial filter even?)))
;=> #'user/count-evens
```

One major difference between metadata and documentation specified with JavaDoc or Doxygen is that metadata is always accessible at runtime. For convenience, there is the `doc` macro in the `clojure.repl` namespace that given the name of a var prints its documentation metadata.

```
(doc count-evens)
; ------------------------
; user/count-evens
; ([coll])
;   Returns the number of even numbers in coll.
;=> nil
(doc map)
; ---------------------------
; map
; ([f coll] [f c1 c2] [f c1 c2 c3] [f c1 c2 c3 & colls])
;   Returns a lazy sequence consisting of the result of applying f to the
;   set of first items of each coll, followed by applying f to the set
;   of second items in each coll, until any one of the colls is
;   exhausted.  Any remaining items in other colls are ignored. Function
;   f should accept number-of-colls arguments.
;=> nil
```

The `:tag` metadata briefly mentioned above plays an important role when inter-operating with Java objects which is the topic of section 6.11 on page 57.

6.10 Namespaces

Clojure code is structured in namespaces. Therefore, a namespace is roughly equivalent to a Java package. More technically, a namespace is a set of dynamic mappings from symbols to Java classes and from symbols to vars, the latter having values such as functions or constants. Therefore, namespaces control symbol resolution, i.e., a namespace defines the meaning of the symbols occurring in it for the Clojure compiler.

When starting a REPL, a namespace `user` is created automatically. When vars are printed, the namespace is always printed and separated from the var name with a slash.

```
*ns*
;=> #<Namespace user>
(def x 1)
;=> #'user/x
(resolve 'x)
#'user/x
x
;=> 1
```

`def` creates a new var with the value 1 and adds a mapping from the symbol x to the newly created var in the current namespace. The function `resolve` can be used to check what a given symbol resolves to in the current namespace.

By default, every namespace *refers* the namespace `clojure.core` where all standard Clojure functions and macros are defined. Referring means that for any public var in the referred namespace, a mapping from a symbol denoting the var's simple name to the referred var is installed in the current namespace. Because of that, every core Clojure function and macro can usually be accessed by its simple name. Furthermore, for every Java classifier in `java.lang` a mapping from a symbol denoting the simple class name to the class object is installed.

```
(resolve 'first)
;=> #'first
Object
;=> java.lang.Object
(class Object)
;=> java.lang.Class
```

Clojure source code files always start with a namespace declaration specified with `ns`. A symbol denotes the name of the namespace, and a single `:refer-clojure` and arbitrary many `:require`, `:use`, and `:import` clauses may follow.

For example, a file `my/example_ns/core.clj` might start with the following declaration. Note that hyphens in the namespace name correspond to underscores in the directory/file name.

```
(ns my.example-ns.core
  (:refer-clojure :exclude [ancestors descendants])
  (:require clojure.pprint
            [clojure.string :as str])
  (:use clojure.pprint
        [clojure.set :only [difference]])
  (:import java.io.Writer
           (java.util ArrayList LinkedList)))
```

The example defines a new namespace `my.example-ns.core`.

The `:refer-clojure` clause says to install symbol-to-var mappings for all public Clojure vars except for `#'ancestors` and `#'descendants`, most probably because this namespace defines functions with the same simple name. The core functions can still be accessed by qualifying them: `clojure.core/ancestors` and `clojure.core/descendants`. If this clause was omitted, mappings would be created for all public vars in `clojure.core` and the compiler would emit warnings at the definition forms defining the two vars in the current namespace.

The namespaces enumerated in the `:require` clause are merely *loaded* but their vars need to be accessed in a qualified manner. The vector notation with the `:as` keyword can be used to define a shorter namespace-local alias for the required namespace. Therefore, in the namespace defined by the listing above, the Clojure pretty-printing namespace is loaded and its functions need to be called qualified like `(clojure.pprint/pprint [1 2 3])`, and `(str/blank? "\n\t")` and `(clojure.string/blank? "\n\t")` are calls of the same function, because `str` is made an alias for `clojure.string` in the current namespace.

The vars of the namespaces enumerated in the `:use` clause are *loaded* and *referred* and can be used in the declared namespace without namespace qualification. The vector notation with the `:only` keyword can be used to make only parts of a namespace's vars accessible[13].

---

[13]The general suggestion is to never use `:use` but `:require` with `:as` to make it obvious where the functions called in a namespace originate from.

Finally, the `:import` clause enumerates Java classes that should be *imported* in order to be accessible without qualification. The list notation allows for importing many classes in one package. Wildcards corresponding to Java's `import pkg.*;` are not supported.

During interactive development at the REPL, the current namespace can be changed using the `in-ns` function which receives the target namespace as a symbol.

```
*ns*
;=> #<Namespace my.example-ns.core>
(in-ns 'user)
;=> #<Namespace user>
*ns*
;=> #<Namespace user>
```

There are also the functions `require`, `use`, and `import` which correspond to the ns-causes of the same name. Those are rarely used in Clojure code but they are the primitives used by the the `ns` macro itself.

Since namespaces are dynamic mappings from symbols to vars, they can be changed without recompiling and reloading the complete namespace. During development, the IDE is always connected to the running JVM via the REPL, and changing a function will only replace the value of a var with the new definition. This makes it possible to fix bugs, add functions, and re-run test cases without ever needing to recompile and restart the system.

6.11 Java Interop

Being able to interoperate easily with existing Java libraries has been a major goal of Clojure right from the beginning. The term Java interop is a bit misleading. In fact, Clojure has direct, wrapper-free access to the JVM abstractions that are the result of compiling programs of JVM-hosted languages. These abstractions happen to be classes with fields and methods, and for Java there is a direct one-to-one correspondence between the classes/methods in the source code and the resulting JVM classes/methods. For other languages such as Clojure, Scala, or JRuby that provide other concepts like first-class functions, traits, or mixins this correspondence is not so clear and merely an implementation detail.

The special form `new` is used to create a new object. It receives a class and any number of arguments which are provided to the class' constructor.

```
(new java.awt.Point 7 10)
;=> #<Point java.awt.Point[x=7,y=10]>
```

The `new` special form is almost never used directly. Instead, the reader supports the shorter notation where the class name suffixed with a dot is in function position.

```
(java.awt.Point. 7 10)
;=> #<Point java.awt.Point[x=7,y=10]>
```

The dot special form is the basic construct for accessing fields and calling methods. For accessing a static field or calling a static method, it receives the class and the field or method name. In case of a method call, more parameters may be specified.

```
(. Math PI)                    ;; static field access
;=> 3.141592653589793
(. Math sqrt 9)                ;; static method call
;=> 3.0
```

If the first element of a dot-form is an object instead of a class, it is an instance field access or method call.

```
(let [p (java.awt.Point. 7 10)]
  [[(. p x) (. p getY)]        ;; instance x-field access & getY-method call
   (do
     (. p move 0 0)
     [(. p x) (. p getY)])])
;=> [[7 10.0] [0 0.0]]
```

Like new, the dot-special form is almost never used in Clojure but the reader supports a more consise and clear notation.

```
Math/PI                        ;; static field access
;=> 3.141592653589793
(Math/sqrt 9)                  ;; static method call
;=> 3.0
(let [p (java.awt.Point. 7 10)]
  [(.x p) (.getX p)])          ;; instance x-field access & getY-method call
;=> [7 7.0]
```

The assignment special form set! can be used to set the values of public Java fields. It receives a field access form and the value to be set for the accessed field.

```
(let [p (java.awt.Point. 7 10)]
  [(.x p) (do
            (set! (.x p) 10)
            (.x p))])
;=> [7 10]
```

Since almost all classes have private or protected fields that are set only in terms of setter methods, set! is very seldomly used.

Of course, being able to access Java fields and call methods is only the lowest level of interoperability. To facilitate a higher level of interoperability, Clojure tries to participate in the most prominent Java abstractions, e.g., the Java Collections Framework. Therefore, all Clojure collection types including (lazy) sequences implement the java.util.Collection interface. Because Clojure collections are immutable, the methods that change a collection's contents throw an UnsupportedOperationException.

```
(.add [1 2 3] 4)
; No message.
;    [Thrown class java.lang.UnsupportedOperationException]
```

But all concrete Java collection classes have a copy constructor receiving an arbitrary collection. Thus, Clojure collections can be easily converted to Java collections for interoperating with libraries mandating mutability.

```
(let [l (java.util.ArrayList. (range 10))]
  (java.util.Collections/shuffle l)
  [(class l) l])
;=> [java.util.ArrayList [0 8 2 6 5 3 1 4 7 9]]
```

Furthermore, Clojure's sequential collection types (list, vectors, sequences) implement java.util.List. Vectors also implement java.util.RandomAccess, sets implement java.util.Set, and maps implement java.util.Map.

Clojure functions also participate in the common Java abstractions in that they implement java.lang.Runnable and java.util.concurrent.Callable, which makes them suited for being distributed to threads.

Since Clojure is dynamically typed, the concrete method to be called cannot be determined at compilation time. Therefore, correct method has to be determined at runtime using reflection which is much slower than a direct method call. However, when calling Java methods, the programmer knows the class or interface of the method receiver and the method's arguments. By providing type hints, he allows the Clojure compiler to create byte-code that is equivalent to a direct method call in Java.

Type hints can be specified using :tag metadata on symbols defined with def, let, loop, binding, or function parameters. Additionally, all forms may be hinted denoting the type of the form's result, with the exception of Java literals (numbers, strings) that don't allow for added metadata. The reader supports the concise ^TypeName notation that is equivalent to ^{:tag TypeName}.

For example, the following example defines a subseq? predicate that simply wraps the boolean String.contains(CharSequence) method. First, it is defined without and then again with type hints. time is a macro that simply prints the time needed for evaluating the given expression. dotimes repeats its body the given number of times for side-effects and always returns nil.

```
(defn subseq? [s cs]
  (.contains s cs))
;=> #'user/subseq?
(time (dotimes [_ 1000000] (subseq? "abcd" "bc")))
; "Elapsed time: 4568.265582 msecs"
;=> nil
(defn subseq? [^String s cs]
  (.contains s cs))
;=> #'user/subseq?
(time (dotimes [_ 1000000] (subseq? "abcd" "bc")))
; "Elapsed time: 33.737549 msecs"
;=> nil
```

As can be seen, the hinted call is more than 100 times faster. Since the method String.contains() is not overloaded, the hinting of the cs parameter can be omitted, because the compiler can infer that the second argument must be a `CharSequence`. The compiler is also able to track the types though chains of method calls, so type hints are only needed for the innermost call. The return type of functions can also be specified by adding a type hint to the function's argument vector(s).

Type hints only have an effect on instance method calls or instance field accesses. Therefore, there is no reason to specify type hints for functions that don't call methods directly. There is a globally defined var `*warn-on-reflection*` which will make the compiler issue warnings whenever it cannot resolve a method call.

There are several more facilities for interoperating with Java which are of no importance for this works. For example, there is a set of functions for working with Java arrays, and special type hints for primitive types and arrays of primitive types. Their main use-case is high-performance numerical computations. And there are `proxy` and `reify` that allow for creating objects of anonymous classes extending and implementing other classes and interfaces.

6.12   Macros

Macros are functions that are run at *compile time* rather than *runtime*. Whereas a function receives concrete values bound to its parameters when being called, macros are called by the Clojure compiler, and the parameters of the macro are bound to the raw, unevaluated forms given to it. It may act on them arbitrarily, and its result is another form called its *expansion* which takes the place of the original macro call. Of course, its expansion may result in a form that contains another macro call which will be expanded again until no macro calls but only function calls and applications of special forms are left over.

The major point separating Clojure or Lisp macros in general from preprocessor macros in C is that the latter are substitutions on strings. Due to Lisp's homoiconicity, i.e., Lisp source code is at the same time the abstract syntax tree represented in the language's own data structures, Lisp macros are essentially endogenous in-place transformations.

In section 6.5 on page 33, it was already mentioned that some of the special forms discussed there are in fact macros. Especially the binding forms that allow for destructuring like `let`, `loop`, or `fn` are actually macros built upon simpler special forms `let*`, `loop*`, and `fn*` that don't provide the destructuring feature.

There are the functions `macroexpand` and `macroexpand-1`. They receive a form and expand it if it is a macro form. The latter function performs exactly one expansion, and the former expands repeatedly until the returned form is no macro form anymore. These functions are usually called by the compiler but they are also very helpful for understanding macros. For example, the following listing shows an expansion of a `let` form using sequential and map destructuring.

```
(let [[a b {:keys [c d] :or {d 17}}] [1 2 {:c 10}]]
  [a b c d])
;=> [1 2 10 17]
(macroexpand '(let [[a b {:keys [c d] :or {d 17}}] [1 2 {:c 10}]]
                [a b c d]))
```

```
;=> (let* [vec__2048 [1 2 {:c 10}]
;          a (nth vec__2048 0 nil)
;          b (nth vec__2048 1 nil)
;          map__2049 (nth vec__2048 2 nil)
;          map__2049 (if (seq? map__2049)
;                      (clojure.lang.PersistentHashMap/create map__2049)
;                      map__2049)
;          d (get map__2049 :d 17)
;          c (get map__2049 :c)]
;     [a b c d])
```

Without going into details, it can be seen that two new symbols `vec__2048` and `map__2049` are created implicitly, that sequential destructuring corresponds to picking out values using `nth`, and that map destructuring picks out values using `get`.

There are only few but good reasons for using macros.

1. *Removing boilerplate*: Clearly, the `let` form with destructuring is much more concise and clear than its expansion. Similarly, function definitions with `defn` are more concise and clear than their expansion, a `def` whose value is a function definition with `fn`. Therefore, definition forms are typically implemented as macros.

2. *Controlling evaluation*: `if` is the only construct that allows for conditional evaluation, i.e., depending on the result of the condition, either its then- or its else-part is evaluated. Upon that, macros can be used to define richer control structures with custom evaluation semantics. For example, the logical operators `or` and `and` should be short-circuiting. Therefore, they cannot be functions, because function arguments are evaluated before the function is called. Instead, they are macros on top of `if`. For example, `(and a b c)` expands to `(if a (and b c) false)` where the inner `and` expands to `(if b c false)` again.

3. *Performance*: Every calculation that does not depend on runtime values can be performed at compile time. As an example, there is the *core.match*[14] library that provides macros for doing pattern matching on Clojure data structures. These macros implement the algorithm described in [Mar08] to generate highly efficient decision trees at compile time, i.e., cascades of `let` and `if` forms.

One important concept for writing macros is *quasi-quoting* or *syntax-quoting*. Quoting with a backtick character ` is similar to quoting with `quote` or ' , except that it allows for *unquoting*, that is, evaluating, inner forms using `~`.

```
`(1 2 ~(+ 1 2) 4)
;=> (1 2 3 4)
```

Furthermore, expressions resulting in sequences can be unquoted with `~@` in which case the result is spliced into the outer form.

```
`(1 2 ~@(range 3 6) 7)
;=> (1 2 3 4 5 7)
```

---

[14]https://github.com/clojure/core.match (last visited: 2015-01-19)

Another quasi-quoting feature is that symbols suffixed with a hash character #
are translated to symbols with guaranteed unique names. If such a symbol occurs
multiple times in the same quasi-quoted form, its translation is always the same.

```
`(a# b# a#)
;=> (a__2473__auto__ b__2474__auto__ a__2473__auto__)
```

The function `gensym` is responsible for generating such unique symbols. Given
an optional string, it returns a symbol whose name starts with the given prefix.
Therefore, this quasi-quoting feature is frequently called *auto-gensym*.

Finally, quasi-quoting qualifies symbols. All symbols denoting vars are qualified
with their defining namespace, all other symbols are qualified with the current
namespace.

```
`(*ns* first subseq? x)
;=> (*ns* first user/subseq? user/x)
```

`*ns*` and `first` are symbols denoting vars defined in Clojure's core namespace,
`subseq?` denotes a var defined in section 6.11 on page 57 in the `user` namespace, and
`x` is a free symbol and thus is qualified with the current namespace `user`.

For defining macros, there is the `defmacro` macro. Its signature is the same as
that of `defn`, i.e., it receives the name of the new macro, an optional docstring, an
argument vector, and arbitrary many body forms. As said, when a macro is called,
its arguments are bound to the raw forms passed to it. Its body may act on them
and has to result in another form that takes the place of the macro form.

For example, let's define a `foreach` macro that mimics the advanced Java for-loop,
i.e., it evaluates a body of arbitrary many expressions for every element in some
seqable object. The desired syntax and semantics are given in the next listing.

```
(foreach [x (range 5)]
  (println x "*" x "=" (* x x)))
;  0 * 0 = 0
;  1 * 1 = 1
;  2 * 2 = 4
;  3 * 3 = 9
;  4 * 4 = 16
;=> nil
```

So `foreach` should receive a binding vector consisting of a symbol denoting the
current element and an expression resulting in a sequence, and a body of one or
many expressions. The individual parts can be picked out easily using destructuring.

```
(defmacro foreach
  "Evaluates body on each elem of coll."
  [[elem coll] & body]
  `(loop [c# ~coll]
     (when (seq c#)
       (let [~elem (first c#)]
```

```
      ~@body
      (recur (rest c#))))))
;=> #'user/foreach
```

The macro's definition mirrors its expansion using quasi-quoting. Clearly, the desired iteration can be based on `loop` and `recur`. Here, a new symbol for binding the value of the sequence expression has to be introduced. This new, implicitly created symbol must not clash with any other symbol in this scope which is guaranteed by the hash-notation. The expansion of the example is given in the following listing. The namespaces are removed for readability.

```
(loop [c__2593__auto__ (range 5)]
  (when (seq c__2593__auto__)
    (let [x (first c__2593__auto__)]
      (println x "*" x "=" (* x x))
      (recur (rest c__2593__auto__)))))
```

There are two important macro writing rules:

1. A macro should never unquote an argument more than once.
2. A macro should never capture other symbols in its scope.

The reason for the first rule is that users of a macro usually expect forms they have written only once to be evaluated only once, too. This can be demonstrated with a naive implementation of a `square` macro.

```
(defmacro square [exp]
  `(* ~exp ~exp))
;=> #'user/square
(square 3)
;=> 9
(square (rand-int 10))
;=> 12
```

The `rand-int` function returns a random integer between 0 and the given number. Clearly, 12 is no square number. The reason for this result is that `exp` is unquoted twice in the macro definition, thus its expansion is (* (rand-int 10) (rand-int 10)).

The second macro rule is concerned with *macro hygiene*. In Clojure, where quasi-quoting qualifies symbols automatically, it is really hard to be unhygienic. For example, trying to correct the `square` macro so that it doesn't evaluate its argument twice might result in the following.

```
(defmacro square [exp]
  `(let [x ~exp]
     (* x x)))
```

But since `x` will be qualified to `user/x`, and `let` cannot bind qualified symbols, any application of this macro won't even compile. Auto-gensyms or using `gensym` explicitly make it easy to stick to hygienic macros. So the following two definitions of `square` are both hygienic and correct, and their expansions will always be the same except for the name of the newly introduced symbol.

```
(defmacro square1 [exp]
  `(let [x# ~exp]
     (* x# x#)))

(defmacro square2 [exp]
  (let [x (gensym)]
    `(let [~x ~exp]
       (* ~x ~x))))
```

Usually, auto-gensyms are preferred over explicit gensyms. However, since an auto-gensym symbol like the x# above denotes only the same symbol inside one single quasi-quoted form, macros that contain many quasi-quoted forms that need to share symbols will need to use explicit gensyms.

Concludingly, macros are good for implementing new control structures, for defining custom binding forms, and for hiding boilerplate code. As such, they enable the definition of domain-specific mini-lisps providing exactly the constructs suited for that domain. However, in contrast to functions, macros are no first-class objects. For example, they cannot be passed to higher-order function.

```
(map square [1 2 3])
; Can't take value of a macro: #'user/square
;    [Thrown class java.lang.RuntimeException]
```

Therefore, macros are only used when a function won't do, and clearly defining square as a macro doesn't make sense at all.

The next section discusses the most important utility macros occurring frequently in Clojure programs.

6.13   Utility macros

This section discusses some of the very frequently used standard macros.

As its name suggests, if-let combines if with let. It receives a binding vector consisting of a symbol and a test expression, a then-form, and an optional else-form. If the test succeeds, the then-form is evaluated with the symbol bound to the value of the test. Else, the else-form is evaluated.

This macro is frequently used by functions that recurse through sequences such as the eager-reduce function in the next listing.

```
(defn eager-reduce [f s coll]
  (loop [acc s, c coll]
    (if-let [r (seq c)]
      (recur (f acc (first c)) (rest c))
      acc)))
;=> #'user/eager-reduce
(eager-reduce + 0 (range 10))
;=> 45
(eager-reduce * 1 (range 1 10))
;=> 362880
```

The when-let macro complements if-let in the same way as when complements if. It has no else-form but arbitrary many then-forms can be specified.

The cond macro receives arbitrary many test/expression pairs and returns the value of the expression that is paired with the first succeeding test. If no test succeeds, nil is returned.

```
(let [x 7]
  (cond
    (= 10 x)        :ten
    (even? x)       :even
    :else           :none-were-true))
;=> :none-were-true
```

Clearly, x is neither equal to 10 nor even. The value of the third clause is the evaluation result not because :else has a special meaning but because :else is a keyword which is neither nil nor false and thus truthy.

The for macro is a *sequence comprehension*. It receives a binding vector of symbol-expression pairs where the expressions must evaluate to seqables, and one body expression. The seqables are iterated in a nested, rightmost fastest fashion, and for each binding the body expression is evaluated. The result of for is the lazy seq of body expression values.

```
(for [x (range 3), y (range 3)]
  [x y])
;=> ([0 0] [0 1] [0 2] [1 0] [1 1] [1 2] [2 0] [2 1] [2 2])
```

The binding vector may also contain the keyword modifiers :let, :when, and :while. :let gets a binding vector, and the introduced symbols are available in all following for-bindings and the body expression. :when gets an expression that is used to impose constraints on values. Only if it is truthy, the for's body expression is evaluated, else the next iteration is started. :while also gets an expression which terminates the iteration preceding it when it becomes logical false.

The following uses these modifiers to compute a seq of triples where the first number in each triple is an integer between 0 and 10, and the second and third number are two factors.

```
(for [x (range) :while (<= x 10)
      y (range (inc x)), z (range (inc x))
      :when (<= y z)
      :let [yz (* y z)]
      :when (= x yz)]
  [x y z])
;=> ([0 0 0] [1 1 1] [2 1 2] [3 1 3] [4 1 4] [4 2 2] [5 1 5] [6 1 6]
;    [6 2 3] [7 1 7] [8 1 8] [8 2 4] [9 1 9] [9 3 3] [10 1 10] [10 2 5])
```

The doseq macro gets a binding vector with the syntax and semantics of for and aritrary many body forms. It evaluates the body for every valid binding and always returns nil. Therefore, it is only of use for its body's side-effects and mostly used when interoperating with Java.

Another Java interop macro is `doto`. It gets an expression and arbitrary many other forms. The expression is evaluated and its result is added as first argument in each following form, finally returning the result. If any of these forms in not a list already, it is created implicitly.

```
(doto (java.util.BitSet.)
  (.flip 0)
  (.flip 3 7))
;=> #<BitSet {0, 3, 4, 5, 6}>
```

The threading macros `->` (*thread first*) and `->>` (*thread last*) get an expression and arbitrary many other forms. The expression is evaluated, and the successive next forms are evaluated on the result of the respective previous form. With `->`, the result is added as first argument, with `->>` it is added as last argument. Like with `doto`, forms that are no lists already are made lists implicitly.

```
(-> (range 10) (conj (rand-int 10)) (conj (rand-int 10)) sort)
;=> (0 1 2 3 4 4 5 6 6 7 8 9)
(->> (range 20) (filter even?) count)
;=> 10
```

6.14   Protocols

Clojure protocols are similar to Java interfaces in that a protocol declares a set of method signatures without providing implementations. Concrete types can participate in arbitrary many protocols just like a Java class can implement many interfaces. And invoking a protocol method performs an efficient polymorphic dispatch based on the method receiver's type.

A protocol is declared using `defprotocol`. It receives a symbol denoting the protocol's name, an optional docstring, and arbitrary many method specifications. Each method specification consists of a name, one or many parameter vectors, and an optional docstring.

For example, the following listing defines a run-length coding protocol consisting of two method signatures.

```
(defprotocol RunLengthCoding
  "A protocol for run-length encoding/decoding."
  (run-length-encode [this]
    "Run-length encodes this.")
  (run-length-decode [this]
    "Run-length decodes this."))
```

One crucial difference between Java interfaces and protocols is that types that should participate in an abstraction defined by interfaces need to implement those. In contrast, Clojure protocols can be dynamically extended upon existing types.

With respect to the `RunLengthCoding` protocol, every type that implements some ordered collection of values can participate in the protocol in a sensible manner. This includes Clojure vectors, lists, and sequences but also strings or Java lists.

The next listing defines a private functions for run-length encoding. The only requirement of the encoding function `rle` is that its argument is some object participating in the sequence abstraction. Its result is a vector of tuples (vectors of length 2), where the first element is a value and the second element is the number of consecutive occurrences in the original seq.

```
(defn- rle [coll]
  (reduce (fn [r e]
            (let [[l n] (peek r)]
              (if (= l e)
                (conj (pop r) [l (inc n)])
                (conj r [e 1)))))
          [[(first coll) 0]]
          coll))
```

The decoding function `rld` given in the next listing assumes this representation and unpacks it to a sequence again.

```
(defn- rld [coll]
  (mapcat (fn [[c l]]
            (repeat l c))
          coll))
```

These two functions are the low-level primitives suited to provide implementations for the `RunLengthCoding` protocol. The following listing shows some example applications on a vector and a string.

```
(rle [1 1 1 2 2 3 4 4 4 4 4])
;=> [[1 3] [2 2] [3 1] [4 5]]
(rld (rle [1 1 1 2 2 3 4 4 4 4 4]))
;=> (1 1 1 2 2 3 4 4 4 4 4)
(rle "aaabbccccc")
;=> [[\a 3] [\b 2] [\c 5]]
(rld (rle "aaabbccccc"))
;=> (\a \a \a \b \b \c \c \c \c \c)
(apply str (rld (rle "aaabbccccc")))
;=> "aaabbccccc"
```

To provide implementations for a protocol, there is the `extend-protocol` macro. It gets the protocol name as a symbol followed by arbitrary many implementation specifications. Each implementation specification consists of a type on which the protocol is extended followed by implementations of the protocol's methods.

In the next listing, the `RunLengthCoding` protocol is extended upon `java.util.List` and `java.lang.String` mostly by delegating to the private functions `rle` and `rld`.

```
(extend-protocol RunLengthCoding
  java.util.List
  (run-length-encode [this]
    (rle this))
  (run-length-decode [this]
```

```clojure
    (let [v (rld this)]
      (if (= String (::orig-type (meta this)))
        (apply str v)
        v)))
  String
  (run-length-encode [this]
    (with-meta (rle this)
      {::orig-type String})))
```

In the case of strings, there is only an implementation of the encoding function, because a string's run-length encoded representation is a vector which implements java.util.List. Metadata is used to ensure that run-length encoding and decoding a string results in a string again rather than a sequence of characters. Keywords like ::orig-type starting with two colons are qualified with the current namespace by the Clojure reader which is appropriate here because this metadata is meant only for internal use.

Chapter 7

Modeling Frameworks

In this chapter, the two modeling frameworks JGraLab and EMF are introduced. They are directly supported by FunnyQT, and their commonalities and differences are highlighted.

7.1 JGraLab

With JGraLab, models are represented as so-called *TGraphs* [ERW08]. A TGraph is a graph where both the vertices and the edges are typed and may be attributed. Even the graph itself is typed and may be attributed, too. Edges are directed but navigation is always possible in both directions. There is a global order upon all vertices in a TGraph, a global order upon all edges, and at every vertex, there is a local order upon all incident edges. Lastly, every vertex and every edge in a TGraph has an integral ID.

Figure 7.1 on the next page shows a visualization of an example TGraph[1]. Many of the TGraph properties can be seen. The vertex $v1$ has the type Female and its name attribute has the value "Jane Smith". The edge $e1$ has the type HasSpouse and its marriageDate attribute has some composite value which encodes the date March 13, 2001. The IDs of this vertex and this edge are both 1, i.e., the prefixes "v" and "e" are only artifacts of the visualization.

As mentioned above, even the graph itself may be attributed. However, in the visualization there is no representation of the graph, only of its vertices and edges.

The global order between all vertices and all edges in the graph is not visible. In general, the IDs of vertices and edges do not indicate the order. A vertex or and edge may be moved forward and backward in the list of a graph's vertices and edges which affects the order but the ID stays stable. Also, if a vertex or edge is deleted, the ID which has become unused will eventually be reused by a new vertex or edge which is by default appended to the graph's list of vertices or edges.

---

[1]This visualization has been generated by FunnyQT's visualization facility which is discussed in section 15.3 on page 158

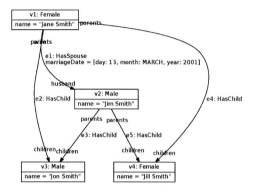

Figure 7.1: An example TGraph

However, in the special case that a graph is created from scratch using only create methods, the IDs correspond to both the global order of vertices and edges, and the IDs of the edges also indicate the incidence order at each vertex. So when assuming this situation, the incidence order at the vertex $v2$ is $e1$ first, then $e3$, and lastly $e5$.

Every TGraph conforms to a *schema*. A schema is a metamodel for a class of TGraphs which is defined as a *GraphUML* class diagram. GraphUML (*grUML*) is a profile of the UML class diagram language [OMG15c] which comprises only those elements that are compatible with graph semantics. For example, the UML supports n-ary associations with $n > 2$ but grUML does not because that would require hypergraphs[2].

The schema the TGraph from fig. 7.1 conforms to is shown in fig. 7.2 on the facing page. This schema defines a *graph class* Genealogy which is the type of all conforming graphs. The graph class has one attribute version of attribute type (*domain*) Integer.

Vertex types (*vertex classes*) are defined as grUML classes, and edge types (*edge classes*) are defined as grUML associations or association classes in case attributes are defined for them. There may be specializations (including multiple inheritance) between the vertex classes on the one hand and between the edge classes on the other hand.

The schema defines three vertex classes: Person, Female, and Male. The Person class is abstract and specialized by the two other vertex classes. Therefore, the name attribute of domain String is inherited by the latter two classes.

---

[2]There is a JGraLab variant supporting Distributed Hierarchical Hyper-TGraphs (DHHTGraphs, [Bil12; BE11]) but it is not supported by FunnyQT.

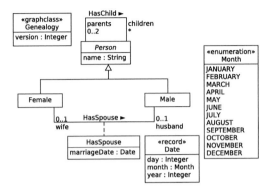

Figure 7.2: The schema of the graph in fig. 7.1 on page 70

The schema also defines two edge classes HasSpouse and HasChild. The HasSpouse edge class starts at the vertex class Female and ends at the vertex class Male, thus edges of this type must always start at a Female vertex and end at a Male vertex[3]. The role names and multiplicities define that every female has at most one husband, and every male has at most one wife.

The domain of the marriageDate attribute of the HasSpouse edge class is Date which is a custom *record domain*. A record domain defines a structured datatype, e.g., similar to a struct in C. Each component of the record domain has a name and a domain. Thus, a Date consists of a day, a month, and a year where the first and the last are integers and the month is an enumeration constant defined by the *enumeration domain* Month which is also defined by the schema.

The concepts available for modeling a TGraph schema are defined by the *grUML metaschema* which is self-describing meaning it is a valid schema on its own. This metaschema is shown in fig. 7.3 on the following page.

It defines that every schema must contain exactly one graph class. Furthermore, it may define any number of vertex classes, edge classes, and domains[4]. As already mentioned above, the graph class, vertex classes, and edge classes may be attributed, and there are separate specialization hierarchies for vertex classes and edge classes, respectively.

The end points of edge classes with their properties are encoded by *incidence classes*. These properties include the multiplicities, a role name (which is optional),

---

[3]This schema is easily understandable and therefore nice for illustration purposes. It is definitely not intended as a statement against same-sex marriage.

[4]The figure does not include the Package class for formatting reasons. Each schema contains one default package which may contain other packages. All named elements are contained in some package, and the graph class and all domains except for record and enum domains must reside in the default package.

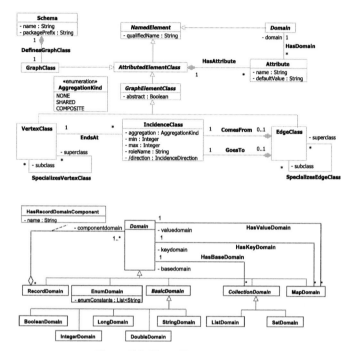

Figure 7.3: The grUML metaschema

and the aggregation kind. The latter is used to encode if an edge class defines a part-of relationship, and at most one incidence class of an edge class may have an aggregation kind different from NONE. An edge class $A2B$ starting at a vertex class A and ending at a vertex class B has a strict containment semantics if the aggregation kind of the incidence class at B is COMPOSITE, i.e., it then corresponds to a UML composition. If it was SHARED, it would have weak containment semantics, i.e., it would then correspond to a UML aggregation. An edge class where both incidence classes have the aggregation kind NONE has no containment semantics and corresponds to a usual UML association.

The lower part of fig. 7.3 shows the different domains available as attribute types. The supported basic domains correspond to the Java types `boolean`, `int`, `long`, `double`, and `String`. As has been seen in fig. 7.2 on page 71, a schema may define custom record and enumeration domains. Furthermore, list- and set-valued homogeneous collection domains are supported which have a given base domain, e.g., the domain List<Integer> in a schema denotes the list domain with base domain integer. Lastly, there is the map domain which has a key domain and a value domain.

Programming with JGraLab. When programming with TGraphs, every graph is an object being an instance of the JGraLab interface Graph. From a graph, all vertices and edges contained by it can be retrieved. Those are instances of the JGraLab interfaces Vertex and Edge, respectively.

Graphs, vertices, and edges are all instances of the interface AttributedElement which declares methods for retrieving and setting attribute values. From all attributed elements, the corresponding attributed element class in the schema can be accessed.

From an edge, the source vertex (*alpha*) and the target vertex (*omega*) can be accessed, and from a vertex, the sequence of all incident edges can be retrieved. And from a vertex, adjacent vertices can also be accessed by the role names defined for far-end incidence classes. Vertices can also be added to a role which then implies the creation of edges.

JGraLab provides two runtime representations for TGraphs. With the generic representation, the graph and its vertices and edges are accessed using the interfaces named above. All constraints imposed by the schema are checked dynamically at runtime, e.g., when trying to create an edge being instance of some edge class between two vertices, it is checked if these vertices are instances of the source and target vertex classes of the edge class. If not, an exception is thrown.

Alternatively, JGraLab can generate an object-oriented API for a given schema. In this case, the standard interfaces mentioned above and the corresponding implementation classes are further specialized so that for any graph class, vertex class, and edge class defined in the schema, a corresponding interface (and implementation class) exists. This generated API ensures most constraints imposed by the schema in terms of static typing already, e.g., the create method for HasSpouse edges requires that a Female start vertex and a Male end vertex is given.

There is almost no measurable difference in performance or memory requirements between the two representations. However, the generated API is much more convenient when programming with TGraphs in Java. Generic tools such as FunnyQT which have to work with any TGraphs no matter the schema can obviously only use the generic API. But since the schema-specific interfaces specialize the generic ones, the generic API is always available.

7.2   The Eclipse Modeling Framework

With the Eclipse Modeling Framework (EMF, [Ste+09]), a model is a set of typed EObject instances (*eobjects* for short) which may be attributed and may reference each other.

Figure 7.4 on the next page shows a visualization of a simple EMF model which represents the same facts as the TGraph in fig. 7.1 on page 70. All three properties of eobjects are clearly visible. The topmost eobject in the visualization has the type Genealogy. Its version attribute is set to 0, and it references five other eobjects: four Female and Male eobjects are referenced with the persons reference, and one Marriage eobject is referenced with the marriages reference.

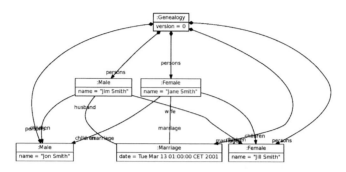

Figure 7.4: An example EMF model

The name attribute values of Female and Male eobjects are obviously strings. However, the type of the date attribute of the Marriage eobject seems to be some kind of timestamp.

With EMF, there is no explicit object representing the model itself. Therefore, an explicit Genealogy object is used in order to be able to assign a version. Furthermore, it is good although not required practice for an EMF model to have some root object which contains all other eobjects directly or indirectly. In the visualization, references denoting containments are visualized with a filled diamond at the side of the container.

References in EMF are just links without an identity. Therefore, whereas an attributed edge has been used to indicate that Jane and Jim are married to each other, the EMF model has to represent this fact with a Marriage eobject which references both Jane and Jim[5].

References in EMF are either unidirectional or bidirectional. For example, the persons reference is a unidirectional containment reference where the unidirectionality is visualized by having a label only at the target side. Bidirectional references are visualized by having a label at both sides. In fact, a bidirectional reference is actually a pair of unidirectional references where the respective other one is set as the opposite reference. For example, the wife reference is the opposite of the husband reference, and together they can be viewed as a bidirectional reference.

Every EMF model conforms to an *Ecore* metamodel which defines the abstract syntax of model instances. The model from fig. 7.4 conforms to the metamodel shown in fig. 7.5 on the facing page.

Metamodels are defined using Ecore diagrams which are EMOF [OMG15a]

---

[5]It is a running gag in our working group to refer to such a thing as a "nedge" (or "*Knante*" in German) because it is a node (ger. *Knoten*) which actually represents a relationship that should be modeled with an edge (ger. *Kante*).

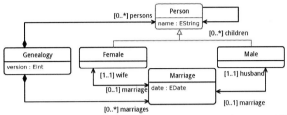

Figure 7.5: The metamodel of the model in fig. 7.4 on page 74

compatible class diagrams. Each class in the diagram defines an EClass with its attributes (EAttribute). Specialization including multiple inheritance is supported between eclasses.

Associations in the diagram define references (EReference). If there is only one role name, a unidirectional reference is defined. If there are role names at both sides of the association, a bidirectional reference is defined, i.e., a pair of two unidirectional references opposite to each other.

Ecore distinguishes only plain references modeled as associations from containment references modeled as compositions, i.e., weak containment semantics cannot be expressed.

So the persons reference is a unidirectional containment reference where a Genealogy is the container of arbitrary many Person eobjects. The children reference is unidirectional and has no containment semantics. Lastly, the references wife and husband are opposite to each other and together form a bidirectional reference without containment semantics.

The concepts available for modeling metamodels are defined by the *Ecore metametamodel* which is depicted in fig. 7.6 on the following page. This is actually a fragmentary version reduced to the core concepts because the actual Ecore metametamodel is quite large and very near to the implementation.

The most important concept is the EClass which may specialize other eclasses and contain structural features which are either attributes or references.

Structural features are typed elements, therefore they have a type. That the eType reference is optional according to the multiplicities has a purely technical reason. In a valid Ecore metamodel, all typed elements have a type[6]. All typed elements have multiplicities. If the upper bound is greater than one, a typed element is said to be multi-valued in which case the many attribute would be set to true. A multi-valued attribute in an Ecore metamodel corresponds to a list-valued attribute in a TGraph schema. Although not shown in fig. 7.6, typed elements can also be set to unique in which case a multi-valued attribute would represent a set. In practice, multi-valued attributes are rarely used.

The eType reference is actually subsetted by two references at EAttribute and

---

[6]Also, every structural feature is contained by some eclass, and every classifier is contained by some epackage.

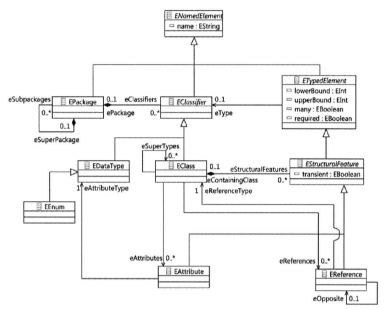

Figure 7.6: The Ecore metametamodel

EReference in order to define that the type of an eattribute is always an EDataType whereas the type of an ereference is always an EClass.

EMF supports more datatypes than JGraLab. Next to all the primitive Java types (`boolean`, `byte`, `short`, `char`, `int`, `long`, `float`, and `double`), strings, and custom enumerations, it also supports dates (`java.util.Date`), big integers (`java.math.BigInteger`), and big decimals (`java.math.BigDecimal`). Furthermore, Ecore allows to define arbitrary custom datatypes. For persistence, the user has to define methods for writing instances of such a datatype to a string and for reading it back. In practice, however, almost all Ecore metamodels use only the primitive Java types, strings, and enumerations for attributes.

Programming with EMF.   Every element in a model is represented as an instance of the EObject interface which provides methods for accessing and setting attribute values and references. Furthermore, there is a method for retrieving the EClass the eobject is an instance of.

Like with JGraLab, a model can be represented generically at runtime (called a *dynamic model instance* in this context), or code may be generated from an Ecore metamodel. In the latter case, many constraints imposed by the schema are already ensured statically but the generated interfaces and classes extend the generic ones, so a generic access is always possible, too.

As said above, with EMF there is no real representation of the model or the metamodel itself. A model is just a set of interrelated eobjects, and a metamodel is in essence just a set of interrelated eclasses. Interestingly, EClass is a subinterface of EObject, thus with EMF, a metamodel is a model, too.

For persistence, there is the Resource interface. A resource is a container for eobjects. When saving a resource, all eobjects are saved which are contained directly or indirectly by the resource[7]. Furthermore, many resources can be combined in one ResourceSet.

When comparing EMF with TGraphs, a TGraph is a closed system whereas EMF models are more open. A TGraph contains its vertices and edges, and edges can only start and end at vertices of the same graph. With EMF, objects are not restricted in that respect. Only for persistence, the objects need to be placed in a resource. Especially with transformations on EMF models, it is common practice to have the traceability information, i.e., which target element has been created for which source element, represented as a model whose elements reference eobjects in the transformation's source and target model. This is a valuable feature which is not possible with TGraphs. On the other hand, TGraphs are more expressive especially due to having typed and attributed edges.

In the next part, a generic view on models including its terminology is conceptualized. All higher-level querying and transformation concepts provided by FunnyQT are based on this generic view and thus agnostic to the actual modeling framework used for representing models at runtime.

---

[7]This is the reason why most Ecore metamodels define a strict containment hierarchy.

Part III

The FunnyQT Approach

Summary

In this part, a high-level overview of the FunnyQT approach is given. First, chapter 8 starting on page 83 discusses several possible options for achieving genericity in model querying and transformations, and then it goes on explaining the option chosen by FunnyQT in more detail.

Chapter 9 starting on page 91 explicates the terminology used throughout this writing and introduces the conventions used when designing the FunnyQT API.

Finally, the way FunnyQT is structured into several namespaces, i.e., its architecture, is explained in chapter 10 starting on page 95.

Chapter 8

On Genericity

As stated in chapter 3 starting on page 13, one of FunnyQT's major goals is to be generic, i.e., to allow for defining queries and transformations on models without having to take into account concrete modeling frameworks and their inherent model representations. Therefore, some kind of a generic view on models has to be realized.

There are various options how genericity can be achieved. The most important ones are discussed along their advantages and disadvantages in section 8.1. The option taken by FunnyQT is then discussed in more detail in section 8.2 on page 88.

8.1 Viable Options for Genericity

In this section, three options for achieving genericity in model querying and transformations are discussed. Two options, the *interface-based approach* discussed in section 8.1.1 and the *protocol-based approach* discussed in section 8.1.3 on page 88, deal with defining a generic view on the existing model representations used by today's modeling frameworks. In contrast, another option is to define a *custom model representation* with import and export facilities for models of existing frameworks as suggested by the approach discussed in section 8.1.2 on page 87.

8.1.1 Interface-Based Genericity

The most obvious option and standard practice for achieving genericity in Java is to define the assumptions and requirements that are relevant in a certain context as a set of interfaces accompanied by documentation specifying the contract of every method declared by the interfaces. Then, the actual functionality is implemented on top of those interfaces and can be obtained from every object whose concrete implementation class implements one or more of those interfaces.

In the context of model querying and model transformation, a generic view on models and metamodels would be needed in order to build querying and transformation capabilities on top. This generic view would need at least the common

CRUD-capabilities[1], i.e., it must provide the abilities to create new model elements, to access and set elements' attributes and references, and to delete model elements from a model again. Furthermore, it also needs to provide at least a read-only view on metamodels, e.g., in order to distinguish and filter elements according to their metamodel classes.

A sketch of how such an interface-based model and metamodel view might look like is shown in fig. 8.1.

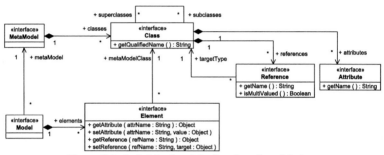

Figure 8.1: A sketch of an interface-based model view

A metamodel consists of arbitrary many classes. For every metamodel class, one can get its qualified name and the sets of direct super- and subclasses. A metamodel class may possess attributes and references which both have a name. Every reference has a metamodel class as target type, and it may either be single- or multi-valued.

Then, a model consists of a set of elements. From a model, one can retrieve the metamodel to which the model conforms to, and from a model element, one can retrieve the metamodel class the element is an instance of. Furthermore, the element interface declares methods for accessing and setting the values of properties.

All in all, the interfaces in fig. 8.1 specify a generic view on models where model elements are typed and attributed, and navigation between elements is performed in terms of reference names. This view is very similar to the standard EMF interfaces except that it is a bit simplified. E.g., the EMF interface EObject fulfills the role of the Element interface in the figure where the methods eGet() and eSet() provide the functionality of Element's attribute and reference getter and setter methods. Likewise, one can have this view also on JGraLab's TGraphs by ignoring first-class edges and only considering the role names as references which are declared for the edge classes.

There are three options with respect to how a concrete modeling framework could be supported with such an interface-based approach.

The first one is that the framework's model and metamodel representation interfaces or classes extend or implement the generic model view interfaces directly.

---
[1]CRUD means create/read/update/delete

This puts the burden of implementing the view on the developers of the respective modeling frameworks, and it adds a mandatory dependency between the modeling framework and the interfaces making up the generic model view. For this reason, this option is very unlikely to happen.

The second option is to use aspect-oriented programming (AOP, [Kic96] and specifically [Kic+01] for AspectJ[2]/Java), especially inter-type declarations, to make a modeling framework's interfaces extend the generic interfaces. There is no way to distinguish if an interface has been implemented directly or if it has been implemented by an advice that wove in the required byte-code at load-time. Thus, the AOP-based approach is equivalent to direct implementation of the generic interfaces with the crucial advantage that it can be performed without touching a concrete modeling framework's interfaces and classes. For inter-type declarations there also shouldn't be a performance penalty involved. On the negative side, aspects introduce a dependency to a concrete AOP framework like AspectJ and require additional tool support in IDEs and build infrastructure.

The third option to access concrete models using the interfaces of the generic view is to write adapter classes (see *Adapter Pattern* in [Gam+95]) which implement the generic interfaces, wrap an object of a concrete modeling framework, and then translate calls of the generic methods to calls of the framework-specific methods.

The following listing shows how such a class for adapting EMF objects would be implemented.

```
class EMFElement implements Element {
    private EObject adaptee;

    public EMFElement(EObject adaptee) {
        this.adaptee = adaptee;
    }

    public Class getMetaModelClass() {
        return new EMFClass(adaptee.eClass());
    }

    public Object getAttribute(String attrName) {
        EClass eclass = adaptee.eClass();
        EStructuralFeature sf = eclass.getEStructuralFeature(attrName);
        if (sf instanceof EAttribute) {
            return adaptee.eGet(sf);
        } else throw new RuntimeException("No such attribute " + attrName);
    }

    // ...
}
```

EMFElement is an Element-adapter for EMF objects. Its method getMetaModel-Class() simply delegates to the wrapped object's eClass() method and wraps its return value in a Class-adapter for EMF EClass objects.

---

[2]https://www.eclipse.org/aspectj/ (last visited: 2015-12-26)

The getAttribute() method's implementation caters for the fact that EObject's eGet() method considers both attributes and references, and receives a structural feature instead of only a name.

A similar adapter could be written for adapting JGraLab's Vertex interface to the generic Element interface.

The positive aspects of such an adapter-based implementation of the generic interfaces is that it can be done without touching the interfaces of a modeling framework similar to the AOP-based implementation approach. In contrast to that, the adapter-based approach does not require additional tool support but this advantage is dearly bought by having (at least) one wrapper object per model element.

In general, positive aspects of an interface-based approach for genericity is that it is relatively easy to implement and still uses the framework-specific model representations. Therefore, a model can be accessed with both the generic and the framework-specific interfaces which makes it possible to use a combination of tools requiring the generic interfaces and native tools working on the concrete modeling framework's interfaces.

A negative aspect of the interface-based approach is that interfaces don't provide adequate means to deal with optionality or variability. The generic model view in fig. 8.1 on page 84 models only the intersection of features provided by different modeling frameworks' model representations. All additional properties a concrete model representation offers (e.g., first-class edges) should be accessible for querying and transformation services, too. However, it is hardly possible to model every combination of supported features in terms of a hierarchy of interfaces.

For example, consider the functionality of accessing attribute values. In the minimal interface sketch in fig. 8.1 on page 84 this is only possible for Element instances which correspond to JGraLab's vertices and EMF's eobjects. But in JGraLab, also edges and even the graph itself might possess attributes. Thus, the functionality of accessing attributes shouldn't be declared in the Element interface but in its own AttributedElement interface which could then be extended by Element. Since in general a model has no attributes on its own, Model should not specialize AttributedElement but we might define a new interface AttributedModel which specializes Model and AttributedElement. Next comes the functionality of retrieving the relationships in a model which can only be implemented if the concrete model representation has first-class edges, thus a new ModelWithRelationships interface is due. And of course, this might come in an attributed version, too. It is easy to see that it is at least very tedious to press each and every functionality that might be supported by some modeling framework in a hierarchy of interfaces.

This problem could be somehow mitigated by not following the standard Java practice that if a class implements an interface, the methods brought in by that interface can be called safely on objects of that class. That is, the interfaces defining the generic model view could model the union of features instead of their intersection. In that case, the implementation of a method which cannot be supported by a concrete model representation, e.g., retrieving the first-class relationships of an EMF model, would simply throw an UnsupportedOperationException. However, there is no good way to test if a method is supported other than to call it to see if it returns a sensible value or throws an exception[3].

8.1.2 A Custom Model Representation

Another way to achieve genericity is to define a custom FunnyQT-specific model representation with import and export facilities for the common modeling frameworks such as EMF and JGraLab. Then all querying and transformation services can be based on a single well-defined data structure, and to add support for another modeling framework only an import and export service needs to be implemented.

Such an approach has some attractiveness. Because FunnyQT is implemented as a Clojure API and Clojure is a functional language, a purely functional model data structure would be a prefect match. A purely functional data structure is a data structure which is immutable and persistent. This means that a modification to the data structure, e.g., the addition of a new element, creates a new version of the structure where the old version is still accessible. These properties can be achieved trivially by a copy-on-write strategy but modern functional data structures such as the ones designed in [Oka98] are much more sophisticated and efficient by having updated versions share large parts of their (usually tree-based) internals with previous versions. All Clojure collection types are such functional data structures.

The crucial benefit of functional data structures is that they can be accessed and manipulated concurrently without any locking because every thread only sees a specific version that can never change and all updates are only visible to the updating thread itself. Clojure provides several reference types which allow for concurrent (and possibly coordinated) atomic updates of state shared by multiple threads. Because any update might need to be retried in case another thread performed an update in the meantime, it is crucial that update actions are free of side-effects which implies that the data structure itself needs to be a functional one.

Some work has been done to come up with a fully functional graph data structure in [Erw97; Erw01] leading to Haskell's *Functional Graph Library (FGL*[4]*)* which provides directed inductive multi-graphs with labeled nodes and edges. However, those graphs are still far off the expressivity and performance of modern modeling frameworks like JGraLab and EMF.

And with a custom model representation, the same considerations with respect to optionality and variability apply. Ideally, it should be able to expose features that are only supported by a subset of model representations for which an import facility exists.

This does not mean that this option is infeasible but it is a hard research problem on its own and thus not tackled by FunnyQT.

---

[3]Another way would be to use Java annotations with `@Retention(RetentionPolicy.RUNTIME)` for marking methods as unsupported and then accessing them using reflection.

[4]`http://hackage.haskell.org/package/fgl` (last visited: 2015-12-26)

8.1.3 Protocol-Based Genericity

The third approach to achieve genericity is protocol-based. This is the approach eventually taken by FunnyQT.

Clojure protocols have already been discussed in section 6.14 on page 66. To recapitulate, a protocol is similar to an interface in that it has a name and declares one or more methods accompanied by documentation without providing implementations. After a protocol has been declared, implementations of its methods can be added for arbitrary interfaces and classes. This is similar to the AOP-based option of implementing interfaces discussed in section 8.1.1 on page 83 except that this extension of applicability to another type happens at runtime rather than compile- or load-time, and there is also no byte-code modification involved.

The crucial difference between interfaces and protocols is that the former complect typing with applicability of method calls whereas protocols only deal with the latter. That is, when a class C implements an interface I in order to provide an implementation for I's doi() method, then C-objects are also I-instances. When a protocol P is extended upon a class C, it only means that the protocol's methods can be called for C-objects (and objects of C's subclasses) without changing C's type hierarchy. And it is possible to test if a given object's class satisfies a protocol.

Every functionality one may assume from a model or model element can be specified as a protocol. One such functionality is to retrieve the value of an attribute. Thus, this protocol has to be extended upon all types that possess attributes. For JGraLab, this is the graph itself and its vertices and edges. For EMF, only eobjects are attributed. That way, FunnyQT can use the native model representations which it accesses in terms of a generic protocol-based API. And by testing if a concrete framework-specific class satisfies a given protocol or set of protocols, it can unlock additional features which require those protocols.

So in conclusion, protocols are an adequate means to achieve genericity. A more detailed description of how FunnyQT uses protocols is given in section 8.2.

8.2 Protocol-Based Genericity for Model Querying and Transformation

FunnyQT uses the native model representations of concrete modeling frameworks. I.e., with EMF a model is a Resource containing EObject instances, and with JGraLab a model is a Graph containing Vertex and Edge instances.

FunnyQT's generic model management and querying API which is discussed later in part IV starting on page 105 defines several protocols for accessing models and model elements. For example, there is a protocol IElements that declares an `elements` method. When being applied to a model, it should return the sequence of elements contained in that model. For EMF, there is an implementation for Resource which returns the sequence of eobjects contained in that resource. For JGraLab, there is an implementation for Graph which returns the sequence of vertices of that graph.

For model representations which provide first-class edges, there is also a protocol

IRelationships declaring a `relationships` method. This protocol is only implemented for JGraLab's Graph interface where it returns the sequence of edges of the given graph.

The model elements and relationships returned by the methods `elements` and `relationships` can be restricted to specific metamodel types in case a type-checking protocol ITypeMatcher is extended upon a concrete framework's types.

Likewise, there is a protocol IAttributeValueAccess declaring the methods `aval` and `set-aval!`. For EMF, this protocol is extended upon the EObject interface. For JGraLab, it is extended upon the AttributedElement interface which is the superinterface of all JGraLab types that may possess attributes namely vertices, edges, and the graph itself.

There are several more such protocols but they all have in common that they are very slim (most of the time they only declare one method) and encode only one single functionality. The most important protocols are:

IElements for retrieving the elements contained in a model
IRelationships for retrieving the relationships contained in a model with first-class edges
IAttributeValueAccess for accessing and setting attribute values
ITypeMatcher for restricting elements and relationships to a certain type
IQualifiedName for retrieving the qualified name of a metamodel class
IMMClass for retrieving a metamodel class by its qualified name or the metamodel class of a given model element
ICreateElement for creating elements in a model
ICreateRelationship for creating a relationship between two elements in a model with first-class edges
IDelete for deleting elements or relationships in a model
IAdjacenciesInternal for navigating between elements in terms of role or reference names

All these protocol realize a *duck-typed*[5] *view* on models. With such a view, it's not a label that classifies a thing, it's the set of observable properties it has. Or in programming language terms: it's not the class of an object that's relevant, it's the set of methods it responds to. So for FunnyQT, it's not an object's type which makes it a model, a model element, or a metamodel element but it's the set of protocol methods which are applicable for the object.

For example, if an object satisfies the IElements and ICreateElement protocol to retrieve its model elements and to create new ones, then FunnyQT may treat this object as a model because it possesses all essential properties one expects from a model. If it also satisfies the protocols IRelationships and ICreateRelationship, then it is even a model with first-class edges. Thus, EMF resources and JGraLab graphs are both models although their only common supertype is java.lang.Object. In the same sense, EMF eobjects and JGraLab vertices are model elements because those are returned by the IElements method `elements`, and JGraLab edges are relationships because those are returned by the IRelationships method `relationships`. And since in a model every object is an instance of a class in the metamodel, we can retrieve this

---

[5]"When I see a bird that walks like a duck and swims like a duck and quacks like a duck, I call that bird a duck." — James Whitcomb Riley

(element or relationship) class with the `mm-class` method declared by the IMMClass protocol.

Chapter 9

Terminology and Conventions

This chapter briefly introduces the terminology around models which is used throughout this thesis and FunnyQT's documentation. This terminology encompasses all generally useful concepts which are likely to exist in many modeling frameworks.

While the terminology is being discussed, also some conventions are introduced. This is done using short code snippets containing exemplary function calls. Those functions are discussed later in chapter 12 starting on page 107, but their exact semantics is not needed for the purpose of exemplifying conventions, anyway.

Figure 9.1 shows a simple example metamodel that models a filesystem structure both as TGraph schema on the left and as Ecore model on the right. This metamodel is used for illustrating important concepts in the following.

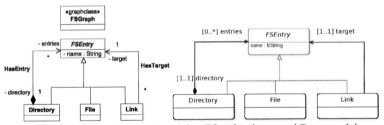

Figure 9.1: A filesystem metamodel as TGraph schema and Ecore model

As said in section 8.2 on page 88, FunnyQT has a duck-typed view on models. As such, a *model* is essentially just a container for *model elements*, i.e., one can retrieve the model elements contained in it, one can create new elements in it, and one can delete elements in it. If the underlying model representation supports first-class edges, then a model may also contain *relationships* that can be enumerated, created, and deleted.

Each model conforms to some *metamodel* which FunnyQT treats as a container of *element classes* and possibly *relationship classes*. That is, for a metamodel it should be possible to enumerate all element and relationship classes, and it should be possible to retrieve a concrete class by its *qualified name*[1]. Furthermore, any model element or relationship should be able to return the metamodel class it is an instance of.

In FunnyQT, wherever a metamodel class has to be specified, it is provided as a Clojure symbol denoting the fully qualified name of that type. With respect to fig. 9.1 on page 91, to create a new File element in a model, one would use (create-element! model 'File) where the symbol File denotes the correspondingly named metamodel class. Or in case the model supports first-class relationships, (relationships model 'HasTarget) would return the sequence of all HasTarget relationships contained in the model.

Depending on the underlying model representation, metamodel element and relationship classes may possess *attributes* whose values may be retrieved and set for instances of those classes. In FunnyQT, wherever an attribute has to be specified, it is provided as a Clojure keyword denoting the name of the attribute. So in order to retrieve the value of a filesystem entry's name attribute, one would write (aval entry :name).

A metamodel class may define *references* that are like attributes whose type is another metamodel class. Modeling frameworks without first-class edges such as EMF have only references whereas modeling frameworks with first-class edges might allow the usage of references in addition to edges. In JGraLab, an edge class may define role names for its source and target ends which can be treated like references in EMF. Therefore, the terms reference and *role name* are used interchangeably.

With respect to fig. 9.1 on page 91, the element class FSEntry has a reference named directory, Directory has an entries-reference, and Link has a target-reference. In FunnyQT, wherever a reference has to be specified, it is provided as a Clojure keyword denoting the reference name. For example, one would write (adj link :target) to get the filesystem entry link points at.

For many metamodels it is sensible and natural to define a strict containment hierarchy. For example, a metamodel for Java might model that a package contains classes, classes contain fields and methods, and methods contain statements. Such *containment references* are commonly visualized as UML compositions. The metamodel class owning the containment reference is called the *whole* or the *container* and the metamodel class on the opposite side is called the *part* or *contents*. Such containment references also denote an existential dependency between the part and the whole. There cannot be a field or a method which is not contained in a class[2]. Usually, this also implies a cascading delete semantics on the instance level. When deleting the container, e.g., a class element, all its contents, e.g, its fields and methods, are deleted, too.

The metamodel in fig. 9.1 on page 91 also defines a strict containment hierarchy. A directory contains filesystem entries, and every filesystem entry is contained in exactly one directory. Thus, the reference entries is a containment reference. In the

---

[1]Optionally, metamodel classes may also be specified using their simple class name in case that is unique and the IUniqueName protocol is satisfied.

[2]Of course, there can be statements not directly contained in a method. This would be modeled by a (0,1) multiplicity on the side of the container, i.e., the method.

TGraph schema on the left, we say that HasEntry is a *containment relationship class*.

Every reference which has no strict containment semantics is called a *cross-reference*. Likewise, relationship classes with no strict containment semantics are called *cross-referencing relationship classes*.

In fig. 9.1 on page 91, the Link class' target-reference is a cross-reference, and the edge class HasTarget is a cross-referencing relationship class.

Next, references can be distinguished in *unidirectional references* and *bidirectional references*. A reference is bidirectional if it has an opposite reference, otherwise it's unidirectional. I.e., a bidirectional reference is actually a pair of two references where one points from A to B and the other from B to A. Modeling frameworks such as EMF automatically synchronize such bidirectional references.

In fig. 9.1 on page 91, the entries-reference is bidirectional because it has the opposite directory-reference. Thus, the latter is also bidirectional[3]. In contrast, target is a unidirectional reference. There is no way to navigate from some filesystem entry to the links pointing to it via a role name. Of course, in the case of JGraLab one can still do that by traversing all incoming HasTarget edges.

The term *property* is frequently used as the superordinate concept of attributes and references. Properties can be *single-valued* or *multi-valued*. A property is single-valued if its multiplicity is (0,1) or (1,1). If its maximum multiplicity is larger than one, it is multi-valued.

With respect to fig. 9.1 on page 91, the references directory and target are single-valued whereas entries is multi-valued. The attribute name is single-valued.

Attributes with multiplicities other than (0,1) are rather uncommon but supported in EMF. With JGraLab, attributes of the domains list, set, or map are considered multi-valued.

Those were all the terms used in the remainder of this thesis when talking about models in general. Models contain elements and possibly relationships and conform to a metamodel which defines element classes and possibly relationship classes. For those metamodel classes, attributes may be defined. For element classes, also references may be defined. References can be distinguished in unidirectional and bidirectional references. References and relationship classes may either be containment- or cross-referencing. And lastly, any property may be either single- or multi-valued.

With respect to conventions, it can be summarized that metamodel class names are always referred to using Clojure symbols denoting their qualified name, and properties are always referred to using Clojure keywords.

---

[3]It would be more correct to say that entries and directory together define one bidirectional reference but because they inherently belong together one usually names only one role name and calls it bidirectional.

Chapter 10

The FunnyQT Architecture

The FunnyQT API is structured into several namespaces (see section 6.10 on page 55). Each namespace provides an API consisting of functions and macros for a specific use-case. These namespaces are illustrated in fig. 10.1 on the following page. The arrows denote dependencies. Each namespace implements its services using the constructs provided by the namespaces it depends on.

In this figure, the namespaces are arranged in layers. On the lowest layer named *Model Management*, there are namespaces that support the basic access to models with their elements and relationships. This is also the layer that defines and implements FunnyQT's protocol-based generic view on models which has been discussed in section 8.2 on page 88.

Above that, there is the *Querying* layer which provides higher-level querying nor transformation services. Furthermore, the namespaces in the *Transformation* layer provide high-level transformation services. Additionally, there are several namespaces printed with blue background color that provide auxiliary utility services that are neither model management nor querying services.

The complete model management API is the topic of part IV starting on page 105. The generic model management API `funnyqt.generic` is discussed in chapter 12 starting on page 107. In this namespace, all the protocols defining FunnyQT's generic model view are declared. This generic API is complemented by two framework-specific APIs residing in the namespaces `funnyqt.tg` for accessing JGraLab TGraphs (see chapter 13 starting on page 123) and `funnyqt.emf` for accessing EMF models (see chapter 14 starting on page 137).

The namespace `funnyqt.query` which among other services defines regular path expressions, and also the namespaces implementing auxiliary services such as model visualization (`funnyqt.visualization`), persistence of model-related data (`funnyqt.edn`), polymorphic functions (`funnyqt.polyfns`), and XML processing (`funnyqt.xmltg`) are also discussed in part IV.

The namespace `funnyqt.pmatch` provides an embedded pattern matching DSL which is discussed in part V starting on page 181. Based on this pattern matching API, the namespace `funnyqt.in-place` provides constructs to define transformation rules that match elements using a pattern and then act on the matched elements.

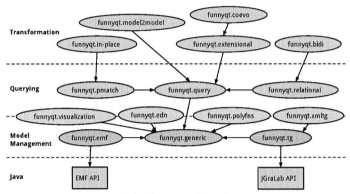

Figure 10.1: The FunnyQT architecture

This namespace is discussed in part VI starting on page 221.

FunnyQT provides two kinds of out-place transformation APIs.

The namespace `funnyqt.model2model` provides an internal DSL for out-place transformations which traverse the source models and incrementally build up the target models. The `funnyqt.extensional` namespace uses a different take on out-place transformations by specifying the target model in terms of extensional semantics. Both are discussed in part VII starting on page 259.

The `funnyqt.relational` namespace provides an API for querying models using a relational paradigm similar to Prolog logic programming language. It is discussed in part VIII starting on page 311.

Based on the `funnyqt.relational` namespace, the `funnyqt.bidi` namespace provides an internal DSL for specifying bidirectional transformations similar to the QVT Relations language [OMG11b]. This namespace is discussed in discussed in part IX starting on page 339.

At last, the namespace `funnyqt.coevo` supplies an API for co-evolution transformations which simultaneously change a model and its metamodel at runtime. For example, it allows to create new metamodel classes and instances thereof. For this purpose, it reuses the concept of extensional semantics used by the `funnyqt.extensional` namespace. The co-evolution transformation API is discussed in part X starting on page 375.

Some of the querying and transformation namespaces shown in fig. 10.1 are complemented by additional namespaces containing framework-specific versions or extensions of the original namespace.

The central point, however, is that any other modeling framework which can be accessed using a Java API can be supported by FunnyQT without touching its internals. Only the protocols declared in the `funnyqt.generic` namespace have to be extended upon that framework's model representation classes, and then the FunnyQT services on the Querying and Transformation layer will just work[1]. Even better, most services require only a subset of protocols to be satisfied. For example, out of the more than thirty protocols defined by FunnyQT, the `funnyqt.pmatch` namespace providing sophisticated pattern matching capabilities requires only four of them to be satisfied.

---

[1]A notable exception is `funnyqt.coevo` which has much higher assumptions and requirements on meta-models.

Chapter 11

Related Work

This chapter discusses model querying and transformation approaches which are related to FunnyQT with respect to comprehensiveness and genericity. At the current point in time, there is only one such approach.

The *Epsilon*[1] framework [Kol+15] is a comprehensive model management, querying, and transformation approach which is integrated tightly into the Eclipse IDE. It shares with FunnyQT the property that it is generic and can be used with various kinds of model representations.

Epsilon is implemented as a set of external DSLs. The Epsilon Object Language (EOL) is a model management language providing constructs for loading and persisting models, for accessing their elements and creating new ones, and for retrieving and setting their properties. All other Epsilon languages are implemented on top of EOL. This is very similar to FunnyQT's architecture where there is one generic core API which is then used in order to provide several higher-level querying and transformation DSLs. A difference is that FunnyQT provides internal DSLs whereas Epsilon is an external DSL where the individual sub-languages extend EOL.

Table 11.1 on the next page shows a comparison between the services provided by Epsilon and FunnyQT. As can be seen, there is a great overlap.

There are some services which have no dedicated support in FunnyQT. Firstly, the Epsilon Wizard Language (EWL) provides means for defining simple and small update transformations which are applied to a set of model elements selected in an Eclipse editor. Such transformations might require user interaction which is provided by graphical user interfaces, i.e., wizards. So wizards are intended for easing the usability when working with Epsilon inside Eclipse. FunnyQT has no support for any specific IDE but any editor with Clojure support is a workable FunnyQT development environment.

Secondly, the Epsilon Generation Language (EGL) offers special support for model-to-text transformations. FunnyQT doesn't need dedicated support for this task since it can use any Clojure or Java templating library for this purpose. For

---

[1]http://www.eclipse.org/epsilon/ (last visited: 2015-10-13)

Service	Epsilon	FunnyQT
Model Management	EOL	`funnyqt.generic`
Querying	EOL	`funnyqt.generic, funnyqt.query`
Constraints	EVL	`funnyqt.generic, funnyqt.query`
Pattern Matching	EPL	`funnyqt.pmatch`
In-Place Transf.	EPL	`funnyqt.in-place`
Out-Place Transf.	ETL	`funnyqt.model2model,`
		`funnyqt.extensional`
Wizard Generation	EWL	(no dedicated support)
Model-to-Text Transf.	EGL	(no dedicated support)
Model Comparison	ECL	(no dedicated support)
Model Merging	EML	(no dedicated support)
Model Migration	Epsilon Flock	`funnyqt.coevo`
Relational Querying	(not supported)	`funnyqt.relational`
Bidirectional Transf.	(not supported)	`funnyqt.bidi`

Table 11.1: Service comparison between Epsilon and FunnyQT

example, the FunnyQT solution to the TTC FIXML case [Hor14a] used the Stencil[2] templating library for implementing a model-to-Java/C++/C#/C transformation, and the FunnyQT-Henshin tool[3] uses FunnyQT's model management and querying APIs and Clojure macros in order to compile Henshin transformations provided as Henshin models to equivalent FunnyQT transformations.

Thirdly, the Epsilon Comparison Language (ECL) provides support for customized model comparisons. FunnyQT only provides an `equal-models?` function which is able to test two models for equality (see section 12.8 on page 115) where the measure of equality is fixed. Two models are equal if and only if every element in one model has exactly one equal element in the other model. Two elements are equal when they have the same type, the same attribute values, and the same references or incident relationships. Optionally, the order of references/incident relationships may be considered, too.

Lastly, Epsilon has dedicated support for model merging with its Epsilon Merging Language (EML) which provides means to suppress duplication when merging models with overlaps, for conformance checking during the merge, and for reconciling and restructuring the merged model after the merge. FunnyQT doesn't provide such a service at the current point in time.

On the other hand, there are also some FunnyQT services which have no counterpart in Epsilon. It has support for declarative logic-based querying (see part VIII starting on page 311), and it allows for defining bidirectional transformations (see part IX starting on page 339).

In-depth comparisons between Epsilon languages (and other languages) and FunnyQT namespaces providing similar capabilities are made later in the related work chapters corresponding to concrete FunnyQT services, i.e., chapter 16 starting on page 173 discusses model management, querying, and constraint approaches, chapter 19 starting on page 217 discusses pattern matching approaches, chapter 24

---

[2]`https://github.com/davidsantiago/stencil` (last visited: 2015-10-13)
[3]`https://github.com/jgralab/funnyqt-henshin` (last visited: 2015-10-13)

starting on page 249 discusses in-place transformation approaches, chapter 28 starting on page 301 discusses out-place transformation approaches, chapter 32 starting on page 335 discusses relational querying approaches, chapter 37 starting on page 369 discusses bidirectional transformation approaches, and chapter 41 starting on page 397 discusses co-evolution approaches.

For achieving genericity, Epsilon has a model connectivity layer where drivers for different model representations can be added. By default, Epsilon supports EMF models, MDR[4] models, MetaEdit[5] models, and it can also treat plain XML files, BibTEX files, and Z specifications as models in a wider sense.

Other drivers can be added, too. Here, Epsilon uses a variant of the interface-based approach discussed in section 8.1.1 on page 83. Whereas the approach sketched in this section suggested providing interfaces for metamodels, metaclasses, models, and model elements, Epsilon uses a more light-weight approach. In essence, there is only one single interface IModel that needs to be implemented which specifies methods for retrieving elements and creating new elements, for type checks, and for retrieving and setting values of element properties. Thus, a driver is just a wrapper class around the framework-specific model representation implementing this interface, and Epsilon uses the native representation for model elements.

One drawback of this approach is that the API is not very appealing. Metamodel types are represented as plain strings, and every action on a model element is initiated from an IModel instance, too. However, this is no problem for Epsilon because the API is only used for implementing EOL itself and no user needs to be aware of it. In contrast, with FunnyQT users have to use the provided APIs directly, so their design is of utmost importance.

Another drawback of Epsilon's approach on genericity is that it considers models as containers for model elements which may be typed and have properties but there is no notion of first-class relationships whereas FunnyQT has optional support for typed and attributed edges.

All in all, the vision and goals of Epsilon and FunnyQT are quite similar. They overlap in a large set of services, and each approach has some additional services which the other one lacks.

One major difference is that Epsilon follows a more traditional imperative and object-oriented paradigm whereas FunnyQT has an overall functional emphasis with some logic-based/relational parts.

A second major difference is that FunnyQT is extremely light-weight compared to Epsilon. FunnyQT's complete implementation consists of about 12.000 lines of Clojure code (without counting comments but including documentation strings) arranged in 22 files. In contrast, Epsilon consists of 4652 files, about 400.000 non-commented lines of Java code, about 40.000 lines of XML configurations, and a complex build infrastructure.

---

[4]MDR (NetBeans MetaData Repository) has been a modeling framework developed by Sun Microsystems in the early noughties as a response to the OMG's Model-Driven Architecture initiative. It has been discontinued long ago.

[5]http://www.metacase.com/mwb/ (last visited: 2015-10-13)

And lastly, Epsilon's EOL atop of which all other Epsilon languages are built is an interpreted language which is not overly performant. FunnyQT and Clojure in general compile to JVM byte-code, and there are no obvious bottlenecks in FunnyQT's implementation. So in general, a query or transformation written in FunnyQT can potentially be as efficient as an equivalent query or transformation written in plain Java.

Part IV

On Model Management and Querying

Summary

In this part, FunnyQT's core model management and querying APIs are discussed. Those consist of a generic core API discussed in chapter 12 starting on page 107 which is applicable to both JGraLab TGraphs and EMF models, and which can be extended to support other modeling frameworks, too.

Next to that, there is a JGraLab-specific core API which is discussed in chapter 13 starting on page 123 and an EMF-specific core API which is discussed in chapter 14 starting on page 137. Whereas the generic core API supports the common duck-typed view on models discussed in section 8.2 on page 88, these framework-specific core APIs also give access to all features that are only present in their respective framework. Furthermore, the functions and constructs of the framework-specific APIs are named according to the terminology inherent to that framework, so JGraLab and EMF users should feel right at home.

Chapter 15 starting on page 147 finally introduces a broad set of generic model management and querying features such as regular path expressions and polymorphic functions which are based on the generic core API discussed in chapter 12.

Chapter 12

Generic Model Management and Querying

The core API implemented in the namespace `funnyqt.generic` declares many protocols for accessing models and model elements in a generic manner. They are extended upon JGraLab's and EMF's interfaces to provide the generic duck-typed view on models which has already been discussed in chapter 8 starting on page 83.

In this view, a model consists of elements and possibly relationships between elements. Both elements and relationships may possess attributes, and one may navigate between elements by traversing relationships or using references.

The central point of the generic API is to provide a foundation on which features can be implemented that instantly work for any supported modeling framework. The protocols declared by the generic core API are all very fine-granular, i.e., most protocols define only one single method. All querying and transformation features discussed in the rest of this work require only a subset of these protocols. Appendix A starting on page 423 names all protocols which need to be extended in order to add support for a certain querying or transformation feature to a modeling framework other than JGraLab and EMF.

12.1 Creating and Deleting Elements and Relationships

Elements are created using the `create-element!` method. It receives the `model` in which to create the element, and a symbol `cls` specifying the metamodel class by its qualified name (see concept 1 on the following page) or unique name (see concept 2 on the next page).

The optional `prop-map` is a map from property names given as keywords to property values to be set, i.e., it may contain entries for attributes and references. In the case of multi-valued properties, the respective entry's value must be a collection.

Protocol: `funnyqt.generic/ICreateElement`
```
(create-element! model cls)
(create-element! model cls prop-map)
```

The `ICreateElement` protocol is extended upon JGraLab's interface Graph where it creates a vertex and EMF's interface Resource where it creates an EObject.

Concept 1: Qualified Name. The *qualified name* of a metamodel class is a symbol consisting of the package path of the class followed by the name of the class. Package names and class name are separated by dots.

Wherever a metamodel type has to be stated, e.g., to create a new element of that type or at a type check, a qualified name has to be specified.

The qualified name of a metamodel class can be retrieved using the `qname` method defined by the `IQualifiedName` protocol.

Protocol: `funnyqt.generic/IQualifiedName`
```
(qname el)
```

The argument `el` can be both a model element or a metamodel element. In the former case, the qualified name of the metamodel class `el` is an instance of is returned.

Note that qualified names given to functions or protocol methods such as `create-element!` (see page 108) need to be quoted in order to protect them from evaluation. In contrast, when given to macros such as `defpolyfn` (see section 15.2 on page 155) they must not be quoted.

Concept 2: Unique Names. A *unique name* of a metamodel class is a symbol denoting the name of the class in its metamodel. If the class name is unique in the metamodel, then the unique name equals the class name. If the metamodel contains multiple classes with that name in different packages, the unique name equals the qualified name (see concept 1).

Unique names can be used wherever qualified names can be used. In addition, the unique name of metamodel classes is used for deriving function names from metamodel classes by several macros which generate custom APIs from metamodels (see section 12.11 on page 120).

The unique name of a metamodel class can be retrieved using the `uname` method defined by the `IUniqueName` protocol.

Protocol: `funnyqt.generic/IUniqueName`
```
(uname el)
```

The argument `el` can be both a model element or a metamodel element. In the former case, the qualified name of the metamodel class `el` is an instance of is returned.

Like with qualified names, unique names must be quoted when given to functions or protocol methods. When given to macros, they must not be quoted.

Relationships are created using the `create-relationship!` function. It receives the `model` in which to create the relationship, the qualified name of the relationship class `cls`, and the `source` and `target` element. The optional `attr-map` is a map from attribute names given as keywords to attribute values to be set.

Protocol: `funnyqt.generic/ICreateRelationship`
`(create-relationship! model cls source target)`
`(create-relationship! model cls source target attr-map)`

The `ICreateRelationship` protocol is extended upon the JGraLab interface Graph where it creates an edge.

The `delete!` method deletes the given element `elem`. The parameter `recursively` (defaulting to `true`) determines if `elem`'s contents should also be deleted. The contents of an element are all adjacent elements which are referenced with a reference with strict containment semantics where `elem` is in the role of the container.

Protocol: `funnyqt.generic/IDelete`
`(delete! elem)`
`(delete! elem recursively)`

The `IDelete` protocol is extended upon the JGraLab interfaces Vertex and Edge, and upon the EMF interface EObject. It is also extended upon java.util.Collection where all elements and relationship contained in that collection are deleted.

12.2   Iterating Elements and Relationships

The elements and relationships of a `model` can be iterated using the protocol methods `elements` and `relationships`. Both return lazy sequences and can be restrict using a type specification `type-spec` (see concept 3).

Protocol: `funnyqt.generic/IElements`   **Protocol:** `funnyqt.generic/IRelationships`
`(elements model)`   `(relationships model)`
`(elements model type-spec)`   `(relationships model type-spec)`

The `IElements` protocols is extended upon JGraLab's Graph interface and EMF's Resource and ResourceSet interfaces. The `relationships` method is only applicable for model representations with first-class edges, so it is extended only upon JGraLab's Graph interface.

Concept 3: Type Specification.   A *type specification* defines a set of metamodel classes.

A simple type specification is a qualified name (see concept 1 on page 108) defining the set containing this class (or data type) and all its subclasses. The qualified name QName may be suffixed with an exclamation mark (!) for excluding the class' subclasses, and it may be prefixed with an exclamation mark for negation:

```
QName      ;; Class QName with its subclasses
QName!     ;; Class QName without its subclasses
!QName     ;; all classes except for QName and its subclasses
!QName!    ;; all classes except for QName
```

If ts1, ts2,... are type specifications, then the following vectors are type specifications, too.

```
[:or ts1 ts2 ...]      ;; disjunction (set union)
[ts1 ts2 ...]          ;; shorthand for [:or ts1 ts2 ...]
[:and ts1 ts2 ...]     ;; conjunction (set intersection)
[:nor ts1 ts2 ...]     ;; non-disjunction
[:nand ts1 ts2 ...]    ;; non-conjunction
[:xor ts1 ts2 ...]     ;; exclusive disjunction (symmetric set difference)
```

A model element matches a type specification if its type is included in the set of metamodel types implied by a type specification.

Type specifications are handled internally by the method type-matcher defined by the ITypeMatcher protocol.

Protocol: funnyqt.generic/ITypeMatcher
(type-matcher model type-spec)

Given a model (used to access its metamodel) and a type specification, it returns a predicate receiving a model element and returning true if and only if the given element's type is included in the set of types defined by the type specification. The returned predicate is called a *type matcher*.

Such a type matcher is also a valid type specification in itself. When given a function as second argument to type-matcher, this function is simply returned. Therefore, type matchers can easily be composed as shown in the next listing.

```
(let [a? (type-matcher model 'A)
      b? (type-matcher model 'B)]
  (elements model [:or a? b?]))
```

This is equivalent to the call (elements model [:or 'A 'B]) but the type matcher used by elements is composed of the two already existing type matchers a? and b?.

For convenience, FunnyQT allows for using unique names (see concept 2 on page 108) in place of qualified names for the definition of type specifications. However, this is an implementation detail which does not need to be followed when extending the ITypeMatcher protocol upon the interfaces or classes of other modeling frameworks.

Note that type names in type specifications given to functions or protocol methods such as elements (see page 109) need to be quoted in order to protect them from evaluation. In contrast, when given to macros such as `type-case` (see page 114) they must not be quoted.

For accessing the source and target elements of a relationship, there is the IRelationshipSourceTarget protocol with its `source` and `target` functions.

Protocol: `funnyqt.generic/IRelationshipSourceTarget`
```
(source rel)
(target rel)
```

This protocol is extended upon the JGraLab interface Edge. Its implementations return a given edge's alpha and omega vertex.

The protocol IIncidentRelationships declares the method `incident-relationships`. This method returns the lazy sequence of relationships incident to a given element `el`. The relationships may be restricted by the given type specification `type-spec`, and they may be restricted by the given direction specification `dir-spec` (see concept 4).

Protocol: `funnyqt.generic/incident-relationships`
```
(incident-relationships el)
(incident-relationships el type-spec)
(incident-relationships el type-spec dir-spec)
```

The IIncidentRelationships protocol is extended upon JGraLab's Vertex interface.

Concept 4: Direction Specification. A *direction specification* defines which relationships are to be considered with respect to a incident vertex. Possible direction specifications are the following:

- The keyword `:in` considers only incoming edges.
- The keyword `:out` considers only outgoing edges.
- The keyword `:inout` and `nil` consider both incoming and outgoing edges.

12.3 Attribute Value Access

For accessing attribute values, there is the `aval` method. It receives an element (or relationship) `elem` and the name of an attribute `attr` given as a keyword. An attribute can be set using the `set-aval!` method receiving an element `elem`, the attribute name `attr` given as keyword, and the value `val` to be set.

Protocol: `funnyqt.generic/IAttributeValueAccess`
```
(aval elem attr)
(set-aval! elem attr val)
```

The IAttributeValueAccess protocol is extended upon JGraLab's AttributedElement and Record interfaces, and upon EMF's EObject interface.

12.4   Role Name Navigation

To navigate to adjacent elements by traversing edges or references, there are several adjacency functions.

The `adj` functions returns the element that can be reached from `elem` by traversing `role` and possibly many other `roles` one after the other. All roles must exist and be single-valued, and no intermediate role may be `nil`.

Function: funnyqt.generic/adj   **Function:** funnyqt.generic/adj*
(adj elem role & roles)   (adj* elem role & roles)

The `adj*` function is like `adj` except that it doesn't signal an error if a role is undefined or an intermediate role is not set. In that case, it simply returns `nil`.

The `adjs` function returns the elements that can be reached form `elem` by traversing `role` and possibly many other `roles` one after the other. All roles may be single- or multi-valued. All roles must exist. The return value is a vector.

Function: funnyqt.generic/adjs   **Function:** funnyqt.generic/adjs*
(adjs elem role & roles)   (adjs* elem role & roles)

The `adjs*` function is like `adjs` except that it simply returns `nil` if some role is undefined instead of throwing an exception.

These four adjacency functions delegate to the method `adjs-internal` of the protocol `IAdjacenciesInternal` which defines a one-step traversal from one element to its adjacent elements with respect to a single role. The method receives an element `elem`, a single `role` given as keyword, and two booleans `allow-unknown-role` and `single-valued` and always returns a collection of adjacent elements.

Protocol: funnyqt.internal/IAdjacenciesInternal
(adjs-internal elem role allow-unknown-role single-valued)

If `allow-unknown-role` is true and `role` is undefined for `elem`, it simply returns an empty collection. Otherwise, an exception is thrown in this situation.

If `single-valued` is true and `role` denotes a multi-valued reference of `elem`, an exception is thrown.

The protocol is extended upon the JGraLab interface Vertex and the EMF interface EObject, and it can be extended upon the model element class or interface of other modeling frameworks to add support for role name navigation.

The `IModifyAdjacencies` protocol declares methods for setting and adding adjacent elements.

`set-adj!` puts `relem` in the single-valued `role` of `elem`. If there is already an element in that role, it is removed beforehand.

`set-adjs!` is `set-adj!`'s counterpart for multi-valued roles. It receives a collection `relems` of elements to be set as adjacencies of `elem`.

Protocol: `funnyqt.generic/IModifyAdjacencies`
```
(set-adj! elem role relem)
(set-adjs! elem role relems)
(add-adj! elem role relem)
(add-adjs! elem role relems)
(remove-adj! elem role relem)
(remove-adjs! elem role relems)
```

The `add-adj!` method allows to add one single element `relem` to `elem`'s `role`, and `add-adjs` allows to add a collection of `relem`s. Both are applicable only for multi-valued roles.

Lastly, the `remove-adj!` and `remove-adjs!` methods allow to remove references to the given element or elements. Again, both are applicable only for multi-valued roles.

12.5 Type Checks

The IElement protocol declares just one `element?` method which returns `true` if and only if the given object `o` is a model element.

Protocol: `funnyqt.generic/IElement`
```
(element? o)
```

Likewise, the IRelationship protocol declares just one method `relationship?` which returns true if and only if the given object `o` is a relationship.

Protocol: `funnyqt.generic/IRelationship`
```
(relationship?)
```

Both protocols have default implementations for Object and `nil` which return `false`, and there are JGraLab and EMF implementations such that `element?` returns true for JGraLab vertices and EMF eobjects, and `relationship?` returns true for JGraLab edges.

The IInstanceOf protocol declares the `is-instance?` method.

Protocol: `funnyqt.generic/IInstanceOf`
```
(is-instance? el mm-class)
```

The method returns `true` if and only the model element `el` is an instance of the metamodel class `mm-class`. Note that `mm-class` must indeed be a metamodel class, i.e., a JGraLab GraphClass or GraphElementClass, or an EMF EClass.

The IInstanceOf protocol is extended upon JGraLab's Graph, Vertex, and Edge interfaces and upon EMF's EObject interface.

Based on the ITypeMatcher protocol (see concept 3 on page 110) there is the `has-type?` function.

Function: `funnyqt.generic/has-type?`
```
(has-type? el type-spec)
```

It receives a model element `el` and a type specification `type-spec` and returns true if and only if the element's type matches the type specification.

Based on `has-type?` there is the `type-case` macro which allows a dispatch between multiple type specifications.

Macro: `funnyqt.generic/type-case`
`(type-case el & clauses)`

Every clause in `clauses` consists of a type specification and an expression. The element `el`'s type is matched against the type specifications one after the other, and the expression paired with the first matching one is evaluated forming the result of the `type-case` expression.

A single default expression may be the last form in a `type-case`. It is evaluated if no type specification matches `el`'s type.

The following example demonstrates `type-case`'s syntax.

```
(type-case el
  ;; each clause has the form:
  ;; type-spec expression
  MMTypeA            (do-a-stuff el)
  [:or MMTypeB MMTypeC] (do-bc-stuff el)
  ;; a single default expression may follow
  (do-default-stuff el))
```

12.6   Containers and Contents

In many models the elements are arranged in a containment tree with only some cross-references turning the tree into a graph. This containment structure can be queried with the methods `container` and `contents` provided by the protocols IContainer and IContents, respectively.

The `container` method returns the container of a given model element `el`. The container is a model element which references `el` with a strict containment reference. Optionally, a type specification (see concept 3 on page 109) on the relationship type or a role name `ts-or-role` may be given.

Protocol: `funnyqt.generic/IContainer`
`(container el)`
`(container el ts-or-role)`

If `el` is not contained by some other element, `nil` is returned. With EMF, every element has at most one container. With JGraLab, the creation of edges with containment semantics does not check if an element is already contained by some other element, thus it is possible that a vertex is contained by more than one other vertex at a given point in time[1]. In that case, `container` returns the container vertex whose corresponding containment edge comes first in the incidence sequence of `el`.

---

[1]Strictly speaking, in this case the graph doesn't conform to its schema. However, it can be useful to have a vertex temporally be contained by more than one other vertex and restoring conformance later on.

The `contents` method declared by the IContents protocol returns the sequence of direct contents of a given model element `el`, i.e., all elements which are referenced by `el` via some containment reference.

Protocol: `funnyqt.generic/IContents`
```
(contents el)
(contents el ts)
```

The contained elements may be restricted to certain element classes using a type specification `ts`.

12.7   Neighboring Elements

Quite similar to the adjacency functions is the `neighbors` method of the INeighbors protocol.

Protocol: `funnyqt.generic/INeighbors`
```
(neighbors elem)
```

Given a model element `elem` it simply returns the sequence of `elem`'s neighboring model elements. Neighboring elements are those which are referenced by `elem` by an arbitrary reference.

12.8   Model Equality

The protocol IEqualModels defines a method `equal-models?` which can be used to test two models for equality.

Protocol: `funnyqt.generic/IEqualModels`
```
(equal-models? m1 m2)
(equal-models? m1 m2 link-order)
```

Two models are considered equal if there is a bijective mapping f between the elements of the first model and the elements of the second model such that $(el_1 \mapsto el_2) \in f \iff equal(el_1, el_2)$. Two elements are considered equal if

1. they are instances of the same metamodel element class,
2. their attribute values are equal,
3. and
   (a) all incident relationships are equal for models with first-class edges, i.e.,
      i. they are instances of the same metamodel relationship class,
      ii. their attribute values are equal,
      iii. their start and end elements are equal, or
   (b) all references contain equal elements for models with only references.

If the `link-order` argument is true, then the order of incident relationships or the order in the reference lists is also considered. The default is `false`.

In other words, two models are considered equal if there exists a *graph isomor-*

phism between the two models which considers not only structural equality but also equality of typing, attribution, and optionally link order.

The protocol is implemented upon the JGraLab interface Graph and the EMF interface Resource. If the models are not equal, `false` is returned. If they are equal, a map which assigns to every element and relationship in the first model its equal counterpart in the second model and vice-versa is returned. However, the protocol only specifies the predicate semantics of `equal-models?`, so this behavior doesn't need to be followed when adding another implementation.

12.9   Copying Models

Sometimes, it is convenient to be able to copy a model, for example, to test a transformation without having to worry that some error in the transformation invalidates it. This can be done with the `copy-model` method specified by the ICopyModel protocol.

Protocol: `funnyqt.generic/ICopyModel`
`(copy-model model)`

The `copy-model` method receives a model and returns a copy. The protocol is extended upon the JGraLab Graph interface and the EMF Resource interface.

The copy of the original model is at least so exact that `(equal-models? original copy true)` would succeed, i.e., they are structurally equal and contain elements which are equal with respect to typing, attribution, and referenced elements where the order of incident relationships or the order of referenced elements is equal, too. However, there can be some minor differences in details. Concretely, for JGraLab TGraphs, the IDs of vertices and edges might differ in case they don't correspond to the creation order.

12.10   Metamodel Access

The generic API also defines some functions and protocols with methods for accessing and querying metamodel elements. Those are rarely useful for writing queries and transformations but they are extensively used internally for implementing several of the more elaborated querying and transformation features in a generic way.

To load a metamodel, there is the `mm-load` function which receives a string denoting a file.

Function: `funnyqt.generic/mm-load`
`(mm-load file)`

Depending on the file's extension, the appropriate framework-specific function is determined and called. This is controlled by the var `mm-load-handlers`.

Var: `funnyqt.generic/mm-load-handlers`

Its value is a map from regular expression matched against the file name to functions for loading a metamodel. By default, it contains entries for the regular expressions `".*\.ecore$"` and `".*\.tg$"` with the appropriate load functions for EMF and JGraLab metamodels.

The `IMMClass` protocol defines a method `mm-class`. The version of arity one returns the metamodel class of a given model element or relationship. The version of arity two gets a `model` and a qualified name `qname` and returns the metamodel class with the given `qname` in the metamodel of `model`. It also declares a method `mm-class?` which given some object returns `true` only if that object is a metamodel class.

Protocol: `funnyqt.generic/IMMClass`
```
(mm-class elem)
(mm-class model qname)
(mm-class? obj)
```

The protocol is extended upon JGraLab's AttributedElement and Schema interfaces, and upon EMF's Resource, ResourceSet, and EObject interfaces. Additionally, there are default implementations for the `mm-class?` predicate for java.lang.Object and `nil` which simply return `false`.

The protocols `IMMElementClass` and `IMMRelationshipClass` define simple predicates `mm-element-class?` and `mm-relationship-class?` which return `true` if and only if the given `obj` is an element or relationship class defined in some metamodel, respectively.

Protocol: `funnyqt.generic/IMMElementClass`
```
(mm-element-class? obj)
```

Protocol: `funnyqt.generic/IMMRelationshipClass`
```
(mm-relationship-class? obj)
```

Both protocols have a default implementations for java.lang.Object and `nil` which return `false`, and there are `IMMElementClass` implementations for JGraLab's VertexClass interface and EMF's EClass interface which return `true`. Additionally, there's an `IMMRelationshipClass` implementation for JGraLab's EdgeClass interface also returning `true`.

The `mm-element-classes` methods specified by the `IMMElementClasses` protocol returns the sequence of metamodel element classes in `mm-or-cls`. `mm-or-cls` may be either a metamodel or a metamodel class. In the latter case, all classes of the metamodel which contains `mm-or-cls` are returned.

Protocol: `funnyqt.generic/IMMElementClasses`
```
(mm-element-classes mm-or-cls)
```

It is extended upon JGraLab's Schema and GraphElementClass interfaces and EMF's Resource, ResourceSet, and EClass interfaces.

For relationship classes, there's the method `mm-relationship-classes`.

Protocol: `funnyqt.generic/IMMRelationshipClasses`
```
(mm-relationship-classes mm-or-cls)
```

The `IMMRelationshipClasses` protocol is extended upon the JGraLab interfaces Schema and GraphElementClass but not upon any EMF interface because EMF doesn't have typed relationships.

The methods `mm-relationship-class-source` and `mm-relationship-class-target` declared by the `IMMRelationshipClassSourceTarget` protocol receive a relationship class and return its source and target element class, respectively.

Protocol: `funnyqt.generic/IMMRelationshipClassSourceTarget`
`(mm-relationship-class-source rel-cls)`
`(mm-relationship-class-source rel-cls)`

The protocol is extended upon the JGraLab interface EdgeClass.

The `mm-direct-superclasses` method of the `IMMDirectSuperclasses` protocol returns the sequence of a given `class`' direct superclasses.

Protocol: `funnyqt.generic/IMMDirectSuperclasses`
`(mm-direct-superclasses class)`

The protocol is extended upon JGraLab's GraphElementClass and EMF's EClass interfaces.

The function `mm-all-superclasses` uses the `mm-direct-superclasses` method in order to compute the set of all superclasses of the given `class`.

Function: `funnyqt.generic/mm-all-superclasses`
`(mm-all-superclasses class)`

The `mm-all-subclasses` method of the `IMMAllSubclasses` protocol returns the sequence of a given `class`' subclasses including both direct and indirect ones.

Protocol: `funnyqt.generic/IMMAllSubclasses`
`(mm-all-subclasses class)`

The protocol is extended upon JGraLab's GraphElementClass and EMF's EClass interfaces.

The `IMMSuperclass` protocol defines the predicate `mm-superclass?` that returns `true` if and only if `super` is a superclass of `sub`.

Protocol: `funnyqt.generic/IMMSuperclass`
`(mm-superclass? super sub)`

It is extended upon JGraLab's GraphElementClass and EMF's EClass interfaces.

The `mm-abstract?` method declared by the `IMMAbstract` protocol returns `true` if and only if the given metamodel `class` is abstract.

Protocol: `funnyqt.generic/IMMAbstract`
`(mm-abstract? class)`

It is extended upon JGraLab's GraphElementClass and EMF's EClass interfaces.

The protocol `IMMContainmentReference` declares the `mm-containment-reference?` method which returns `true` if and only if `ref` (given as keyword) is a containment reference of the element class `cls`.

Protocol: `funnyqt.generic/IMMContainmentReference`
`(mm-containment-reference? cls ref)`

It is extended upon the JGraLab interface VertexClass and the EMF interface EClass.

The method `mm-referenced-element-class` which is declared by the protocol `IMMReferencedElementClass` receives an element class `cls` and a reference name `ref` given as a keyword and returns the element class being the target of the reference.

Protocol: `funnyqt.generic/IMMReferencedElementClass`
`(mm-referenced-element-class cls ref)`

The protocol is extended upon the JGraLab interface VertexClass and the EMF interface EClass.

The `IMMBooleanAttribute` protocol declares the method `mm-boolean-attribute?` which returns `true` if and only if `attr` is a boolean attribute of `cls`.

Protocol: `funnyqt.generic/IMMBooleanAttribute`
`(mm-boolean-attribute? cls attr)`

It is extended upon the JGraLab interface AttributedElementClass and the EMF interface EClass.

The `IMMAttributes` and `IMMReferences` protocols declare methods `mm-attributes` and `mm-references` which return the sequence of attributes and references declared for the class `cls`, respectively. The attributes and references are returned as keywords.

Protocol: `funnyqt.generic/IMMAttributes`
`(mm-attributes cls)`
Protocol: `funnyqt.generic/IMMReferences`
`(mm-references cls)`

The protocols are extended upon JGraLab's AttributedElementClass and EMF's EClass interfaces.

The functions `mm-all-attributes` and `mm-all-references` return the sets of attributes and references declared for class `cls` or any of its superclasses.

Function: `funnyqt.generic/mm-all-attributes`
`(mm-all-attributes cls)`
Function: `funnyqt.generic/mm-all-references`
`(mm-all-references cls)`

Again, the attributes and references are returned as keywords.

Lastly, there is the `IMMMultiValuedProperty` protocol which declares a method `mm-multi-valued-property?`. It returns `true` if and only if `prop` (given as keyword) is a multi-valued property of `cls`.

Protocol: `funnyqt.generic/IMMMultiValuedProperty`
`(mm-multi-valued-property? cls prop)`

The protocol is extended upon the JGraLab AttributedElementClass interface and the EMF EClass interface.

12.11 Generating a Metamodel-Specific API

Given a metamodel, FunnyQT can generate a specialized API for accessing models conforming to this metamodel. This generated API contains functions for creating and iterating elements of all classes declared in the metamodel, for retrieving and setting attribute values, and for retrieving and setting referenced elements. The functions of the generated API are only convenience shorthands for the generic functions discussed in the previous sections. However, their usage allows for even more concise and understandable code. E.g., instead of writing (`aval el :id`) to retrieve the value of `el`'s id attribute the generated API contains a getter for this attribute so that the same effect is achieved with just (`id el`).

The metamodel-specific API is generated by the `generate-metamodel-functions` macro.

Macro: `funnyqt.generic/generate-metamodel-functions`
`(generate-metamodel-functions mm-file)`
`(generate-metamodel-functions mm-file nssym)`
`(generate-metamodel-functions mm-file nssym alias)`
`(generate-metamodel-functions mm-file nssym alias prefix)`

The macro receives the metamodel file name `mm-file` as a string. The metamodel needs to be loadable using the `mm-load` method (see section 12.10 on page 116).

The second argument `nssym` is a symbol denoting a namespace into which the API should be generated. If the namespace doesn't exist, it will be created. If omitted or `nil`, the functions are generated into the current namespace.

The third argument `alias` is a symbol denoting an alias under which the namespace denoted by `nssym` should be required. If omitted, the current namespace won't have an alias for the namespace `nssym`.

The last argument `prefix` is a symbol which will be prepended to all names of the generated functions. This is useful for preventing name clashes with existing vars when generating the API into an existing namespace.

The generated API consists of the following functions.

For every element class E, there is a function (`create-E! model`) which creates a new E instance and adds it to the `model`, a function (`all-Es model`)[2] which returns the possibly lazy sequence of E instances of `model`, and a predicate (`isa-E? el`) which returns `true` only if `el` is an instance of element class E.

For every relationship class R, there is a function (`create-R! model src trg`) which creates a relationship between the elements `src` and `trg` and adds it to the `model`, a function (`all-Rs model`) which returns the possibly lazy sequence of R instances of

---

[2]The properly inflected plural form of E is used here.

model, a function (`incident-Rs el dir-spec`) which returns the possibly lazy sequence of R relationships incident to the element `el` which may be restricted by the optional direction specification `dir-spec` (see concept 4 on page 111) and a predicate (`isa-R? rel`) which returns `true` only if `rel` is an instance of relationship class R.

For every attribute name attr, there is a getter function (`attr el`) which returns the given attributed element's attr value, and a setter function (`set-attr! el val`) which sets `el`'s attr value to `val`. In case attr is a boolean attribute and the protocol `IMMBooleanAttribute` is extended appropriately, the getter function is named `attr?` instead.

For every reference name ref, there is a getter function (`->ref el`) which returns the element if ref is single-valued or the elements referenced by `el`, a setter function (`->set-ref! el refed`) which sets the value of `el`'s ref reference to `refed`, and for a multi-valued reference, there are two additional adder functions (`->add-ref! el refed & more`) and (`->addall-ref! el rs`). `->add-ref!` is for adding individual elements, `->addall-ref!` adds all elements in the collection `rs`.

The macro `metamodel-api-generator` is the underlying facility used to create the metamodel-specific API. It is also exposed to users to provide a convenient way to generate custom APIs for given metamodels.

Macro: `funnyqt.generic/metamodel-api-generator`
```
(metamodel-api-generator mm-file nssym alias prefix element-class-fn
 ↪ relationship-class-fn attr-fn ref-fn)
(metamodel-api-generator mm-file nssym alias prefix element-class-fn
 ↪ relationship-class-fn attr-fn ref-fn extension-hook)
```

The arguments `mm-file`, `nssym`, `alias`, and `prefix` have the same meaning as the arguments of the `generate-metamodel-functions` macro above.

`element-class-fn`, `relationship-class-fn`, `attr-fn`, and `ref-fn` are all functions that are called automatically and should return code, e.g., function definitions.

`element-class-fn` is a function receiving an element class and the `prefix`. It will be called once for every element class defined by the metamodel. `element-class-fn` may be nil in which case no code is generated for element classes.

Similarly, `relationship-class-fn` is a function receiving a relationship class and the `prefix` which is called for each relationship class in the metamodel.

`attr-fn` is a function receiving an attribute name as keyword, a set of attributed element classes declaring an attribute of that name, and the `prefix`. It is called for every attribute name occurring at one or many attributed element classes defined in the metamodel.

Lastly, `ref-fn` is a function receiving a reference name as keyword, a set of element classes having a reference of that name, and the `prefix`. It is called once for every reference name occurring at one or many element classes defined in the metamodel.

The optional last argument `extension-hook` is a function which can be used for generating auxiliary definitions which don't fall into the categories of element classes, relationship classes, attributes, or references. The extension hook function receives the loaded metamodel and should return a collection of definition forms.

Chapter 13

Managing and Querying TGraphs

In this chapter, FunnyQT's core JGraLab API defined in the namespace `funnyqt.tg` is discussed. This API consists of the elementary model management functions like loading and saving graphs and schemas (section 13.1), functions for creating elements (section 13.2 on the following page), element access and traversal functions (section 13.3 on page 125, section 13.4 on page 125, and section 13.6 on page 127), functions for accessing and modifying the element order (section 13.5 on page 126) and attribute values (section 13.7 on page 128), type predicates (section 13.11 on page 131), and functions for accessing a graph's schema (section 13.12 on page 131).

It also contains functions and macros for JGraLab's subgraph restriction concept (section 13.14 on page 133), a macro for generating schema-specific APIs (section 13.13 on page 132), and several auxiliary functions (section 13.8 on page 129, section 13.9 on page 129, and section 13.10 on page 130).

13.1 Loading and Saving Graphs and Schemas

A TGraph can be loaded with the function `load-graph`.

Function: `funnyqt.tg/load-graph`
`(load-graph file)`
`(load-graph file impl)`

It loads the graph from the given `file` as a generic graph and returns it. `file` has to be a string denoting a file name. The implementation type `impl` to be used can be specified, too. It must be either `:generic` (the default if omitted) or `:standard` in which case classes for the graph's schema are generated and compiled in memory in case they are not found by the current class loader.

A TGraph schema can be loaded with the `load-schema` function.

123

Function: `funnyqt.tg/load-schema`
```
(load-schema file)
(load-schema file impl)
```

In the aritiy one version, it loads the schema from the given `file` and returns it as a generic schema, i.e., an instance of the JGraLab class SchemaImpl. `file` has to be a string denoting a file name.

In the arity two version, again the implementation type is specified using the `impl` parameter. Possible values are `:generic` (the default) and `:standard` in which case classes are generated for that schema and compiled in memory. An instance of the generated schema class is returned.

A TGraph can be saved to a file using the function `save-graph`.

Function: `funnyqt.tg/save-graph`
```
(save-graph g file)
```

The argument `g` is the graph to be saved, and `file` is a string denoting a file name. Usually, the file name should have a `.tg` suffix. If the suffix is `.tg.gz`, the file will automatically be zipped.

Likewise, there is a function `save-schema` for saving a schema to a file.

Function: `funnyqt.tg/save-schema`
```
(save-schema s file)
```

The argument `s` is the schema to be saved, and `file` is a string denoting a file name. Like with `save-graph`, if the file name has a `.gz` suffix, it will be zipped.

13.2   Creating Graphs, Vertices, and Edges

To create a new, empty graph, there is the `new-graph` function.

Function: `funnyqt.tg/new-graph`
```
(new-graph schema)
(new-graph schema gid)
(new-graph schema gid impl)
```

The `schema` of the graph has to be given. Optionally, the graph's ID (a string) and its implementation type may be specified. The graph ID defaults to a timestamp denoting the creation time. The implementation type may be `:generic` (the default) or `:standard` in which case classes are generated and compiled in memory for the given `schema` if they do not exist already. Objects of those classes are then used to represent the graph, its vertices, and its edges.

For creating vertices in an existing graph, there is the function `create-vertex!`.

Function: `funnyqt.tg/create-vertex!`
```
(create-vertex! g vc)
(create-vertex! g vc prop-map)
```

Its first argument `g` is the graph in which to create the vertex, `vc` is either the VertexClass or the qualified name of the vertex class (see concept 1 on page 108) which is the type of the new vertex, and `prop-map` is an optional map from property names given as keywords to values to be set. Properties encompass both attributes and role names. In the latter case, edges are created implicitly.

For creating edges in an existing graph, there is the `create-edge!` function.

Function: `funnyqt.tg/create-edge!`
```
(create-edge! g ec from to)
(create-edge! g ec from to attr-map)
```

Its first argument `g` is the graph in which to create the edge and `ec` is either the EdgeClass or the qualified name of the edge class which is the type of the new edge. Furthermore, the start vertex `from` and target vertex `to` of the new edge have to be specified. Lastly, `attr-map` is an optional map from attribute names given as keywords to values to be set.

13.3 Accessing Graph Elements by ID

As discussed in section 7.1 on page 69, all vertices and edges in a graph have a unique ID, a positive integer value. This ID can be retrieved with the `id` function.

Function: `funnyqt.tg/id`
```
(id elem)
```

The `id` function may also be called with a graph. It returns the graph's ID in this case (a string).

The other way round, elements can be retrieved by their ID using the functions `vertex` and `edge`. Both functions are constant-time operations looking up the elements in the graph's array of vertices/edges which is indexed by the IDs.

Function: `funnyqt.tg/vertex`   **Function:** `funnyqt.tg/edge`
```
(vertex g id)                          (edge g id)
```

The `edge` function returns the oriented edge with the given `id`, that is, if the given ID is negative, the reversed edge of the edge with ID `(Math/abs id)` is returned.

13.4 Accessing Vertices and Edges by their Order

The vertices and edges in a graph as well as the incidences at some vertex are represented by double linkage. E.g., the graph knows its first and last vertex, and every vertex knows its previous and next vertex in the global order of the graph's vertices. The same is true for the edges in a graph. With incidences, a vertex knows the first and last edge incident to it, and every edge knows the previous and next incident edge with respect to the vertex.

This is exposed by the following six functions.

Function: `funnyqt.tg/first-vertex`   **Function:** `funnyqt.tg/last-vertex`
```
(first-vertex g)                             (last-vertex g)
(first-vertex g pred)                        (last-vertex g pred)
```

Function: `funnyqt.tg/first-edge`   **Function:** `funnyqt.tg/last-edge`
```
(first-edge g)                             (last-edge g)
(first-edge g pred)                        (last-edge g pred)
```

Function: `funnyqt.tg/first-inc`   **Function:** `funnyqt.tg/last-inc`
`(first-inc v)`   `(last-inc v)`
`(first-inc v pred)`   `(last-inc v pred)`

If a predicate `pred` is given, the functions don't return the logical first/last element but the first/last element for which the predicate succeeds.

As said, every vertex references the previous vertex and the next vertex in the graph's vertex sequence, every edge references the previous edge and the next edge in the graph's edge sequence. Similarly, every incidence references the previous incidence and the next incidence in the incidence sequence of the corresponding vertex. This is exposed by the following functions.

Function: `funnyqt.tg/next-vertex`   **Function:** `funnyqt.tg/prev-vertex`
`(next-vertex v)`   `(prev-vertex v)`
`(next-vertex v pred)`   `(prev-vertex v pred)`

Function: `funnyqt.tg/next-edge`   **Function:** `funnyqt.tg/prev-edge`
`(next-edge e)`   `(prev-edge e)`
`(next-edge e pred)`   `(prev-edge e pred)`

Function: `funnyqt.tg/next-inc`   **Function:** `funnyqt.tg/prev-inc`
`(next-inc e)`   `(prev-inc e)`
`(next-inc e pred)`   `(prev-inc e pred)`

If a predicate `pred` is given, the functions don't return the logical next/previous element but the next/previous element for which the predicate returns true.

13.5   Querying and Manipulating Element Order

The order upon the vertices or edges of a graph can be tested explicitly using the predicates `before?` and `after?`.

Function: `funnyqt.tg/before?`   **Function:** `funnyqt.tg/after?`
`(before? a b)`   `(after? a b)`

Both functions must be given either two vertices or two edges a and b. If given the same vertex or edge twice, they return `false`.

The order may be changed using the functions `put-before!` and `put-after!`.

Function: `funnyqt.tg/put-before!`   **Function:** `funnyqt.tg/put-after!`
`(put-before! a b)`   `(put-after! a b)`

Again, a and b must either be two vertices or two edges. `put-before!` puts a immediately before b in the graph's vertex/edge sequence, and `put-after!` puts a immediately after b.

Likewise, the functions `before-inc?` and `after-inc?` test if an incidence a comes before/after another incidence b.

Function: `funnyqt.tg/before-inc?`   **Function:** `funnyqt.tg/after-inc?`
`(before-inc? a b)`   `(after-inc? a b)`

In case a and b are not incident to the same vertex, `false` is returned.

The incidence order can be manipulated using the functions `put-before-inc!` and `put-after-inc!`.

Function: `funnyqt.tg/put-before-inc!`
`(put-before-inc! a b)`

Function: `funnyqt.tg/put-after-inc!`
`(put-after-inc! a b)`

`put-before-inc!` puts a immediately before b in the corresponding vertex's incidence sequence, and `put-after-inc!` puts a immediately after b. In case a and b are not incident to the same vertex, an exception is thrown.

13.6 Lazy Vertex and Edge Sequences

As discussed in section 7.1 on page 69, in a TGraph there is a global order upon all vertices and all edges, and for every vertex, there is a local order upon all incident edges. These vertex, edge, and incidence sequences are exposed by the functions `vseq`, `eseq`, and `iseq`.

Function: `funnyqt.tg/vseq`
`(vseq g)`
`(vseq g ts)`

Function: `funnyqt.tg/eseq`
`(eseq g)`
`(eseq g ts)`

Function: `funnyqt.tg/iseq`
`(iseq v)`
`(iseq v ts)`
`(iseq v ts ds)`

All these functions return lazy sequences of the graph g's vertices and edges or the vertex v's incident edges. The sequences may be restricted to vertices/edges matching the type specification ts (see concept 3 on page 109). The sequence of incidences `iseq` of a vertex may also be restricted to only incoming or outgoing edges by providing a direction specification ds (see concept 4 on page 111).

The function `vseq` may also be called with a vertex g instead of a graph. In that case, it returns the lazy sequence of vertices following that vertex in the global vertex sequence. Likewise, `eseq` may be called with an edge g instead of a graph to get the lazy sequence of edges following the given edge, and `iseq` may be called with an edge v to get the lazy sequence of incidences following the given edge.

Because all vertex and edge sequences in TGraphs are doubly linked, all lazy element sequence functions have reverse counterparts.

Function: `funnyqt.tg/rvseq`
`(rvseq g)`
`(rvseq g ts)`
Function: `funnyqt.tg/riseq`
`(riseq v)`
`(riseq v ts)`
`(riseq v ts ds)`

Function: `funnyqt.tg/reseq`
`(reseq g)`
`(reseq g ts)`

If given a graph g, `rvseq` returns the lazy reversed vertex sequence of that graph. If given a vertex g, it returns the lazy reversed sequence of vertices preceding that vertex in the global vertex sequence.

If given a graph g, `reseq` returns the lazy reversed edge sequence of that graph. If given an edge g, it returns the lazy reversed sequence of edges preceding that edge in the global edge sequence.

Lastly, if given a vertex v, `riseq` returns the lazy reversed sequence of incidences of that vertex. If given an incidence v instead, it returns the lazy reversed sequence of incidences preceding the given one.

13.7   Attribute Value Access

For retrieving the value of some attributed element's attribute, there is the `value` function.

Function: `funnyqt.tg/value`
`(value ae attr)`

The `value` function receives an attributed element `ae` and an attribute name `attr` given as keyword and returns the value of that attribute on that element. `ae` may also be a record instead of an attributed element, in which case the value of the record's `attr` component is returned.

For setting the value of some element's attribute, there is the function `set-value!`.

Function: `funnyqt.tg/set-value!`
`(set-value! ae attr val)`

It receives an attributed element `ae`, an attribute name `attr` given as keyword, and the value `val` to be set.

When setting an attribute whose domain is list, set, or map the value may be a Clojure collection which will be converted to a corresponding PCollection[1]. Concretely, Clojure sequences and vectors are converted to PVector instances, Clojure sets are converted to PSet instances, and Clojure maps are converted to PMap instances.

When setting numeric attribute values, Clojure ratios are converted to double values. Furthermore, long values are converted to integers when setting an attribute of domain Integer[2]. If the value is too small or large to be represented as an integer, an exception is thrown.

To set the value of an attribute of an enumeration domain, the concrete enumeration constant has to be provided. The `enum-constant` function can be used to retrieve it.

Function: `funnyqt.tg/enum-constant`
`(enum-constant ae qname)`

It gets some attributed element `ae` and returns the enumeration constant with the qualified name `qname` defined in the schema of that element. The qualified name is given as a symbol, e.g., `'dates.Month.JANUARY`.

To set the value of an attribute of a record domain, a concrete record instance has to be provided. Such an instance can be created using the `record` function.

Function: `funnyqt.tg/record`
`(record ae qname m)`

---

[1]JGraLab uses immutable pcollections for storing collection-valued attributes.
[2]Remember that Clojure uses Long values for integral numbers by default (see section 6.3 on page 29).

It receives an attributed element `ae`, the qualified name of the record domain `qname`, and a map `m` from keywords denoting record component names to the values to be set for the components. The provided map must specify all of the record's components.

13.8 Auxiliary Graph Functions

The graph containing a given vertex or edge can be retrieved using the `graph` function.

Function: `funnyqt.tg/graph`
`(graph ge)`

The other way round, the functions `contains-vertex?` and `contains-edge?` can be used to test if a given graph g contains some given vertex v or given edge e.

Function: `funnyqt.tg/contains-vertex?`   **Function:** `funnyqt.tg/contains-edge?`
`(contains-vertex? g v)`   `(contains-edge? g e)`

Note that `(contains-vertex? g v)` is not equivalent to `(= g (graph v))` in the presence of traversal contexts (see section 13.14 on page 133).

To get the number of vertices or edges of a graph, there are the `vcount` and `ecount` functions.

Function: `funnyqt.tg/vcount`   **Function:** `funnyqt.tg/ecount`
`(vcount g)`   `(ecount g)`
`(vcount g ts)`   `(ecount g ts)`

The versions of arity one return the total number of vertices or edges, and they are constant-time operations. The arity two versions return the number of vertices or edges matching a given type specification `ts`, and their complexity scales linearly to the total number of vertices or edges.

13.9 Auxiliary Vertex Functions

The degree of a vertex, i.e., the number of incident edges, can be retrieved with the `degree` function.

Function: `funnyqt.tg/degree`
`(degree v)`
`(degree v ts)`
`(degree v ts ds)`

It may be restricted to incidences matching a given type specification `ts` and direction specification `ds` (see concept 4 on page 111).

To delete incidences at a vertex v, there is the `unlink!` function.

Function: `funnyqt.tg/unlink!`
`(unlink! v)`
`(unlink! v ts)`
`(unlink! v ts ds)`

The incident edges to be deleted may be restricted by type using a type specification `ts` and a direction specification `ds`.

Lastly, the `relink!` function provides a convenient way to relocate the incidences of a vertex `from` to some other vertex `to`.

Function: `funnyqt.tg/relink!`
```
(relink! from to)
(relink! from to ts)
(relink! from to ts ds)
```

Again, the incidences to be relinked may be restricted by a type specification `ts` and a direction specification `ds`.

13.10   Auxiliary Edge Functions

Every edge `e` in a graph has one start and one end vertex which are also called the *alpha-* and *omega-vertex* of that edge. Those can be retrieved by the functions `alpha` and `omega`.

Function: `funnyqt.tg/alpha`   **Function:** `funnyqt.tg/omega`
```
(alpha e)
```
```
(omega e)
```

The start and end vertex of an edge `e` can be set to some vertex `v` using the functions `set-alpha!` and `set-omega!`.

Function: `funnyqt.tg/set-alpha!`   **Function:** `funnyqt.tg/set-omega!`
```
(set-alpha! e v)
```
```
(set-omega! e v)
```

When obtaining an edge incident to some vertex, e.g., using `first-inc`/`next-inc` or `iseq`, it is either outgoing or incoming. Outgoing incidences are called *normal edges*, incoming incidences are called *reversed edges*. To distinguish both, there is the `normal-edge?` predicate.

Function: `funnyqt.tg/normal-edge?`
```
(normal-edge? e)
```

To get the corresponding normal edge form a reversed edge, there is the *normal-edge* function.

Function: `funnyqt.tg/normal-edge`
```
(normal-edge e)
```

If the given edge `e` already is the normal edge, `e` is returned again.

Likewise, the `reversed-edge` function returns the reversed edge of the edge `e`.

Function: `funnyqt.tg/reversed-edge`
```
(reversed-edge e)
```

If `e` already is the reversed edge, it is returned again.

The `inverse-edge` function returns the reversed edge if the given edge `e` is normal. Otherwise it returns the normal edge.

Function: `funnyqt.tg/inverse-edge`
```
(inverse-edge e)
```

The vertex from which an incidence is retrieved is called the *this-vertex* in JGraLab parlance. The vertex at the opposite side is called the *that-vertex*. They can be retrieved using the this and that functions.

Function: funnyqt.tg/this
(this e)

Function: funnyqt.tg/that
(that e)

For normal edges, the this-vertex is the alpha-vertex and the that-vertex is the omega-vertex. For reversed edges, it is the other way round.

The this- and that-vertex may also be modified with the set-this! and set-that! functions.

Function: funnyqt.tg/set-this!
(set-this! e v)

Function: funnyqt.tg/set-that!
(set-that! e v)

13.11 Type Predicates

The core JGraLab API also contains several predicates for testing if an object is an instance of the central JGraLab classes. On the instance level, there are the following functions.

Function: funnyqt.tg/graph?
(graph? g)

Function: funnyqt.tg/vertex?
(vertex? v)

Function: funnyqt.tg/edge?
(edge? e)

Function: funnyqt.tg/graph-element?
(graph-element? ge)

Function: funnyqt.tg/attributed-element?
(attributed-element? ae)

Similar predicates exist to test if an object is an instance of one of the classes that constitute a TGraph schema.

Function: funnyqt.tg/schema?
(schema? s)

Function: funnyqt.tg/graph-class?
(graph-class? gc)

Function: funnyqt.tg/vertex-class?
(vertex-class? vc)

Function: funnyqt.tg/edge-class?
(edge-class? ec)

Function: funnyqt.tg/graph-element-class?
(graph-element-class? gec)

Function: funnyqt.tg/attributed-element-class?
(attributed-element-class? aec)

13.12 Schema Access

The core TGraph API contains only a very slim schema access part because it is usually not needed when writing queries and transformations. The few functions are mostly used internally.

The function schema allows to get the schema of an element.

Function: funnyqt.tg/schema
(schema elem)

elem may be an attributed element, an attributed element class, or a domain.

The function `domain` returns the domain with the given `qname` in the schema of element `elem`.

Function: `funnyqt.tg/domain`
`(domain elem qname)`

`elem` may be a schema, an attributed element, an attributed element class, or a domain. `qname` has to be the qualified name of a JGraLab domain, e.g., `'Integer` or `'String`. For JGraLab's collection domains, a vector notation is used. For example, `'[Map Integer [Set String]]` is the qualified name of the domain `Map<String, Set<Integer>>`.

The function `attributed-element-class` returns the attributed element class of a given attributed element `ae`. In the arity two version, it returns the attributed element class with the qualified name `qname` in the schema of `elem`.

Function: `funnyqt.tg/attributed-element-class`
`(attributed-element-class ae)`
`(attributed-element-class elem qname)`

Like with the `domain` function, `elem` may be a schema, an attributed element, an attributed element class, or a domain.

13.13   Generating a Schema-Specific API

The `funnyqt.tg` namespace also contains the macro `generate-schema-functions` which generates a schema-specific API encompassing functions for element creation, element traversal, and attribute access. It is the TGraph-specific counterpart to the generic `generate-metamodel-functions` macro (see section 12.11 on page 120). In contrast to the latter, the functions it generates are named according to the TGraph terminology and delegate to functions in the `funnyqt.tg` namespace instead of their generic protocol method counterparts.

Macro: `funnyqt.tg/generate-schema-functions`
`(generate-schema-functions schema-file)`
`(generate-schema-functions schema-file nssym)`
`(generate-schema-functions schema-file nssym alias)`
`(generate-schema-functions schema-file nssym alias prefix)`

The macro receives the TG file `schema-file` containing the schema as its first argument.

The second argument `nssym` is a symbol naming the namespace in which the API should be generated. That namespace will be created if it doesn't exist. If `nssym` is `nil` or not given, then the API is generated in the current namespace.

If `nssym` has been given, this namespace can be referred to by the `alias` (a symbol) given as third argument.

Lastly, an optional `prefix` (a symbol) may be given in which case the names of all functions of the generated API are prefixed with it. This can be used to prevent name clashes when generating the API in an already existing and populated namespace, although it is generally advisable to designate one new namespace for each generated schema-specific API.

The actual generated API consists of the following functions.

For every vertex class with unique name VC (see concept 2 on page 108) defined in the schema saved in `schema-file`, there is a function (`create-VC!` g) that creates a new vertex of type VC in the graph g, a function (`vseq-VC` g) that returns the lazy sequence of VC vertices in the graph g, and a predicate (`isa-VC?` v) that returns `true` only if v is a vertex of type VC.

Likewise, for every edge class with unique name EC defined in the schema, there is a function (`create-EC!` g alpha omega) that creates a new edge of type EC starting at vertex `alpha` and ending at vertex `omega` in the graph g, a function (`eseq-VC` g) that returns the lazy sequence of EC edges in the graph g, and a predicate (`isa-EC?` e) that returns `true` only if e is an edge of type EC.

For every attribute attr name, there is a getter function (`attr` ae) and a setter function (`set-attr!` ae val). Since attribute names are not necessarily unique, the functions are applicable to all attributed elements ae that are instances of classes that have such an attribute. For boolean attributes, the getter function is named (`attr?` ae). (If attr is both a name of a boolean attribute and of an attribute of some other domain, then both getter functions are generated.)

For every role name role, there is a getter function (`->role` v) and a setter function (`->set-role!` v val). The setter function implicitly created edges. If role is single-valued, the getter function returns the vertex in that role or `nil` if there is none. If there are more than one vertex in that role, an exception is thrown[3]. If role is multi-valued, the sequence of vertices in that role is returned. Likewise, the setter function requires val to be a single vertex if role is single-valued. Otherwise, val must be a collection of vertices. If, because role names aren't unique, role denotes both as single- and a multi-valued role, then v's type is used to determine which one is meant. For multi-valued roles, additional adder functions (`->add-role!` v ov & more) and (`->addall-role!` v vs) are generated, too.

13.14 Traversal Contexts

Sometimes it is convenient to be able to concentrate on certain parts of a graph while ignoring other parts. For example, one might want to navigate through a graph only over edges of a specific type. One way to achieve this is to use type specifications matching only edges of this type everywhere where some traversal function is called.

An alternative approach is offered by JGraLab's *traversal contexts*. A traversal context restricts all navigation and traversal related functions to act only on a *subgraph* of the original complete graph.

To create such a traversal context, there are the functions `vsubgraph` and `esubgraph`.

Function: `funnyqt.tg/vsubgraph`
(`vsubgraph` g pred)
(`vsubgraph` g pred precalc)

Function: `funnyqt.tg/esubgraph`
(`esubgraph` g pred)
(`esubgraph` g pred precalc)

Both receive the graph g to be restricted and a predicate pred which is applied to

---

[3]JGraLab doesn't treat multiplicities strictly.

a graph element to test if that element is included in the subgraph. For vsubgraph, the predicate is applied to vertices, for esubgraph, it is applied to edges.

For convenience, pred may also be a type specification or a collection of vertices (for vsubgraph) or edges (for esubgraph). In the former case, all vertices/edges matching the type specification are included in the subgraph, in the latter case, all elements being member of the collection are included.

The optional argument precalc is a boolean value (defaulting to true) determining if the subgraph should be pre-calculated. Pre-calculation costs are linear in the number of vertices and edges of the complete graph but navigation over a pre-calculated subgraph is about as fast as navigating in a unrestricted graph. Without pre-calculation, pred will be called before any traversal step. The major benefit of omitting pre-calculation is that it allows the traversal context to adapt to changes in the graph. For example, a pre-calculated vsubgraph for a type specification 'T includes all vertices of type T that existed at subgraph creation time. If new T-vertices are created afterwards, they are not included. Without pre-calculated, they are included.

vsubgraph creates a *vertex-induced subgraph* meaning that it includes all vertices for which pred holds plus all edges between included vertices.

Likewise, *esubgraph* creates an *edge-induced subgraph* meaning that it includes all edges for which pred holds plus all vertices being the alpha or omega of an included edge.

Simply creating a traversal context with vsubgraph or esubgraph has no side-effect and doesn't make it effective. To restrict a graph to the subgraph induced by the traversal context, there is the on-subgraph macro.

Macro: funnyqt.tg/on-subgraph
(on-subgraph [g tc] & body)

It receives a vector containing the complete graph g and a traversal context tc, and arbitrary many forms as body. The body code (including its dynamic extent) is then evaluated on the subgraph imposed by tc, and its result is the result of the on-subgraph form. When control flow exits the on-subgraph form, the subgraph restriction is removed from the graph g again even if the exit is caused by an exception.

The macros on-subgraph-intersection and on-subgraph-union allow to restrict the current subgraph restriction even more or to relax it a bit. Like on-subgraph, they receive a vector containing the complete graph g, a traversal context tc, and a body of code.

Macro: funnyqt.tg/on-subgraph-intersection
(on-subgraph-intersection [g tc] & body)

on-subgraph-intersection makes a new subgraph effective that includes only those elements that are included in both the current subgraph and the subgraph imposed by tc.

Macro: funnyqt.tg/on-subgraph-union
(on-subgraph-union [g tc] & body)

on-subgraph-union makes a new subgraph effective that includes only those elements that are included in the current subgraph or the subgraph imposed by tc.

Lastly, to temporally remove a subgraph restriction, there is the `on-graph` macro.

Macro: `funnyqt.tg/on-graph`
`(on-graph [g] & body)`

It removes the current subgraph restriction from the graph g, executes body, and re-establishes the subgraph restriction again.

The following contrieved example demonstrates the usage of the various subgraph restriction macros.

```
(+ (vcount g)                          ;; (1)
   (on-subgraph [g tc1]
     (- (vcount g)                     ;; (2)
        (on-subgraph-intersection [g tc2]
          (vcount g))                  ;; (3)
        (on-subgraph-union [g tc3]
          (+ (vcount g)                ;; (4)
             (on-graph [g]
               (vcount g)))))))        ;; (5)
```

The `vcount` call at position (1) is not restricted by any traversal context, thus it returns the number of vertices in the complete graph. The call at position (2) returns the number of vertices in the subgraph imposed by traversal context tc1. The call at position (3) returns the number of vertices that are contained in both the subgraph imposed by tc1 and the subgraph imposed by tc2. The call at position (4) returns the number of vertices that are contained in the subgraph imposed by tc1 or the subgraph imposed by tc3. Lastly, the call at position (5) returns the number of vertices in the complete graph just like the call at position (1).

Chapter 14

Managing and Querying EMF Models

In this chapter, the core EMF API is discussed. It consists of the basic model management functions for managing resources (section 14.1), functions for creating and deleting elements (section 14.2 on the following page), element access functions (section 14.3 on page 139), and property access functions (section 14.4 on page 140).

Additionally, there are functions to access the conceptual edges contained in an EMF model (section 14.5 on page 141), macros for generating metamodel-specific APIs (section 14.8 on page 144), and several auxiliary functions.

14.1 Managing Resources

As mentioned in section 7.2 on page 73, in the Eclipse Modeling Framework model elements, i.e., EObject instances, are not existentially dependent on some model structure. Only for the sake of persistence model objects have to be added to some *resource* which can be saved to a file and loaded again. Every object can be contained in at most one resource, however the objects of one single conceptual model may be separated in several resources.

To load such a resource and the objects it contains, there is the `load-resource` function.

Function: `funnyqt.emf/load-resource`
`(load-resource f)`

The parameter `f` has to be a string denoting a file name, a java.io.File, an org.eclipse.emf.common.util.URI, or a java.net.URL.

To load a resource containing an Ecore model, i.e., an EMF metamodel, there is the `load-ecore-resource` function.

Function: `funnyqt.emf/load-ecore-resource`
`(load-ecore-resource f)`

In addition to loading and returning the resource, it registers the metamodel's packages at the global EMF package registry thus making the classes and data types defined in the metamodel available.

Lastly, there is the `save-resource` function for saving a resource.

Function: `funnyqt.emf/save-resource`
```
(save-resource resource)
(save-resource resource f)
```

The version with two arguments associates the given `resource` with the file denoted by `f` and saves it. The version with just one single argument saves the given `resource` which has to be associated with a file already. If it is not, an exception is thrown.

A new resources can be created with the `new-resource` function.

Function: `funnyqt.emf/new-resource`
```
(new-resource)
```

Objects can be added and removed from a resource using the functions `eadd!`, `eaddall!`, `eremove!`, and `eremoveall!`.

Function: `funnyqt.emf/eadd!`   **Function:** `funnyqt.emf/eaddall!`
```
(eadd! resource eo)                (eaddall! resource coll)
```

Whereas `eadd!` adds just one single object `eo` to the given `resource`, `eaddall!` adds all objects contained in a collection `coll`.

Likewise, `eremove!` removes one single object `eo` from the given `resource` whereas `eremoveall!` removes all objects in the given collection `coll`.

Function: `funnyqt.emf/eremove!`   **Function:** `funnyqt.emf/eremoveall!`
```
(eremove! resource eo)                (eremoveall! resource coll)
```

All four functions return the given resource again.

Note that the four functions are overloaded and are also used to modify multi-valued properties (see section 14.4 on page 140).

14.2 Creating and Deleting EObjects

To create new elements, there is the function `ecreate!`.

Function: `funnyqt.emf/ecreate!`
```
(ecreate! resource ec)
(ecreate! resource ec prop-map)
```

It creates a new eobject of type `ec` and adds it to `resource` which may be `nil`. `prop-map` is an optional map from property names given as keywords to values to be set for these properties (see function `eset!` in section 14.4 on page 140).

The parameter `ec` denotes the EClass, i.e., the metamodel class, of the new object. It may be an EClass instance or a unique name or qualified name of an eclass.

FunnyQT registers epackages at the global EMF package registry, and there eclasses are looked up by their unique or qualified name. However, the registry maps from EPackage namespace URIs to EPackage, so it is perfectly fine to have two epackages of the same name but with different namespace URIs registered that in turn contain eclasses of the same name. For example, there could be two versions

of a metamodel registered, one with the namespace URI http://mypkg/1.0 and one
with the namespace URI http://mypkg/1.1.

Therefore, a unique or qualified name may also be expressed as a map containing
one single entry in which a namespace URI given as string maps to a symbol denoting
the unique or qualified name, e.g., {nsURI QName}. For such a unique/qualified name,
the eclassifier lookup is restricted to the epackage with the given namespace URI.

Alternatively, the eclassifier lookup can be restricted to certain epackages with
the with-ns-uris macro.

Macro: funnyqt.emf/with-ns-uris
```
(with-ns-uris [uris] & body)
```

It receives one or many namespace uris as a vector, and then every eclassifier
lookup in the dynamic extent of body is restricted to those namespace URIs.

To delete an eobject, there is the function edelete!.

Function: funnyqt.emf/edelete!
```
(edelete! eo)
(edelete! eo recursively)
(edelete! eo recursively unset-uni-crossrefs)
```

It receives the eobject eo to be deleted and then unsets all of eo's references and
removes it from its containing eobject and resource. The return value is eo again. If
recursively is true (the default), then it first calls edelete! on the objects contained by
eo. If unset-uni-crossrefs is true, then also unidirectional cross-references pointing
to eo from other objects contained in the same root object, resource, or resource
set as eo are unset. This is a very expensive operation, so the default value of
unset-uni-crossrefs is false.

14.3 Lazy Content Sequences

The function econtents returns the lazy sequence of objects directly contained by
some container.

Function: funnyqt.emf/econtents
```
(econtents container)
(econtents container ts)
```

The container may be an eobject, a collection, a resource, or a resource set.
The sequence may be restricted to objects matching a type specification ts (see
concept 3 on page 109).

The eallcontents function returns the lazy sequence of transitively contained
objects of container.

Function: funnyqt.emf/eallcontents
```
(eallcontents container)
(eallcontents container ts)
```

Again, container may be an eobject, a collection, a resource, or a resource set,
and the sequence may be restricted to objects matching the type specification ts.

Conversely, every eobject can be asked for its containing eobject with the `econtainer` function, and it can be asked for its containing resource with the `eresource` function.

Function: `funnyqt.emf/econtainer`   **Function:** `funnyqt.emf/eresource`
(econtainer eo)   (eresource eo)

For `eresource`, the returned resource may contain `eo` directly or indirectly.

14.4   EObject Structural Feature Access

In EMF, there's no strict separation between attributes and references. Both are so-called *structural features*, and their value can be retrieved using the functions `eget` and `eget-raw`.

Function: `funnyqt.emf/eget`   **Function:** `funnyqt.emf/eget-raw`
(eget eo sf)   (eget-raw eo sf)

Both functions get an eobject `eo` and the name of a structural feature `sf` given as keyword. The difference is that `eget` converts mutable EMF collections to immutable Clojure collections; UniqueEList instances are converted to sets, EMap instances are converted to maps, and EList instances are converted to vectors. In contrast, `eget-raw` returns the feature value without any conversion, so calling `eget-raw` on a multi-valued reference returns an EList that can be mutated.

The values of structural features can be set with the `eset!` function.

Function: `funnyqt.emf/eset!`
(eset! eo sf value)

It receives an object `eo`, the name of a structural feature `sf` given as keyword, and the `value` to be set. For multi-valued features, any Clojure collection of elements of the expected element type of the feature may be given. When setting numeric attribute values, Clojure ratios are converted to double values. Furthermore, long values are converted to integers when setting an attribute of type EInt[1]. If the value is too small or large to be represented as an integer, an exception is thrown.

To set the value of an attribute whose type is an enumeration, the concrete enumeration constant has to be provided. The `eenum-literal` function can be used to retrieve it.

Function: `funnyqt.emf/eenum-literal`
(eenum-literal qname)

It receives the qualified name `qname` of the enumeration's literal to retrieve.

The `eunset!` function can be used to unset a structural feature.

Function: `funnyqt.emf/eunset!`
(eunset! eo sf)

Unsetting a multi-valued reference clears the EList holding the referenced eobjects. Unsetting a single-valued reference sets it to null. Unsetting an attribute sets its value to the default value specified in the metamodel, or to an appropriate default value depending on its type, e.g., 0 for EInt and ELong.

---

[1] Remember that Clojure uses Long values for integral numbers by default (see section 6.3 on page 29).

New values can be added to multi-valued features using eadd! and eaddall!.

Function: funnyqt.emf/eadd!   **Function:** funnyqt.emf/eaddall!
(eadd! eo sf value & more)   (eaddall! eo sf coll)

Both receive an eobject eo and the name of a structural feature sf given as a keyword. eadd! then receives one value and possibly more values to be added. eaddall! receives a collection coll of values.

Likewise, there are the functions eremove! and eremoveall! for removing values of multi-valued features.

Function: funnyqt.emf/eremove!   **Function:** funnyqt.emf/eremoveall!
(eremove! eo sf value & more)   (eremoveall! eo sf coll)

Both receive an eobject eo, the name of a structural feature sf, and the values to be removed, the former as variable number of arguments and the latter as a collection.

Note that the add- and remove-functions are overloaded and are also used to modify the contents of resources (see section 14.1 on page 137).

14.5 Access to Referenced Objects and Conceptual Edges

The erefs function is used to get the objects referenced by some object eo.

Function: funnyqt.emf/erefs
(erefs eo)
(erefs eo rs)

In the version of arity one, it receives just one object eo and returns a sequence of all objects referenced by it no matter by which EReference. In the arity two version, the sequence is restricted by an *ereference specification* rs (see concept 5) which allows to consider only a subset of eo's references.

Concept 5: EMF Reference Specification. An *EMF reference specification* restricts the traversal of an eobjects references. The possible values are:

• nil allows the traversal of any reference.

• An EReference instance allows the traversal of exactly this reference.

• A keyword :ref allows the traversal of references named ref.

• A predicate (fn [r] ...) taking an EReference r allows the traversal of all references for which it returns true.

• If rs1, rs2, etc. are valid ereference specifications, then a vector [rs1 rs2 ...] is a reference specification, too, which allows the traversal of the union of references allowed by the individual specifications (logical or).

While `erefs` considers all references, the `ecrossrefs` function considers only cross-references, i.e., non-containment references.

Function: `funnyqt.emf/ecrossrefs`
```
(ecrossrefs eo)
(ecrossrefs eo rs)
```

The arguments are the same as for `erefs`.

Analogously, there is a function `econtentrefs` that considers only containment-references.

Function: `funnyqt.emf/econtentrefs`
```
(econtentrefs eo)
(econtentrefs eo rs)
```

Note that `econtentrefs` returns only children of `eo` and not `eo`'s parent. `(econtentrefs eo)` is equivalent to `(econtents eo)` but using their respective second argument, the former allows to restrict the references whereas the latter allows to restrict the types of the referenced objects.

The next two functions allow to query which other objects reference a given object `eo` using a reference allowed by the reference specification `rs`.

Function: `funnyqt.emf/inv-erefs`   **Function:** `funnyqt.emf/inv-ecrossrefs`
```
(inv-erefs eo)                                (inv-ecrossrefs eo)
(inv-erefs eo rs)                             (inv-ecrossrefs eo rs)
(inv-erefs eo rs container)                   (inv-ecrossrefs eo rs container)
```

If `container` is not given or `nil`, then only `eo`'s opposite reference are checked if they match `rs`. In that case, `(inv-erefs eo rs)` is equivalent to `(erefs eo [or1 or2])` where `or1` and `or2` are all opposite references of a reference accepted by `rs`. Thus, the versions of arity one and two cannot return objects that reference `eo` with a unidirectional reference. Therefore, a `container` may be provided. If it is an eobject, a resource, or a resource set, all objects directly or indirectly contained in it referencing `eo` with a reference matching `rs` are returned. If the `container` is a collection, then only the objects directly contained in it are tested.

FunnyQT also provides three functions for accessing pairs of eobjects referencing each other. Such a pair is conceptually an edge when the EMF model is viewed as a graph.

Function: `funnyqt.emf/epairs`
```
(epairs r)
(epairs r src-rs trg-rs)
(epairs r src-rs trg-rs src-ts trg-ts)
```

Function: `funnyqt.emf/ecrosspairs`
```
(ecrosspairs r)
(ecrosspairs r src-rs trg-rs)
(ecrosspairs r src-rs trg-rs src-ts trg-ts)
```

Function: `funnyqt.emf/econtentpairs`
```
(econtentpairs r)
(econtentpairs r src-rs trg-rs)
(econtentpairs r src-rs trg-rs src-ts trg-ts)
```

The `epairs` function receives a resource or resource set `r` and returns the lazy sequence of all [src trg] eobject pairs where src references trg with a reference matching trg-rs whose opposite reference matches src-rs. Additionally, the types of src and trg have to match src-ts and trg-ts, respectively. If both a src-rs and trg-rs are non-nil, unidirectional edges are excluded. To include unidirectional edges, src-rs must be nil.

ecrosspairs is like epairs except that it only considers cross-references, and econtentpairs only considers containment references. Here, the source object is always the container and the target object is part of its contents.

All three functions take care of not returning inverse duplicates caused by considering both a reference and its opposite reference. The identity of a conceptual edge is a tuple [#{src trg} #{src-ref trg-ref}] where src references trg with its trg-ref EReference and src-ref is its opposite reference. That is, if both [eo1   eo2] and [eo2 eo1] are contained in the result sequence, then the corresponding #{src-ref trg-ref} sets are disjoint.

14.6   Type Predicates

The core EMF API also contains several predicates for testing if a given object is an instance of one of the central EMF classes.

Function: funnyqt.emf/eobject?
(eobject? eo)

Function: funnyqt.emf/eclass?
(eclass? ec)

Function: funnyqt.emf/eattribute?
(eattribute? ea)

Function: funnyqt.emf/ereference?
(ereference? er)

Function: funnyqt.emf/epackage?
(epackage? ep)

Note that EClass is a subclass of EObject, so for an EClass ec both (eclass? ec) and (eobject? ec) are true.

14.7   Metamodel Access

Several functions are used to access metamodel elements. Any eobject eo can be asked for its metamodel class with the eclass function.

Function: funnyqt.emf/eclass
(eclass eo)

The sequence of all eclasses registered at the global package registry can be retrieved with the eclasses function[2].

Function: funnyqt.emf/eclasses
(eclasses)
(eclasses ecore-resource)

---

[2]Also see the with-ns-uris macro on page 139 to get to know how to restrict the eclass lookup to only packages with certain namespace URIs.

If it is called with an `ecore-resource`, then only the sequence of contained eclasses are returned.

The `eclassifiers` function returns the sequence of classifiers registered at the global package registry. Classifiers are both EClass and EDataType instances, e.g., EInt, EString, or custom EEnum subtypes. If given an `ecore-resource` (a Resource or ResourceSet), the function only returns the eclassifiers contained in that resource.

Function: `funnyqt.emf/eclassifiers`
`(eclassifiers)`

The `eclassifier` function returns an eclassifier given its simple or qualified name `qname`.

Function: `funnyqt.emf/eclassifier`
`(eclassifier qname)`

`esuperclasses` returns the sequence of direct superclasses of the eclass `ec`, and `eallsuperclasses` returns the sequence of direct and indirect superclasses.

Function: `funnyqt.emf/esuperclasses`   **Function:** `funnyqt.emf/eallsuperclasses`
`(esuperclasses ec)`   `(eallsuperclasses ec)`

Analogously, `esubclasses` returns the sequence of direct subclasses of the eclass `ec`, and `eallsubclasses` returns the sequence of direct and indirect subclasses.

Function: `funnyqt.emf/esubclasses`   **Function:** `funnyqt.emf/eallsubclasses`
`(esubclasses ec)`   `(eallsubclasses ec)`

The direct subpackages of an EPackage `epkg` can be retrieved with `esubpackages`.

Function: `funnyqt.emf/esubpackages`   **Function:** `funnyqt.emf/eallsubpackages`
`(esubpackages epkg)`   `(eallsubpackages epkg)`

The `eallsubpackages` function returns direct and indirect subpackages.

14.8 Generating an Ecore-Model-Specific API

A metamodel-specific API encompassing creation, traversal, and property access functions can be generated for a given Ecore model using the `generate-ecore-model-functions` macro. It is the EMF-specific counterpart to the generic `generate-metamodel-functions` macro (see section 12.11 on page 120). In contrast to the latter, the functions it generates are named according to the EMF terminology and delegate to functions in the `funnyqt.emf` namespace instead of their generic protocol method counterparts.

Macro: `funnyqt.emf/generate-ecore-model-functions`
`(generate-ecore-model-functions ecore-file)`
`(generate-ecore-model-functions ecore-file nssym)`
`(generate-ecore-model-functions ecore-file nssym alias)`
`(generate-ecore-model-functions ecore-file nssym alias prefix)`

The macro receives the Ecore file `ecore-file` containing the metamodel as its first argument.

The second argument `nssym` is a symbol naming the namespace in which the API should be generated. That namespace will be created if it doesn't exist. If `nssym` is `nil` or not given, then the API is generated in the current namespace.

If `nssym` has been given, this namespace can be referred to by the `alias` (a symbol) given as third argument.

Lastly, an optional `prefix` (a symbol) may be given in which case the names of all functions of the generated API are prefixed with it. This can be used to prevent name clashes when generating the API in an already existing and populated namespace, although it is generally advisable to designate one new namespace for each generated metamodel-specific API.

The generated API consists of the following functions.

For any eclass with unique name EC (see concept 2 on page 108), there is a create function (`create-EC!` r) that creates a new instance of the eclass and adds it to the resource r which may be `nil`. There is also a (`all-ECs!` r)[3] function that returns the lazy sequence of EC objects in r where r may be an eobject, a collection, a resource, or a resource set. Lastly, there is a function (`isa-EC?` eo) testing if eo is an instance of EC.

For any eattribute name attr, there is a getter function (`attr` eo) and a setter function (`set-attr!` eo val). Since attribute names are not necessarily unique, the functions are applicable to all eobjects eo that are instances of eclasses that have such an attribute. For boolean attributes, the getter function is named `attr?`. If attr is both a name of a boolean attribute and a name an attribute of some other type, then both getter functions are generated.

For any ereference name ref, there is a getter function (`->ref` eo) and a setter function (`->set-ref` eo val). If ref is single-valued, the getter function returns the referenced eobject or `nil` if there is none. If ref is multi-valued, the collection of referenced eobjects is returned (in terms of `eget`). Likewise, the setter function requires val to be a single object if ref is single-valued. Otherwise, val must be a collection of eobjects. If, because reference names aren't unique, ref denotes both as single- and a multi-valued reference, then eo's type is used to determine which one is meant. For multi-valued references, additional adder functions (`->add-ref!` eo reo & more) and (`->addall-role!` eo reos) and a remove function (`->remove-ref!` eo reo & more) are generated, too.

---

[3]`ECs` is a proper plural inflection for the singular noun `EC`, e.g., for an eclass named `Shelf` the function would be called `all-Shelves`.

Chapter 15

Generic Querying and Model Management Features

In this chapter, miscellaneous FunnyQT querying and model management features are going to be discussed. The first one are *regular path expressions* (section 15.1) that allow for the computation of the set of reachable elements given a start element or set of start elements and a regular path expression specifying the paths in the model that may be traversed.

The next feature going to be discussed are *polymorphic functions* (section 15.2 on page 154) which allow the definition of functions that dispatch between different implementations based on the metamodel type of their first argument. As such, they are similar to methods in object-oriented programming languages.

Lastly, section 15.6 on page 168 discusses further querying functions such as *quantified expressions*, *higher-order combinator functions*, and several *utility sequence functions* which are useful for model querying.

15.1 Regular Path Expressions

A FunnyQT *regular path expression* (*RPE* in short) defines a set of paths in a model using edge symbols or role names and regular operators such as sequence, option, alternative, or iteration. RPEs allow the computation of all elements that can be reached by a path matching the RPE from a given start node or a set of start nodes.

As such, they are quite similar to regular expressions on strings. The regular expression `#"a"` allows reading the character "a" in a string. Likewise, the edge symbol `-->` in an RPE allows the traversal of an outgoing edge. The regular expression `#"a|b"` allows reading the character "a" or the character "b". Likewise, the RPE `[p-alt --> <--]` allows the traversal of an outgoing or an incoming edge.

In the next few paragraphs, the generic version of FunnyQT's regular path expression API is introduced. Thereafter, section 15.1.1 on page 152 discusses some framework-specific extensions.

Simple Path Expressions.   Simple path expressions allow a one-step traversal, i.e., given a start node or a set of start nodes incident edges matching the simple path expression may be traversed to compute the set of adjacent nodes. The `funnyqt.query` namespace defines eight functions being simple RPEs.

The protocol methods `-->` and `<--` return the adjacent nodes that can be reached by either outgoing or incoming edges.

Protocol: `funnyqt.query/ISimpleRegularPathExpression`

```
(--> n)
(--> n spec)
(--> n spec pred)
(<-- n)
(<-- n spec)
(<-- n spec pred)
```

The mandatory argument `n` is the start node or a set of start nodes. `spec` is a specification used to restrict the edges to some given kind. For JGraLab, it is a type specification (see concept 3 on page 109) matched against the edge class. For EMF, which doesn't have typed edges, it is an ereference specification. The `pred` argument is a predicate applied to the edge in order to test if its traversal is allowed. Because there are no first-class edges in EMF, the versions with arity three are not implemented for it.

It should be noted that on EMF models, the backward-directed simple path expressions (`<-- n`) and (`<-- n :role`), i.e., the set of nodes that reference `n` (using their role-reference), only traverse bidirectional references for performance reasons. If unidirectional references were also considered, every element in the complete model would have to be tested if it references `n` (with its role-reference). Section 15.1.1 on page 154 discusses some EMF-specific simple path expressions which don't have this limitation, but in general it is advisable to use only forward-directed simple path expressions with EMF if possible.

The protocol methods `--->` and `<---` are very similar to the `-->` and `<--` methods discussed above. Again, they return the set of nodes reachable via either outgoing or incoming edges but with the additional restriction that only cross-referencing edges may be traversed.

Protocol: `funnyqt.query/ISimpleRegularPathExpression`

```
(---> n)
(---> n spec)
(---> n spec pred)
(<--- n)
(<--- n spec)
(<--- n spec pred)
```

The next two protocol methods `<->` and `<-->` return the set of adjacent nodes no matter what the direction of the edge is. Analogously to above, `<-->` considers only cross-referencing edges.

Protocol: `funnyqt.query/ISimpleRegularPathExpression`
```
(<-> n)
(<-> n spec)
(<-> n spec pred)
(<--> n)
(<--> n spec)
(<--> n spec pred)
```

    `(<-> n spec)` is equivalent to `(set/union (--> n spec) (<-- spec))`.

    The last two protocol methods `<>--` and `--<>` return the nodes reachable via a containment edge, either from the container to its contents or vice versa.

Protocol: `funnyqt.query/ISimpleRegularPathExpression`
```
(<>-- n)
(<>-- n spec)
(<>-- n spec pred)
(--<> n)
(--<> n spec)
(--<> n spec pred)
```

    In contrast to the backward-directed edge functions `<--` and `<---` discussed above, containment edges are always traversable in both directions even in EMF models. Usually, Ecore models define containments unidirectionally where only the container references its parts but every EObject can retrieve its container anyhow.

    Finally, when occurring in a regular path expression, *every keyword is a simple path expression* resulting in the set of nodes reachable by traversing edges whose far-end role is named like the keyword.

Regular Path Operators. The "regular" in RPEs comes from the regular path operators going to be introduced in this paragraph. The first regular path operator is the *regular path sequence* function `p-seq`.

Function: `funnyqt.query/p-seq`
```
(p-seq n & ps)
```

    It gets a start node or set of start nodes `n` and arbitrary many RPEs `ps`, and it returns the set of nodes that can be reached by traversing paths matching the RPEs in `ps` one after the other. For example, `(p-seq n --> :next)` returns the set of nodes that can be reached from `n` by following an arbitrary outgoing edge and then a reference named `next`.

    The next regular path operator is the *regular path option* function `p-opt`.

Function: `funnyqt.query/p-opt`
```
(p-opt n p)
```

    It receives a start node or set of start nodes `n` and an RPE `p` and returns the set containing `n` extended by the nodes reachable from `n` by traversing a path matching `p`. In set-theoretic terms, `(p-opt n p)` is equivalent to `(set/union n (p n))`.

    Next, there is the *regular path alternative* function `p-alt`.

Function: `funnyqt.query/p-alt`
`(p-alt n & ps)`

It receives a start node or set of start nodes `n` and returns the set of nodes reachable from `n` by traversing a path that matches any RPE in `ps`. In set-theoretic terms, `(p-alt n p1 p2 p3)` is equivalent to `(set/union (p1 n) (p2 n) (p3 n))`.

Then, there is the *regular path exponent* function `p-exp`.

Function: `funnyqt.query/p-exp`
`(p-exp n l u p)`
`(p-exp n i p)`

It gets a start node or set of start nodes `n`, non-negative integer values `l` and `u` with (`<= l u`) or a non-negative integer `i`, and an RPE `p`. It returns the nodes reachable from `n` via a path that matches `p` `i` times or at least `l` (lower bound) and at most `u` (upper bound) times. Clearly, `(p-exp n 0 1 p)` is equivalent to the path option `(p-opt n p)`. `(p-exp n i p)` is equivalent to a regular path sequence that repeats `p` `i` times.

There are the two *regular path iteration* functions `p-*` and `p-+`. `p-*` is the *reflexive transitive closure*, `p-+` is the *transitive closure*.

Function: `funnyqt.query/p-*`   **Function:** `funnyqt.query/p-+`
`(p-* n p)`   `(p-+ n p)`

`p-*` gets a start node or set of start nodes `n` and an RPE `p` and returns the set of nodes that can be reached from `n` by traversing a path matching `p` zero or many times. `p-+` returns the set of nodes that can be reached by traversing a path matching `p` one or many times.

Lastly, there is the *regular path restriction* function `p-restr`.

Function: `funnyqt.query/p-restr`
`(p-restr n ts)`
`(p-restr n ts pred)`

It receives a node or set of nodes `n` and returns the subset of nodes in `n` that match the type specification `ts` (see concept 3 on page 109) and the predicate `pred`. This function is used to filter nodes in a path expression.

Composition of Regular Path Expressions. The regular path operators discussed in the previous paragraph are all higher-order functions receiving a regular path expression `p` or a sequence `ps` thereof. Those are ordinary functions, thus, RPEs can be composed simply by providing regular path functions as arguments, possibly wrapped in anonymous functions when some arguments should have concrete values.

The following listing shows an example. Starting at some node or set of nodes `n`, the set of nodes reachable by traversing one `foo` reference followed by traversing a bar or baz-reference one or many times is computed and then filtered to nodes of type Quux.

```
(p-seq n :foo
       (fn [n]
         (p-+ n (fn [n]
                  (p-alt n :bar :baz))))
       (fn [n]
         (p-restr n 'Quux)))
```

While this is perfectly legal code, it is not easy to understand or write. The important parts are obscured by the three anonymous functions needed to pass through the start nodes argument n and to define the arguments of each call.

Therefore, any RPE may be expressed concisely as a possibly nested vector. In every vector, the first element is the regular path function to be applied, and the remaining elements are the function's arguments where the start node argument n which is the first argument of any regular path function is omitted. Such a regular path expression in vector notation can be applied using the function p-apply.

Function: funnyqt.query/p-apply
(p-apply n p)

It receives a start node or set of start nodes n and a regular path expression in vector notation p and returns the set of nodes reachable from n via paths matching p.

Using regular path expressions in vector notation and p-apply, the regular path expression above can be rewritten as follows.

```
(p-apply n [p-seq :foo
                  [p-+ [p-alt :bar :baz]]
                  [p-restr 'Quux]])
```

This version is clearly more concise and much better to understand.

Internally, all regular path operator functions also use p-apply to execute the regular path expressions being their arguments. Therefore, it needs to deal not only with RPEs in vector notation but also with keywords and plain functions. Thus, in a call (p-apply n p)

(1) if p is a function, (p n) is called,
(2) if p is a vector [rpe & args], (apply rpe args) is called, and
(3) if p is a keyword, the adjs* function discussed on page 112 is called for any node in n with the keyword p and the results are combined in a set.

The items (1) and (2) reveal that users can easily define custom regular path functions. Every function that receives a node or a set of nodes as its first argument and returns a set of nodes again can be used in a regular path expression and applied by p-apply.

For example, many models have a strict containment hierarchy where every element except one single root element is contained by some other element. In such cases, the computation of all elements contained directly or indirectly in some other element might be used very frequently, so a shorthand p-contents could be valuable.

```
(defn p-contents
```

```
([n]    (p-apply n [p-+ <>--]))
([n ts] (p-apply n [p-seq [p-+ <>--] [p-restr ts]]))))
```

With this definition, the expression

```
(p-apply function [p-seq [p-+ <>--] [p-restr 'Variable] :type])
```

computing the set of variable types in a function contained in a model conforming to some hypothetical programming language metamodel could be written more concise as shown in the next listing.

```
(p-apply function [p-seq [p-contents 'Variable] :type])
```

15.1.1 Framework-Specific Simple Path Expressions

The generic simple path expressions -->, <--, --->, <---, <->, <-->, <>--, and --<> discussed above have the advantage that they work on every model representation upon whose node representation the ISimpleRegularPathExpression has been extended. As said above, by default, it is extended upon JGraLab's Vertex interface and EMF's EObject interface, and java.util.Collection. When the methods are called with a collection of nodes, the collection implementation simply calls itself recursively for each node in the collection and combines the results of the calls.

The disadvantage of this approach its overhead. When ns is a collection of nodes, then (--> ns) first dispatches to the Collection implementation of --> which in turn calls (--> n) for every node n in ns. This means that evaluating (--> ns) results in (+ 1 (count ns)) protocol dispatches to find the implementation responsible for ns's type which is then called. Because the number of (intermediate) nodes when evaluating a regular path expression can become large, this admittedly small overhead for traversal step may cumulate and become significant.

Therefore, FunnyQT provides framework-specific simple path expression functions in the funnyqt.query.tg and funnyqt.query.emf namespaces. Those assume that the start node argument is a JGraLab Vertex or an EMF EObject or a collection thereof and omit any dispatch or recursive calls. For that reason, they are faster and their performance benefit increases with the size of the node set. With larger models and complex RPEs, the performance difference can be factor two or even more.

An even more important justification for also having framework-specific simple RPE functions is that those can be sensible to a concrete framework's characteristic features. With the generic simple RPEs, one can distinguish traversal of cross-referencing edges and traversal of containment edges. However, as discussed in section 7.1 on page 69, JGraLab has two kinds of containment edges. There are edges with strict containment semantics (like UML's compositions) and edges with weak containment semantics (like UML's aggregations). The JGraLab-specific simple RPEs allow to distinguish those, too.

JGraLab-Specific Simple Path Expressions

The following six JGraLab-specific simple path expressions are completely equivalent to the generic ones of the same names discussed above.

Function: `funnyqt.query.tg/-->`
`(--> v)`
`(--> v ts)`
`(--> v ts pred)`

Function: `funnyqt.query.tg/<--`
`(<-- v)`
`(<-- v ts)`
`(<-- v ts pred)`

Function: `funnyqt.query.tg/--->`
`(---> v)`
`(---> v ts)`
`(---> v ts pred)`

Function: `funnyqt.query.tg/<---`
`(<--- v)`
`(<--- v ts)`
`(<--- v ts pred)`

Function: `funnyqt.query.tg/<->`
`(<-> v)`
`(<-> v ts)`
`(<-> v ts pred)`

Function: `funnyqt.query.tg/<-->`
`(<--> v)`
`(<--> v ts)`
`(<--> v ts pred)`

For all of them, `v` is a Vertex or a collection of vertices, `ts` is a type specification (see concept 3 on page 109) used to restrict the edges to the specified types, and `pred` is a predicate on the edges determining wether an edge may be traversed.

In contrast to EMF, JGraLab has not only cross-referencing edges and strict containment edges but like with UML every edge class may be modeled as an association (cross-referencing edge), an aggregation with weak containment semantics, or as a composition with strict containment semantics. The simple path expressions given in the following allow a more fine-granular distinction.

The aggregation path expressions implemented by the functions `<?>--` and `--<?>` return the set of vertices reachable from `v` via an edge with aggregation or composition semantics.

Function: `funnyqt.query.tg/<?>--`
`(<?>-- v)`
`(<?>-- v ts)`
`(<?>-- v ts pred)`

Function: `funnyqt.query.tg/--<?>`
`(--<?> v)`
`(--<?> v ts)`
`(--<?> v ts pred)`

The `<?>--` function defines a traversal from the whole `v` to its parts, `--<?>` defines a traversal from parts to the wholes.

The aggregation-only path expression defined by the functions `<->--` and `--<->` returns the set of vertices reachable by traversing an edge with aggregation semantics (but no composition semantics).

Function: `funnyqt.query.tg/<->--`
`(<->-- v)`
`(<->-- v ts)`
`(<->-- v ts pred)`

Function: `funnyqt.query.tg/--<->`
`(--<-> v)`
`(--<-> v ts)`
`(--<-> v ts pred)`

Again, with `<->--` traversal is from the whole to its parts, with `--<->` it's from the parts to the wholes.

Lastly, there is the composition-only path expression defined by the functions `<>--` and `--<>` which returns the set of vertices reachable by traversion an edge with strict composition semantics.

Function: `funnyqt.query.tg/<>--`   **Function:** `funnyqt.query.tg/--<>`
`(<>-- v)`   `(--<> v)`
`(<>-- v ts)`   `(--<> v ts)`
`(<>-- v ts pred)`   `(--<> v ts pred)`

So `<>--` and `--<>` are equivalent to the generic simple path expressions `<>--` and `--<>` in the `funnyqt.generic` namespace.

EMF-Specific Simple Path Expressions

The following EMF-specific path expressions have the very same semantics as their generic counterparts.

Function: `funnyqt.query.emf/-->`   **Function:** `funnyqt.query.emf/--->`
`(--> obj)`   `(---> obj)`
`(--> obj rs)`   `(---> obj rs)`

Function: `funnyqt.query.emf/<>--`   **Function:** `funnyqt.query.emf/--<>`
`(<>-- obj)`   `(--<> obj)`
`(<>-- obj rs)`   `(--<> obj rs)`

The argument `obj` is an EObject or a set of eobjects, and `rs` is an ereference specification.

Since EMF doesn't have first-class edges, in contrast to the generic protocol methods of the same name, there are no versions of arity three which also accept a predicate on the edges.

The EMF-specific backward-edge functions `<--` and `<---` are a bit more powerful than their generic versions.

Function: `funnyqt.query.emf/<--`   **Function:** `funnyqt.query.emf/<---`
`(<-- obj)`   `(<--- obj)`
`(<-- obj rs)`   `(<--- obj rs)`
`(<-- obj rs container)`   `(<--- obj rs container)`

They accept an optional third argument `container`. If that is `nil` or omitted, then the functions behave equivalently to the generic protocol methods. In contrast, if `container` is an EObject, a Resource, or a ResourceSet, then all direct and indirect contents of `container` are tested if they reference `obj` with a reference matching `rs`. `container` may also be a collection of eobjects in which case only those are tested but not their contents.

15.2 Polymorphic Functions

FunnyQT supports the definition of *polymorphic functions* (*polyfns* in short) by providing two macros in its `funnyqt.polyfns` namespace. Such a polyfn possesses different behaviors depending on the metamodel type of its first argument which needs to be a model element. Therefore, they are similar to abstract methods in object-oriented languages which are declared in some class or interface and then implemented or overridden in subclasses or classes implementing the interface.

A FunnyQT polyfn has to be declared once, and then implementations for different metamodel classes can be added. The declaration is done once using the `declare-polyfn` macro.

Macro: `funnyqt.polyfns/declare-polyfn`
`(declare-polyfn name doc-string? attr-map? [args] & body)`

The macro receives the `name` of the new polymorphic function, an optional documentation string `doc-string`, an optional `attr-map` of options, an argument vector `args`, and an optional `body` of code being the default implementation. The first argument in `args` must denote a model element.

Implementations for instances of a given metamodel type can be added using the `defpolyfn` macro.

Macro: `funnyqt.polyfns/defpolyfn`
`(defpolyfn name type args & body)`

The argument `name` denotes the name of the polyfn for which an implementation should be added. `type` is the qualified name of the metamodel class for which this implementation is responsible (see concept 1 on page 108) given as a symbol. It may also be a list of qualified name symbols in which case this implementation is added to all those types. `args` is an argument vector which must equal the argument vector of the polyfn declaration except that argument names can be chosen freely[1]. Lastly, the `body` of code implementing the behavior follows.

When calling such a polyfn, a polymorphic dispatch based on the function's first argument is performed to find and execute the implementation applicable for the first argument's metamodel class. If there is no applicable implementation, the default behavior provided at the polyfn declaration is invoked. If no default behavior was provided, an exception is thrown. In the presence of multiple inheritance in a metamodel multiple implementations could be applicable. In this case, an exception is thrown and developer has to add another implementation for the metamodel type in question to remove the ambiguity.

Which protocols have to be extended in order to add support for polymorphic functions on models of modeling frameworks other than JGraLab and EMF is discussed in appendix A.2 on page 423

15.2.1 Implementation

The declaration of a polyfn using `declare-polyfn` creates a function-valued var in the declaring namespace. By default, this var has as metadata a specification table and a dispatch table, both initialized with empty hash-maps.

Whenever an implementation for some metamodel type is added using `defpolyfn`, a mapping from the qualified name of the type to an anonymous function being the implementation for instances of that type is added to the specification table of the polyfn var.

---

[1] In other words, only the number and order of arguments is significant.

When the polyfn is called the very first time, the dispatch table is built according to the contents of the specification table. Whereas the specification table only contains entries for the types an implementation has been added for, the dispatch table contains entries for every metamodel class for which there is an applicable implementation. E.g., if the specification table contains just one entry for some metaclass A, the dispatch table contains entries for A and for all direct and indirect subclasses of A, too. Furthermore, the keys of the dispatch table are metamodel classes and not only the qualified names of the metamodel classes. During this dispatch table build process, an exception is thrown if any ambiguities are detected, i.e., if there is some metamodel class for which multiple polyfn implementations are applicable.

For the second and later calls, the polyfn simply looks up the implementation responsible for the first argument's metaclass in the dispatch table. If there is one, it is invoked. If there is none, either the default behavior gets executed (if it was provided) or an exception is thrown.

It should be noted that evaluating a `defpolyfn` form clears the dispatch table. Thus, new implementations can be added even at runtime where the respective next call of the polyfn will cause a regeneration of the dispatch table.

The dispatch table approach offers a good performance because only the first call computes the implementations responsible for all metaclasses of the complete metamodel and any later call only looks that up from a hash-map. However, if the metamodel changes at runtime, the information in the dispatch table may become invalid. In part X starting on page 375, transformations are discussed that evolve a model's metamodel in-place while at the same time keeping the model in conformance. Such transformation allow for example the addition of a new metamodel class as a subclass of an existing class. If a polyfn with already built dispatch table was called for an instance of this new metaclass an exception would be thrown because the dispatch table wouldn't contain an implementation for that. Therefore, the `:no-dispatch-table` option can be set to `true` in the `attr-map` of a `declare-polyfn` form. It can also be added as metadata to the polyfn's name. In this case, the polyfn won't have a dispatch table and the implementation responsible for the metaclass of the first argument is computed anew on every call.

15.2.2   Examples

The polymorphic dispatch should be exemplified using the (quite contrived) meta-model shown in fig. 15.1 on the facing page.

Let's assume the following polyfn `foo`. It is declared to take one argument `el` and no default behavior is specified. Line 2 defines one implementation for the metamodel class A which simply returns the keyword `:a`.

```
1  (declare-polyfn foo [el])
2  (defpolyfn foo A [el] :a)
3
4  (foo a-instance) ;=> :a
5  (foo b-instance) ;=> :a
6  (foo c-instance) ;=> :a
```

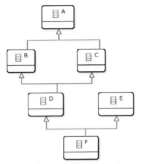

Figure 15.1: An example metamodel

```
7  (foo d-instance) ;=> :a
8  (foo e-instance) ; Exception: No polyfn implementation defined for type E
9  (foo f-instance) ;=> :a
```

Whenever this polyfn is called with a direct or indirect instance of class A, the single implementation is executed and returns :a. In line 8 it is called with a direct instance of class E. This class does not inherit the implementation defined for class A and since no default behavior is specified, an exception is thrown.

Now let's assume another polyfn bar. It is also declared to take one argument el and is possesses a default behavior which simply returns the keyword :default.

Line 2 defines an implementation for class A which returns :a, and line 3 defines another implementation for class B which returns :b.

```
1   (declare-polyfn ^:no-dispatch-table bar [el] :default)
2   (defpolyfn bar A [el] :a)
3   (defpolyfn bar B [el] :b)
4
5   (bar a-instance) ;=> :a
6   (bar b-instance) ;=> :b
7   (bar c-instance) ;=> :a
8   (bar d-instance) ; Exception: Multiple bar polyfn impls for type D.
9   (bar e-instance) ;=> :default
10  (bar f-instance) ; Exception: Multiple bar polyfn impls for type F.
```

When being called with a direct A-instance it returns :a. When it is called with a direct B-instance it returns :b. The implementation for class A is inherited by class C, so the call in line 7 returns :a.

For class D the implementations for class B and class A (inherited via C) are both applicable, thus the call in line 8 throws an exception to inform the developer of this ambiguity.

For class E there is no implementation defined. Therefore, the default behavior gets executed in line 9 returning :default.

Lastly, for F-instances the implementations for A and B are applicable again, so the call in line 10 triggers another exception.

To remove the ambiguities, the developer has to define another polyfn implementation for class D which would then be inherited also by class F.

If the polyfn declaration for bar didn't have specified the :no-dispatch-table option, then the two ambiguities would have been detected already at the first call while building the dispatch table.

15.3   Model Visualization

FunnyQT supports generating model visualizations with its funnyqt.visualization namespace. It doesn't implement any graph layout algorithms on its own but instead provides a convenient interface to *GraphViz*[2]. In order to use FunnyQT's visualization facility, the GraphViz program dot needs to be installed on the system.

The visualization namespace provides only the single function print-model.

Function: funnyqt.visualization/print-model
(print-model m f & opts)

The function receives the model m to be printed, the file name f where the visualization should be saved, and a sequence of further options opts.

The file type is determined by the extension of f, e.g., when the value of this argument is "test.pdf", the visualization will be saved as a PDF file. The supported file formats are DOT, XDOT, PS (PostScript), SVG, SVGZ, PNG, GIF, and PDF. In addition, f may also be one of the keywords :gtk or :image. If f is :gtk, the visualization is displayed immediately in the GraphViz viewer instead of saving it to a file. If f is :image, the visualization is returned as a java.awt.Image object which can then be displayed in a graphical user interface.

There is a large set of options which can be provided using the opts parameter. All options consist of a keyword and a value.

:name The name of the visualization which must be a valid DOT ID, i.e., it must not contain whitespaces. Depending on the output format, the value may or may not be used. When generating a PDF visualization, the value is used as the PDF's title.

:exclude A sequence of model elements which should be excluded from visualization.

:include A sequence of model elements which should be included in the visualization. If omitted or set to nil, all elements are included implicitly. When both :include and :exclude are given, the elements in the former which do not occur in the latter are visualized.

:exclude-attributes A map of the form {pred [attr1 attr2 ...], ...} defining that the attributes attr1, attr2, etc. should not be printed for all elements for which the predicate pred returns true.

---

[2]http://graphviz.org/

:mark A sequence of model elements which are to be marked (printed in red instead of black). The value may also be a predicate which is applied to elements and should return true if and only if that element should be marked.

:node-attrs A map of the form {pred node-attrs, ...}. The predicate pred is applied to model elements, and if it returns true, node-attrs is appended to the given node's DOT definition[3]. This can be used, e.g., to colorize elements by their type. For example,

```
:node-attrs {#(g/has-type? % 'Person)  "fillcolor=\"green\""
             #(g/has-type? % 'Address) "fillcolor=\"blue\""}
```

will print elements of the metamodel class Person with a green background and elements of the Address metamodel class with a blue background.

:edge-attrs The same as :node-attrs except that here the predicate is applied to relationships. Obviously, this option has only an effect for models with first-class edges.

:qualified-names If set to true, the types of elements and relationships are printed as qualified names. If set to :unique, the unique type names are printed. If omitted or set to nil or false, only the simple type names are printed.

In addition to these special options which are handled by print-model itself, arbitrary DOT graph attributes[3] may be given. For example, the call (print-model m "test.pdf" :layout "circo" :fontname "Helvetica" :fontsize 9) prints a visualization of the given model m to the given file. Instead of the default DOT layout algorithm, the *circo* circular layout algorithm is used. Furthermore, the call defines that the *Helvetica* font in size 9 is to be used for rendering the text in the visualization.

15.4 XML Processing

XML[4] is an ubiquitous format. Therefore, treating XML documents as a kind of model which can be queried and transformed is reasonable.

There are two implementation choices how this can be achieved. Firstly, FunnyQT could treat XML DOM[5] trees as models in a wider sense, i.e., the applicability of the generic model management protocol methods discussed in chapter 12 starting on page 107 could be extended to the interfaces and classes of some concrete DOM API. The second option is to use JGraLab graphs or EMF models as representation and convert XML documents to models conforming to some generic XML metamodel.

While the first alternative seems very elegant and an XML document can in fact be seen as a model conforming to a metamodel defined by its XML schema or DTD on an abstract level, there are some difficulties in details because XML and the DOM API don't really fit too well into the generic view on models discussed in chapter 8 starting on page 83. For example, having an XML schema or DTD is only optional but when it is provided, it might change semantics. E.g., it might declare that some attribute declared for an XML element type has the type IDREF which

---

[3]The DOT graph, node, and edge attributes are documented at http://www.graphviz.org/content/attrs (last visited: 2015-09-24)

[4]http://www.w3.org/TR/2006/REC-xml11-20060816/ (last visited: 2015-10-19)

[5]*Document Object Model*, http://www.w3.org/DOM/ (last visited: 2015-10-19)

turns it into something more similar to a reference than an attribute. Also, with models in the strict sense, the main facility for navigation are named references or typed edges but with XML, the only generally available navigation concepts is (anonymous) containment of elements inside of other elements. FunnyQT defines a protocol method `contents` (see page 115) which could be used for retrieving all elements returned by a given element but XML elements may also contain character contents which are just plain strings and thus don't fit into the contract of `contents`.

For these reasons, FunnyQT uses the second implementation choice and its `funnyqt.xmltg` API provides functions for converting between XML documents and TGraphs conforming to the schema shown in fig. 15.2.

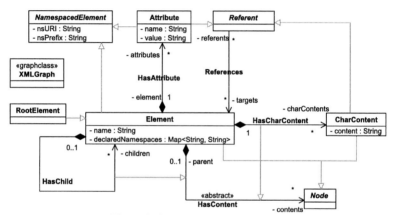

Figure 15.2: FunnyQT's XML Schema

With this schema, an XML document is represented by an XMLGraph. Such a graph has exactly one RoolElement which is a special Element. Elements may have attributes, each Attribute having a name and a value. Elements may also have contents which is a sequence of elements and CharContent objects.

Attributes and character contents may encode references to other elements in case their type is IDREF or IDREFS. This capability is modeled by the Referent class.

XML's namespace concept is also supported. Every element and attribute is a NamespacedElement having a nsPrefix and a nsURI, and every Element may declare more namespaces with its declaredNamespaces attribute which is a map from namespace prefixes to namespace URIs.

The function `xml2xml-graph` converts the given XML file f into a new XML graph conforming to the metamodel shown in fig. 15.2.

Function: `funnyqt.xmltg/xml2xml-graph`
`(xml2xml-graph f)`
`(xml2xml-graph f attr-type-fn)`
`(xml2xml-graph f attr-type-fn text-type-fn)`
`(xml2xml-graph f attr-type-fn text-type-fn xml-graph)`

If the XML file references a DTD file or contains an embedded DTD, then References edges for attributes of types IDREF and IDREFS are created automatically. If not, an additional `attr-type-fn` may be provided which is a function receiving an element's qualified name[6], an attribute name, and a corresponding attribute value. The function should return the type of the attribute where the following types are recognized: `"ID"` (other elements may reference this element using this attribute value), `"IDREF"` (a reference to some other element with an attribute of type ID), `"IDREFS"` (a reference to a sequence of other elements), `"EMFFragmentPath"` (an XPath-like navigation expression used in XMI documents of the Eclipse Modeling Framework), or `nil` (no special type).

Although no real XML concept, in practice IDs and references to other elements are frequently encoded as character contents. For example, an XML document might contain <person><id>SOME-ID</id> ... </person> instead of the more correct definition <person id="SOME-ID">...</person>. For tracking such IDs and creating References edges, an additional `text-type-fn` may be provided. It receives three arguments: the parent element's qualified name, the current element's qualified name, and the character contents as string. It should return the type of the character contents where again the values `"ID"`, `"IDREF"`, `"IDREFS"`, `"EMFFragmentPath"`, and `nil` are considered.

Lastly, instead of creating a new XML graph, an existing `xml-graph` may be provided. In this case, the existing given graph is populated and returned again[7].

The function `xml-graph2xml` simply serializes the XML graph g back to its XML representation and stores it in the file f.

Function: `funnyqt.xmltg/xml-graph2xml`
`(xml-graph2xml g f)`

The two functions `xml2xml-graph` and `xml-graph2xml` provide the core of the namespace `funnyqt.xmltg`. After an XML document has been converted to a graph, all generic and TGraph-specific model management and querying functions discussed so far can be used with it. However, there are some more auxiliary functions provided which ease working with XML graphs.

The functions `ns-prefix` and `ns-uri` return the namespace prefix and URI of the given XML element or attribute `elem-or-attr`.

Function: `funnyqt.xmltg/ns-prefix`
`(ns-prefix elem-or-attr)`
Function: `funnyqt.xmltg/ns-uri`
`(ns-uri elem-or-attr)`

If the given element doesn't declare a namespace itself, the respective parent elements are consulted recursively.

---

[6]A qualified name in this context is a string of the form `"nsPrefix:tag-name"` for namespaced elements and just the tag name for non-namespaced elements.
[7]In this case, the graph contains one RootElement per XML document read into it.

The next three functions return different kinds of names of a given element or attribute `elem-or-attr`.

Function: `funnyqt.xmltg/declared-name`
`(declared-name elem-or-attr)`
Function: `funnyqt.xmltg/qualified-name`
`(qualified-name elem-or-attr)`
Function: `funnyqt.xmltg/expanded-name`
`(expanded-name elem-or-attr)`

The `declared-name` is the name as written in the XML file, i.e., it includes a namespace prefix only if it has been specified in the XML file, too. The `qualified-name` is a name in the form `"nsPrefix:name"`, i.e., it always contains the namespace prefix unless the element or attribute is not namespaced. Lastly, the `expanded-name` has the form `"{nsURI}name"`, i.e., it always includes the namespace URI unless the element or attribute is not namespaced.

The `children` function returns the sequence of children elements of the given element `elem`. The children may be restricted to a given `name` which may be given as a plain tag name, a qualified, or an expanded name.

Function: `funnyqt.xmltg/children`
`(children elem)`
`(children elem name)`

The `siblings` function returns the siblings of a given element `elem` as a vector `[pred-sibs succ-sibs]` such that `(concat pred-sibs [elem] succ-sibs)` is equal to `(children elem)`, i.e., `pred-sibs` is the sequence of the children of `elem`'s parent preceding `elem`, and `succ-sibs` is the sequence of the children of `elem`'s parent following `elem`.

Function: `funnyqt.xmltg/siblings`
`(siblings elem qn)`

Lastly, the `attribute-value` function returns the value of `elem`'s `attr` attribute.

Function: `funnyqt.xmltg/attribute-value`
`(attribute-value elem attr)`

The attribute may be given as a plain or qualified attribute name. In case the element doesn't have such an attribute, an exception is thrown.

15.5   Persistence of Model-Related Data

When querying and transforming models, there is often a need to persist auxiliary data for later use such as query results or transformation traces. Such data may contain arbitrary objects, e.g., sets of lists of model elements, and there is no universal data format which can be used for the task as-is.

EMF-based tools usually capture such data as models where the model's elements may reference elements in the queried or transformed models using unidirectional references. Then, these query result or transformation trace models can be persisted using EMF's usual XMI [OMG14c] serialization. For JGraLab, there is no such predefined format.

In any case, since FunnyQT allows to query and transform different kinds of models arbitrarily mixed, a persistence format is needed which supports persisting references to models and model elements of arbitrary kinds. In addition, this format has to be extensible. When a user adds support for another modeling framework next to JGraLab and EMF by extending the FunnyQT protocols, the user must also be able to extend the persistence facilities.

15.5.1 The Extensible Data Notation

The *Extensible Data Notation* (*EDN*[8]) proposed by the Clojure author Rich Hickey is a light-weight alternative to XML. In essence, EDN is a subset of Clojure data comprising the null value (`nil`), booleans (`true` and `false`), characters (`\x`), symbols (`example`), keywords (`:kw`), integers (`-17`), floating point numbers (`-0.1`), strings (`"a string"`), sets (`#{1 2 3}`), lists (`(1 2 3)`), and maps (`{1 :one, 2 :one}`).

EDN aims to be an *interoperable* format, and indeed there are EDN reading and writing libraries for at least Clojure, Java, Ruby, C, C++, JavaScript, .NET, ObjectiveC, Python, Erlang, Haskell, PHP, and Scala. Although its standard types and their serialization format originate from Clojure, its not the exact runtime type of an object that defines the suitable EDN type but rather its semantics. For example, the EDN vector is meant to be used for collection types which have random access capabilities. Clojure vectors exhibit this semantics as well as arrays in Clojure, Scala, Java, Ruby, Python, or JavaScript.

EDN is also *extensible*. Applications and libraries can define their own EDN format for their custom data types and corresponding readers. For this purpose, EDN uses *tagged values*. As the name suggests, a tagged value consists of a tag and a value. The tag is a symbol prefixed with # consisting of an owner and a name component, and the value may be an arbitrary EDN datum. For example, `#de.myshop/OrderItem [18 2 2.99]` is a valid tagged value. The value is a vector of two integers and one floating point number, and the tag specifies that this vector represents an item in an order of some web shop. Usually, domains or namespace names like `de.myshop` are used as owner component of the tag symbol.

To read such a custom EDN datum, a reader function has to be defined and registered for the custom tag's symbol. For example, for the order items, a custom reader function might look like this:

```
(defn order-item-reader [[article-no quantity price]]
  (OrderItem. article-no quantity price))
```

The reader defines the semantics of the tagged value. Here, the reader defines that the first integer in the vector is the article number, the second integer is the quantity, and the final floating point number is the price. It simply uses these values to create and return a new OrderItem instance.

EDN itself defines two standard tagged value formats in addition to the standard untagged types listed above. Those can be recognized by their tags not having

---

[8]`http://edn-format.org` (last visited: 2015-05-28)

an owner component. Firstly, there are instants in time in RFC-3339 [KN02] format (`#inst "1985-04-12T23:20:50.52Z"`), and secondly, there are universally unique identifiers (UUID, [LMS05]) (`#uuid "f81d4fae-7dec-11d0-a765-00a0c91e6bf6"`).

With EDN, there may be alternative readers suitable for a given tagged value. and user is free to choose which one to use.

In the following, the FunnyQT extensions to the EDN format are discussed including with the corresponding functions for writing and reading data containing references to models and model elements.

15.5.2 EDN Format Extensions

FunnyQT defines EDN format extensions for storing references to models and model elements. The tags for those use as owner component the FunnyQT namespaces dealing with these kinds of models, e.g., `funnqt.tg` for references to JGraLab TGraphs, vertices, and edges, and `funnyqt.emf` for references to EMF resource sets, resources, and eobjects.

Concretely, this is the EDN format for JGraLab TGraphs, vertices, and edges.

```
;; Reference to a TGraph
#funnyqt.tg/Graph "918348b4-5153b25a-5668c393-2767b494"
;; Reference to a Vertex in a TGraph
#funnyqt.tg/Vertex [#funnyqt.tg/Graph "918348b4-5153b25a-5668c393-2767b494", 1]
;; Reference to an Edge in a TGraph
#funnyqt.tg/Edge [#funnyqt.tg/Graph "918348b4-5153b25a-5668c393-2767b494", 1]
```

A reference to a graph is written using the tag `#funnyqt.tg/Graph`, and the value is the graph's unique identifier which is computed when a graph is created and won't change afterwards.

A reference to a vertex is written using the tag `#funnyqt.tg/Vertex`, and the value is a vector of two components. The first one is a reference to the graph containing that vertex, and the second component is the ID of the vertex.

References to edges are written with the tag `#funnyqt.tg/Edge`, and the value is again a vector containing the reference to the containing graph and the edge's ID.

As said, a graph's unique identifier is stable and won't change over time, thus it is very suitable for the task. The IDs of vertices and edges also don't change in general, however if a vertex or edge with a given ID gets deleted, this ID will eventually be reused for a new element. That said, as long as the referenced elements aren't deleted and new elements are created, the EDN representation stays valid.

The EDN format for EMF resources, resource sets, and eobjects is given in the following listing.

```
;; References to Resources
#funnyqt.emf/Resource "example.families"
#funnyqt.emf/Resource #funnyqt.emf/URI
  ↪ "file:/home/horn/Repos/uni/funnyqt/test/input/example.families"
```

```
;; Reference to a ResourceSet
#funnyqt.emf/ResourceSet #{#funnyqt.emf/Resource "example.families",
 ↪  #funnyqt.emf/Resource "Families.ecore"}
;; Reference to an EObject
#funnyqt.emf/EObject [#funnyqt.emf/Resource "example.families", "//@families.2"]
```

A reference to a resource is written using the tag `#funnyqt.emf/Resource`, and the value is either the simple name of the resource, or the EDN representation of the resource's URI. A URI is written using the tag `#funnyqt.emf/URI`, and the value is a string denoting that URI. Which representation is used depends on the value of the following dynamic var whose default value is true.

Var: `funnyqt.edn/*edn-emf-store-resources-by-simple-name*`

EMF resources don't have a unique identifier which could be used to unambiguously identify it, so the file name or the resource's URI is the best thing one can use to reference them. But when using simple names, it is not possible to reference two different resources having the same name but residing in different directories. And when using URIs, the references become invalid and need to be updated as soon as resources are moved. And of course both representations are invalidated when a resource is renamed.

A reference to a resource set is written using the tag `#funnyqt.emf/ResourceSet`, and the value is a set of resources.

A reference to an EObject contained in some resource is written using the tag `#funnyqt.emf/EObject`, and the value is a vector of two components. The first is the containing resource, the second is the EMF fragment path denoting the eobject inside the resource. Such an EMF fragment path is an ID in case the metamodel defines an attribute with ID semantics for the type of that element. If this is not the case like in the example above, the fragment path denotes the path to that element starting at the root element. This representation is fragile because it depends on element order, e.g., the fragment path above denotes the third eobject in the root object's families reference. If an object occurring earlier in this list gets deleted, the reference is invalidated, i.e., it points to the eobject that comes after the originally referenced object.

With all these problems discussed above in mind, the solution to solve them is very simple. When a model for which data has been saved is going to be modified in a way which would invalidate the EDN data, this data needs to be loaded before the modification and persisted again afterwards.

The actual functions for writing and reading EDN data are discussed in the following two sections. Lastly, section 15.5.5 on page 167 describes how the EDN format can be extended.

15.5.3 Writing EDN Data

The following four functions are responsible for writing EDN data. They all have the same names as the core Clojure data printing functions.

Function: funnyqt.edn/pr   **Function:** funnyqt.edn/prn
(pr obj)   (prn obj)

Function: funnyqt.edn/pr-str   **Function:** funnyqt.edn/spit
(pr-str obj)   (spit obj file)

The function pr prints the given object's EDN representation to the current value of the dynamic var clojure.core/*out* which is standard output by default but can be bound to any java.io.Writer, e.g., in order to write to a file, or to send the EDN text over the network. prn is just like pr but prints a final newline.

The pr-str function is like pr but returns obj's EDN representation as a string, i.e., it is a shorthand for using pr to print into a java.io.StringWriter and then returning its contents.

Lastly, the function spit saves the EDN representation of obj into a file which may be either a string denoting the file's name or a java.io.File object. If the specified file already exists, it will be overwritten.

15.5.4 Reading EDN Data

There are three functions for reading EDN data: read, read-string, and slurp.

Function: funnyqt.edn/read   **Function:** funnyqt.edn/read-string
(read reader models)   (read-string string models)
(read opts reader models)   (read-string opts string models)

Function: funnyqt.edn/slurp
(slurp file models)
(slurp opts file models)

The read functions reads one datum from the given reader which must be a java.io.PushbackReader or a subclass instance. The read-string function reads from a given string instead from a reader. Lastly, slurp reads from a file which may be given as java.io.File or as a string denoting the file name.

In all three cases, a collection of models must be provided. Whenever a reference to a model or model element is read, it is resolved with respect to this collection. If a referenced model or model element cannot be resolved, an exception is thrown.

read and read-string delegate to the functions of the same name in the Clojure standard library's clojure.edn namespace, and slurp is only a shorthand for reading from a PushbackReader wrapping a java.io.FileReader. These Clojure standard library functions accept a map of options (opts) which can optionally be provided when using the FunnyQT variants. The map of options may contain the following entries:

:eof The value of this key is the value to be returned when reading from a reader or string which doesn't contain another value anymore. By default, an exception is thrown.

:default A default reader function of two arguments. Whenever a tagged value is encountered for which no reader is defined, this function is called with the tag symbol and the value. By default, tagged values for which no reader is available trigger an exception.

:readers A map from symbols denoting tags to corresponding reader functions responsible for reading such tagged values.

By default, the FunnyQT EDN read functions call the Clojure versions with the
:readers map initialized with readers appropriate for reading references to models
and model elements. If a :reader map is given in the opts, this map is merged with
the default map where entries in the explicitly given map may override default ones,
i.e., the reader functions defined by FunnyQT may be swapped with custom ones.

15.5.5 Extending the EDN Format

Extending the EDN format in order to add support for new kinds of models and
elements requires two steps: the extension of the writing and the reading part.

To extend the writing part, the FunnyQT IWriteEDN protocol has to be extended.

Protocol: funnyqt.edn/IWriteEDN
(write-edn obj out)

The write-edn method receives an object obj and a java.io.Writer out and should
write obj's EDN representation to the writer. For example, this is the definition for
JGraLab vertices.

```
(extend-protocol IWriteEDN
  de.uni_koblenz.jgralab.Vertex
  (write-edn [v out]
    (.write out "#funnyqt.tg/Vertex ")
    (write-edn [(tg/graph v) (tg/id v)] out)))
```

First, the tag is written to out, and then the write-edn method is invoked recursively to write the vector forming the value of the #funnyqt.tc/Vertex tag.

To be able to read a tagged value, a reader function has to be provided and
registered for EDN elements with a given tag. This registration is done by altering
the value of the var edn-readers.

Var: funnyqt.edn/edn-readers

Its default value is given in the following which illustrates that for any tag denoting
a JGraLab or EMF model or model element, there is a corresponding reader function.

```
{'funnyqt.tg/Graph       #'edn-tg-graph-reader
 'funnyqt.tg/Vertex      #'edn-tg-vertex-reader
 'funnyqt.tg/Edge        #'edn-tg-edge-reader
 'funnyqt.emf/Resource   #'edn-emf-resource-reader
 'funnyqt.emf/ResourceSet #'edn-emf-resource-set-reader
 'funnyqt.emf/EObject    #'edn-emf-eobject-reader
 'funnyqt.emf/URI        #'edn-emf-uri-reader}
```

Every reader function receives the value associated with the tag it is responsible
for and should return the value corresponding to the EDN datum. The models given
at a call to read, read-string, or slurp are available to readers in terms of the dynamic
var *models* and can then be used for resolution of models and model elements.

Var: `funnyqt.edn/*models*`

Note that EDN readers receive the already read and resolved value, i.e., reading a nested EDN structure works bottom-up. For example, these are the definitions of the readers for TGraphs and TGraph vertices.

```
(defn ^:private edn-tg-graph-reader [id]
  (q/the #(and (instance? de.uni_koblenz.jgralab.Graph %)
               (= id (tg/id %)))
         *models*))

(defn ^:private edn-tg-vertex-reader [[g vid]]
  (tg/vertex g vid))
```

The value of a TGraph reference is its ID (see page 164). In order to return the actually referenced graph, the collection of `*models*` is searched for the model which is a TGraph with the given ID.

The value of a vertex reference EDN tagged value is a vector containing a reference to the graph, and the ID of the vertex in this graph. However, the reader receives a vector containing the already resolved graph and the vertex ID, i.e., the `edn-tg-graph-reader` has already been invoked on the TGraph reference before the `edn-tg-vertex-reader` gets invoked.

15.6   Miscellaneous

In this section, several miscellaneous querying functions are discussed. First, section 15.6.1 introduces FunnyQT's quantified expressions on sequences, then section 15.6.2 on the next page explains several utility sequence functions, section 15.6.3 on page 171 defines several higher-order functions for composing predicates, and lastly section 15.6.4 on page 171 provides some logic functions complementing Clojure's standard logic macros.

15.6.1   Quantified Expressions

There are three quantified expression predicates on sequences in FunnyQT. They all receive a predicate and a seqable object.

The `forall?` quantified expression predicate returns true if and only if `(pred el)` returns true for any `el` in the collection `coll`.

Function: `funnyqt.query/forall?`
`(forall? pred coll)`

`forall?` is short-circuiting, i.e., it stops testing elements and returns false as soon as the first element not satisfying `pred` has been encountered. This is an important property in case `coll` is a lazy (possibly infinite) sequence.

The exists? predicate returns true if and only if (pred el) holds for at least one element el in coll.

Function: funnyqt.query/exists?
(exists? pred coll)

exists? is also short-circuiting. It stops testing elements and returns true as soon as the first element satisfying pred has been encountered.

Finally, exist-n? returns true if and only if there exist exactly n elements el in coll for which (pred el) returns true.

Function: funnyqt.query/exist-n?
(exist-n? n pred coll)

Also exist-n? is short-circuiting returning false as soon as the (+ n 1)-th element for which pred holds has been found.

15.6.2 Utility Sequence Functions

The funnyqt.query namespace defines several additional sequence utility functions.

The first one is the function the.

Function: funnyqt.query/the
(the xs)
(the pred xs)

Given a sequence xs, it returns the single element in the sequence, or the single element for which pred holds. If the sequence does not contain exactly one element (for which pred holds), then this function throws an exception. Therefore, the is useful for specifying explicitly that some sequence must only contain one single element (satisfying pred). Everything else would mean there is a bug.

The member? predicate returns true if and only if a given element e is member of the given sequence xs.

Function: funnyqt.query/member?
(member? e xs)

This function is similar to contains? (see page 44) but the latter has the peculiar property of checking if the given collection contains the given object as a key[9]. For sets, the keys are the elements themself thus contains? and member? are equivalent but for vectors (contains? 1 [3 4 5]) returns true because that vector does indeed have the key 1 since the keys of a vector are its indices.

The functions pred-seq and succ-seq receive a sequence xs and return the lazy predecessor and successor sequences.

Function: funnyqt.query/pred-seq   **Function:** funnyqt.query/succ-seq
(pred-seq xs)   (succ-seq xs)

In the lazy predecessor sequence, each element of xs is given as a pair of its predecessor in xs and itself. nil is used as the first element's predecessor. Likewise,

---

[9]Thus, it would have been better if it was named contains-key?, but that ship has sailed long ago.

in the lazy successor sequence, each element of xs is given as pair of the element itself and its successor in xs and nil is used as the last element's successor. The following example demonstrates this behavior.

```
(pred-seq [1 2 3 4])
;=> ([nil 1] [1 2] [2 3] [3 4])
(succ-seq [1 2 3 4])
;=> ([1 2] [2 3] [3 4] [4 nil])
```

And there is the lazy predecessor and successor sequence function pred-succ-seq.

Function: funnyqt.query/pred-succ-seq
(pred-succ-seq xs)

In the returned lazy sequence, every element in xs is represented as a triple of its predecessor in xs, the element itself, and its successor in xs as demonstrated by the following example. Again, nil is used to represent the nonexisting predecessor of the first element and successor of the last element.

```
(pred-succ-seq [1 2 3 4])
;=> ([nil 1 2] [1 2 3] [2 3 4] [3 4 nil])
```

The seq-comparator function composes comparators in order to sort collections containing tuples of homogenous values. To recapitulate, a comparator (see section 6.6.7 on page 47) is a function receiving two objects and returning a negative integer if the first object is less than the second object, a positive integer if the first object is greater than the second object, or zero otherwise.

Function: funnyqt.query/seq-comparator
(seq-comparator & cmps)

It receives a varargs sequence of comparator functions and returns a new comparator. The returned comparator assumes that the two object given as its arguments are sequences. It compares the i-th element of each sequence with the i-th comparator given to seq-comparator until the first one returns a non-zero value. The following example demonstrates its semantics.

```
(sort (seq-comparator compare #(- %2 %1))
      [["Peter" 29] ["Alice" 31] ["James" 17] ["Peter" 17]])
;=> (["Alice" 31] ["James" 17] ["Peter" 29] ["Peter" 17])
```

A vector containing name-age pairs is to be sorted. The comparator returned by the seq-comparator call compares the names using the compare function and the ages by substracting the first pair's age from the second pair's age. Thus, in the result sequence the pairs are sorted lexicographically with respect to the names, and for equal names the pairs are sorted descendingly with respect to the age.

The last sequence utility function is sort-topologically.

Function: funnyqt.query/sort-topologically
(sort-topologically deps-fn els)

It receives a sequence of elements `els` and a dependencies function `deps-fn`. The dependency function is called once for each element in `els` and has to return that element's "dependencies", i.e., the set of elements that should be sorted before it. `sort-topologically` returns a topologically sorted vector of the elements in `els` or false if there is a dependency cycle. Thus, this function also acts as a acyclicity test with respect to `deps-fn`.

15.6.3   Higher-Order Predicate Combinators

FunnyQT provides several higher-order functions for combining predicates.

Function: `funnyqt.query/and-fn`
(and-fn & ps)

Function: `funnyqt.query/or-fn`
(or-fn & ps)

Function: `funnyqt.query/nand-fn`
(nand-fn & ps)

Function: `funnyqt.query/nor-fn`
(nor-fn & ps)

Function: `funnyqt.query/xor-fn`
(xor-fn & ps)

All these functions receive a varargs sequence of predicates ps and return a new predicate combining the given predicate in the provided order using the logic operation being the first part of their name. For example, (or-fn odd? zero?) yields a predicate which returns true if and only if the given argument (which must be an integer) is odd or zero.

The predicates returned by the combinator functions are all short-circuiting, e.g., the predicate returned by or-fn tests only one predicate after the other until one returns true.

15.6.4   Logic Macros and Functions

Clojure provides the short-circuiting logic macros and and or. FunnyQT adds some more.

Macro: `funnyqt.query/nand`
(nand & xs)

Macro: `funnyqt.query/nor`
(nor & xs)

Macro: `funnyqt.query/xor`
(xor & xs)

All three macros receive arbitrary many values. (nand ...) is a shorthand for (not (and ...)), and (nor ...) is a shorthand for (not (or ...)). xor returns true if and only if an odd number of its arguments are true.

FunnyQT provides the functionality of the logic operator macros also as functions.

Function: `funnyqt.query/and*`
(and* & xs)

Function: `funnyqt.query/or*`
(or* & xs)

Function: `funnyqt.query/nand*`
(nand* & xs)

Function: `funnyqt.query/nor*`
(nor* & xs)

Function: `funnyqt.query/xor*`
(xor* & xs)

As functions, they are not short-circuiting because all arguments are evaluated before a function gets executed. This property might be useful in some scenarios but the major justification of their existence is that as functions they are first-class objects which can be passed to higher-order functions as demonstrated in the following example.

```
(apply and* [1 false true true nil])
;=> false
(apply or* [1 false true true nil])
;=> 1
(apply nand* [1 false true true nil])
;=> true
(apply nor* [1 false true true nil])
;=> false
(apply xor* [1 false true true nil])
;=> true
```

With respect to their return value, these functions are completely equivalent to their macro counterparts. For example, or* returns the first truthy argument value as does or.

Chapter 16

Related Work

In this chapter, related querying approaches are discussed. Approaches whose main querying facility is pattern matching are discussed later in chapter 19 starting on page 217. Similarly, related logic-based querying approaches are discussed separately in chapter 32 starting on page 335.

The querying parts of FunnyQT have been strongly influenced by the declarative TGraph querying language *GReQL* [EB10]. Its most common querying construct is the `from ... with ... report ... end` expression which is a comprehension. The `from` part binds variables to domains, the `with` part filters these bindings using constraints, and the `report` part defines the structure of the result.

Furthermore, GReQL supports quantified expressions and comes with an extensible function library. In order to add a new custom function to GReQL, only a class implementing a simple predefined interface needs to be implemented.

Regular path expressions also come from GReQL. Essentially, GReQL supports the same set of regular path operators as FunnyQT. However, the implementation is quite different. Whereas FunnyQT implements regular path expressions in terms of function composition, with GReQL, a deterministic finite automaton is constructed from the RPE which is then used to steer a local search though the queried graph.

This automaton-based implementation has some benefits. In general, many RPEs are evaluated slightly faster with GReQL than corresponding RPEs with FunnyQT. Furthermore, the GReQL implementation provides more features. Whereas FunnyQT's RPEs allow only to compute the set of reachable elements given a start element or a set of start elements, GReQL can also compute the inverse, i.e., all possible start vertices for a given RPE and a target vertex or a set of target vertices. And GReQL allows to compute a path system or a trace from a given RPE and a start vertex. A path system contains one single path from the start vertex to any reachable vertex, and this path is also guaranteed to be a shortest path. A trace is the set of all vertices which are reachable from the start vertex or which are contained in a path from the start vertex to at least one of the reachable vertices.

The benefit of the FunnyQT implementation is that it is much simpler and easier to extend. For example, defining a custom regular path operator like `p-contents` on section 15.1 on page 151 is not possible for a GReQL user as it would require modifications at least to the GReQL parser and the evaluator.

GReQL's tender spot is that it is only an expression language, i.e., it lacks adequate abstractions supporting reuse of existing queries which would allow for defining libraries of related queries where one query might use other queries.

Concepts similar to regular path expressions are also used or have been proposed for querying other tree- or graph-like structures, e.g., for querying XML documents using XPath [W3C10], or for querying RDF[1] graphs using an extended version of SPARQL [W3C08; ABE09].

Although initially designed only as a constraint language, the *Object Constraint Language* (*OCL*, [OMG14b]) is the standard model querying language nowadays, and many transformation approaches use (variants of) it for their querying parts. There is also a stand-alone OCL implementation[2] for EMF models developed as part of the Eclipse project.

At its heart, OCL supports the definition of constraints in the context of metamodel elements, e.g., in the form of invariants that have to hold for instances of a given metamodel class, or in the form of pre- and postconditions which have to hold for operations defined in a UML [OMG15c] model. Additionally, initial values of properties and expressions defining the values of derived properties can be specified. The behavior of operations can be specified by providing an OCL body expression, too. However, since OCL is a side-effect free language, only querying operations can be defined.

For the same reason, OCL is not suitable for model management. The OMG's QVT standard [OMG11b] also specifies an extension to OCL called *Imperative OCL* which provides operations for changing models and model elements, however this extension is not supported by the Eclipse OCL implementation.

For querying purposes, OCL provides a large library consisting of operations returning all instances of a given class, collection operations for filtering (`select` and `reject`), mapping (`collect`), and reducing/folding (`iterate`), and there are also quantified expressions (`forAll` and `exists`). Having filtering, mapping, and reducing functions at hand, it seems plausible to assume that OCL is a functional language. However, operations cannot be passed as parameters to other operations because the concept of an operation is on the metametamodel level whereas OCL's type world is the metamodel of the model being queried (in addition to OCL's own scalar and collection types).

OCL provides a concise notation for navigating objects using its dot and arrow operators, e.g., `obj.srole.mrole->forAll(...)` navigates from `obj` to the element in its single-valued `srole` role and from there it retrieves the set of elements in the multi-valued role `mrole` which results in a set on which a universally quantified expression is tested.

OCL also supports a `closure` operation which returns the reflexive transitive closure of a navigation expression, e.g., `persons->closure(children)` returns the set

---

[1]http://www.w3.org/RDF/ (last visited: 2015-10-14)
[2]http://www.eclipse.org/modeling/mdt/?project=ocl (last visited: 2015-10-2015)

containing persons, their children, their grandchildren, etc. The closure expression is required to return a collection of elements but may be chosen freely otherwise which provides navigation possibilities similar to regular path expressions. E.g., the closure operation corresponds to the path iteration, its expression may navigate multiple roles which corresponds to the path sequence, it may take the union of several roles which corresponds to the path alternative.

The *Epsilon Object Language* (*EOL*, [Kol+15]) is the model management language of the Epsilon framework atop of which all other Epsilon languages are built. Its querying parts are very similar to OCL, i.e., it provides largely the same kinds of features with respect to role name navigation including transitive closures, quantified expressions, and collection functions.

In addition, it provides variables, assignments, and typical imperative control flow structures such as if and switch statements and loops. Even exceptions can be thrown which can then be caught from Java.

Furthermore, it provides all means for model management and low-level model manipulation, i.e., models can be loaded and persisted, elements can be created and deleted, and properties can be retrieved and set.

EOL also supports the definition of custom operations. Those can be defined in the context of a metamodel class in which case they are essentially methods of this class. They may also be defined without context in which case they are plain procedures. Operations may be annotated with a precondition and a postcondition. Furthermore, there is an additional @cached annotation adding memoization to an operation.

The Epsilon framework also provides a language specialized for model validation in terms of constraint checking called *Epsilon Validation Language* (*EVL*). The expressions that have to be tested are defined using EOL.

EVL allows for defining constraints and critiques which have different levels of importance. Whereas invalidating a constraint is considered an error, critiques can be used to implement style guidelines which are gently suggested to the user but not strictly enforced. In the following, only the term constraint is used but it always includes critiques as well.

Constraints are defined in the context of a metamodel class where they define an invariant which all instances of that class have to satisfy.

Each constraints has a name and a boolean expression indicating if the constraint is satisfied or not.

Optionally, a constraint may have a guard expression which can be used to restrict the constraint to only a subset of instances of the context. This and the fact that constraints are named makes it possible to express that some constraint depends on another constraint. E.g., there may the two constraints that the names of entities must not be undefined, and they must start with a capital letter. Clearly, when already the first constraint fails, there is no value in testing the second one. Thus, the guard of the second constraint may specify that the first constraint has to be satisfied already.

Every constraint may also have a message which is shown to the user in case the constraint is not satisfied for a set of elements.

Lastly, every constraint may have arbitrary many fixes which are actions that would resolve the issue. For example, a fix for an undefined name could be to ask the user for a value. Each fix may have a title which is presented to the user, it may have a guard controlling when it is enabled, and a block of EOL statements implementing the actual repair actions of the fix.

In the past, there have been various other querying languages for EMF models: *EMF ModelQuery, EMF ModelQuery2,* and *EMFPath.*

The first provided a Java API for programming queries mostly in the style of SQL-like comprehensions, i.e., selection of model elements of a given type and filtering using constraints.

Its successor EMF ModelQuery2 intended to increase the efficiency when querying large models in terms of indexing and lazy loading of resources. Additionally, next to its API it provided a SQL-like DSL for defining queries.

Lastly, EMFPath also went into the same direction as EMF ModelQuery2 by trying to increase efficiency in terms of lazy loading of models. Again, it was provided as an API for querying EMF models, and it used Google's *Guava* library which provides function and predicate interfaces that can be used in mapping and filtering operations on immutable Guava collections in order to provide some functional programming capabilities[3].

However, all three querying approaches have been discontinued.

The *.NET Modeling Framework* (*NMF*[4]) is a light-weight modeling framework implemented in C#. Amongst other features, the framework provides *NMF Expressions* [HH15] which allow to define queries on NMF models which can either be evaluated in a batch-mode or incrementally. Queries are defined using LINQ[5] [PR10], the querying DSL embedded in all .NET languages. LINQ is a querying DSL similar to SQL, i.e., it allows to define nested comprehensions and provides several constructs for aggregating, sorting, or grouping values.

However, neither the NMF homepage[4] nor the few NMF-related publications explicit which LINQ constructs are actually supported by NMF Expressions.

Adding behavior to models is an obvious desire which can be achieved with most if not all modeling frameworks. Usually, interfaces and implementation classes can be generated from a metamodel, and the simplest approach to add behavior is to add method declarations to the interfaces and implementations to the classes. The problem here is that in case the metamodel is changed, the code needs to be re-generated and manual changes get overridden.

EMF allows the declaration of methods already on the metamodel level where even the body may already be specified, too. And special comments in the generated

---

[3]This part of Guava can be seen as a kind of predecessor of Java 8's new streams API.
[4]https://nmf.codeplex.com/ (last visited: 2015-09-30)
[5]*Language Integrated Query*

code allow to protect custom methods from being overridden when the code is re-generated after a metamodel change.

Both JGraLab and EMF also allow for specializing the generated interfaces and classes which provides another means for adding custom methods.

Also aspect-oriented programming [Kic96], especially inter-type declarations, can be used for adding methods to the generated interfaces. This approach is taken by KerMeta [MFJ05] which provides, among others, a concise and statically-typed DSL that allows for defining operations for metamodel classes. Those are compiled to aspects that are eventually woven in into the interfaces and classes generated for the metamodel. The benefit of having a special DSL instead of defining the behavior with plain AspectJ [Kic+01] directly is that the KerMeta DSL has direct support for typical metamodeling concepts such as opposite references, associations, or derived properties.

Part V

On Pattern Matching

Summary

This part's topic is pattern matching. Chapter 17 starting on page 183 opens with a discussion of pattern matching facilities in functional languages and pattern matching on graphs.

Chapter 18 starting on page 193 then describes FunnyQT's embedded pattern matching DSL with all its features including positive and negative application conditions, patterns with alternatives, and nested patterns.

Finally, chapter 19 starting on page 217 closes this part with a discussion of related work.

Chapter 17

Introduction

Pattern matching is a widely used term in both functional programming languages and graph transformations. A *pattern* usually equals or at least mimics the shape of the data structure it is matched against and contains variables or placeholders.

Then, the intrinsic idea of pattern matching is to compute a total assignment where every variable in the pattern gets assigned an element in the data structure being matched against. If such an assignment exists, it is called a *match* of the pattern.

It is important to emphasize that the match has to be total. Every variable in the pattern needs to get assigned an object of the data structure being matched against.

A different way to look at pattern matching is to consider it a means for finding a substitution for the placeholders (variables) in a pattern such that when applying the substitution, the pattern equals the matched data structure.

Patterns may also contain constructs for restricting matches. For example, a pattern may declare that some element must be of a certain type in order for a possible match to be valid, or it may declare that some element must satisfy a given predicate.

With pattern matching in functional languages, patterns are notated textually. With pattern matching in graph transformation systems, patterns are frequently notated visually but textual notations are not uncommon, too.

In section 17.1 on the next page, a short introduction of the pattern matching facilities available in the functional languages Clojure and Haskell[1] is given. Section 17.2 on page 188 then generalizes the idea of pattern matching to graphs.

Starting with chapter 18 starting on page 193, FunnyQT's pattern matching approach is discussed in detail. It provides an embedded DSL for defining patterns that can be matched on arbitrary models. Related approaches are then discussed in chapter 19 starting on page 217. appendix A.3 on page 424 discusses how the pattern matching DSL can be extended to support models of modeling frameworks other than JGraLab and EMF.

---

[1] `http://www.haskell.org` (last visited: 2015-01-19)

17.1   Pattern Matching in Functional Languages

Clojure's destructuring capabilities, which have been discussed in section 6.7 on page 48, are a simple form of pattern matching. For example, in the following listing

```
(let [[a b & more] (range 10)]
  {:a a, :b b, :more more})
;=> {:a 0, :b 1, :more (2 3 4 5 6 7 8 9)}
```

the destructuring form [a b & more], i.e., the pattern, is matched against the sequence containing the numbers from 0 to 9. The pattern defines that the variable a should map to the first element in the sequence, b should map to the second element, and more should map to the remainder of the sequence. Such a destructuring form works for all kinds of sequential collections, e.g., lists, sequences, vectors, and even strings.

Additionally, there is also support for destructuring on maps as shown by the next example.

```
(let [person {:first-name "Jim", :last-name "Miller",
              :address {:street "Graham Road 17", :town "London"}}
      {fname :first-name
       lname :last-name
       {s :street, t :town} :address} person]
  [fname lname s t])
;=> ["Jim" "Miller" "Graham Road 17" "London"]
```

In there, person is a map representing a person. The person's address is modeled as a nested map with entries for the street and the town. The destructuring form picks out the first name, the last name, the street, and the town and binds them to the variables fname, lname, s, and t, respectively. Note that for picking out the street and town values from the nested :address map a nested destructuring form is used.

Similar destructuring capabilities are also available in most other Lisp dialects such as Common Lisp and Scheme.

As said above, with pattern matching one usually expects the match to be total. Every variable in the pattern must get a value assigned. This aspect is not true for Clojure destructuring, e.g., in

```
(when-let [[a b] [1]]
  [a b])
;=> [1 nil]
```

the variable b has no assigned value because the vector being matched against contains only one single element. Therefore, Clojure destructuring has been introduced as a simple form of pattern matching. It exhibits the variable assignment part of pattern matching but doesn't enforce that the match function is total.

The *clojure.core.match* library[2] provides much more extensive pattern matching capabilities which also enforce that matches are total. It provides a match macro

---

[2]https://github.com/clojure/core.match (last visited: 2015-01-19)

which gets a data structure to be matched against and arbitrarily many pattern/result form pairs. Each pattern is matched against the data structure one after the other and if it succeeds, the corresponding result form is the value of match. An optional :else clause may end the match expression. Its result form is the value of the match expression in case no pattern matches. If there is no :else clause and no pattern matches, an exception is thrown.

The following listing provides an example.

```
(for [x [[1 2]
         [1 2 3]
         [1 2 3 4]
         {:a 17, :b 2}
         {:a 23, :b 7}]]
  (match [x]
    ;; patterns                   ;; result forms
    [[a b c]]                     [c b a]
    [{:a a, :b 2}]                {:a a}
    [{:a (a :guard odd?), :b b}]  {:a a, :b b}
    :else                         :no-match))
;=> (:no-match [1 2 3] :no-match {:a 17} {:a 23, :b 7})
```

The variable x is bound to three different vectors and two different maps one after the other. Each x value is then matched against the given patterns until one succeeds. If no pattern succeeds, the :else clause defines the value of the match expression to be :no-match.

The first pattern [[a b c]] matches vectors with exactly three elements and binds those to the variables a, b, and c. These variables are only accessible in the corresponding result form which returns a vector of the form [c b a], i.e., the reversed vector.

The second pattern [{:a a, :b 2}] matches any map which has at least the keys :a and :b. Additionally, the value of the :b key needs to be the number 2. In that case, the value of the :a key is bound to the variable a, and the map {:a a} is returned.

The third pattern [{:a (a :guard odd?), :b b}] again matches maps which have at least the keys :a and :b. The values are bound to the variables a and b. The :guard attached to a additionally specifies that the value of the :a key needs to be an odd integer for a match to succeed.

The :else clause finally defines that for values of x where no pattern matches, the result of the match expression is :no-match.

The return value of the complete for comprehension is also printed in the listing. For x being the vector [1 2] there is no match because the single vector pattern matches only vectors of size 3. This matches only the second x value [1 2 3] but not the third one [1 2 3 4] which is too long. The first map bound to x matches the pattern [{:a a, :b 2}] because its :b key's value is 2. Note that it would also match the third pattern of the match expression but earlier patterns are always preferred to later ones. Lastly, the map {:a 23, :b 7} can only be matched by the third pattern in the match because the value of the :a key is odd. It cannot be matched by the second pattern because the :b value is not 2.

It should be noted that the example match expression only demonstrates a small

number of *clojure.core.match*'s features but it still suffices to give an idea about
the underlying concept, e.g., the computation of a total assignment of variables in
a pattern to elements in a matched structure which are restricted by the type of
the data structure, the size of the data structure, the contents of the data structure,
and arbitrary predicates on parts of the content.

One especially important aspect of *clojure.core.match* is that it performs *lazy
pattern matching*. This means that the match macro expands into a decision tree[3]
according to the algorithm described in [Mar08]. This decision tree based approach
is called lazy because every test is executed only if needed and at most once.

The decision tree generated for the match expression above is visualized in
fig. 17.1. In there, edges going to the left state the parent test succeeded and
edges going to the right state the parent test did not succeed. We can see that the

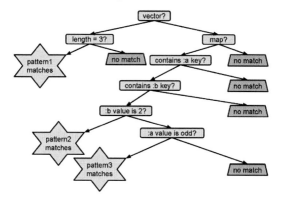

Figure 17.1: The decision tree of the *clojure.core.match* example

common tests relevant for the second and third pattern are only tested once. I.e.,
since both patterns only match maps which contain at least an :a and a :b key, the
corresponding tests are shared. Because the third pattern may only match in case
the second pattern does not match, even the test if the :b value is 2 is shared. If the
test succeeds, then the second pattern matches. If not, then the third pattern might
match in case the :a value is odd.

Haskell's pattern matching capabilities are quite similar to those provided by
clojure.core.match, i.e., they allow for destructuring with variable binding and
restricting based on contents and arbitrary predicates. In contrast to Clojure,
pattern matching is an essential part of the language.

For example, the function patternDemo defined in the next listing

```
patternDemo (a:b:[])        = [b,a]
patternDemo (1:2:xs)        = xs
```

---

[3]Concretely, the decision tree is a deeply nested cond expression.

```
patternDemo l | sum l == 5     = reverse l
              | length l >= 5 = sort l
              | True           = []
-- patternDemo [1,2]            -> [2,1]             (1)
-- patternDemo [1,2,3,4,5]      -> [3,4,5]           (2)
-- patternDemo [2,0,3]          -> [3,0,2]           (3)
-- patternDemo [2,0,3,-12,1] -> [-12,0,1,2,3]  (4)
-- patternDemo [0,1,2]          -> []               (5)
```

is defined to receive and return a list of integers[4]. The definition is split into three equations. Equations usually have the form functionName pattern = body.

The pattern (a:b:[]) of the first equation matches a list with exactly two elements. The first element is bound to a and the second element is bound to b. The result is the reversed two-element list [b,a]. Call (1) demonstrates this case.

The second equation's pattern matches any list with at least two elements. The first and second element must be 1 and 2, respectively. The remainder of the list is bound to xs and is the result of the function as demonstrated by the call (2). Note that both this pattern and the first equation's pattern match the list [1,2]. In such cases the declaration order is significant and resolves the ambiguity.

The third equation's pattern binds the given list to the variable l, and then so-called guards are used to test for certain properties of l. Every guard is a boolean expression. Only if its result is true, the corresponding body is evaluated.

The first guard tests if the sum of the given list's elements is 5. In this case, the result of the function is the reversed list as shown by call (3).

The second guard tests if the length of the list is greater than or equal to 5. If so, the result is the sorted list as demonstrated by call (4).

The last guard is a catch-all case which is always true. So any list which neither has exactly two elements, nor starts with 1 and 2, nor has the sum 5, nor has a length greater than or equal to 5 results in the empty list []. Call (5) shows that [0,1,2] is such a list.

Patterns can also match depending on the type of the data structure being matched on as shown by the following example.

```
data Shape = Square Float | Rectangle Float Float | Circle Float

surface (Square x)    = x * x
surface (Rectangle x y) = x * y
surface (Circle r)     = pi * r ^ 2
-- surface (Square 2)      -> 4.0
-- surface (Rectangle 3 2) -> 6.0
-- surface (Circle 1)      -> 3.1415927
```

The algebraic data type **Shape** is defined to be either a **Square** defined by its side length, a **Rectangle** defined by its x and y lengths, or a **Circle** defined by its radius.

---

[4]The type [Int] -> [Int] can be omitted because the compiler is able to infer it from the patterns and the result expressions.

The surface function can then be defined by three equations whose patterns match one of the three alternative types and bind their relevant components to variables that are used in the equation bodies.

17.2   Pattern Matching on Graphs

Pattern matching on graphs is a quite intuitive extension to the pattern matching approaches present in functional programming languages that were briefly illustrated in the previous section. Here, a pattern is a graph consisting of nodes and edges. When such a pattern is matched on a graph, which is frequently called the *host graph* in this context, an assignment from pattern graph nodes and edges to host graph nodes and edges is computed. Such a match has to conform to the connection constraints defined by the pattern's edges, i.e., it has to be a *subgraph homomorphism*.

Formally speaking, let the pattern graph be $G_p = (V_p, E_p)$ and the host graph be $G_h = (V_h, E_h)$, and let there be src and trg functions that map edges to their source and target nodes.

$$src_p: \ E_p \longrightarrow V_p, \ \ trg_p: \ E_p \longrightarrow V_p$$
$$src_h: \ E_h \longrightarrow V_h, \ \ trg_h: \ E_h \longrightarrow V_h$$

Then a match is a pair of total functions

$$match_V: \ V_p \longrightarrow V_h, \ \ match_E: \ E_p \longrightarrow E_h$$

that map all pattern graph nodes to host graph nodes and all pattern graph edges to host graph edges such that

$$\forall e \in E_p: match_V(src_p(e)) = src_h(match_E(e))$$
$$\wedge \ match_V(trg_p(e)) = trg_h(match_E(e)),$$

i.e., the host graph node matched by a pattern edge e's source node is the source node of the host graph edge matched by e, and likewise, the host graph node matched by e's target node is the target node of the host graph edge matched by e. The definition also implies that an edge can only be matched if both its source and target node match.

Note that this definition allows that two different nodes in the pattern graph are matched to the same host graph node, and the same applies to edges. In other words, $match_v$ and $match_E$ don't need to be injective in order to comply with the definition. For many graph pattern matching approaches, injectivity is enforced or can optionally be enabled. In that case, one speaks of *isomorphic matching* or the match function being a *subgraph isomorphism*.

With modern modeling frameworks where graphs and models conform to metamodels, the nodes and edges of a pattern are usually augmented with typing information. Then a host graph node can only be matched by a pattern graph node if it is an instance of the metamodel type declared for the pattern node, and the same applies to edges.

Likewise, if nodes or edges possess attributes, then patterns can define additional restrictions on their values.

One crucial difference between the pattern matching facilities of functional programming languages discussed in the previous section and pattern matching on graphs and models is that with the former, a pattern either matches a given data structure or it does not. With the latter, a pattern can match multiple times because the host graph can contain multiple subgraphs that comply the typing, connection, and attribute value constraints imposed by the pattern. Therefore, one frequently calls a match an occurrence of the pattern in the host graph. A pattern matching approach may provide the ability to deliver one such occurrence, or it might be able to enumerate all occurrences of the pattern in the host graph.

Figure 17.2 illustrates an example using a visual notation[5]. The pattern on the left side defines that two Buddy nodes n1 and n2 and a Likes edge e starting at n1 and ending at n2 have to be matched.

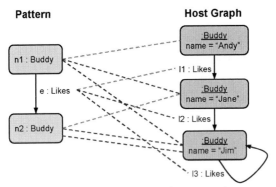

Figure 17.2: A pattern matching example

The host graph is visualized on the right side. There are three Buddy nodes representing Andy, Jane, and Jim. Andy likes Jane, Jane likes Jim, and Jim being a peacocky guy likes himself.

With homomorphic pattern matching, there are three matches of the pattern in the host graph. In the first (green) match, n1 maps to Andy, e to l1, and n2 to Jane. In the second (blue) match, n1 maps to Jane, e to l2, and n2 to Jim. In the third and last match (red), both n1 and n2 map to Jim, and e maps to l3.

In contrast, with isomorphic pattern matching there are only two matches: the green and the blue one. The red one is no valid match because with isomorphic matching distinct nodes in the pattern must be mapped to distinct nodes in the host graph.

---

[5]As a Clojure library for programming queries and transformations, FunnyQT uses a textual notation for patterns. The example pattern would be specified as n1<Buddy> -e<Likes>-> n2<Buddy>.

Finding matches for kinds of patterns discussed so far which consist of typed nodes and edges and possibly constraints on attribute values are the essentials of pattern matching on graphs and models. But many approaches support more advanced pattern matching concepts.

A feature which is widely common are *positive* and *negative application conditions* called *PACs* and *NACs* for short. The nodes and edges defined by a PAC merely define an existential assertion, i.e., occurrences of such nodes and edges have to exist but they are not part of the matches.

Figure 17.3 shows an example of a pattern with positive application condition[6].

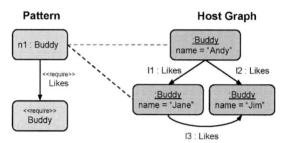

Figure 17.3: A pattern with positive application condition

The edge and the node marked with «require» make up the PAC. The complete pattern matches all Buddy nodes which have an outgoing Likes edge ending at some Buddy. However, the edge and the liked buddy are not part of the match. It's only their existence which matters. This pattern has two matches, namely Andy and Jane.

Note that there would be three matches if the edge and the liked buddy node were matched, too, instead of modeling their existence only using a PAC. In that case, there would be two matches for Andy: one for him and Jane, and one for him and Jim.

Negative application conditions are the inverse of PACs. They enforce that some nodes and edges of the pattern must not match. Figure 17.4 on the facing page gives an example[7].

The edge and the node marked with «forbid» make up the NAC. The pattern matches all Buddy nodes which have no outgoing Likes edges leading to some Buddy node. In the example's host graph, Jim is the only buddy who doesn't like anyone else.

There are several other features which are provided by different graph pattern matching approaches, e.g., *alternative patterns* which allow for defining variable parts inside a pattern, or patterns containing *nested patterns* which are matched in the context of a match of the surrounding pattern.

---

[6]In FunnyQT, this pattern would be expressed as n1<Buddy> -<Likes>-> <Buddy>.

[7]This pattern would be expressed as n1<Buddy> -!<Likes>-> <Buddy> in FunnyQT.

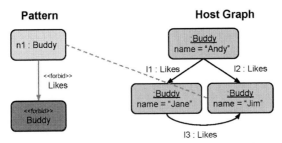

Figure 17.4: A pattern with negative application condition

In the remainder of this part, FunnyQT's take on pattern matching is discussed in detail[8]. It supports all pattern matching concepts discussed in this section, i.e., basic patterns consisting of typed nodes and edges, arbitrary constraints, positive and negative application conditions, alternative patterns, and also nested patterns.

Chapter 18 starting on page 193 introduces the FunnyQT macros for defining patterns including the exact pattern syntax and semantics, and chapter 19 starting on page 217 discusses related pattern matching approaches. Appendix A.3 on page 424 eventually explains how FunnyQT's pattern matching facility can be extended to support model representations other than JGraLab and EMF.

---

[8]A brief overview of FunnyQT's pattern matching DSL has already been published in [Hor15a]

Chapter 18

Defining Patterns

FunnyQT uses an applicative notion of patterns. A pattern is a function that receives a model as an argument and returns the lazy sequence of matches. An embedded DSL is used to specify what is matched by a pattern. Because FunnyQT uses the term pattern for the function that computes and returns the matches, the declarative specification of what a pattern matches is named a *pattern specification* in the following.

Patterns can be defined with three pattern definition forms. All these definition forms are macros which receive a declarative pattern specification written in FunnyQT's internal pattern DSL which is going to be discussed in detail in section 18.1 on page 195, and they expand to plain Clojure function definitions. The code in these functions' bodies is generated from the pattern specification and performs a search for matches in the model given at call-time.

The first and most important pattern definition form is `defpattern`.

Macro: `funnyqt.pmatch/defpattern`
```
(defpattern name docstring? attr-map? [args] [pattern-spec])
(defpattern name docstring? attr-map? ([args] [pattern-spec])+)
```

A pattern has a `name` (a symbol), an optional `docstring`, an optional `attr-map` containing options affecting the pattern's behavior, a vector of formal arguments `args` where the first argument must denote the model the pattern is evaluated on, and a pattern specification `pattern-spec` specifying the structure of the subgraph to be matched. In the simplest case, a pattern specification consists of only node symbols and connecting edge symbols but many more sophisticated features are available, too (see section 18.1 on page 195).

As can be seen from the second signature, a pattern can be overloaded on arity just like usual Clojure function definitions with `defn` (see page 37).

The following listing shows an example pattern definition. The pattern's name is `difficult-relationships`. It has a documentation string and its only formal argument is `m`. The pattern specification defines that two Person elements are to be matched where p1 references p2 with its loves-reference, and p2 references p1 with

193

its hates-reference.

```
(defpattern difficult-relationships
  "A pattern matching two persons `p1` and `p2`
  where `p1` loves `p2 and `p2` hates `p1`."
  [m]
  [p1<Person> -<:loves>-> p2<Person> -<:hates>-> p1])
```

As already said, a pattern definition like the one above expands into a plain Clojure function definition. Evaluating the pattern definition above defines a function named difficult-relationships in the current namespace which receives one argument m. When the function is called, this argument must be bound to the model the pattern is to be evaluated on. The code in the function's body is generated from the pattern specification and computes the lazy sequence (see section 6.6.2 on page 42) of matches in the queried model m. By default, each match is represented as a map where the identifiers (as keywords) of the pattern specification's symbols are the keys and the matched model elements are the values. Thus, every match of the pattern above has the structure {:p1 #<x:Person>, :p2 #<y:Person>}.

There are three options that can be set in the attr-map of a defpattern form. First, there is the :eager option. If it is set to true, then the pattern will be evaluated eagerly when being called and returns a fully realized sequence of matches instead of a lazy sequence. If there is more than one CPU available to the JVM, then FunnyQT automatically parallelizes the pattern matching process. The second available option :sequential suppresses this parallelization. The third option available is :pattern-expansion-context with possible values :generic (the default), :tg, and :emf. The last two values allow for making the pattern definition expand into framework-specific code which is slightly faster because of less indirection. Furthermore, when doing pattern matching on JGraLab's TGraphs with the expansion context set to :tg, patterns can also match edges (see section 18.2 on page 212). The options can also be provided as metadata (see section 6.9 on page 53) attached to the pattern name.

Where defpattern defines a function-valued var in the current namespace, the letpattern macro defines one or many local named patterns without creating vars in the current namespace. Therefore, defpattern stands to letpattern like defn stands to letfn (see page 37).

Macro: funnyqt.pmatch/letpattern
(letpattern [patterns] attr-map? & body)

It receives a vector of patterns, an optional attr-map, and arbitrary many body forms. Each pattern in patterns is represented analogously to defpattern:

```
(pattern-name attr-map? [args] [pattern-spec])
(pattern-name attr-map? ([args] [pattern-spec])+)
```

The attr-map of the letpattern applies to all defined local patterns in patterns, and those may add or override individual options.

Finally, there is the pattern macro which defines an anonymous pattern. Therefore, defpattern stands to pattern like defn stands to fn (see page 35).

Macro: funnyqt.pmatch/pattern
(pattern name? attr-map? [args] [pattern-spec])
(pattern name? attr-map? ([args] [pattern-spec])+)

It receives an optional name, a map of options attr-map, an argument vector args, and a vector containing the pattern specification pattern-spec. Again, overloading on arity is supported.

In the next section, the exact syntax and semantics of the pattern specification provided as pattern-spec argument to the three pattern definition forms is going to be discussed.

18.1 Pattern Syntax and Semantics

By default, FunnyQT performs homomorphic pattern matching. To discuss the syntax and the semantics of FunnyQT patterns, the metamodel and model shown in fig. 18.1 is used.

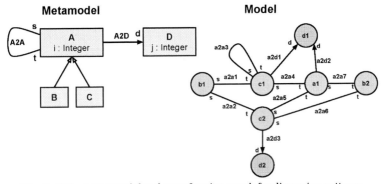

Figure 18.1: A metamodel and a conforming graph for discussing patterns

The metamodel on the left defines a node class A with integer-valued attribute i and two subclasses B and C. There is a node class D with integer-valued attribute j. A-nodes may be connected with edges of type A2A with roles s and t, and there may be A2D-edges starting at A-nodes and ending at D-nodes where only one role d is defined.

The right part of the figure shows a conforming example graph. For reasons of conciseness, the element types and attribute values have been encoded in labels. So b1 is an instance of the class B where the attribute i has the value 1. For the edges, the numbers only serve the purpose of making them unambiguously identifiable. When writing down the match results in the remainder of this section, the example graph nodes are notated as #<label>, e.g., #<c1> denotes the node c1 in fig. 18.1.

In the following, the generic features of FunnyQT's pattern specification DSL are discussed. Those are used to define patterns that can be applied to all models containing typed nodes that reference each other without having first-class edges. Clearly, this exactly matches EMF models, and it also matches JGraLab's TGraphs when ignoring edge types and just using the role names. In section 18.2 on page 212, some framework specific extensions are discussed. The extension for TGraphs exploits the fact that edges are first-class entities which can also be matched.

After introducing all constituents of FunnyQT's pattern specification DSL with their syntax and semantics, section 18.1.18 on page 212 provides a concise summary in terms of an EBNF.

18.1.1 Basic Pattern Specifications

A basic pattern specification consist of only *node symbols* which might be connected using *edge symbols*.

The most basic pattern conceivable is (`pattern` [m] [a<A>]) whose pattern specification consists of only one single node symbol a<A>. This pattern matches nodes which are an instance of metamodel class A or a subclass thereof. When applied to the model in fig. 18.1 on page 195, the pattern matches all nodes except for d1 and d2.

The node type may be prefixed with ! as a negation. For example, a pattern with the pattern specification x<!A> matches any node which is not an instance of class A. Thus, there are two matches: {:x #<d1>} and {:x #<d2>}.

The node type may also be suffixed with ! for restricting to direct instances. Therefore, a pattern with the pattern specification a<A!> yields only the match {:a #<a1>} which is the only direct instance of metamodel class A.

Both modifiers may be combined, so a pattern with the pattern specification x<!A!> matches all nodes which are not direct instances of metamodel class A. In the example model in fig. 18.1 on page 195, those would be {:x #<b1>}, {:x #<c1>}, {:x #<c2>}, {:x #<b2>}, {:x #<d1>}, and {:x #<d2>}.

The type in a node symbol is optional. A pattern with the pattern specification x<> or even shorter just x matches any node in the host graph regardless of its type.

In a pattern specification, two node symbols may be connected by an edge symbol. The pattern

```
(pattern [m] [c<C> -<:t>-> a<A>])
```

matches all occurrences of a C-node c and an A-node a where c references a with its t-reference. As always in FunnyQT, reference/role names are specified as keywords. In the example graph in fig. 18.1 on page 195, this pattern has four matches: {:c #<c1>, :a #<a1>}, {:c #<c2>, :a #<a1>}, {:c #<c2>, :a #<b2>}, and also {:c #<c1>, :a #<c1>} because FunnyQT does homomorphic matching by default.

Like with node symbols, the reference name in an edge symbol is optional. A pattern with the pattern specification c<C> -<>-> a<A> or even shorter c<C> --> a<A>

matches all occurrences of a C-node c and an A-node a where c references a with an arbitrary reference. With respect to the example model in fig. 18.1 on page 195, this pattern results in seven matches: {:c #<c1>, :a #<b1>}, {:c #<c1>, :a #<c1>}, {:c #<c1>, :a #<a1>}, {:c #<c2>, :a #<b1>}, {:c #<c2>, :a #<a1>}, and {:c #<c2>, :a #<b2>}.

There are also the edge symbols <>-- and --<> which only match edges with strict containment semantics, e.g., a pattern with pattern specification a <>-- b matches all elements a and b where a contains b. Like with normal edge symbols, a role name may be given, e.g., a <:bs>-- b matches all elements a and b where a contains b using a containment reference bs.

Every edge symbol must connect two node symbols. If a pattern should match a series of nodes connected by references, the pattern specification may be written as a sequence of alternating node and edge symbols. Alternatively, one may also specify nodes and edges separately. The following two patterns are completely equivalent:

```
(pattern [m]
 [n1<A> -<:t>-> n2<A> -<:t>-> n3<A>])

(pattern [m]
 [n1<A> -<:t>-> n2<A>
  n2     -<:t>-> n3<A>])
```

Note that in the second pattern, the node symbol n2 is notated twice. This is perfectly valid[1]. Every node symbol identifier may occur arbitrarily often in a pattern specification, and it always denotes the very same node. The type information, e.g., <A> for n2, may be omitted from all but one occurrence.

18.1.2 Anonymous Nodes

The identifier of node symbols is optional, too. Omitting it means that such a node has to exist in the matched subgraph but it shouldn't be part of the matches. Thus, it models a kind of *positive application condition*.

For example, the pattern specification in

```
(pattern [m]
 [b<B> -<:t>-> <C> -<:t>-> <> -<:t>-> a<A>])
```

contains an anonymous node <C> and another anonymous node <>. The pattern matches all occurrences of a B-node b and an A-node a where a path exists which starts at b, follows a t-reference to some C-node, then follows another t-reference to some arbitrary node, and finally follows yet another t-reference to a. In the model in fig. 18.1 on page 195, there are three matches for this pattern: {:b #<b1>, :a #<c1>}, {:b #<b1>, :a #<a1>}, and {:b #<b1>, :a #<b2>}.

---

[1]Notating a node symbol twice is the only way to specify a pattern matching a node that references itself: (pattern [m] [a<A> -<:t>-> a])

Note that anonymous nodes only implement a restricted form of positive application conditions because only the existence of single nodes can be asserted but not
the existence of a subgraph consisting of many interconnected nodes. E.g., in the
pattern above it's not possible to specify that there is another edge connected to one
of the anonymous nodes because that would require a node identifier for notation.
Full PACs are supported by positive patterns which are going to be discussed in
section 18.1.11 on page 204.

18.1.3 Negative Edges

Negative edges implement a simple form of *negative application conditions* which
forbid the existence of certain edges. A negative edge is an edge marked with !.
For example, the pattern

```
(pattern [m] [a<A> -!<:d>-> <>])
```

matches all occurrences of an A-node a which doesn't reference any node using
its d-reference. With respect to fig. 18.1 on page 195, there are the two matches
{:a #<b1>} and {:a #<b2>}.

The pattern

```
(pattern [m] [a<A> -!<:t>-> <C>])
```

matches all occurrences of an A-node a whose t-reference does not point to any
C-node. For this pattern, there are three matches with respect to the example graph:
one match for a1, one for c2, and one for b2.

If the target node of a negative edge is also bound, i.e., the target node symbol
has an identifier, then the semantics is to find all pairs of start and target nodes
where the start node doesn't reference the target node using a reference of the
given kind. E.g., the pattern

```
(pattern [m] [a1<A> -!-> a2<A!>])
```

matches all occurrences of two nodes a1 and a2 of the specified types where a1
doesn't reference a2. This pattern yields two matches: {:a1 #<a1>, :a2 #<a1>} and
{:a1 #<b1>, :a2 #<a1>}.

As said, negative edges only implement a restricted form of negative application
conditions as they can only forbid the existence of single edges but not the existence
of complex subgraphs. Full NACs are supported by negative patterns which are
going to be discussed in section 18.1.12 on page 205.

18.1.4 Isomorphic Matching

By default FunnyQT performs homomorphic matching, i.e., it is possible that multiple
node symbols in a pattern are matched to the very same host graph node. To suppress

this behavior and switch to isomorphic matching, the :isomorphic keyword can be used.

For example, the pattern

```
(pattern [m]
 [c<C> -<:t>-> a<A>
  :isomorphic])
```

only has three matches. The first one is {:c #<c1>, :a #<a1>}, the second one is {:c #<c2>, :a #<a1>}, and the third one is {:c #<c2>, :a #<b2>}. Without the :isomorphic keyword, it would also result in the match {:c #<c1>, :a #<c1>} as already discussed in section 18.1.1 on page 196.

18.1.5 Constraints

Arbitrary constraints can be embedded in a pattern using :when clauses. If there are multiple :when clauses, all of them have to evaluate to logical true. The pattern

```
(pattern [m]
 [c<C> --> a<A>
  :when (= 1 (aval c :i))
  :when (= 1 (aval a :i))])
```

yields these four matches: {:c #<c1>, :a #<b1>}, {:c #<c1>, :a #<c1>}, {:c #<c1>, :a #<c1>} again, and {:c #<c1>, :a #<a1>}. Like with the pattern [c<C> --> a<A>] discussed in section 18.1.1 on page 196 the match {:c #<c1>, :a #<c1>} is in the result twice because there is one match for c1 referencing itself using the t-reference and another match for c1 referencing itself using the s-reference.

It should be noted that due to the way FunnyQT evaluates patterns, all variables used in constraint expressions have to be declared before the constraint in the pattern specification, else a compile-time exception is thrown.

18.1.6 Patterns with Node Arguments

As stated in chapter 18 starting on page 193, the first argument of a pattern must refer to the model the pattern is evaluated on and an arbitrary number of additional parameters may follow.

If a pattern specification includes an argument as node identifier, then this node must always match to the node given as argument. If the argument is nil, the pattern cannot match. Likewise, if the pattern declares a node type but the actual argument is a node of a different type, the pattern cannot match.

For example, the following pattern has an additional argument a denoting a node of strict node type A in the host graph which references a B-node using its t-reference.

```
(pattern [m a]
 [a<A!> -<:t>-> b<B>])
```

When being applied to the model in fig. 18.1 on page 195 and `nil`, there are no matches. When being applied to the model and any node except for a1, there are no matches again because the argument `a` is not a direct instance of class A. Lastly, when this pattern is applied to the model and node a1, it returns the sequence containing the single match {:a #<a1>, :b #<b2>}.

It should be noted that it is advisable that patterns with node arguments start the pattern with one of those for performance reasons. This advise is followed in the above pattern. The result is that FunnyQT performs a local search starting at the given node `a`. The next example defines the same pattern the other way round.

```
(pattern [m a]
  [b<B> -<:s>-> a<A!>])
```

The result of this pattern is the same as for the pattern above but because the argument node `a` doesn't start the pattern, its evaluation will consider every B-node in the complete model `m` and test if it references `a` with its s-reference which is clearly less performant[2].

It is also possible to have patterns asserting that two nodes given as arguments are connected in some way like its done in the next example.

```
(pattern [m a b]
  [a<A!> -<:t>-> b<B>])
```

When being applied to the model in fig. 18.1 on page 195, a1, and b2, it returns the sequence containing one single match {:a #<a1>, :b #<b2>}. For all other combinations of node arguments, it cannot find a match and returns the empty sequence.

18.1.7   Local Bindings

Additional variables can be introduced and bound in a pattern using a `:let` clause which gets a vector of symbol-expression pairs with the same syntax and semantics as Clojure's special form `let` (see page 34). The new variables can then be used in later parts of the pattern, and they are also part of the pattern's matches.

The following pattern matches occurrences of a node `c` of metamodel class C and a referenced node `d` of metamodel class D. The i attribute value of `c` and the j attribute value of `d` are bound to the new variables i and j.

```
(pattern [m]
  [c<C> --> d<D>]
  :let [i (aval c :i)
        j (aval d :j)]])
```

---

[2]FunnyQT emits a compile-time warning whenever a pattern with argument nodes doesn't start with one of them.

The matches of this pattern in the model shown in fig. 18.1 on page 195 are {:c #<c1>, :d #<d1>, :i 1, :j 1} and {:c #<c2>, :d #<d2>, :i 2, :j 2}.

In addition to :let, there is also the pattern binding keyword :when-let. It is followed by a vector of exactly one variable-expression pair. Like with :let, the variable is bound to the value of the expression. The difference, however, is that with :when-let the variable value has to be logical true in order for a match to occur. Essentially, :when-let [x (exp ...)] is a shorthand for a :let [x (exp ...)] followed by the constraint :when x.

As with constraints, the expressions of a :let or :when-let clause may only access variables declared earlier in the pattern specification.

18.1.8 Comprehension Bindings

A pattern may also include iterated bindings using a :for clause which has the syntax and semantics of the standard Clojure sequence comprehension for (see page 65). It receives a vector of variable-expression pairs (just like :let), but the expressions have to evaluate to seqables. The variables are bound to the elements of the sequences in a nested, rightmost fastest fashion.

For example, the following pattern produces a match for any C-node c which references a D-node d using its d-reference together with any node f that can be reached from c by traversing a t-reference one or many times[3].

```
(pattern [m]
  [c<C> -<:d>-> d<D>
   :for [f (p-+ c :t)]])
```

With respect to the example model in fig. 18.1 on page 195, this pattern has five matches: {:c #<c1>, :d #<d1>, :f #<c1>}, {:c #<c1>, :d #<d1>, :f #<a1>}, {:c #<c1>, :d #<d1>, :f #<b2>}, {:c #<c2>, :d #<d2>, :f #<a1>}, and {:c #<c2>, :d #<d2>, :f #<b2>}.

As with constraints and bindings with :let and :when-let, the expressions of a :for clause may only access variables declared earlier in the pattern specification.

18.1.9 Patterns Calling Patterns

As discussed in section 18.1.7 on page 200, a pattern can define local bindings using a :let clause which receives a vector of variable-expression pairs. Of course, the expressions may be applications of patterns again thus allowing to define patterns where parts of the matches are sequence of matches of other patterns or of the same pattern again.

---

[3](p-+ c :t) is a regular path expression. Those are discussed in section 15.1 on page 147

For example, the following `successors` pattern is defined recursively. Given a model `m` and a model element `cur` it returns the lazy sequence of matches containing the current node `cur`, a node `next` which is referenced by `cur` with its t-reference, and the lazy sequence `nnexts` of matches of the same pattern where the current node is the `next`. The arity two version simply delegates to an arity three version where the set of `known` nodes is initialized with an empty set. This additional parameter in combination with the `:when` constraint is used as the base case of the recursion.

```
(defpattern successors
  ([m cur] (successors m cur #{}))
  ([m cur known]
   [:when (not (known cur))
    cur<A> -<:t>-> next<A>
    :let [nnexts (successors m next (conj known cur))]]]))
```

When this pattern is applied to the model in fig. 18.1 on page 195 and b1 as current node, it results in the following sequence of matches.

```
(successors model b1)
;=> ({:cur #<b1>,
;      :next #<c1>,
;      :nnexts ({:cur #<c1>,
;               :next #<c1>,
;               :nnexts ()}
;              {:cur #<c1>,
;               :next #<a1>,
;               :nnexts ({:cur #<a1>,
;                        :next #<b2>,
;                        :nnexts ()})})}
;     {:cur #<b1>,
;      :next #<c2>,
;      :nnexts ({:cur #<c2>,
;               :next #<a1>,
;               :nnexts ({:cur #<a1>,
;                        :next #<b2>,
;                        :nnexts ()})}
;              {:cur #<c2>,
;               :next #<b2>,
;               :nnexts ()})})
```

There are two matches: one match where c1 is the next node, and one where c2 is the next node. When looking at the first match's `:nnexts` matches, we can see that c1 has the two successors c1 and a1. In turn, a1 has b2 as successor. For c1, the set `known` and the constraint ensure that the recursion ends after c1 has been reported as current node once.

Note that the `successors` pattern would be valid even if the third parameter `known` and the constraint testing if the current node is known were removed. In that case, the match where `cur` and `next` are both c1 contains itself again as first match of its `nnexts` sequence. But because the pattern returns a lazy sequence, the matches are not realized until they are accessed. Thus, we could retrieve the first match in the :nnexts sequence of any match, and in the case where the match is {:cur #<c1>, :next #<c1>, :nnexts (...)} we can do that an infinite number of times always resulting in the same match. This would not cause a stack-overflow because with each step, only one further step is realized. However, everything that causes a full realization of the sequence of matches, e.g., printing the sequence of matches or declaring the pattern with the :eager option set to true, causes a stack-overflow.

18.1.10 Match Representation

As said, by default a pattern's matches are represented as maps where keywords named according to the node identifiers and variables map to nodes matched in the host graph and values assigned in the binding clauses :let, :when-let and :for. The match representation can be overridden with an :as clause which gets an arbitrary expression which has access to all identifiers and variables of the pattern and evaluates to a custom match representation.

For example, the following pattern represents each match as a vector where the matched nodes and attribute values are ordered by their first occurrence in the pattern.

```
(defpattern c-d-with-vals [m]
  [c<C> --> d<D>
  :let [i (g/aval c :i)
        j (g/aval d :j)]
  :as [c d i j]])
```

Applied to the graph in fig. 18.1 on page 195, this pattern results in the two matches [#<c1> #<d1> 1 1] and [#<c2> #<d2> 2 2].

Representing the matches as vectors can be very convenient depending on how the results of a pattern are used, especially if the parts of the matches are to be bound to individual variables again using destructuring (see section 6.7 on page 48). For example, the following listing demonstrates how the individual parts of each match can be extracted again using sequential destructuring.

```
(map (fn [[c d i j]]
       (do-something-with c d i j))
     (c-d-with-vals model))
```

Since do-something-with has the arity four, it can also be called with a vector representing a match using apply (see page 50).

```
(map #(apply do-something-with %)
     (c-d-with-vals model))
```

Maps can also be destructured but the syntax is more complex and harder to understand, and it is also slightly less efficient. So if the above pattern had no :as clause and thus matches were represented as maps, the same code would need to be written as one of the two variants shown in the next listing.

```
;; Variant 1
(map (fn [{:keys [c d i j]}]
        (do-something-with c d i j))
      (c-d-with-vals model))

;; Variant 2
(map (fn [{c :c, d :d, i :i, j :j}]
        (do-something-with c d i j))
      (c-d-with-vals model))
```

Therefore, FunnyQT provides the shorthand :as :vector which is equivalent to
the clause :as [c d i j] above. Matches are represented as vectors where the
values are ordered according to the first occurrence in the pattern. For reasons
of symmetry, the shorthand :as :map is equivalent to omitting the :as clause, i.e.,
matches are represented as maps.

18.1.11   Positive Patterns

In section 18.1.2 on page 197, anonymous nodes have been discussed which implement a weak form of positive application conditions. Those require the existence of
single nodes but they don't suffice to require the existence of a complex subgraph
consisting of many arbitrarily interconnected nodes.

Positive patterns fill this gap by implementing full-blown PACs. The specification
of a positive pattern starts with the keyword :positive followed by a vector containing
the positive pattern specification. Arbitrarily many positive patterns may be specified
in a pattern. The semantics is that a pattern containing positive patterns can only
match if all of its positive patterns have at least one match.

A positive pattern specification may include identifiers of the surrounding pattern.
Those are bound to the nodes matched by the outer pattern and used to connect the
nodes of the outer pattern with the nodes of the positive pattern.

The following listing shows an example pattern which includes a positive pattern.

```
(defpattern b-with-positive-pattern [m]
  [b<B>
   :positive [b -<:t>-> c1<C> -<:t>-> a<A>
              b -<:t>-> c2<C> -<:t>-> a
              :isomorphic]])
```

It matches all B-nodes b which are connected to two C-nodes c1 and c2 which
both reference the same A-node a. All nodes have to be pairwise disjoint because of
the :isomorphic keyword.

When looking at fig. 18.1 on page 195 we can see that the positive pattern exactly
corresponds to the nodes b1, c1, c2, and a1. Thus, its only match is {:b #<b1>}.

In the pattern above, the outer pattern and the positive pattern were connected
by the common node b. This is not required. If they are not connected, then the
positive pattern specifies a global PAC, i.e., the positive pattern must have a match

in the complete host graph. Due to the way patterns are evaluated in FunnyQT, it is advisable to specify global PACs (and global NACs) as the first elements in a pattern specification.

Positive patterns always inherit the :pattern-expansion-context of the surrounding pattern. Again, that can be overridden by attaching metadata to the positive pattern vector. Also the :eager and :sequential options can be set in this way although it is unreasonable to compute all matches of a positive pattern when already the first match suffices to make the surrounding pattern match.

Positive patterns are only a convenient shorthand notation of the general case of patterns calling other patterns (see section 18.1.9 on page 201). The pattern b-with-positive-pattern above is a shorthand for the following pattern.

```
(defpattern b-with-positive-pattern [m]
  [b<B>
   :when (seq ((pattern [m b]
                [b -<:t>-> c1<C> -<:t>-> a<A>
                 b -<:t>-> c2<C> -<:t>-> a
                 :when (not= c1 c2)])
               m b))])
```

A B-element b is only a valid match if the anonymous pattern also matches when being applied to the model m and b, i.e., when its sequence of matches is non-empty.

18.1.12 Negative Patterns

In section 18.1.3 on page 198 negative edges have been introduced. They implement a weak form of negative application conditions which only allow to forbid the existence of particular edges. What they do not allow is the specification of a complete subgraph which is interconnected with the positive part of the pattern in arbitrary ways and which must not be matched.

Negative patterns fill this gap by implementing full-blown NACs. The specification of a negative pattern starts with the keyword :negative followed by a vector containing the negative pattern specification. There may be arbitrarily many negative patterns defined in a pattern. The semantics is that a pattern containing negative patterns can only match if all its negative patterns don't match.

Like with positive patterns, negative pattern may include the node identifiers of its surrounding pattern. Those are bound to the nodes matched by the outer pattern and used to connect the outer pattern with the nodes of the negative pattern.

The following listing shows an example pattern which includes a negative pattern.

```
(defpattern b-with-negative-pattern [m]
  [b<B>
   :negative [b -<:t>-> c1<C> -<:t>-> a<A>
              b -<:t>-> c2<C> -<:t>-> a
              :isomorphic]])
```

This pattern matches all B-nodes b which are not connected to two different C-nodes c1 and c2 that both reference the same A-node a. Because of the :isomorphic keyword, all nodes have to be pairwise disjoint.

When looking at fig. 18.1 on page 195, we can see that the negative pattern matches the nodes b1, c1, c2, and a1. Therefore, b1 cannot be a valid match for b-with-negative-pattern. Thus, its only match is {:b #<b2>}.

Like with positive patterns, a negative pattern does not need to be connected with the surrounding pattern. If both don't share at least one node, then it acts as a global NAC. As already mentioned, due to implementation details, global NACs and global PACs should be specified as first elements in a pattern specification.

Like with positive patterns, negative patterns inherit the :pattern-expansion-context of the surrounding pattern which can be overridden by attaching metadata to the negative pattern vector. Likewise, the :eager and :sequential options can be set in this way although it is unreasonable to compute all matches of a negative pattern when already the first match suffices to specify that the surrounding pattern cannot match.

Negative patterns are also only a convenient shorthand notation. The pattern b-with-negative-pattern above is a shorthand for the following pattern.

```
(defpattern b-with-negative-pattern [m]
  [b<B>
   :when (empty? ((pattern [m b]
                    [b -<:t>-> c1<C> -<:t>-> a<A>
                     b -<:t>-> c2<C> -<:t>-> a
                     :when (not= c1 c2)])
                  m b))])
```

A B-element b is only a valid match if the anonymous pattern does not match when being applied to the model m and b, i.e., when its sequence of matches is empty.

18.1.13 Logically Combined Patterns

Logically combined patterns are an extension of PACs and NACs. They allow to specify that a pattern matches only if the results of several subpatterns combined with a logical operation return true.

The specification of a logically combined pattern starts with one of the keywords :and, :or, :xor, :nand, or :nor denoting the logical operations of the same names. Then a vector of vectors follows where each inner vector contains a pattern specification. The semantics is that the surrounding pattern can only match if the logically combined patterns match according to the given logical operation.

Like with positive and negative patterns, logically combined patterns may include node identifiers of the surrounding pattern. If they don't, they specify a global application condition, and again, such global conditions should be written as first elements in a pattern specification.

The following listing shows an example pattern that contains two subpatterns combined with the logical OR.

```
(pattern [m]
 [c<C>
  :or [[c -<:t>-> c]          ;; (1)
       [c -<:t>-> <B>]]])     ;; (2)
```

This pattern matches C-nodes c which reference themselves using their t-reference as specified by the subpattern (1), or which reference a B-node b using their t-reference as specified by the subpattern (2). Of course, :or is non-exclusive, so candidates for c for which both alternatives apply are also valid matches. With respect to fig. 18.1 on page 195, this pattern has the two matches {:c #<c1>} (because of the first alternative) and {:c #<c2>} (because of the second alternative).

Logically combined patterns are again only a shorthand notation for patterns calling other patterns. The pattern above is a shorthand notation for the pattern given in the next listing.

```
(pattern [m]
 [c<C>
  :when (or (seq ((pattern [m c]
                   [c -<:t>-> c :as {}])
                  m c))
            (seq ((pattern [m c]
                   [c -<:t>-> <B> :as {:b b}])
                  m c)))])
```

As can be seen, the :or keyword translates into an application of Clojure's or macro, and the same applies to :and which translates to Clojure's and macro. The other keywords :xor, :nand, and :nor translate into the FunnyQT macros of the same name discussed in section 15.6.4 on page 171. All these macros have short-cutting semantics, so each logically combined pattern is only evaluated if needed.

Since logically combined patterns are an extension or generalization of positive and negative patterns, there are some equivalences. I.e., combining subpatterns with :and is equivalent to specifying each subpattern as a :positive pattern. And combining subpatterns with :nor is equivalent to specifying each subpattern as :negative pattern.

18.1.14 Alternative Patterns

Positive, negative, and logically combined patterns are all pure application conditions, i.e., they only serve as constraints. Even if a positive pattern contains node symbols that aren't part of the surrounding pattern, those don't contribute to the matches of the surrounding pattern.

However, sometimes it is convenient to allow expressing certain alternatives in a
pattern just like with logical patterns combined with :or but still have the elements
matched by the subpatterns available in the surrounding pattern. This is exactly
the use case of alternative patterns.

The specification of alternative patterns starts with the keyword :alternative
followed by a vector of vectors. Each inner vector contains the pattern specification of an alternative subpattern. The semantics is similar as with :or-combined
subpatterns, i.e., the outer pattern can only match if at least one alternative subpattern matches. However, the crucial difference is that the nodes matched by the
alternative subpatterns are also part of the outer pattern's matches.

The following listing shows an example pattern containing alternative patterns.

```
(pattern [m]
 [c<C>
  :alternative [[c -<:t>-> a<A!>]                    ;; (1)
               [c -<:t>-> x<A> -<:s>-> a<A!>]]       ;; (2)
  a -<:d>-> d<D>])
```

It matches a C-node c, a strict A-node a, an A-node x, and a D-node d where c
directly references a with its t-reference as specified by subpattern (1), or where c
references x with its t-reference which in turn references a with its s-reference as
specified by subpattern (2). Additionally, a references d with its d-reference.

All matches of the example pattern have the keys :c, :a, :x, and :d. In case a
match is produced by the first alternative subpattern, the value of the :x key is nil.

Alternative patterns are also a shorthand notation for patterns that call patterns
and bind their results using comprehension bindings as discussed in section 18.1.8
on page 201. The pattern above is a shorthand notation for the following pattern[4].

```
(pattern [m]
 [c<C>
  :for [[a x] (funnyqt.utils/no-dups
                (concat ((pattern [m c]
                          [c -<:t>-> a<A!> :as [a nil]])
                         m c)
                        ((pattern [m c]
                          [c -<:t>-> x<A> -<:s>-> a<A!> :as [a x]])
                         m c)))]
  a -<:d>-> d<D>])
```

18.1.15   Nested Patterns

Patterns can define nested patterns using :nested clauses. After the keyword follows
a vector of variable-pattern pairs where the patterns are notated as vectors. With

---

[4]no-dups is a simple utility function.
Function: funnyqt.utils/no-dups
(no-dups coll)

   It returns a lazy sequence view of a given collection coll where duplicate elements are removed.

nested patterns, as soon as the outer pattern has found a match, the nested patterns compute their matches in the context of the match of the outer pattern. That is, each match of the outer pattern contains lazy sequences of matches of the nested patterns.

Here is an example pattern with three nested patterns.

```
(pattern [m]
  [c<C>
   :nested [ds [c -<:d>-> d :as d]
            ss [c -<:s>-> s :as s]
            ts [c -<:t>-> t :as t]]])
```

The outer pattern simply matches all C-nodes c in the model. Whenever a match for c has been found, the three nested patterns are applied. The first one matches all nodes d-referenced by the already matched c, the second all nodes s-referenced, and the third matches all nodes referenced by c's t-reference.

By default, the inner patterns' matches would be represented as maps where only the new nodes matched by the pattern are contained but not the nodes already matched by the outer pattern. Thus, the first nested pattern would have matches of the form {:d #<d1>}. Like with every pattern, an :as clause can be used to use a different match representation. Since all three patterns only match one new node, that node is defined to be the complete match.

The results of nested patterns are lazy sequences of matches. In the example above, those are bound to the variables ds, ss, and ts respectively. When the example pattern is applied to the model in fig. 18.1 on page 195, it results in the two matches {:c #<c1>, :ds (#<d1>), :ss (#<b1> #<c1>), :ts (#<c1> #<a1>)} and {:c #<c2>, :ds (#<d2>), :ss (#<b1>), :ts (#<a1> #<b2>)}.

Like normal patterns, nested patterns support the :eager and :sequential options discussed at the beginning of this chapter. They can be specified as metadata attached to the individual nested pattern vectors. Nested patterns always inherit the :pattern-expansion-context of the surrounding pattern, though even that can be overridden by the metadata.

Patterns can be nested arbitrarily deep, i.e., nested patterns can have nested patterns themselves. The next example shows a pattern with nesting-depth two.

```
(pattern [m]
  [a<A> -<:d>-> d<D>
   :nested [f1 [a -<:t>-> a1
            :nested [f2 [a1 -<:t>-> a2 :as a2]]]]])
```

The outer pattern matches occurrences of an A-node a referencing a D-node d with its d-reference. For every match, the nested pattern matches all nodes referenced by a via its t-reference. This nested pattern has another nested pattern which matches all nodes t-referenced by a1.

All in all, the complete pattern matches A-nodes a that have a D-node together with all t-successors of a, and all t-successors of each successor. Thus, when applied to the example model, these three matches are found:

```
({:a #<c1>, :d #<d1>, :f1 ({:a1 #<c1>, :f2 (#<c1> #<a1>)}
                          {:a1 #<a1>, :f2 (#<b2>)})}
  {:a #<c2>, :d #<d2>, :f1 ({:a1 #<a1>, :f2 (#<b2>)}
                          {:a1 #<b2>, :f2 ()})}
  {:a #<a1>, :d #<d1>, :f1 ({:a1 #<b2>, :f2 ()})})
```

Like with positive and negative patterns, nested patterns are only a convenient shorthand notation of the more general case of patterns calling other patterns that has been discussed in section 18.1.9 on page 201. The doubly-nested pattern in the last listing is equivalent to the following definition.

```
(pattern [m]
  [a<A> -<:d>-> d<D>
   :let [f1 ((pattern [m a]
               [a -<:t>-> a1
                :let [f2 ((pattern [m a1]
                            [a1 -<:t>-> a2
                             :as a2])
                          m a1)]])
             m a)]])
```

This version defines the nested patterns as anonymous patterns that are applied immediately to the model and elements of the containing match.

18.1.16 Distinct Matches

A pattern may contain the keyword :distinct. In that case, it will return only distinct matches, i.e., duplicate matches are removed. This feature is especially useful in conjunction with an :as clause. The following pattern matches all occurrences of two different nodes n1 and n2 where n1 references n2. The matches are represented as sets which posses no order, and only distinct matches are requested.

```
(defpattern connected-nodes [m]
  [n1 --> n2
   :isomorphic
   :as #{n1 n2} :distinct])
```

When applied to the model in fig. 18.1 on page 195, there are nine matches, one match for any pair of nodes where one references the other or both reference each other.

If the :distinct keyword was removed, the pattern would have 15 matches because every match #{n1 n2} being caused by n1 referencing n2 with its t-reference has an opposite match #{n2 n1} which is caused by n2 referencing n1 with its s-reference.

If the :as clause was removed, the pattern would have 15 matches, too, because all matches would be distinct in which match key maps to which node. E.g., where the sets #{#<x> #<y>} and #{#<y> #<x>} are equal, the maps {:n1 #<x>, :n2 #<y>} and {:n1 #<y>, :n2 #<x>} are not.

18.1.17 Pattern Inheritance

FunnyQT supports a kind of inheritance between patterns. A pattern may extend one or many other patterns using :extends clauses. The meaning is that the extending pattern's specification is the concatenation of all the pattern specs of the extended patterns plus the additional specifications it defines besides its :extends clause.

An :extends clause has the form :extends [& extends-specs] where every extends specification in extends-specs can take one of the following forms.

```
extended-pattern                    ;; (1)
(extended-pattern 1)                ;; (2)
(extended-pattern :a a1 :b b2)      ;; (3)
(extended-pattern 1 :a a1 :b b2) ;; (4)
```

In all cases, extended-pattern is the name of the pattern to be extended. Its pattern specification, i.e., its node and edge symbols, constraints, and bindings are included in the extending pattern. Since patterns can be overloaded on arity, an extends spec may include the index of the version whose pattern spec to include as shown in (2). The index starts with 0, and extended-pattern is equivalent to (extended-pattern 0).

An extends spec may also define renamings of node symbol identifiers and variables bound by :let, :when-let, :for, and :nested. In (3), extended-pattern is extended but what is called a in extended-pattern is called a1 in the extending pattern. Likewise, what is called b in extended-pattern is renamed to b2 in the extending pattern.

Finally, (4) demonstrates that an extends spec may specify both the index in an overloaded pattern and renamings. In this case, the order is significant, i.e., first the index of the pattern spec to be extended has to be given, then the renamings.

An example for pattern inheritance is given in the following listing which defines the three patterns a-A, a-having-d, and a-with-a-having-d.

```
(letpattern [(a-A [m] [a<A>])
             (a-having-d [m a d]
             [:extends [a-A]
              a -<:d>-> d<D>])
             (a-with-a-having-d [m]
             [a1 -<:t>-> a2
              :extends [(a-having-d :a a1)
                        (a-having-d :a a2)]])])
  (a-with-a-having-d model))
```

The a-A pattern matches nodes of metamodel class A. a-having-d extends a-A and additionally specifies that a should reference a D-node d. Here, the information that a has to be an A-node is inherited from a-A. The third pattern a-with-a-having-d defines that a1's t-reference targets a2, and it extends a-having-d twice. The first extends-spec defines a renaming from a to a1, the second a renaming from a to a2. As a result, the extending pattern defines two nodes a1 and a2 of type A (as indirectly inherited from a-A) which both reference the same D-node d.

As said, pattern inheritance is a mechanism for inclusion of existing pattern specs with possible renamings of the extended pattern's symbols. The included specs

are spliced in at the position of the :extends clause. The pattern a-with-a-having-d
could have been defined equivalently without pattern extension as shown in the
next listing.

```
(pattern a-with-a-having-d [m]
 [a1 -<:t>-> a2
  a1<A> -<:d>-> d<D>
  a2<A> -<:d>-> d<D>])
```

When the pattern a-with-a-having-d is applied to the model in fig. 18.1 on
page 195, it results in the two matches {:a1 #<c1>, :a2 #<c1>, :d #<d1>} and {:a1
#<c1>, :a2 #<a1>, :d #<d1>}.

A pattern which is overloaded on arity may extend a different arity of itself as
shown in the following example.

```
(defpattern ex-extends
  ([g]    [a<A> -<:d>-> d<D>
           a -<:s>-> b<B> -<:s>-> c<C>])
  ([g a] [:extends [(ex-extends 0)]]))
```

Here, the implementation of arity two simply reuses the pattern spec defined for
the arity one version.

It should be noted that the pattern modifier keywords :isomorphic (see section 18.1.4 on page 198) and :distinct (see section 18.1.16 on page 210) as well as
:as-clauses (see section 18.1.10 on page 203) are not propagated from extended
to extending patterns, thus it is up to the extending pattern to define if isomorphic
matching and distinct matches are enabled, and to define the representation of
matches.

18.1.18   Pattern Specification Summary

Listing 1 presents the syntax of the complete pattern specification DSL using a BNF-
like notation. In there, every uppercase identifier is a non-terminal. Parentheses
are used for grouping. The [] character separates alternatives, ? denotes an option,
* denotes a zero-or-many repetition, and + denotes a one-or-many repetition. Every
other symbol is a terminal that appears in a pattern specification as-is. Additionally,
parentheses enclosed by single-quotes are terminals. This only occurs in the definition of EXTENDS-SPEC.

18.2   Framework-Specific Patterns

As mentioned in the beginning of this chapter, FunnyQT patterns can expand into
generic or framework-specific code. This is controlled by the pattern definition forms'
:pattern-expansion-context option. The possible values are :generic (the default),
:emf, and :tg.

With the :generic expansion context the generated code is protocol-based and applicable to both EMF models and JGraLab TGraphs, and to all model representations that support the relevant protocols. These required protocols are discussed later in appendix A.3 on page 424.

With :emf and :tg, the respective patterns can only be applied to models of the corresponding framework, i.e., EMF and JGraLab, respectively.

EMF-specific patterns. The EMF variant is almost completely identical to the generic variant except that the expansion uses functions defined in the funnyqt.emf namespace directly. Thus, patterns with this expansion context are only applicable to EMF models, and then their evaluation might be slightly more efficient due to less indirection. Other than that, there are neither syntactic extensions to the pattern specification DSL nor semantic differences to the evaluation.

JGraLab-specific patterns. With the :pattern-expansion-context option set to :tg, the pattern's expansion uses functions from the funnyqt.tg namespace instead of generic protocol methods. Therefore, the evaluation of such a pattern might be slightly more efficient compared to the evaluation of a pattern with :generic expansion context.

In contrast to the EMF variant, the JGraLab variant is also slightly extended both syntactically as well as semantically in order to support first-class edges instead of only references. The following additional extensions are available.

In edge symbols, an edge class name can be specified in place of a reference name. In this case, the direction of edges is also considered. E.g., a pattern with the pattern spec a -<A2A>-> b matches two vertices a and b that are connected by an A2A-edge which starts at a and ends at b.

Like for node symbols, the edge class name may be prefixed with ! for negation and suffixed with ! for restricting to direct instances.

Furthermore, reversed edge symbols may be used. For example, the last pattern spec can be specified as [b <-<A2A>- a], too.

Edges can be matched in addition to vertices by providing an identifier for the edge symbol. E.g., every match of a pattern with the pattern spec a -e<A2A>-> b contains two nodes a and b, and one edge e.

An edge symbol with a reference name, e.g., -<:role>->, is treated as a reference compatible with the generic variant. That is, a -<:s>-> b matches a vertex a and a vertex b which is in the role s from a's point of view. The direction of the underlying edge is not considered in this case. Again, for compatibility to the generic version, an untyped edge symbol like in a --> b is also treated as a reference without considering the edge direction.

That -<:role>-> treats edges as references without considering the direction is sensible not only for compatibility to the generic version but because role name navigation implies viewing a model as a set of elements that reference each other. However, that --> is treated as a reference is only due to compatibility. In order to allow untyped pattern edges where the edge direction is considered during matching, the edge type may be specified as _ (underscore). E.g., the a pattern with pattern spec a `-e->` b has twice as many matches as a pattern with spec a `-e<_>->` b because the first pattern treats every edge as a pair of a reference and its opposite reference whereas the second pattern only considers edges which start at a and end at b.

```
    PATTERN-SPEC ::= ( PATTERN-SYMS | CONSTRAINT | BINDING | SUBPATTERN-SPEC
                       | EXTENDS-CLAUSE )*
                     | AS-CLAUSE? | MODIFIER*
    PATTERN-SYMS ::= NODE-SYM ( EDGE-SYM NODE-SYM )*
        NODE-SYM ::= IDENT | IDENT<NODE-TYPE?> | <NODE-TYPE?>
        EDGE-SYM ::= -IDENT?-> | <-IDENT?-
                     | -IDENT?<EDGE-TYPE>-> | <-IDENT?<EDGE-TYPE>-
                     | <EDGE-TYPE<>-IDENT?- | -IDENT?-<EDGE-TYPE?>
                     | NEG-EDGE-SYM
    NEG-EDGE-SYM ::= -!-> | <-!- | -!<EDGE-TYPE?>-> | <-!<EDGE-TYPE?>-
                     | <EDGE-TYPE?>-!- | -!-<EDGE-TYPE?>
       NODE-TYPE ::= ;; a symbol denoting a metamodel element class qname;
                     ;; may be prefixed/suffixed with ! with the same semantics
                     ;; as in type specifications
       EDGE-TYPE ::= ;; a keyword denoting a reference name, or a symbol denoting
                     ;; a metamodel relationship class qname which  may be
                     ;; prefixed/suffixed with ! with the same semantics as in
                     ;; type specifications
           IDENT ::= ;; every legal Clojure symbol not containing < or > and not
                     ;; equal to !
      CONSTRAINT ::= WHEN-CONSTRAINT | APP-COND
 WHEN-CONSTRAINT ::= :when EXPRESSION
      EXPRESSION ::= ;; an arbitrary Clojure expression
        APP-COND ::= POS-APP-COND | NEG-APP-COND | LOG-APP-COND
    POS-APP-COND ::= :positive [PATTERN-SPEC]
    NEG-APP-COND ::= :negative [PATTERN-SPEC]
    LOG-APP-COND ::= LOG-OP [( [PATTERN-SPEC] )*]
          LOG-OP ::= :and | :or | :xor | :nand | :nor
         BINDING ::= LET-BINDING | WHEN-LET-BINDING | FOR-BINDING
     LET-BINDING ::= :let [( DIDENT EXPRESSION )*]
          DIDENT ::= IDENT | DESTRUCT-FORM
WHEN-LET-BINDING ::= :when-let [DIDENT EXPRESSION]
     FOR-BINDING ::= :for [( ( DIDENT SEQ-EXP )
                           | WHEN-CONSTRAINT
                           | LET-BINDING
                           | WHEN-LET-BINDING )*]
         SEQ-EXP ::= ;; an arbitrary Clojure expression resulting in a sequable
   DESTRUCT-FORM ::= ;; a Clojure destructuring form
 SUBPATTERN-SPEC ::= ALT-PATTERN | NESTED-PATTERN
     ALT-PATTERN ::= :alternative [( [PATTERN-SPEC] )+]
  NESTED-PATTERN ::= :nested [( IDENT [PATTERN-SPEC] )+]
  EXTENDS-CLAUSE ::= :extends EXTENDS-SPEC
    EXTENDS-SPEC ::= PATTERN-NAME | '('PATTERN-NAME INDEX? RENAMING*')'
    PATTERN-NAME ::= ;; a symbol denoting the pattern which to extend
           INDEX ::= ;; zero or a positive integer
        RENAMING ::= KEYWORD IDENT
         KEYWORD ::= ;; a Clojure keyword
       AS-CLAUSE ::= :as EXPRESSION
        MODIFIER ::= :isomorphic | :distinct
```

Listing 1: An EBNF grammar for the FunnyQT pattern specification DSL

Chapter 19

Related Work

In this chapter, approaches providing pattern matching as a stand-alone service are discussed. In-place and graph transformation approaches which are usually heavily based on pattern matching capabilities are discussed later in chapter 24 starting on page 249 after FunnyQT's in-place transformation DSL has been introduced.

EMF-IncQuery [Ujh+15] is a graph pattern matching approach for EMF models which has a special focus on incremental pattern matching.

In contrast to traditional pattern matching approaches as provided by FunnyQT, evaluating a pattern does not imply a search for matches in the queried model. Instead, with the incremental approach, a special data structure based on RETE networks [For82] is created from a pattern where every node in the network represents a part of the pattern. I.e., the top nodes in such a network represent typing constraints, and a single bottom node represents the complete pattern. Nodes in between model further constraints, e.g., connection constraints or constraints about attribute values.

Every node in the network caches all elements in the model matching the (sub-)pattern represented by that node. When elements are added to or deleted from the model or attribute values are changed, the EMF notifications framework is used in order to inform the network about the changes which are then propagated for updating the caches accordingly. Thus, all matches of all patterns are accessible at all times and they are updated immediately when the model changes. However, when the model to be queried is initially loaded, the network and its caches have to be populated first which essentially means that notifications for every element, every set reference, and every set attribute in the model have to be processed. This initialization phase is very time-consuming, and of course the caches cause a high memory overhead.

Therefore, the incremental pattern matching approach realized by EMF-IncQuery is very adequate when the same set of queries needs to be re-evaluated over and over again over an extended period of time on the same model. A prime example for such a scenario is a model editor where an always up-to-date list of all elements invalidating certain constraints should be displayed. Every edit operation performed by the user can possibly introduce one or many new problems or fix one or many current problems. With a non-incremental approach, the queries finding elements invalidating some constraint would need to be re-evaluated after every edit operation but with the incremental approach, the matches are automatically updated with minimal effort as soon as the model changes.

Recently, EMF-IncQuery got an alternative implementation [Búr+15] based on local search, and the user can decide on a per-pattern basis which implementation to choose. For future work, even hybrid patterns are considered where some subpatterns are evaluated incrementally and others are evaluated by local search giving the user even more flexibility for fine-tuning for a particular use-case.

Looking at its features, EMF-IncQuery supports only simple (structural) patterns with constraints on attribute values. Patterns may call other patterns which defines a kind of positive application condition. Furthermore, there are negative pattern calls which implement negative application conditions. However, there is no support for expressing alternatives, nested patterns, or other more advanced pattern matching concepts.

The *Scala MTL* discussed in [GWS12] is a type-safe model transformation language implemented as an internal DSL in Scala borrowing the general transformation concepts from ATL [Jou+08].

The approach also enables the use of Scala's built-in pattern matching construct `match` by generating case classes for all classes in a given metamodel. However, Scala's pattern matching facility only allows to test a given element against a number of `case` patterns which may pose constraints on the element's type and properties, and may bind adjacent elements to variables.

SIGMA[1] [KCF14] provides a set of embedded Scala DSLs for model management and transformation tasks. As such, its goals are quite similar to the goals of FunnyQT although its current scope is only on model management, model-to-model transformations, and model-to-text transformations.

SIGMA integrates well with Scala's built-in features, e.g., Scala's static typing and type inference also works for metamodel types, its pattern matching constructs `match/case` constructs can be used on model elements similar to the previously discussed approach, and Scala's `for` expression can be used for encoding patterns in the form of a comprehension for which all matches are to be retrieved from a model.

In the related work chapter for in-place transformation approaches (chapter 24 starting on page 249), several more languages and tools with pattern matching capabilities are discussed.

---

[1]Scala Internal Domain-Specific Languages for Model Manipulation, http://fikovnik.net/Sigma/ (last visited: 2015-09-30)

Part VI

On In-Place Transformations

Summary

This part is dedicated to in-place transformations which change a given model in place in a rule-based manner. Chapter 20 starting on page 223 gives an introduction into the topic and its inherent concepts.

Thereafter, chapter 21 starting on page 227 describes FunnyQT's embedded in-place rule definition DSL, and chapter 22 starting on page 231 explains how the control flow between rules can be defined using higher-order combinators and how the behavior of rules can be modified at call-time.

Chapter 23 starting on page 237 then depicts FunnyQT's state space exploration facilities which can be used in order to analyze in-place transformations.

The part closes with a discussion of related work in chapter 24 starting on page 249.

Chapter 20

Introduction

In contrast to out-place transformations which query a given source model to produce a new target model, *in-place transformations* are transformations that change a given model in place, i.e., the given model is both the source and the target of the transformation. Usually, pattern matching is used to match subgraphs in the model under transformation which are then modified.

The most prominent representatives of this kind of transformations are *graph transformation systems* such as AGG [Tae03], Henshin [Are+10; BET12], GROOVE [Gha+12], GrGen.NET [Gei08], or VIATRA2 [1].

In those systems, a transformation is represented as a set of rules where each rule consists of a *left-hand side (LHS)* and a *right-hand side (RHS)*. The left-hand side is a pattern which is matched in the host graph. The right-hand side is a template describing the effects of applying the rule to the elements matched by the LHS. When a rule is applied, a match of the LHS is searched. The matched elements that occur in both the LHS and the RHS are preserved, the matched elements that occur only in the LHS are deleted, and the elements that occur only in the RHS are created.

Many graph transformation languages use a visual notation for rules similar to the one shown in fig. 20.1 on the following page. This rule named releaseRule is part of a larger transformation which simulates a mutual exclusion algorithm where many processes compete for resources and the transformation rules implement a locking strategy. This transformation is discussed in [VSV05] which suggests it as a benchmark for evaluating the performance of graph transformation systems.

The notation used in fig. 20.1 on the next page clearly separates the rule's LHS and RHS. The LHS matches a resource r which is held by a process p. The negative application condition specifies that this process p must not request another resource. If the LHS matches for some process and resource, the changes induced by the RHS are applied. Here, the held_by reference is deleted because it is not part of the RHS, and a new release link is created between the resource and the process because it occurs only in the rule's RHS. The resource and the process are preserved because they occur in both the LHS and the RHS.

---

[1]http://incquery.net/viatra2 (last visited: 2015-01-19)

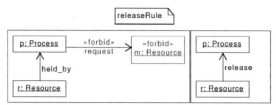

Figure 20.1: A transformation rule with separated LHS and RHS in a visual notation

The visual notation with a strict separation of LHS and RHS can be found in AGG for example. However, most visual graph transformation tools such as GROOVE or Henshin prefer the notation of the LHS and RHS in the very same diagram where colors and annotations are used for distinguishing which elements are to be matched and deleted and which elements are to be created. Figure 20.2 also shows the releaseRule from fig. 20.1 using this combined notation.

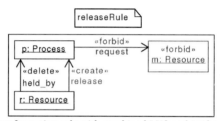

Figure 20.2: A transformation rule with combined LHS and RHS in a visual notation

In this rule definition, the fact that the held_by link has to be matched and then deleted is indicated by its blue color and the «delete» annotation, and the fact that a new release link has to be created between the resource and the process is indicated by its green color and the «create» annotation.

With tools having a textual syntax for rule definitions, the LHS and RHS are strictly separated. For example, listing 20.1 shows the definition of the releaseRule in the textual GrGen.NET syntax.

```
1  rule releaseRule () {
2    r:Resource —hb:held_by—> p:Process;
3    negative {
4      p —req:request—> m:Resource;
5    }
6    replace {
7      r —rel:release—> p;
8    }
9  }
```

Listing 20.1: The releaseRule in textual GrGen.NET syntax

Because the held_by edge hb matched the by the rule's pattern does not occur in the RHS formed by the **replace** part is is deleted by a rule application. In contrast, both the resource r and the process p occur in the RHS, so they are preserved. The release edge rel is only specified in the **replace** part, thus it is created.

The algebraic approach to graph transformations [Cor+97; Ehr+97] is well-founded on graph and category theory, and there are two major formalizations to rule applications. One is the *double-pushout (DPO)* approach, the other is the *single-pushout (SPO)* approach.

With the double-pushout approach, the LHS and the RHS of a rule are related by an intermediate *interface or gluing graph* containing the elements that occur in both the LHS and the RHS, i.e., the elements which are to be preserved by a rule application. When a rule is applied, first a match of the LHS is searched. In a first rewriting step, the elements which are matched but have no counterparts in the gluing graph are deleted. In a second rewriting step, elements which are only defined by the RHS are created.

With DPO, the match of a rule's LHS must satisfy the so-called *gluing condition* which consists of two sub-conditions. (1) If the rule specifies the deletion of a node, then it must also specify the deletion of all edges incident to that node (*dangling condition*). (2) Every element which is to be deleted by the application of a rule must be matched injectively, i.e., it must not have been matched to more than one element of the LHS (*identification condition*).

The dangling condition ensures that there are no dangling edges after the application of a rule, i.e., edges without a start or end node. In most if not all modeling frameworks, dangling edges are not possible. Deletion of a node implies the deletion of all incident edges. However, the strictness enforced by the dangling condition provides additional safety because it prevents accidental deletion of edges, that is, deletion of edges which simply weren't considered by the transformation developer.

The identification condition prevents conflicts between deletion and preservation which occur if a single host graph node is matched by two separate nodes in the LHS where only one of them occurs also in the gluing graph. In this case, the matched node would need to be deleted and preserved at the same time.

With the single-pushout approach, there is no intermediate gluing graph interfacing between a rule's LHS and RHS but the changes implied by a rule are performed in one step. Also, the matches of a rule don't need to satisfy the gluing condition. If a rule specifies the deletion of a node, the deletion of all incident edges is implied implicitly. And in case of a conflict between deletion and preservation, deletion always takes preference.

The differences between the DPO and the SPO approach can be easily illustrated with the pattern and host graphs shown in fig. 20.3 on the next page. The pattern matches two nodes of metamodel type A which are connected by an edge of type E. The start node of the edge is preserved but the edge and its end node are deleted.

With the DPO approach, the rule cannot be applied to any of the two host graphs in the figure. It can't be applied to host graph 1 because the dangling condition doesn't hold. If it was applied to the match (a, e, c) and e and c were deleted, the edge f would be left dangling because its deletion has not been specified. If it was applied to the other possible match (b, f, c) and f and c were deleted, the edge e would be left dangling.

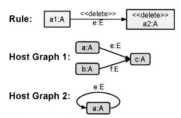

Figure 20.3: Illustration of differences between DPO and SPO

The rule is also not applicable to host graph 2 because of the identification condition. Since $a2$ is specified to be deleted, it must be matched injectively, i.e., it must be matched to a different node than $a1$.

With the SPO approach, the rule can be applied to both host graphs. In case of host graph 1, the deletion of node c implies the deletion of all incident edges. Thus, depending on which of the two matches is chosen, after the rule application the host graph either only contains the node a or b.

In case of host graph 2, the conflict between deletion and preservation is solved in favor of deletion, thus after the rule application, the host graph is empty.

In comparison, the DPO approach is safer than the SPO approach because it ensures that there can't be any effects on the model under transformation which are not explicitly defined by the transformation rules, i.e., rules are free of side-effects. But the SPO approach is more expressive and viable for many practical purposes because the dangling condition does not have to be satisfied.

Out of the cited languages above, AGG, Henshin, and GrGen.NET support both the DPO and SPO approaches where the the approach to be used can be configured on a per-rule basis. GROOVE only implements the SPO approach.

Chapter 21

Defining In-Place Rules

FunnyQT's in-place transformation rules combine patterns, which have already been discussed in the previous part, with actions to be applied on the elements matched by the patterns.

Similar to patterns, FunnyQT provides the three different in-place rule definition macros: `defrule`, `letrule`, and `rule`. They allow defining rules analogously to how Clojure functions are defined.

The `defrule` macro defines a new rule in the current namespace.

Macro: `funnyqt.in-place/defrule`
```
(defrule name doc-string? attr-map? [args] [pattern-spec] & body)
(defrule name doc-string? attr-map? ([args] [pattern-spec] & body)+)
```
The macro receives the `name` of the rule to be defined (a symbol), an optional `doc-string`, an optional `attr-map` containing options affecting the rule's behavior, a vector of formal arguments `args`, a vector containing a `pattern-spec` specifying what elements the rule matches, and a `body` of arbitrary many forms.

The second signature shows that rules can be overloaded on arity just like patterns or plain Clojure functions.

The first formal parameter in `args` must denote the model the rule is applied to just like with patterns. The `pattern-spec` may use all pattern features discussed in section 18.1 on page 195 with the exception of `:as` clauses. A rule's pattern spec may also contain `:extends` clauses for including the pattern specs of other patterns or rules. `:extends` clauses only include pattern specs, i.e., when a rule has an `:extends` clause naming some other rule, only the other rule's pattern spec is included in the extending rule's pattern spec. The bodies of the two rules are not merged.

The `body` forms have access to all variables bound by the pattern, i.e., the forms in the body are executed in an environment in which for every keyword used as key in an entry of the map representing the pattern's match there is a variable of the same name which is bound to the value of that entry. For example, if the pattern is specified by `[a<A> -<:x>-> b<B> :let [c (foo b)]]`, the body is executed in an environment where the variables `a` and `b` are bound to the matched elements and `c` is bound to the value of calling `foo` with `b`.

The body may contain arbitrary forms including recursive calls and recur-forms if the rule should call itself tail-recursively.

The semantics of a rule when being applied to a model given as its first argument is to find a match of the rule's pattern, and then the rule's body is executed in the context of the match, and the return value is the value of the last expression in the body which should be logically true by convention[1]. If there is no match of the pattern, the rule returns nil.

Because the body is made up of arbitrary forms, the graph transformation terms DPO and SPO are not applicable to FunnyQT in-place transformation rules. However, the behavior is very similar to the SPO approach because FunnyQT's delete operations for nodes always delete all incident edges, too.

The example rule which has been shown in a visual notation in fig. 20.1 and fig. 20.2 on page 224 in the introduction could be specified with FunnyQT as shown in the next listing.

```
(defrule release-rule
  "Matches a resource held by a process which does not request more
  resources, and lets the process releases that resource."
  [g]                                                    ;; arguments
  [r<Resource> -hb<HeldBy>-> p<Process> -!<Request>-> <>]  ;; pattern
  (delete! hb)                                           ;; body
  (create-edge! g 'Release r p))
```

The rule matches a Resource vertex r being held by a Process p which does not request any resources. If such a resource and process exist, the HeldBy edge hb is deleted, and a new Release edge starting at the resource and ending at the process is created and is the return value of the rule application.

Like patterns, rule definitions expand to plain Clojure function definitions having the name, documentation string, and arguments as defined by the defrule form.

Rule options. The attr-map that may be given to a rule definition may contain several options. The first one is the :pattern-expansion-context option with possible values :generic (the default), :tg, and :emf which specifies if the pattern should be expanded to generic or slightly faster framework-specific code. This option has already been discussed in chapter 18 starting on page 193.

If the :forall option is enabled, an application of the rule first evaluates the rule's pattern eagerly in order to find all matches. Then, the rule's actions are applied to all matches one after the other. The eager evaluation of the pattern gives rise to parallelization which can be suppressed using the :sequential option. The return value of a forall-rule is logical false if no match could be found. Otherwise, it returns a vector containing the values of applying the rule's body to each match. If the vector of application results is not needed, its creation can be suppressed using the :no-result-vec option. If it is enabled, the forall-rule only returns the number of matches of the rule's pattern.

---

[1]Since recur-forms are valid in a rule's body, this convention cannot be enforced because recur-forms have to be in tail-position.

Note that there can be rules whose effects can create a new match of the same rule. This implies that after the application of a forall-rule, there can still be matches of the rule's pattern in the model under transformation, namely the subgraphs consisting of elements which became matches because of applying the rule's effects to other matches.

The situation above is harmless. However, when the effects of a rule can modify a subgraph in such a way that it is no match of the same rule's pattern anymore although it has been before, a much more severe situation occurs, i.e., the rule's body is going to be applied to a match which has become invalid in the meantime. If a rule's definition allows for this situation to occur, it should have the :recheck option enabled. This option causes each pre-calculated match to be re-validated to test if it still satisfies the pattern just before the rule's body is applied in its context. If it is no match anymore, the effects are not applied.

As with FunnyQT patterns, the attr-map options may alternatively be given as metadata attached to a rule's name.

Parameter passing. In some transformation scenarios, if a rule r_1 gets applied it is very likely or even certain that another rule r_2 can be applied to the elements that are preserved or created by r_1. In such cases, the involved rules may use *parameter passing* to improve performance. Parameter passing means that the elements which are a likely match of r_2 are passed from r_1 to an overloaded arity version of r_2 explicitly. Then r_2 only needs to test if these elements indeed match its pattern instead of performing a global search for matching elements in the model. Depending on the context, the overloaded arity version of r_2 may even test with only a simpler pattern, or the check can be omitted completely.

The mutual exclusion transformation discussed in [VSV05] contains some rules that can benefit from parameter passing as shown below.

```
(defrule take-rule [g]
  [p<Process> -rq<Request>-> r<Resource> -t<Token>-> p]
  (delete! t)
  (delete! rq)
  [r (create-edge! g 'HeldBy r p) p])

(defrule release-rule
  ([g] [r<Resource> -hb<HeldBy>-> p -!<Request>-> <>]
   (release-rule g r hb p))
  ([g r hb p] [p -!<Request>-> <>]
   (delete! hb)
   (create-edge! g 'Release r p)))
```

The take-rule matches a process requesting a resource where it's the process' turn to act on the resource as indicated by the token. The effect is that the token and request edges are deleted and the resource is assigned to the process by a new HeldBy edge.

A resource being held by a process is exactly what the pattern of release-rule matches except for the additional requirement that the process must not request other resources, too. Thus, for the results of the `take-rule` only the latter condition needs to be checked by the `release-rule`.

To enable parameter passing, the `release-rule` is overloaded on arity. The version which only receives the graph g specifies the full pattern and performs a search in the graph when being applied. The version of arity four receives the graph and all elements which the arity one version searches with its pattern and assumes that those already have the right structure. Its pattern only ensures that the process doesn't request additional resources.

The `take-rule`'s value when being applied is a vector of a resource, a HeldBy edge, and a process. Thus, when the two rules are applied as (apply release-rule g (take-rule g)) and `take-rule` matches, the arity four version of the `release-rule` is called. If the `take-rule` doesn't match, then the arity one version of the `release-rule` is called.

In the above case, it is likely that the `release-rule` can be applied to the result of a `take-rule` application. Sometimes, the applicability of a rule is not only likely but absolutely certain. In those cases, there are no additional restrictions that need to be checked when an overloaded version of a rule gets called. Therefore, the pattern is actually optional in a FunnyQT rule definition. If it is omitted, a rule is completely equivalent to a function, i.e., it simply executes its body in the context of its arguments.

The `defrule` macro discussed above defines a new function-valued var in the current namespace. The `letrule` macro defines one or many named rules as specified by `rule-specs` which are accessible only in the lexical scope of `body`. As such, `letrule` stands to `defrule` like `letfn` (see page 37) stands to `defn`.

Macro: funnyqt.in-place/letrule
(letrule [rule-specs] attr-map? & body)

Each rule in `rule-specs` is represented analogously to `defrule`.

```
(rule-name attr-map? [args] [pattern-spec] & body)
(rule-name attr-map? ([args] [pattern-spec] & body)+)
```

The optional `attr-map` of the `letpattern` can be used to specify options which apply to all defined rules, and those may add or override individual options.

The `rule` macro defines an anonymous rule. Therefore, `rule` stands to `defrule` like fn (see page 35) stands to `defn`.

Macro: funnyqt.in-place/rule
(rule name? attr-map? [args] [pattern-spec] & body)
(rule name? attr-map? ([args] [pattern] & body)+)

The `rule` macro receives an optional `name`, an optional `attr-map`, a vector containing a `pattern-spec`, and a `body`. Like with anonymous functions, the `name` is only accessible from within the rule itself and can be used for recursive calls. Again, anonymous rules may be overloaded on arity as indicated by the second signature.

Chapter 22

Defining Control Flow and Modifying Behavior

As said in the last chapter, any rule defined with the rule definition macros `defrule`, `letrule`, and `rule` expands into a plain Clojure function. Together with the contract that a rule must only return logical false if it is not applicable, the standard Clojure control structures may be used for controlling rule application. For example, `(or (rule-1 m) (rule-2 m) (rule-3 m))` applies the first applicable rule[1] to the model m and returns its value due to the short-circuiting nature of `clojure.core/or`.

Nevertheless, for frequently re-occurring rule application patterns such as as-long-as-possible iteration and non-deterministic choice, FunnyQT defines several higher-order rule combinators. These are discussed in section 22.1.

When applying a rule, it searches a match of its pattern. If a match can be found, the rule's actions are executed in the match's context. This means that there is no way to test if a rule is applicable without actually applying it. Section 22.2 on page 235 introduces two rule application modifier macros which allow for testing a rule for applicability and for retrieving the matches of a rule's pattern.

22.1 Higher-Order Rule Combinators

In this section, several higher-order rule combinator functions are introduced. They provide concise means to compose existing rules to new rules which support frequently occurring rule application patterns in in-place transformations. These patterns are

(1) sequential application of several rules to the same arguments,
(2) sequential application of several rules until one fails,
(3) sequential application of several rules until one succeeds,
(4) repeated application of one rule (either a fixed number of iterations or as long

---

[1]Actually, the rules are applied in sequence but if a rule can't find a match (is inapplicable) it returns `nil` and or evaluates the next rule application.

as possible), or the
(5) application of one randomly chosen applicable rule from a given collection of rules.

The rule combinators which might apply more than one rule or the same rule multiple times have a starred variants supporting *parameter passing* which means that values can be passed from one rule to the next rule.

It should be noted that all these combinators are not restricted to in-place transformation rules. Their semantics only depend on the contract that a rule returns a logically true value if it could be applied and logically false otherwise. All other non-rule functions fulfilling this contract can be used with the higher-order combinators discussed in the remainder of this section, too. Most importantly, the functions returned by the combinators can be composed using the combinators again.

The first rule combinator is `sequential-rule`.

Function: `funnyqt.in-place/sequential-rule`
`(sequential-rule & rules)`

It receives a sequence of `rules` and returns a function of variable arguments. This function applies each rule to its arguments in sequence collecting the individual application results in a vector. It returns logical false if no rule could be applied. Otherwise, i.e., if at least one rule could be applied, it returns the vector of application results.

The `conjunctive-rule` combinator returns a function which behaves like a logical and of the applications of the combined rules.

Function: `funnyqt.in-place/conjunctive-rule`
`(conjunctive-rule & rules)`

The returned varargs function applies all rules to its arguments in sequence until an inapplicable rule is encountered. In this case, the function returns false. If all rules could be applied, the return value is the value of the last rule application. I.e., `((conjunctive-rule r1 r2 r3) m)` is equivalent to `(and (r1 m) (r2 m) (r3 m))`.

In some transformation scenarios, applying some rule `r1` might result in the creation of a subgraph which is likely to be matched by another rule `r2`. In this case, the rule `r1` could return a vector which is suitable as sequence of actual parameters for `r2`. The rule combinator `conjunctive-rule*` supports such a kind of parameter passing between multiple rules.

Function: `funnyqt.in-place/conjunctive-rule*`
`(conjunctive-rule* & rules)`

It receives a sequence of `rules` again. The returned varargs function applies the first rule to its arguments. Any later rule is applied to the return value of the previous rule application. Like with `conjunctive-rule`, the first inapplicable rule stops the overall application and false is returned. If all rules could be applied, then the result is the value of the last rule's application. Thus, for `conjunctive-rule*` the equivalence in the following listing holds.

```
(= ((conjunctive-rule* r1 r2 r3) m x)
   (when-let [ret (r1 m x)]
     (when-let [ret (apply r2 ret)]
```

```
(when-let [ret (apply r3 ret)]
  ret))))
```

The next combinator, `disjunctive-rule`, returns a function which behaves like a logical `or` of the applications of the combined rules.

Function: funnyqt.in-place/disjunctive-rule
(disjunctive-rule & rules)

Again, it receives a sequence of `rules` and it returns a varargs function. This function applies the first applicable rule to the function's arguments and returns the value of the rule application. If none of the rules could be applied, logical false is returned. I.e., `((disjunctive-rule r1 r2 r3) m)` is equivalent to `(or (r1 m) (r2 m) (r3 m))`.

For applying a rule a fixed number of times, there is the `repeated-rule` combinator.

Function: funnyqt.in-place/repeated-rule
(repeated-rule rule)
(repeated-rule n rule)

The combinator receives one single `rule` and an optional positive integer n. The returned varargs function applies the given rule as long as possible but at most n times and returns the number of successful applications.

The function returned by `(repeated-rule r1)` has the signature `(fn [n & args])`, i.e., the number of repetitions has to be provided when the function is called whereas it is already fixed when using the version of arity two. Thus, `((repeated-rule r1) 10 m)` is equivalent to `((repeated-rule 10 r1) m)`.

The `repeated-rule*` combinator is similar to its counterpart without the star except that it exhibits the same parameter passing feature as discussed above with `conjunctive-rule*`.

Function: funnyqt.in-place/repeated-rule*
(repeated-rule* rule)
(repeated-rule* n rule)

The returned function's behavior equals the behavior of the one returned by `repeated-rule`. However, the given rule is only applied to the returned function's arguments once. All repeated rule calls receive the result of the previous application.

The next combinator, `iterated-rule`, returns a function performing an as-long-as-possible iteration.

Function: funnyqt.in-place/iterated-rule
(iterated-rule rule)

The combinator receives a single rule and returns a varargs function. When being called, that function applies the rule to its arguments as long as the rule returns a logically true value[2]. The function returns the number of successful rule applications or false if it couldn't be applied at least once.

The `iterated-rule*` combinator is the parameter passing variant of `iterated-rule`.

---

[2]As a consequence, if rule can be applied indefinitely, the function returned by `(iterated-rule rule)` will not terminate when being called.

Function: `funnyqt.in-place/iterated-rule*`
`(iterated-rule* rule)`

The function being returned applies the rule to the arguments given to the function once and then applies it iteratively to the value of the respective previous application. Again, the number of successful applications is returned or false if the rule couldn't be applied at least once.

The `random-rule` combinator implements a non-deterministic choice.

Function: `funnyqt.in-place/random-rule`
`(random-rule & rules)`

The combinator receives a sequence of rules and returns a varargs function. This function randomly selects one applicable rule and applies it to its arguments. The value of the selected rule is the value of the overall application. If no rule is applicable, then logical false is returned.

22.1.1   Interactive Rule Application

The `interactive-rule` combinator is a bit special and mainly intended for debugging purposes because the returned function doesn't implement some well-defined control flow between the given `rules` but it provides a facility for steering rule applications interactively.

Function: `funnyqt.in-place/interactive-rule`
`(interactive-rule & rules)`

Calling the returned function will fire up a dialog window as shown in fig. 22.1.

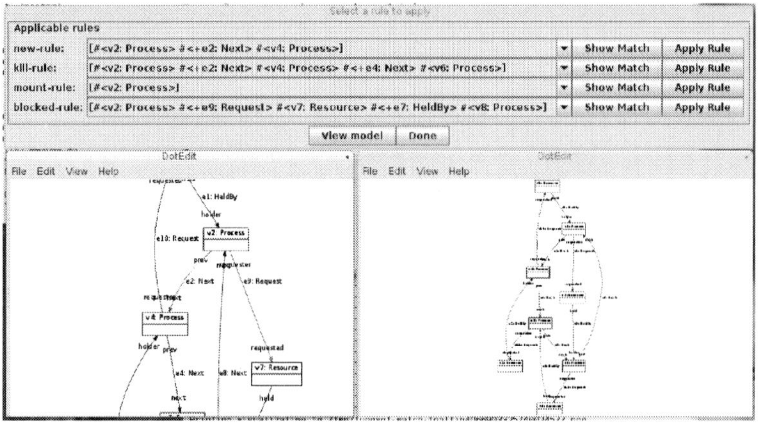

Figure 22.1: The graphical user interface of an interactive rule

The dialog's main compartment lists all rules which are currently applicable, one rule per line. The label starting each line states the rule's name[3].

The second component in each line is a combo box which shows a print representation of the match which is currently selected for that rule. Initially, this is the first match a rule is able to find but the user may select any match using the combo box's drop-down list.

The *Show Match* button allows for viewing the currently selected match in the visualized model. In the screenshot, the bottom-left window shows the currently selected match of the new-rule. The matched elements are highlighted in red color. The match visualization always consists of all matched elements plus their neighboring elements in order for the user to understand the context of the match.

Using the *Apply Rule* button, the user can apply the rule to the currently selected match. As a result, the dialog vanishes and reappears with a refreshed list of applicable rules and their matches.

At the bottom of the dialog, there are two more buttons. The *View model* button opens a window visualizing the complete model. The window in the bottom-right of the screenshot has been spawned by pressing this button. The *Done* button simply quits the dialog without applying any rule.

The return value of the function returned by interactive-rule is either the number of rules which have been applied, or it is nil in case no rule has been applied. If an interactive rule is called and none of its rules has any match, then it returns immediately with value nil.

22.2 Rule Application Modifiers

When a rule is executed, it searches for a match of its pattern and invokes its actions in the context of this match. If there is no match, it returns logical false. Thus, the test for applicability and the actual modification of the model in terms of the rule's actions are indivisible by default, e.g., when calling a rule like in (rule-1 model). To be able to separate the test for a rule's applicability from its actions, FunnyQT defines two *rule application modifier macros*.

The first modifier is as-pattern which allows to apply a rule as a pattern.

Macro: funnyqt.in-place/as-pattern
(as-pattern rule-application)

So calling (as-pattern (rule-1 model)) returns the lazy sequence of matches of rule-1's pattern. The rule's actions are completely disabled.

Being able to get all matches from a rule without having to apply its effects is a valuable feature, and if (seq (as-pattern (rule-1 model))) returns logical true, then rule-1 is indeed applicable, i.e., its sequence of matches is not empty.

However, this is not the best test for applicability. If the rule was called without as-pattern afterwards, it would restart searching for a match again.

For testing a rule for applicability including the possibility to apply it afterwards,

---

[3]It is allowed to give anonymous rules to interactive-rule but those show up with generated names like anon-rule22979--22984.

there is the `as-test` modifier macro.

Macro: `funnyqt.in-place/as-test`
`(as-test rule-application)`

Calling `(as-test (rule-1 model))` returns logical false if `rule-1` is not applicable. If it is applicable, it returns a parameter-less closure (a *thunk*) capturing the rule's first match and the rule's actions. Applying the thunk executes the actions on the captured match.

Thus, the following code tests `rule-1` for its applicability, and if it is applicable, a coin toss decides if the rule's actions are applied to the captured match.

```
(when-let [t (as-test (rule-1 model))]
  (when (>= (Math/random) 0.5)
    (t)))
```

If `rule-2` is a forall-rule, i.e., a rule with `:forall` option enabled, then the value of the expression `(as-test (rule-2 model))` is a vector of thunks, one thunk per match of `rule-2`'s pattern in the model.

Note that rules called as tests can exhibit the same problem as forall-rules, i.e., between the point in time where a match has been found and the time of the application of the rule's actions on this match, the model might have been modified in a way which invalidates the match. Therefore, the `:recheck` rule option discussed in chapter 21 starting on page 227 also applies to the thunks returned by calling rules as tests. E.g., if `rule-1` was declared with the `:recheck` option enabled, then the thunk t would check if its captured match still conforms to the pattern before applying the effects.

Chapter 23

Exploring State Space

State space exploration is a technique for analyzing in-place transformations. A typical scenario is that there is a model representing a system in its current state and a set of in-place transformation rules. When a rule matches and its actions are applied, the system transitions into another state.

As example system, a simple counter with two digits is used in this chapter. Its metamodel is shown in fig. 23.1.

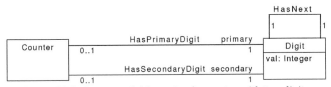

Figure 23.1: A metamodel for a simple counter with two digits

The system of a counter consists of one Counter element and many Digit elements. The latter have an integral value, e.g., the numbers from zero to nine. Every digit knows the previous and next digit of the counter. Furthermore, the counter element references one digit as its primary digit, and one digit as its secondary digit. These two edges represent the clock hands of the counter when imagining it as an analog clock, e.g., the HasPrimaryDigit edge represents the hand for minutes, and the HasSecondaryDigit edge represents the hand for seconds.

Figure 23.2 on the following page shows three states of an example counter graph. In order to keep the visualizations small and clear, a two-digit ternary counter is used, i.e., there are three Digit elements with val attribute values from 0 to 2.

The leftmost graph represents the state 0:0, the graph in the middle represents the state after ticking once, i.e., 0:1, and the rightmost graph represents the state after ticking once again, i.e., 0:2. The next state induced by ticking once more would be 1:0 where the secondary digit is 0 again and the primary digit advances to 1. Then follow the states 1:1, 1:2, 2:0, 2:1, 2:2, and finally the initial state 0:0 is reached again, i.e., in normal operation such a two-digit ternary counter is in one of

237

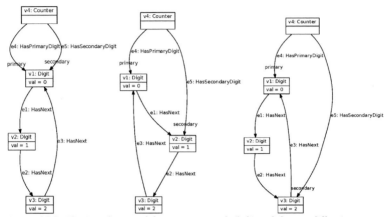

Figure 23.2: The initial state of the counter graph (left) and the two following states when ticking forward

$3^2 = 9$ different states at each time.

The transformation rules modifying the state of the counter are given in the following. They are designed in a way which makes them applicable to any two-digit counter no matter if it has digits from 0-2 or 0-60 or something else.

The tick-forward rule advances the counter. It uses :alternative patterns to distinguish the situations where (1) only the secondary digit has to be advanced and (2) where both the secondary and the primary digit have to be advanced. In both cases, the advancement is realized by setting the target vertex of the respective HasSecondaryDigit or HasPrimaryDigit edge to the digit which is connected to the current one in terms of an outgoing HasNext edge.

```
(defrule tick-forward [g]
  [c<Counter> -sec<:secondary>-> <> -<HasNext>-> next
   :alternative [[:when (not (zero? (value next :val)))]       ;; (1)
                 [:when (zero? (value next :val))              ;; (2)
                  c -prim<:primary>-> <> -<HasNext>-> next2]]]
  (when prim
    (set-omega! prim next2))
  (set-omega! sec next))
```

The tick-backward rule is similar to the tick-forward rule except that its application decreases the counter's value and enables its usage as a countdown timer.

```
(defrule tick-backward [g]
  [c<Counter> -sec<:secondary>-> cur <-<HasNext>- prev
   :alternative [[:when (not (zero? (value cur :val)))]        ;; (1)
                 [:when (zero? (value cur :val))               ;; (2)
```

```
                c -prim<:primary>-> <> <-<HasNext>- prev2]]]
(when prim
  (set-omega! prim prev2))
(set-omega! sec prev))
```

The reset-counter resets the counter back to the state 0:0. It is applicable to all states except for 0:0 in which case a reset would be a no-op anyway.

```
(defrule reset-counter [g]
  [c<Counter> -<:secondary>-> d1
   c          -<:primary>->   d2
   :when (or (not (zero? (value d1 :val)))
             (not (zero? (value d2 :val))))]
  (let [digit-zero (the #(zero? (value % :val))
                        (vseq g 'Digit))]
    (set-adj! c :secondary digit-zero)
    (set-adj! c :primary digit-zero)))
```

State space exploration helps analyzing scenarios where a set of rules modify a system's state by making these states explicit, i.e., during the exploration, an explicit model consisting of states and rule-induced transitions is created. This model is called the *state space graph* in the following, and its schema is shown in fig. 23.3.

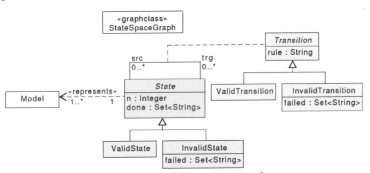

Figure 23.3: FunnyQT's state space schema

Every State in the state space graph corresponds to one or multiple equivalent states of the model under transformation and every state of the model under transformation corresponds to exactly one state in the state space graph[1]. States are created with increasing values of their n attribute starting with 1. When a rule gets applied to the model, a corresponding Transition edge having the rule's name set as value of the rule attribute is created which starts at the State corresponding to the

---

[1]Actually, every state of the model under transformation is represented as a separate copy of the model with some changes

model before the rule application and ends at the State corresponding to the model after the rule application.

When a rule's application results in a model which is equivalent (according to a customizable definition of equivalence) to an earlier model, the State vertex representing this earlier state of the model is reused. For example, when exploring the state space of the counter example with respect to only the `tick-forward` rule starting with the initial model representing the state 0:0, repeated rule application creates states corresponding to 0:1 to 2:2. An appropriate definition of equivalence in this scenario is that two models representing counter states are equivalent if and only if both the primary and secondary hands point to digits with the same values. Thus, when applying `tick-forward` after the creation of the state corresponding to 2:2 the resulting model is equivalent to the initial model representing the state 0:0 and thus its State vertex in the state space graph is reused.

All rules which were tried to be applied to the model corresponding to a state are saved in the state's done attribute. As soon as all rules have been applied to the models corresponding to all State vertices in the state space graph, the state space exploration is finished. Of course, depending on the system being modeled and the transformation rules, it is possible that the rules always transition the system into new states and this stop criterion is never met. For these cases, other stop criteria may be defined which are going to be discussed in the remainder of this chapter where FunnyQT's state space exploration functions are discussed.

Step-wise state space generation. The function `state-space-step-fn` is the most important FunnyQT state space generation construct. It receives an initial model `init-model` of the system under transformation, a comparison function `comparefn`, a collection of `rules`, and an optional map of `options`.

The `comparefn` receives two models representing the states before and after a rule's application and should return true if and only if the two models are equivalent. A predefined comparison function is `funnyqt.generic/equal-models?` which has already been discussed in section 12.8 on page 115.

Function: `funnyqt.in-place/state-space-step-fn`
```
(state-space-step-fn init-model comparefn rules)
(state-space-step-fn init-model comparefn rules options)
```

The return value of `state-space-step-fn` is a function for step-wise state space generation. This function is overloaded on arity and possesses two metadata entries as shown in the next listing.

```
(with-meta (fn ([] ...)
              ([select-rules-fn] ...)
              ([select-rules-fn select-state-fn] ...))
  {:state-space-graph #<StateSpaceGraph>
   :state2model-map   #<volatile {#<State> #<CounterGraph>}>})
```

The `:state-space-graph` metadata key's value is the state space graph, and the `:state2model-map` metadata key's value is a map assigning to each state in the state space graph the corresponding model representing this state. This map is wrapped in a volatile because it changes over time. Thus, by dereferencing the value of

:state2model-map one retrieves the state-to-model map which is current at that point in time.

Initially, that is, immediately after a state space step function has been created and it has not been applied yet, the state space graph contains exactly one State vertex with attribute n set to 1. This single state represents the initial model.

When the state space step function gets called, first the rules to be applied in this step are computed by calling (select-rules-fn rules). The default select-rules-fn is clojure.core/identity, i.e., all rules given to state-space-step-fn are to be applied. A custom select-rules-fn can be used select only a subset of rules (or even a completely separate set of rules) for application in this step.

After the rules selection, an unfinished state is selected by calling (select-state-fn unfinished-states). An unfinished state is a state to which at least one of the selected rules hasn't been applied yet, i.e., a state whose done attribute doesn't contain all the names of the selected rules. The default state selection function is clojure.core/first. The function clojure.core/rand-nth which picks a random element of a collection is a likely candidate for a select-state-fn in case the state space generation should be performed in a non-deterministic order.

After an unfinished state has been selected, the step function applies all selected rules to it. Hereby, each rule is actually applied to a copy of the model under transformation corresponding to the selected state. The copy is created using the funnyqt.generic/copy-model function already discussed in section 12.9 on page 116.

Once a rule has been applied, the modified model is compared to the models corresponding to the state space graph's states using the comparefn one after the other. If there exists a model which is equivalent to the current one, its corresponding state is re-used as target of a new Transition edge which starts at the state corresponding to the model before the rule application. If all models of existing states are different, then a new State is created as target vertex of the new Transition and associated with the current model. In both cases, the transition's rule attribute is set to the name of the rule.

A state space step function returns false if the select-state-fn returned nil which usually only happens if there are no unfinished states anymore. Otherwise, it returns a logically true value. Thus, as long as the state space step function returns a logically true value, the state space generation has not been completed yet.

The map of options given at the call to state-space-step-fn map contain entries with the following keys:

:additional-args The value of this option is a sequence of additional arguments for rule applications. The step-wise state space generation function applies rules using (apply rule model (:additional-args options)).

:select-rules-fn The value of this option is a function that receives the collection of rules given to state-space-step-fn and should return a collection of rules to be applied in a step. If omitted, the collection rules given as argument is used as-is and defines the order. The argument of the same name of the step-wise state space generation function overrides the value of this entry.

:select-state-fn The value of this option is a function that receives the lazy sequence of unfinished states and should return one of them. If omitted, the selected rules are always applied to the first unfinished state's model. The argument of the same name of the step-wise state space generation function overrides the value of this entry.

:state-preds The value of this option is a collection of predicates on the model under transformation. Each time the step function is going to create a new State for the current state of the model, each of those predicates is tested on this model. If all predicates return a logically true value, the new state's vertex class is ValidState. Otherwise, its vertex class is InvalidState and the failed attribute names all predicates which returned a logically false value.

The :state-preds option should be used for specifying invariants of the model under transformation which must not be infringed by the transformation rules. If they do nonetheless, this is an error in the rules whose transitions lead to the invalid state. An example invariant is given in the following listing.

```
(defn exactly-two-clock-hands? [cg]
  (and (= 1 (ecount cg 'HasPrimaryDigit))
       (= 1 (ecount cg 'HasSecondaryDigit))))
```

Every counter graph in the example needs to have exactly one HasPrimaryDigit edge and exactly one HasSecondaryDigit edge.

:transition-preds The value of this option is a map whose keys are (a subset of) the transformation rules and whose values are collections of predicates, e.g., {rule-1 [p1 p2], rule-2 [p3]}. When a rule has been applied to the model corresponding to some state, each of the rule's predicates p is called like (p old-model match new-model), i.e., the predicate receives the model in the state before the application, the match of the rule's pattern, and the model in the state after the application.

If all predicates associated with the applied rule return a logically true value, then the edge class of the transition being created for the rule application is ValidTransition. Otherwise, it is an InvalidTransition and the transition's failed attribute names all predicates which returned a logically false value.

The :transition-preds option is intended to be used for specifying post-conditions of the transformation rules. An example transition predicate could assert that after the rule reset-counter has been applied, the two clock hands represented by the HasSecondaryDigit and HasPrimaryDigit edges must point to a Digit vertex with val equaling 0 as tested by the counter-at-0:0? predicate shown below.

```
(defn counter-at-0:0? [old-model match new-model]
  (let [val-of (fn [ec]
                 (value (omega (the (eseq new-model ec))) :val))]
    (and (= 0 (val-of 'HasPrimaryDigit))
         (= 0 (val-of 'HasSecondaryDigit)))))
```

It only asserts the condition stated above in the new-model without considering the old-model and the match.

:state-space-preds The value of this option is a collection of predicates on the state space graph itself. They don't have an effect on the state space graph but can be tested when needed.

This option should be used to specify invariants on the state space graph itself. For example, with counter models and the transformation rules from the example, it is clear that the state space graph's number of states is bounded. Concretely, with a ternary counter with two digits, there can be at most nine different states in the state space graph. This invariant can be made explicit by using at-most-9-states? being defined as

```
(defn at-most-9-states? [ssg]
  (<= (vcount ssg) 9))
```

as a state space predicate.

After discussing the validation options, the return value of the state space step function can be concretized. Above, it has been said that it returns a logically true value if the select-state-fn returned some unfinished state and thus rules have been applied. In this case, the actual return value is a vector of the form

```
[invalid-states invalid-transitions failed-state-space-preds]
```

where invalid-states is the lazy sequence of State vertices for which at least one predicate in :state-preds failed, invalid-transitions is the lazy sequence of Transition edges for which at least one predicate in :transition-preds failed, and finally, failed-state-space-preds is the lazy sequence of predicates in :state-space-preds which fail when being applied to the current state space graph.

These sequences can be inspected by the caller of the state space step function. For example, a caller might call the step function repeatedly until either the complete state space graph has been built and the step function returns false or until some predicate failed.

Exhaustive state space generation. The function create-state-space can be used to conveniently create the complete state space for a given inital model and a collection of rules. It has the same arguments as the state-space-step-fn discussed above, i.e., it receives an initial model init-model, a comparison function comparefn, a collection of transformation rules, and an optional map of options.

Function: funnyqt.in-place/create-state-space
```
(create-state-space init-model comparefn rules)
(create-state-space init-model comparefn rules options)
```

In fact, create-state-space uses a step-wise state space creation function returned by state-space-step-fn internally where the arguments of the former are passed to the latter.

By default, create-state-space repeatedly calls its internal step-wise state space creation function until either

(1) that returns false in which case the complete state space graph has been created, or

(2) at least one predicate in :state-preds, :transition-preds, or :state-space-preds failed.

The return value of create-state-space is a vector of the form

```
[state-space-graph state2model-map step-fn-retval]
```

where state-space-graph is the final state space graph, state2model-map is the final map assigning to State vertices in the state-space-graph the corresponding models, and step-fn-retval is the return value of the internal step-wise state space creation function. The returned vector has :state-space-step-fn metadata attached. Its value is the internal step-wise state space creation function. Thus, it can be used to drive the state space creation further if `create-state-space` returned because of failed predicates.

In addition to the options which are also applicable to `state-space-step-fn`, `create-state-space` supports an entry with key `:recur-pred` in its map of `options`. The value of this entry must be a function of five arguments.

```
(fn [ssg s2m-map invalid-states invalid-transitions failed-state-space-preds]
  ↪ ...)
```

This function receives the current state space graph `ssg`, the current value of the state-to-model map `s2m-map`, the lazy sequences of invalid states `invalid-states`, the lazy sequence of invalid transitions `invalid-transitions`, and the lazy sequence of state space predicates `failed-state-space-preds` which fail on the current state space graph.

The `:recur-pred` predicate is called whenever the internal step-wise state space function returned a logically true value, i.e., the state space generation hasn't been finished yet. If the predicate returns logically true, then the state space generation resumes. Otherwise, `create-state-space` returns immediately.

The final state space graph created by the call of `create-state-space` in the next listing is shown in fig. 23.4 on the facing page.

```
(create-state-space
 initial-counter-graph
 #(g/equal-models? %1 %2 false)
 [tick-forward tick-backward reset-counter]
 {:state-preds [exactly-two-clock-hands?]
  :transition-preds {reset-counter [counter-at-0:0?]}
  :state-space-preds [at-most-9-states?]})
;=> [#<StateSpaceGraph> {...} false]
```

The `initial-counter-graph` is the counter graph in state 0:0 as shown in the left part of fig. 23.2 on page 238. This graph corresponds to the State vertex v1. The state vertices v2 and v3 correspond to the counter graphs after applying the `tick-forward` or `tick-backward` rule once to the initial graph, respectively, i.e., v2 represents the counter graph in state 0:1 and v3 represents the counter graph in state 2:2.

As can be seen, there are exactly nine state vertices which is expected. In every state, the `tick-forward` and `tick-backward` rules have been applied, and corresponding Transition edges have been created. The `reset-counter` rule has been applied in every state except for the initial state v1. Again, this is expected because the rule explicitly checks that the secondary or the primary digit is non-zero. Therefore, it is inapplicable in the initial state where the model represents the counter value 0:0.

The absence of InvalidState vertices and the return value of the `create-state-space` call indicate that the invariant `exactly-two-clock-hands?` was satisfied by all states' models. Likewise, the absence of InvalidTransition edges and the return value of the `create-state-space` call indicate that the `reset-counter` post-condition `counter-at-0:0?` has always been satisfied. Lastly, the return value also indicates that at all times, the invariant `at-most-9-states?` has been satisfied by the state space graph.

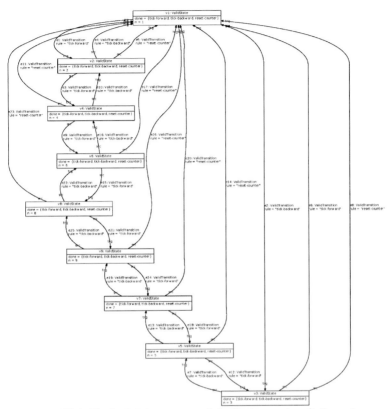

Figure 23.4: The final state space graph for the ternary two-digit counter

Interactive state space generation and exploration. The `explore-state-space` function provides means to create and explore the state space interactively using a simple graphical user interface. It has the same arguments as `state-space-step-fn`, and in fact, it utilizes a step-wise state space creation function internally.

Function: `funnyqt.in-place/explore-state-space`
`(explore-state-space init-model comparefn rules)`
`(explore-state-space init-model comparefn rules options)`

Figure 23.5 on the following page shows a screenshot of the `explore-state-space` GUI. The call to `explore-state-space` had the same arguments as the call to `create-state-space` above except that one additional rule `erase-clock-hands` has been specified. This rule erases the HasPrimaryDigit and HasSecondaryDigit edges from the counter graph. Of course, this is not a sensible rule but it is used here only in order to be able to illustrate how failing predicates are indicated in the GUI.

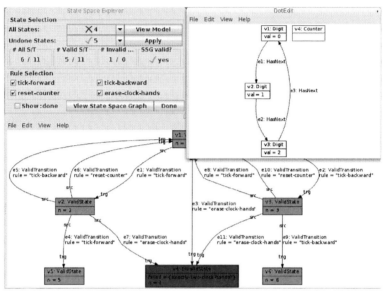

Figure 23.5: Screenshot of the `explore-state-space` GUI

The *State Selection* panel contains two combo boxes which allow the user to select a state for viewing a visualization of the selected state's model or for applying the transformation rules to the model of that state. The combo boxes for state selection use green checkmarks for valid states and red crosses for invalid states. When the mouse hovers over an invalid state, a tooltip displays the names of the invariants in :state-preds which returned false for the model corresponding to this state.

The window on the right visualizes the model corresponding to the invalid state number 4. This state is the result of applying the erase-clock-hands rule to the initial model, and as can be seen, the Counter vertex has no outgoing HasPrimaryDigit and HasSecondaryDigit edges anymore. Thus, the exactly-two-clock-hands? predicate fails which is the reason why this model is represented by an InvalidState vertex in the state space graph.

The bottom part of the panel displays some statistics about the current state space graph, i.e., the number of states and transitions, and if all state space predicates are satisfied by the current state space graph. Again, a green checkmark indicates that all predicates are satisfied, and a red cross would indicate that there are failing predicates which would be displayed in a tooltip.

The *Rule Selection* panel displays checkboxes for all rules which have been provided at the call to explore-state-space. Only the checked rules are considered when applying rules to the model corresponding to some state.

Below the rule selection panel, there is a button to view the current state space graph as shown in the lower window in the screenshot. Valid states are displayed with a green background and invalid states are displayed using a red background. If there were invalid transitions, those would be displayed in red, too. As can be seen from the value of the failed attribute, v4 is an invalid state because the invariant exactly-two-clock-hands? returns false when being applied to this state's model.

The checkbox *Show :done* toggles if the value of the states' done attribute should be displayed in the visualization. Because this makes the state visualizations very wide and thus degrades the layout, the option is disabled by default.

The *Done* button closes the GUI and makes explore-state-space return. The return value is a vector of the form [ssg s2m-map] where ssg is the state space graph and s2m-map is the state-to-model map assigning to state vertices the corresponding models. Like with create-state-space, the returned vector has the step-wise state space generation function used internally attached as :state-space-step-fn metadata.

Chapter 24

Related Work

In this chapter, several in-place transformation approaches are briefly discussed, and similarities and differences with FunnyQT's pattern matching and in-place transformation DSLs are revealed.

The Epsilon framework [Kol+15] supports defining patterns and in-place transformation rules using its *Epsilon Pattern Language* (*EPL*) which is a textual DSL. A pattern consists of a name, one or many element declarations called *roles*, and an optional *match expression*.

In the simplest form, each role consists of a variable and an element type meaning that the variable can be bound to any element in the model being an instance of this type. The match expression is a boolean EOL expression which may restrict the pattern by defining connection constraints or constraints on attribute values. In such a simple pattern, the match expression acts as a filter on the Cartesian product of all possible bindings of the declared variables which is obviously inefficient.

Therefore, the possible bindings of a role may additionally restricted using a *domain* and a *guard* both being EOL expressions. The domain must result in a collection of model elements of the role's declared type and only the elements of this collection are considered valid bindings of the role instead of all instances of the declare type. Usually, domain expressions navigate references of previously declared roles encoding a local search. The guard expression is evaluated once for every possible binding of a role, and only if its value is true, the binding is considered.

Roles can also be negated in which case they define a simple form of negative application conditions comparable to FunnyQT's negative edges. Furthermore, roles can be restricted with a cardinality consisting of a lower and an upper bound. Then, a role has valid bindings if and only if its domain's size fits into these bounds.

Roles may be declared as optional. In this case, if the pattern matches does not depend on the optional roles. If they have no possible binding with respect to their domains and guards, the pattern may still match. The optionality of a role may also depend on other roles, e.g., it is possible to declare that a role is optional if and only if some other role has found a match. This allows for defining alternatives similar to FunnyQT's alternative patterns. However with FunnyQT, the alternatives are complete subpatterns which may match arbitrary many elements instead of only one element.

Lastly, roles can be declared as active only in certain conditions like some other optional role having no binding. The difference between optional and inactive roles is that for the latter, it won't even be attempted to find a match whereas an optional role will always match if its domain contains an element satisfying its guard.

Patterns may also contain three special blocks containing EOL statements which effectively change a pattern from a querying construct to an in-place transformation rule. There may be an *onmatch* block which is invoked for every binding of the declared roles satisfying all guards and the match expression. There may also be a *nomatch* block which is invoked for all bindings of roles for which at least one guard or the match expression does not hold. These two blocks are called during the search, and their statements must not modify the model because this could break iterators. Finally, there may be a *do* block which has the same semantics as the onmatch block except that it is invoked after the search for all matches has already been finished. Here, EOL statements may be placed which actually change the model.

Patterns can be invoked in a one-off or an iterated manner. With the former, all matches are computed once (and then possibly acted upon), with the latter the process is repeated until no matches can be found anymore or a fixed upper bound of iterations has been performed. The one-off semantics correspond to FunnyQT's forall-rules and the iterated semantics correspond to repeating or iterating a forall-rule with the rule combinators `repeated-rule` or `iterated-rule`.

AGG [Tae03] is a general graph transformation approach closely following the algebraic approach to graph transformations [Cor+97; Ehr+97]. It uses the SPO approach by default but DPO can be enabled, too.

AGG has its own graph representation where graphs consist of nodes and directed arcs which are first-class objects. Both nodes and arcs may be typed and attributed where the typing may be defined either as simple sets of possible labels for nodes on the one hand and arcs on the other hand. Alternatively, a more strict typing which also specifies the allowed start and end node types for arcs of some type, a type graph may be defined which is a metamodel for a class of graphs. Multiple inheritance is supported for node types. One specialty of AGG is that the nodes and arcs of a graph may be attributed with arbitrary Java objects.

Transformation rules are defined visually with the left-hand side (LHS) and the right-hand side (RHS) being separated, and the morphism mapping elements of the LHS to elements of the RHS may be specified freely. For example, it is possible to define a non-injective morphism where multiple nodes of the LHS are mapped to one single node in the RHS which implies that these nodes are to be merged into one single node which takes over all incident edges. Aside from the structural condition implied by the LHS, attribute conditions and negative application conditions are supported but more advanced pattern matching concepts such as alternative or nested patterns are not.

Rules can be executed in two modes, the step mode and the interpretation mode.

In the step mode, the user can select one single rule and one of the rule's matches interactively and execute the rule on the selected match. In interpretation mode, a random applicable rule is selected and executed and this step is repeated until either no rule is applicable anymore or the user stops the process.

I simple form of control flow is enabled by layering where rules can be assigned to layers ≥ 0. With layered graph transformations, the rules of layer n are executed only after all rules of layer $n-1$ have become inapplicable. Furthermore, every layer may have exactly one trigger rule. If the trigger rule is not applicable, then all rules of this layer are skipped.

AGG allows also to define consistency constraints which are invariants that have to be satisfied by the initial graph under transformations and all graphs derived by rule applications. From these global consistency constraints, so-called post application constraints can be generated for selected rules. Such rules are only applicable if the graph after the rule's application still satisfies the constraint.

Furthermore, AGG supports critical pair analysis in order to show that a graph transformation system consisting of multiple rules is confluent [HKT02], i.e., no matter in which order the rules are applied to which matches, the final result graph is always the same.

For testing if a given graph is member of the possibly infinite set of graphs derivable by a graph grammar from a given initial graph, AGG provides a graph parser. In essence, this parser inverts all rules of the grammar[1] and then tries to derive the initial graph from the given one.

GROOVE[2] is a general graph transformation approach with a special emphasis on verification of graph transformations. GROOVE uses simple labeled graphs and the SPO approach for rewriting. Matching is performed non-injectively, i.e., distinct nodes in the pattern may be matched to the same node in the host graph but special edges labeled != may be inserted to define inequalities.

Rules are defined visually and the LHS and RHS of a rule are defined as single diagrams where colors specify which elements are to be preserved, deleted, or created.

GROOVE supports arbitrary constraints on attribute values, negative application conditions, and nested rules allowing to match and rewrite all occurrences of a subpattern in the context of a match of a surrounding pattern. Furthermore, GROOVE allows for regular expressions as edge labels which are similar to regular path expressions (see section 15.1 on page 147), e.g., an edge *-father+->* between two pattern nodes matches two nodes in the host graph which are connected by one edge with label *father* or a sequence of multiple such edges.

By default, all rules are applied to an initial graph in parallel and as long as possible leading to the state space induced by the initial graph and the set of rules. Rules can have priorities in which case rules with a lower priority are inapplicable as long as a rule with a higher priority is applicable (similar to AGG's layered approach). Additionally, there is a textual rule application language giving richer means for defining the control flow between rules.

---

[1] This is not feasible in the general case thus the graph parsing capability depends on the grammar.
[2] http://groove.cs.utwente.nl (last visited: 2015-10-05)

As mentioned, GROOVE focuses on verification of graph transformation systems. From a given initial graph and a set of rules, the state space can be generated and analyzed using a model checker which is able to verify properties expressed in *linear temporal logic (LTL)* or *computational tree logic (CTL)*.

A problem with state space analysis in general is that the number of states induced by a set of transformation rules and an initial graph is possibly unbounded. In [Gha+12], an abstraction concept of is introduced where parts of concrete graphs are aggregated in abstractions called shapes. Every node and every edge in a shape represents many concrete nodes and edges in the host graph. It can be shown that using these abstractions, the state space stays finite and a simple logic expressing certain properties on the graph's nodes is preserved.

Like AGG, GROOVE also supports checking the confluence of a graph transformation system using critical pair analysis.

SDMLib[3] [Eic+14] is a light-weight modeling framework implemented in Java with an emphasis on programming. It provides Java APIs with *fluent interfaces*[4] which allow to program metamodels. From these metamodels, code can be generated which in turn allows to program models conforming to these metamodels.

In addition to the model API, a metamodel-specific pattern matching API can be generated. In combination with the framework's standard pattern matching API, patterns can be constructed and evaluated in plain Java. Beside structural constraints, pattern may define attribute and cardinality constraints, negative application conditions, and subpatterns. Subpatterns may be declared as being optional. From every pattern it is possible to iterate all matches, thus when a pattern contains a subpattern from which all matches are retrieved, this is equivalent to nested patterns in FunnyQT.

Patterns may include calls to modification operations, i.e., for deleting matched elements, creating new elements, or setting attributes and references, thus turning a pattern into in-place transformation rules. Of course, in addition to these basic modification operations on matched elements, arbitrary Java methods may also be called.

Patterns and rules encoded in plain Java using the SDMLib API can be visualized in which case a rule is drawn as a kind of object diagram comprising both the LHS and the RHS where colors and stereotypes and further annotations indicate which elements are preserved, deleted, or created, and which parts of a pattern forms a NAC, an optional subpattern, or an iterated subpattern.

Henshin [Are+10; BET12] is a graph transformation language for EMF models. Transformations rules are specified as extended object diagrams using an Eclipse-based visual editor. Both the LHS and the RHS of a rule are drawn as one diagram and stereotypes and colors are used to define which elements are to be preserved, deleted, or created. For rewriting, the SPO and the DPO approach can be used and arbitrarily mixed on a per-rule basis. The injectivity of pattern matching, i.e., if two

---

[3]https://sdmlib.org/ (last visited: 2015-10-07)
[4]http://www.martinfowler.com/bliki/FluentInterface.html (last visited: 2015-10-07)

distinct elements in the pattern must be matched to distinct elements in the host graph, may also be defined on a per-rule basis.

Concerning pattern matching and transformation features, Henshin supports positive and negative application conditions, arbitrary constraints on attribute values (specified as JavaScript expressions), parametrization of rules, and nested rules. The latter implement a for-all semantics, i.e., for a match of the surrounding kernel rule, all matches of the nested rule are found and rewritten. This is very similar to FunnyQT's nested patterns. However, with nested patterns in FunnyQT, the action of a rule has access to all matches of the nested pattern whereas a nested rule in Henshin has a strictly local perspective. It has access only to the match of the surrounding pattern and the current match of the nested pattern.

The control flow between rules is also defined visually using different so-called units. Rules are units, too, and there are further units for sequential execution, conditional execution, execution by priorities, and iterated execution. Units may have parameters allowing to pass values from one unit to the next unit.

Henshin comes with an efficient interpreter engine and alternatively provides a code generator which emits Java code that utilizes Apache Giraph [5] for executing rules on large models in a distributed and massively parallel manner.

For verification purposes, Henshin provides configurable state space generation and analysis features with interfaces and exports to external tools. In the simplest case, invariants can be defined using OCL but more properties can be checked using external model checkers such as CADP[6], mCRL2[7], and PRISM[8].

For example, Henshin supports stochastic graph transformation systems as defined in [HLM06]. Here, rules model transitions between different states of a system, e.g., a formerly working connection between two nodes in a network goes down. Rules are annotated with rates expressing how frequently such transitions are to be expected. With such graph transformation systems, the state space analysis does not only enumerate all states which are possible given the set of rules but for every state, the likelihood of its occurrence is computed, too. A similar approach also supported by Henshin are probabilistic graph transformation systems [KG12] where a rule has one left-hand side and arbitrary many right-hand sides each associated with a given probability.

The pattern matching and in-place transformation features of FunnyQT and Henshin are quite similar. A prototypical translator from Henshin transformations to equivalent FunnyQT transformations has been developed[9]. This translator allows to define transformations using the visual Henshin editor in Eclipse and then export it to a transformation defined using the FunnyQT in-place transformation DSL.

GrGen.NET [Gei08; JBK10; JBG15] is a graph transformation approach with a special emphasis on graph rewriting in the context of compiler construction.

As its name suggests, GrGen.NET is based on the .NET platform. Therefore,

---

[5]http://giraph.apache.org/ (last visited: 2015-10-05)
[6]http://cadp.inria.fr/ (last visited: 2015-10-05)
[7]http://www.mcrl2.org/ (last visited: 2015-10-05)
[8]http://www.prismmodelchecker.org/ (last visited: 2015-10-05)
[9]https://github.com/jgralab/funnyqt-henshin (last visited: 2015-10-07)

it comes with its own metamodel and model representations and provides textual languages to define metamodels and models. The GrGen graph representation considers edges as first-class entities similar to JGraLab, i.e., edges are typed and may be attributed. The types of nodes and edges are modeled in a type graph as node and edge classes with their attributes, and multiple inheritance between node classes on the one hand and edge classes on the other hand is supported, too.

Rules are defined using a concise textual notation and, in the simplest case, consist of a pattern part and a rewriting part. The definition of stand-alone patterns for plain querying purposes is supported, too. By default, rewriting is performed according to SPO semantics but can be switched to DPO using a rule modifier. Additionally, it is also possible to require either only the identification or the dangling condition to be ensured and there is an additional exact matching mode which allows nodes to be matched only if all their incident edges are matched, too. Thus, the exact mode in essence enforces the dangling condition also for nodes which are not going to be deleted. Like with FunnyQT, GrGen.NET supports performing the pattern matching process in parallel for specifically annotated rules in order to increased efficiency.

GrGen.NET is very expressive and supports arbitrary constraints, negative and positive application conditions, and patterns may contain subpatterns. There are iterated subpatterns similar to FunnyQT's nested patterns, optional subpatterns, and alternative subpatterns. Every subpattern may define its own rewriting part.

In addition to usual graph rewriting, GrGen.NET allows for retyping both nodes and edges. The attributes and incident edges in the case of a retyped node which are allowed for both the old and the new type are retained.

Patterns and rules may be parametrized and they may define their return values similar to FunnyQT's custom match representations. Patterns and rules may call other patterns and rules, and defining recursive rules is possible.

GrGen.NET uses extended graph rewrite sequences (XGRS) for controlling rule executions. For example, if r, s, and t are rules, then r+ || s & t[2,17] executes r as long as possible but at least once. Only if r couldn't be applied at least once, then s and t (the latter at least twice and at most 17 times) are executed (|| is the short-circuiting logical OR), and the sequence yields success if both the executions of s and t[2,17] were successful (& is the non-short-circuiting logical AND). XGRS also supports assigning the results of a pattern or rule to a variable, and every rule can be called as a pattern in which case its matches are returned without performing the rule's rewriting step similar to FunnyQT's `as-pattern` rule application modifier.

Extra features provided by GrGen.NET are good graph visualizing capabilities, and a visual debugger for rules which allows for inspecting matches. Additionally, the execution of XGRS can be traced.

The new *VIATRA* (version 3, [Ber+15]) introduces itself as a platform for reactive model transformations where rules are triggered by events instead of being invoked explicitly. Such reactive transformations are enabled by VIATRA's event-driven virtual machine and executed continuously as reactions to changes applied to the underlying models.

A reactive transformation rule consists of at least two parts: a pattern describing a precondition and actions to be performed on events fired for occurrences of this pattern.

The patterns are defined using EMF-IncQuery which has already been discussed in chapter 19 starting on page 217. EMF-IncQuery is an incremental pattern matching approach, which means that all matches of a pattern are cached in a special data structure which is updated automatically whenever the model is changed. Therefore, all matches of all patterns are available at all times and appear or disappear as soon as a corresponding change in the model is performed.

Actions are specified using plain Xtend[10] code, thus like with FunnyQT, actions are not limited to performing changes on the model but they can do arbitrary computations.

There can be several different actions for each rule, each action being associated with a specific event. The supported events are *appearance*, i.e., a new match of the rule's pattern came into being, *disappearance*, i.e., the elements of a previous match have been deleted or modified in such a way that they form no match anymore, or *update*, i.e., the elements of a previous match have been updated in a way which make them stay a valid match of the rule's pattern.

With reactive transformations, rules are triggered by events instead of explicitly invoking them and there is a possibility that multiple rules are triggered for a given change in the model. VIATRA allows for defining custom conflict resolvers which select the rule to be executed next from the set of all activated rules. There are also several predefined resolvers implementing standard strategies such as FIFO, FILO, random choice, rule prioritization, or interactive selection by the user.

---

[10]http://www.eclipse.org/xtend/ (last visited: 2015-10-05)

Part VII

On Out-Place
Transformations

Summary

This part deals with the definition of out-place transformations which create new or populate existing target models based on given source models. First, chapter 25 starting on page 261 gives an introduction into the topic.

After the introduction, FunnyQT's two approaches for realizing such transformations are described. On the one hand, there is an embedded rule-based DSL discussed in chapter 26 starting on page 265, and on the other hand, there is an operational API discussed in chapter 27 starting on page 281 where the target model of a transformation is defined in terms of the extensions of its metamodel's constituents.

Finally, chapter 28 starting on page 301 closes this part with a discussion of the related work in this field.

Chapter 25

Introduction

In contrast to in-place transformations which modify a given model and have been discussed in part VI starting on page 221, out-place transformations are transformations between two or more models. In the case of two models, one model acts as the source model and is only queried while the other acts as the target model in which elements are created.

Frequently, the terms *model-to-model transformation* or just *model transformation* are used as a synonym for out-place transformations.

The classical scenario for out-place transformations as propagated by the Object Management Group[1] is illustrated in fig. 25.1.

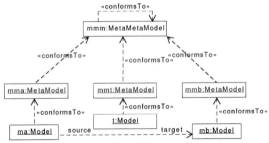

Figure 25.1: The classical out-place transformation scenario

At the bottom layer, there is a source model m_a and a target model m_b, and a transformation t which translates the source model to the target model. Usually, the metamodels of source and target model are different, i.e., mm_b is a different language than mm_b but they conform to the same metametamodel mmm. For example, if the metametamodel is Ecore, then the metamodels are Ecore models and the source and target models of the transformation are EMF models. Or if the metametamodel

[1]http://www.omg.org (last visited: 2015-05-21)

is grUML, then the metamodels are TGraph schemas, and the source and target models of the transformation are TGraphs.

In the figure, the transformation t is a model conforming to a transformation metamodel mm_t itself[2]. This is true for most model transformation approaches and it has the nice property that transformations can be subject to transformations themselves, i.e., transformations can be refactored by in-place transformations or transformations can be queried or produced by out-place transformations. However, this is not a strict requirement for transformations.

In contrast to the illustration in the figure, out-place transformations may have more than just one source and one target model.

A bidirectional transformation is also an out-place transformation. With respect to fig. 25.1 on page 261, a bidirectional transformation is a transformation where the transformation's direction can be switched. The model m_b can be produced from the model m_a but the reverse is also true. In this part, only unidirectional out-place transformations are considered while bidirectional transformations and their specification with FunnyQT are described in part IX starting on page 339.

FunnyQT provides two conceptually very different APIs for defining out-place transformations.

Chapter 26 starting on page 265 describes a typical rule-based approach for specifying model-to-model transformations. With this approach, a transformation consists of a set of rules. Every rule receives elements from a source model as inputs and creates elements in a target model as outputs. The applicability of rules can be restricted by specifying the allowed metamodel types of input elements and further constraints. For traceability purposes, the mapping from input to output elements is managed on a per-rule basis and can be used during and after the transformation execution.

Chapter 27 starting on page 281 describes an approach for defining model-to-model transformations using a concept of extensional semantics. Instead of having rules which produce output elements from input elements, there is a slim API which allows for specifying the extensions of metamodel constituents. The extension of an element class is its set of instances. For a relationship class, the extension is its set of instances plus an incidence function which assigns to each relationship its start and end element. And the extension of an attribute is just a function which assigns values to the elements or relationships for which this attribute is defined. Clearly, extensions cannot be specified directly but a concept based on archetype sets is used which also forms the traceability concept of the approach.

Both approaches have several properties in common. Transformations are functions, i.e., in contrast to the classical scenario illustrated in fig. 25.1 on page 261, a FunnyQT out-place transformation is not a model itself and thus cannot be subject to transformations. On the positive side, this means that there are no restrictions about what a transformation can do. If a transformation needs to query a database or communicate with some remote server, this can be done quite easily.

Support for multiple input and output models is also a feature supported by both

---

[2]In this case, the transformation is merely a specification which is executed by an interpreter or transformation engine.

approaches. And in contrast to the illustration in fig. 25.1 on page 261, the involved models don't need to be of the same modeling framework which implies that there doesn't need to be a unique metametamodel mmm as well. That is, it is perfectly possible to have a transformation which queries a TGraph and produces an EMF model or vice versa.

Also, both approaches don't create the target models. Instead, target models have to be provided and then are populated with new elements. Usually, empty models are provided as target models but it is also allowed to use existing, non-empty target models.

Chapter 26

Defining Rule-Based Transformations

The FunnyQT namespace `funnyqt.model2model` provides an embedded DSL for defining unidirectional out-place transformations similar in the style to well-known transformation languages such as ATL [Jou+08] or QVT Operational Mappings [OMG11b].

Transformations consist of a set of mapping rules which describe how source elements are to be translated to target elements, i.e., each rule takes one or many source model elements as input and produces one or many output elements in the transformation's target models. To initialize the references of a newly created target element, rules may call other rules. Frequently, the transformation traverses the containment hierarchy of the source models and thereby creates elements in the target models.

When a rule creates new target elements from source elements, the mapping is implicitly saved with respect to the rule and used during the transformation. The complete mapping is also the result of the transformation and can be used for traceability purposes once the transformation's execution has finished.

In the following, section 26.1 describes the rule-based out-place transformation DSL with all its details and then section 26.2 on page 276 gives an example. Appendix A.4 on page 426 gives insights on how this embedded DSL can be extended in order to add support for modeling frameworks other than JGraLab and EMF.

26.1 Transformation Definitions

A rule-based out-place transformation is defined using the `deftransformation` macro.

Macro: `funnyqt.model2model/deftransformation`
`(deftransformation name [args] extends-clause? & rules-and-functions)`

A transformation has a `name`, a vector of arguments `args`, an optional `extends-clause` which allows the defined transformation to inherit and override the rules of another transformation (see section 26.1.8 on page 275), and arbitrary many `rules-and-functions`.

The `deftransformation` macro expands to an ordinary Clojure function which implements the transformation. This function has the given `name` and `args` and is defined in the current namespace. When it is applied, it performs the transformation as specified by the transformation's rules and functions, and it returns the traceability mappings established by the transformation's rules. The details of the traceability mappings are going to be discussed in section 26.1.2 on page 268.

Usually, a transformation has at least one input and one output model. Those are declared as arguments in `args`. Thereby, the metadata annotations `^:in`, `^:out`, and `^:inout` are used to define which argument is an input, an output, or an input-output model. Here are some examples:

```
(deftransformation t1 [^:in m1 ^:out m2] ...)
(deftransformation t2 [^:in m1 ^:in m2 ^:out m3] ...)
(deftransformation t3 [^:inout m1 ^:out m2 x y] ...)
```

The transformation `t1` takes one input model and one output model. The transformation `t2` takes two input models `m1` and `m2` and creates elements in the single output model `m3`. The transformation `t3` takes two models `m1` and `m2` where `m1` serves both as input and output model, and `m2` is only an output model. Additionally, the transformation `t3` takes two additional arguments `x` and `y` which are not defined to be either input or output models.

A transformation with a model annotated with `^:inout` like `m1` in `t3` could be considered to be an in-place transformation at least in parts. In fact, the model `m1` can be queried and modified at the same time so it is an in-place transformation from a technical point of view. However, in contrast to the FunnyQT in-place transformation DSL discussed in part VI starting on page 221 which allows to match subgraphs in a model and replace them, the rule-based out-place transformation discussed here has only additive semantics, e.g., the transformation `t3` may query `m1` in order to create additional elements in it[1].

Note that FunnyQT out-place transformations do not instantiate output models. Instead, they have to be provided (as possibly empty models) when calling the transformation.

26.1.1 Mapping Rules

The most important constituents of a transformation are its mapping rules. The general syntax of such a rule is as follows:

```
(rule-name
 :from [...]
 :to   [...]
 body?)
```

---

[1]As will be discussed below, rules may have a body of arbitrary forms, so deletion of elements is actually possible. However, the rule-based out-place transformation API is intended and best suited for typical out-place transformation scenarios.

Every rule has a `rule-name`, a `:from` clause defining its input elements, i.e., the elements accepted by a rule, and a `:to` clause defining its output elements, i.e., the elements which are created by the rule. An optional `body` of arbitrary forms may be the last constituent of a rule definition.

When a rule is applied to some arguments, usually one or many source model elements, it is tested if the arguments are accepted by the rule's `:from` clause. If they are, target model elements are created as specified by the rule's `:to` clause. Thereafter, the rule's `body` is executed which has access to all input and output elements declared by the `:from` and `:to` clauses.

Most of the time, rules can be defined without providing a body because the `:to` clause already provides the means to create target model elements and to set their properties. However, the body can be used for auxiliary services, e.g., it can be used to log rule executions in some file or to visualize a target model (see section 15.3 on page 158) after the execution of a specific rule for debugging purposes. Additionally, it can be used gainfully with rules with input identities and disjunctive rules which are introduced in section 26.1.4 on page 270 and section 26.1.5 on page 273, respectively

Defining input elements. In the simplest case, a `:from` clause only defines the number of the rule's arguments and gives a name to them just like a plain Clojure function argument vector. For example, the clause `:from [a b c]` declares that the current mapping rule accepts exactly three arguments named a, b, and c. The arguments could be anything, i.e., they don't need to be model elements but could be strings, numbers, or any other JVM object as well.

However, usually a mapping rule accepts only model elements of a given metamodel type. For that purpose, a type specification (see concept 3 on page 109) may be following each argument. For example, the clause `:from [a 'A, x '[:or B C]]` defines that the rule accepts exactly two arguments a and x where a must be an instance of metamodel class A and x must be an instance of metamodel class B or C.

Rule definitions expand to local functions internally, so if a rule is called with a wrong number of arguments, an exception is thrown. In contrast, if a rule is called with the correct number of arguments but the provided arguments don't match the types declared in the `:from` clause, then the rule is called correctly but not applicable in which case it returns `nil`.

Defining output elements. The `:to` clause specifies which elements have to be created in the target model (or the target models) if the arguments given at a rule call match the rule's `:from` clause.

In the simplest case, the `:to` clause is vector of variable names paired with metamodel type names[2]. For example, the clause `:to [u 'U, v 'V]` defines that two output elements u and v have to be created in the target model where u has the target metamodel type U and v has the target metamodel type V.

---

[2]Type names can always be specified as qualified names (see concept 1 on page 108) and also as unique names (see concept 2 on page 108) in case the corresponding protocol is extended upon the interfaces or classes of the output model's modeling framework. This is true for the directly supported frameworks JGraLab and EMF.

Instead of providing the target metamodel type as a symbol, it is also allowed to specify an expression evaluating to a metamodel type or symbol denoting a target metamodel type name. E.g., :to [u 'U, v (choose-type s)] is a valid :to clause where the function call (choose-type s) returns a target metamodel based on s which could be a source model element matched by the :in clause.

In case a transformation has two or more output models, :in clauses can be used to define in which output model an element needs to be created. For example, the clause :to [u 'U :in out1, v 'V :in out2] again defines that two elements of the types U and V have to be created but u has to be created in the output model out1 and v has to be created in the output model out2. In this case, the models out1 and out2 have to be declared with ^:out or ^:inout metadata annotation in the transformation's argument vector as described on page 266.

If a transformation has multiple output models but there is no :in clause specified for an element in the :to clause, then the first output model is used as default.

It is also possible to set the newly created elements' attributes and references in the :to clause. For that purpose, an output element's specification may contain a property map from keywords denoting attribute and reference names to the values to be set for their attributes and references. This map must come after the output element's type and either before or after an :in clause. For example, the following hypothetical rule java-class2uml-class

```
(java-class2uml-class
 :from [jc 'JavaClass]
 :to   [uc 'UMLClass {
          :name (aval jc :name)
          :attributes (map field2attribute (adjs jc :fields))
        }])
```

creates a UMLClass element for any given JavaClass element. The map defines that the value of the name of the new UML class element should be set to the name of the corresponding Java class element, and the attributes reference should be set to the sequence of applying another rule, field2attribute, to the elements referenced by the Java class element's fields reference[3].

A rule's :to clause also defines its return value. If the rule's :to clause declares only one single output element, this element is the return value of the rule. If it declares many output elements, then a vector of output elements in the declaration order in :to is the return value.

Note that even if a rule has a body following the :to clause which may consist of arbitrary expressions, the rule's return value is still defined by the :to clause.

26.1.2 Traceability Mappings

Mapping rules implicitly create traceability relationships. When a rule gets applied to some input elements matching its :from clause, it creates output elements as declared by its :to clause, and the mapping from input elements to output elements

---

[3]See section 12.3 on page 111 for the aval function and section 12.4 on page 112 for the adjs function.

is saved. If it gets applied another time with the same input elements, it simply returns the output elements that have been created previously. Thus, both the creation of target elements and the resolution of source elements to target elements is performed by calling rules and rules define a one-to-one mapping between their inputs and outputs.

The complete traceability mappings of all rules are the return value of a transformation. The mappings are represented as a nested map where the outer map assigns rule names represented as keywords to that rule's traceability map, i.e., the traceability map has the following form:

```
{:rule1 {in1 out1, ...}              ;; single input / single output
 :rule2 {[inA inB] outA, ...}        ;; 2 inputs     / single output
 :rule3 {inU [outU outV], ...}       ;; single input / 2 outputs
 :rule4 {[inX inY] [outX outY], ...}} ;; 2 inputs     / 2 outputs
```

As can be seen, the structure of a rule's mappings depend on the number of input and output elements it declares in its :from and :to clauses. If the :from clause declares only one single element, then this element is used for the keys of the rule's traceability map. If it declares multiple input elements, a vector containing all of them in declaration order is used. The same applies to the values of a rule's traceability map, i.e., the values are either plain elements in case the rule has only one output element or the values are vectors of output elements if the rule has multiple output elements. In the latter case, the vector contains the elements in the declaration order in :to.

For example, the java-class2uml-class from the last section 26.1.1 on page 266 receives one single java class input element and creates one single UML class output element, thus its entry in the transformation's traceability map has the form {:java-class2uml-class {jc-1 uc-1, jc-2 uc-2, ...}}, i.e., it assigns to any input object jc-n being a JavaClass element a corresponding and newly created UMLClass output element uc-n.

In general, the traceability relationship of each rule of a transformation is an injective function, i.e., distinct inputs are translated into distinct outputs. The input of a rule is either one arbitrary object or a vector of two or more arbitrary objects. Likewise, the output of an applicable rule is either one target element or a vector of two or more target elements.

In section 26.1.4 on the following page, rules with input identities are introduced. Such rules define a custom rule-specific equality semantics on their inputs. If such a rule is called twice with distinct[4] inputs which however are equal according to the rule's custom equality semantics, then the second call returns the outputs that have been created on the first call. Thus, the traceability relationships of a rule with input identities is not necessarily injective anymore. It may map distinct inputs to the very same outputs.

---

[4]"distinct" in the sense of not identical.

26.1.3 Constraints and Local Bindings

While the :from clause of a mapping rule already allows for specifying constraints on the input elements' types, :when clauses can be used to define arbitrary constraints. A rule may possess multiple :when clauses and in order for a rule to be applicable to the given input elements, the expressions of all :when clauses must be true.

Local bindings can be established using :let clauses. The value of a :let clause is a vector of variables paired with expressions.

Lastly, there are :when-let clauses which combine local bindings with constraints. The value is a vector of variables paired with expressions just like with :let clauses, however the rule is only applicable if all expressions evaluate to a logically true value, i.e., all variables are bound to values which are neither nil nor false.

The following example rule member2male illustrates constraints and local bindings.

```
(member2male
 :from [m 'Member]
 :when (male? m)
 :let  [w (wife m)]
 :to   [p 'Male {:spouse (and w (member2female w))}]
```

This rule is only applicable to input elements m which are an instance of the metamodel class Member. Additionally, m must also satisfy the helper predicate male?. If so, the wife of m is computed by a helper function wife and bound to the local variable w. This variable is then used in the :to clause which creates an output element p of class Male and sets its spouse reference to the result of applying another rule member2female to the wife w but only if w is non-nil.

A mapping rule may have any number of :when, :let, and :when-let clauses. They are evaluated in their order of declaration and always after the :from clause and before the :to clause. Thus, any constraint or local binding may refer to variables bound by an earlier local binding clause or the :from clause but they cannot refer to the variables bound by the :to clause.

26.1.4 Input Identities

As described earlier, a rule creates output elements for any unique combination of input elements accepted by the rule. If it is called another time with the same input elements, the output elements created at the first call are returned instead of creating new element again. So by default, a rule returns for any valid input a new output and there is a one-to-one correspondence between valid inputs and outputs.

However, there are situations where distinct elements in the source models actually have the very same meaning and should be treated as if they were identical. For example, consider some UML class model has been extended independently by two developers and now a transformation should merge the two extended versions into a new class model which contains the union of all classes, associations, and attributes of the two extended versions. Of course, all classes which have been modeled in the base version already are contained in the two extended versions, too. However, they are represented as different model elements which are neither identical nor equal. Thus, when a normal mapping rule class2class was applied to a given class pkg.C in the first extended model and then to the same class in the other extended model, each call would result in the creation of a corresponding class in the output model.

Input identities allow for specifying rules which translate different inputs to the same (identical) outputs, i.e., for these rules there may be a many-to-one correspondence between the valid inputs and the outputs. One can think of input identities as a way to define custom equality semantics between input elements on a per-rule basis.

By using an input identity which is specified using an :id clause whose value is a vector of one variable and one expression which has access to all variables bound by the :from clause. The variable is bound to the value of the expression, and then different inputs to the rule are considered equal if and only if they result in the same value.

In our example, a transformation developer may define that two classes represent the very same thing if and only if their qualified name is equal, i.e., the identity of a class is its qualified name, as shown in the next example listing.

```
(class2class
 :from [ic 'UMLClass]
 :id   [qn (aval c :qualifiedName))
 :to   [oc 'UMLClass {:qualifiedName qn}])
```

In this case, the rule creates a class in the output model only once for every unique qualified name of a class in one of the input models. With respect to the example above, when the rule is called first with the class element with qualified name pkg.C from the first extended model, a corresponding output class oc is created. When the rule is called again with a different class element with the same qualified name from the second extended model, no further element is created in the target model but the element created at the first call is returned.

Rules with input identities also establish additional traceability mappings. Concretely, there is one mapping for any unique :id value the rule has been called with and there are additional mappings for all inputs having this identity, i.e., rules with input identities define many-to-one mappings. With respect to the example, the traceability map of the class2class rule might have the following structure.

```
{"pkg.C"        #<UMLClass@23>   ;; mapping for the id
 #<UMLClass@1> #<UMLClass@23>   ;; mapping for first element with id "pkg.C"
 #<UMLClass@2> #<UMLClass@23>   ;; mapping for second element with id "pkg.C"
 ...}
```

As can be seen, the rule maps at least two different model elements #<UMLClass@1> and #<UMLClass@2> to the very same output element #<UMLClass@23> and there is an additional mapping for the identity both input elements have in common, i.e., the string "pkg.C" denoting the qualified name of the classes #<UMLClass@1> and #<UMLClass@2>.

The class2class rule above lets us create one unique class element in the output model from any number of input class elements which are different but actually represent the same class. However, in our example scenario, the class pkg.C in the first model could have been extended with an additional attribute x, and in the second model it could have been extended with an additional attribute y. Therefore, the corresponding class element in the output model should have the union of the attributes defined by both representatives in the two input models.

For such kinds of problems, there is the :dup-id-eval option. If set to true, the rule's body is evaluated also for inputs which happen to have an :id value that has been encountered earlier. The :to clause is not evaluated, i.e., no new output elements are created. However, the output elements created at the first call are resolved and bound to the variables of the :to clause. Then, multi-valued properties of the outputs can be altered with the add-operations of FunnyQT's model management API in the rule's body instead of specifying them in the property maps of the output elements in the :to clause.

The following extended class2class rule gives an example.

```
(class2class
 :from [ic 'UMLClass]
 :id    [qn (aval c :qualifiedName))
 :dup-id-eval true
 :to    [oc 'UMLClass {:qualifiedName qn}]
 (add-adjs! oc :attributes (map attribute2attribute (adjs ic :attributes)))))
```

In contrast to the previous version, here the :dup-id-eval option is enabled. The qualified name of the output UMLClass element is again set using a property map in the :to clause of the rule. However, the attributes reference is altered only in the rule's body which will be run even for input elements ic which have an :id value which has been encountered before. Here, the list of elements referenced by oc's attributes reference gets added the elements returned by calling the attribute2attribute rule on any attribute of ic.

In the above example rule, the attributes created by the attribute2attribute rule, which is also assumed to be a rule with input identity, are simply added to the attributes reference of oc. If this is a correct approach depends on the target model. With EMF, most multi-valued references are defined to be unique, i.e., references are ordered but don't allow duplicates. In contrast, with JGraLab the above body can create parallel edges from some class element to some attribute element. So if the output model was a TGraph, the attributes returned by the map call would need to be filtered to those which aren't an attribute of oc already.

It should be noted that when a rule with input identity is able to retrieve an output element created earlier for some other element with the same :id value, no constraints (:when or :when-let) will be checked and no local bindings (:let) will be established anymore. This is partly for performance reasons but also has a semantic explanation: input identities define per-rule equality semantics, so if two different elements are to be considered equal by the rule, then it is a legitimate assumption that any expression on them must return the same value.

26.1.5 Disjunctive Rules

A special variant of rules are disjunctive rules. Instead of producing output elements themselves, they just delegate to other rules for this task.

A disjunctive rule has no :to clause but instead a :disjuncts clause. Its value is a vector of disjunct rules which may be ordinary rules or other disjunctive rules again. When a disjunctive rule gets called and is applicable with respect to its :from clause and its constraints, it tries to execute the disjunct rules one after the other until the first one succeeds. The value of the succeeding disjunct rule is the value of the disjunctive rule.

The next listing gives an example.

```
(member2person
 :from [m 'Member]
 :disjuncts [member2male member2female])
(member2male
 :from [m]
 :when (male? m)
 :to   [p 'Male])
(member2female
 :from [m 'Member]
 :when (not (male? m))
 :to   [p 'Female])
```

The member2person rule is a disjunctive rule dispatching between the ordinary rules member2male and member2female, i.e., if member2person is called with a Member element m, it tries to execute member2male first and if that fails, it tries to execute member2female.

The two disjunct rules member2male and member2female transform the given Member element either to a target Male or Female element depending on the value of (male? m).

Rule disjunction can be seen as a kind of rule inheritance where the disjunctive rule is a kind of super-rule for the disjunct rules. However, in contrast to typical inheritance scenarios, the dispatch doesn't need to be based on the input element's type but can also be based on constraints like above. Additionally, there might be multiple applicable disjunct rules but since the :disjuncts clause imposes an order, disjunct rules occurring earlier have a higher priority than later disjunct rules.

A disjunctive rule may bind the result of the disjunct rule which eventually succeeded using an :as clause which must be the very last item in the :disjuncts clause. This is convenient when the results of the disjunct rules are instances of some base class because it allows to set the base class properties in the disjunctive rule's body instead of duplicating the code in each disjunct rule.

For example, in the example above, the two disjunct rules create Male or Female elements which are subclasses of the metamodel class Person. Thus, all properties a Person may possess can be set in member2person as shown in the following redefinition of the rule.

```
(member2person
 :from [m 'Member]
 :disjuncts [member2male member2female :as p]
 (set-aval! p :fullName (str (aval m :firstName) " "
                             (aval (family m) :lastName))))
```

Here, the result of either `member2male` or `member2female` is bound to the variable `p` using an `:as` clause. In the disjunctive rule's body, the new person's full name is set instead of doing that in both `member2male` and `member2female`.

26.1.6 Local Helper Functions

Next to a transformation's rules, there may be local function definitions. Function and rule definitions may be arbitrarily mixed and can access each other regardless of declaration order. Functions are defined with the syntax of `letfn` (see page 37).

For example, the predicate `male?` already used above is defined as shown in the next listing.

```
(male? [m]
  (or (aval m :familyFather)
      (aval m :familySon)))
```

26.1.7 Top-level Rules and Main Functions

Above it has been discussed how a transformation's mapping rules and helper functions can be defined. Rules and functions can call other rules and functions, however until now, it hasn't been said which rules or functions get applied when a transformation is called initially.

There are two ways to define the entry points of a transformation: either by defining *top-level rules* or by defining a *main function*.

A top-level rule is a rule to whose name `^:top` metadata is attached. A transformation must have at least one top-level rule unless it has a main function. Top-level rules are restricted to have exactly one input element in their `:from` clauses. When the transformation is executed, all elements contained in the input models (the arguments declared with `^:in` or `^:inout` metadata) and matching at least one top-level rule's input element's type specification are applied to all top-level rules.

The following `example` transformation receives one input model `i`, one input-output model `io`, and one output model `o`.

```
(deftransformation example [^:in i ^:inout io ^:out o]
  (^:top rule-1
   :from [a 'A]
   ...)
  (^:top rule-2
   :from [b 'B]
   ...)
  ...)
```

The rules `rule-1` and `rule-2` are declared as top-level rules. Thus, when the transformation is invoked, both rules are applied to all elements of the models `i` and `io` which match the combined type specification [:or 'A 'B].

Alternatively, instead of annotating some rules as top-level rules, a `main` function of arity zero may be defined. This function is called automatically when the transformation is applied and is responsible to call the transformation's rules appropriately.

The `example` transformation above can be specified semantically equivalent using a `main` function as shown below.

```
(deftransformation example [^:in i ^:inout io ^:out o]
 (rule-1
  :from [a 'A]
  ...)
 (rule-2
  :from [b 'B]
  ...)
 (main []
  (doseq [input-models [i io]]
    (doseq [el (elements input-model [:or 'A 'B])]
      (rule-1 el)
      (rule-2 el)))))
```

Top-level rules are simpler, more concise, and more declarative whereas a transformation developer gains more control when using a main function. When a transformation contains both top-level rules and a main function, the latter takes precedence. This situation doesn't occur with a single transformation where one could always either remove the `^:top` metadata annotations or the `main` function but it can occur with transformation inheritance which is discussed in the next paragraph.

26.1.8 Transformation Inheritance

A transformation may extend one or many other transformations by specifying an `:extends` clause right after the vector of arguments. The value of this clause is either a symbol denoting the extended transformation's name or a vector of symbols in case multiple other transformations are to be extended as illustrated in the next listing.

```
(deftransformation extends-example-1 [...]
  :extends example-base
  ;; rules & functions
  )

(deftransformation extends-example-2 [...]
  :extends [example-base-1 example-base-2]
  ;; rules & functions
  )
```

The transformation `extends-example-1` extends some other transformation `example-base`. The transformation `extends-example-2` extends two other transformations `example-base-1` and `example-base-2`.

The effect of transformation inheritance is that the extending transformation contains the union of all the functions and rules of all extended transformation. The extending transformation may define additional rules and functions and it may override inherited rules and functions by defining new ones with the same name as the inherited ones.

Inherited top-level rules are top-level rules also in the extending transformation. In case this doesn't fit the intended semantics of the extending transformation, the latter should have a main function as entry point which may define the control flow appropriately and makes the top-level annotations of inherited rules ineffective.

In general, the argument vectors of the extending transformation should be compatible with the argument vectors of the extended transformation especially with respect to the order and the names of the input-output and output models. Remember that a clause `:to [a 'A, b 'B :in out2]` creates an A element in the first output model and a B element in the output model named `out2`. There are no such strict dependencies on the pure input models, however it is possible that input models are referenced by name in a rule's body, too. So it is advisable to have extending transformations re-use the argument vector of an extended transformation and append additional arguments to the end.

26.2 Example

In this section, the rule-based out-place transformation DSL is illustrated using a simple example transformation which translates a model conforming to the families metamodel shown in fig. 26.1 on the next page to a model conforming to the genealogy metamodel shown in fig. 26.2 on the facing page[5].

A FamilyModel contains Family and Member elements. Families carry the last name and address information, members only know about their first name. The different roles a member can have in a family are modeled via references. Every family has exactly one father and one mother, and there may be arbitrary many sons and daughters.

The target genealogy metamodel has a more tree-like structure. A Person has a full name and may be either a Male or a Female. Any person has at most two parents and may have an arbitrary number of children. Additionally, a male and a female may be liaised as indicated by the HasSpouse relationship class. Lastly, any person lives at exactly one Address.

The general correspondences between source and target metamodel are quite easy to see. Members correspond to persons, the different roles a member may

---

[5]This transformation is an extension of the ATL tutorial transformation available at `https://wiki.eclipse.org/ATL/Tutorials_-_Create_a_simple_ATL_transformation` (last visited: 2015-06-16). The transformation and the corresponding metamodels center around a very traditional family model which is simple and well-suited for illustration purposes but should not be advertised as being the right model in the real world.

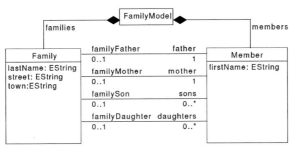

Figure 26.1: The source metamodel (Ecore)

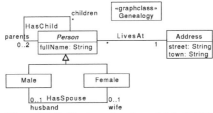

Figure 26.2: The target metamodel (grUML)

have in a family correspond to HasChild or HasSpouse relationships, and families
somehow correspond to addresses although there may be multiple families with the
same street and town attribute values which should still relate to one single Address.

Before illustrating the actual transformation from family models to genealogy
graphs, first some helper functions are introduced which aid in querying the source
model.

```
(defn family
  "Returns the main family of member m."
  [m]
  (or (adj m :familyFather) (adj m :familyMother)
      (adj m :familySon)    (adj m :familyDaughter)))

(defn male?
  "Returns true, iff member m is male."
  [m]
  (or (adj m :familyFather) (adj m :familySon)))

(defn parents
  "Returns the set of parent members of m."
  [m]
  (p-seq m
         [p-alt :familySon :familyDaughter]
```

```
      [p-alt :father :mother]))

(defn wife
  "Returns the wife member of member m."
  [m]
  (adj* m :familyFather :mother))
```

The family function receives a member and returns the family where this member is in a parental role. The male? predicate checks if the given member is male where a member is considered to be male if and only if he is either a father or a son of some family. The parents helper returns the (at most two) members which are the parents of the given member using a regular path expression (see section 15.1 on page 147). Lastly, the wife function returns the member being the wife of the given member.

Using these helpers, the actual transformation definition is very simple. The transformation families2genealogy has two arguments: an input model families conforming to the metamodel from fig. 26.1 on page 277 and an output model genealogy conforming to the metamodel from fig. 26.2 on page 277.

```
(deftransformation families2genealogy
  "Transforms a family model to a genealogy model."
  [^:in families ^:out genealogy]
  (^:top member2person
   :from [m 'Member]
   :disjuncts [member2male member2female :as p]
   (set-aval! p :fullName (str (aval m :firstName) " "
                               (aval (family m) :lastName)))
   (set-adj! p :address (family2address (family m)))
   (set-adjs! p :parents (map member2person (parents m))))
  (member2male
   :from [m 'Member]
   :when (male? m)
   :let [w (wife m)]
   :to [p 'Male {:wife (member2female (wife m))}])
  (member2female
   :from [m 'Member]
   :when (not (male? m))
   :to [p 'Female])
  (family2address
   :from [f 'Family]
   :id [st [(aval f :street) (aval f :town)]]
   :to [adr 'Address {:street (first st), :town (second st)}]))
```

The transformation's rules are explained in order of increasing complexity. The member2female rule receives a member m, and if that member is not male, it creates and returns a new female element p.

The member2male rule is very similar except that when creating a new target male element for a given male member, the male's wife is also set by applying the member2female rule to the member's wife[6] and assigning the result.

---

[6]The member2person rule could have been used here, too.

The `member2person` rule is a disjunctive rule which receives a member `m` and then applies the first matching rule in the given `:disjuncts` vector, i.e., it applies either `member2male` or `member2female`. The result of the matching disjunct rule is bound to the variable `p` using an `:as` clause. This variable is then used in the rule's body in order to set all attributes and references males and females have in common. One of these common properties is the address a person lives at. This role is set to the value returned by applying the `family2address` rule to the member's main family.

The `family2address` rule transforms families to addresses. There can be multiple families with the same street and town attribute values, i.e., families living at the same address. However, the Address elements in the target genealogy model should be unique. For this purpose, the rule defines an input identity which specifies that two families should be considered equal by the rule if they have the same street and town values. Note that the input identity value is bound to the variable `st` and then accessed later in the property map in the `:to` clause.

Chapter 27

Defining Extensional Transformations

The out-place transformation DSL discussed in the previous chapter supported specifying transformations as a set of rules. Each rule takes one or many source model elements optionally restricted by type and arbitrary constraints and translates them to one or many corresponding target model elements. Thereby, the rule also sets the properties of the new target elements.

In contrast, the transformation approach discussed in this section is not rule-based at all. Instead, it provides a small set of operations which let the transformation developer specify the target model of a transformation in terms of the extensions of its metamodel's constituents.

With such a viewpoint of *extensional semantics*, a metamodel defines the set of possible instance models that may exists. Every class defined in a metamodel stands for a set of instances of that class in a concrete model. An abstract class defines that at all times, the set of this class' instances is the union of all subclass instances. Likewise, an attribute of a class stands for a function which assigns to every instance of this class a corresponding value of the domain defined by the attribute's type. That is, a model is just one specific extension of a metamodel, i.e., for every class defined by the metamodel there is a concrete set of instances, and for any attribute declared for a metamodel class, the corresponding instances have one concrete value.

The out-place transformation API provided by the funnyqt.extensional namespace provides functions that let the transformation writer define one specific target model in terms of the extensions of its metamodel constituents. The metamodel constituents to be considered are element classes, attributes, and either relationship classes or references depending on which flavor of linking elements is supported by a concrete modeling framework. Additionally, the generalization hierarchy has to be considered because a property defined for a metamodel element or relationship class is implicitly also part of its subclasses.

Furthermore, this extensional transformation API forms the instance-only transformation part of the co-evolution transformation API which will be discussed in part X starting on page 375. These transformations enable the simultaneous evolution of a metamodel and a conforming model at runtime.

In the following, section 27.1 formally defines the relevant metamodel constituents and their respective extensions. It is shown that each model can be specified unambiguously on a per-constituent basis. Then, section 27.2 on page 284 shows how the extensions of each metamodel constituent can be specified, and section 27.3 on page 285 describes the traceability concept of the extensional transformation approach. The concrete functions provided by the API are introduced in section 27.4 on page 287, and lastly, section 27.5 on page 294 discusses an example transformation.

How the extensional transformation API can be extended in order to support models of different kinds than JGraLab and EMF is explained in appendix A.5 on page 426.

27.1   Metamodel Constituents and Their Extensions

As said above, a metamodel consists of element classes which may possess attributes and either the elements classes declare references or there are explicit relationship classes. In the latter case, also the relationship classes may possess attributes and there may be generalizations between element classes on the one side and relationship classes on the other side.

Formally, let

- $Element$ be a universe of elements,
- $Relationship$ be a universe of relationships,
- $TypeId$ be a universe of type identifiers,
- $PropId$ be a universe of property identifiers, and
- $Value$ be a universe of attribute values.

Then, a model M can be defined as

$$M = \begin{cases} (E, R, inc, type, value) & \text{if } M \text{ has first-class relationships, e.g., a TGraph} \\ (E, type, ref, value) & \text{if } M \text{ has only references, e.g., an EMF model} \end{cases}$$

where

(i) $E \subseteq Element$ is an *element set*,

(ii) $R \subseteq Relationship$ is a *relationship set*,

(iii) $inc : R \to E \times E$ is an *incidence function* assigning to each relationship its source and target element,

(iv) $type : E \cup R \to TypeId$ is a *typing function* assigning to each element or relationship its type,

(v) $ref : E \to (PropId \to \{\langle e_1, e_2, \dots \rangle \mid e_i \in E\}$ where $\forall x, y \in E : type(x) = type(y) \implies dom(ref(x)) = dom(ref(y))$ is a *reference function* assigning to each element a function which assigns a sequence of referenced elements to each defined reference, and

(vi) $value : E \cup R \to (PropId \to Value)$ where $\forall x, y \in E \cup R : type(x) = type(y) \implies dom(value(x)) = dom(value(y))$ is an *attribute function* assigning to each element and relationship a function which assigns a value to each attribute defined for the type of the element or relationship.

It must also hold that $\forall e \in E : dom(ref(e)) \cap dom(value(e)) = \emptyset$, i.e., there mustn't be a property identifier which is used as both a reference and an attribute name.

Further constraints are imposed by the metamodel. The available element and relationship types are defined including their generalization hierarchies, the source and target element types of all relationship types are defined, the available reference and attribute names are defined on a per-type basis, the types of attributes and references are defined, and for references also their cardinality is restricted (essentially single-valued or multi-valued). So for example, the *inc* function is restricted such that it ensures that only direct or indirect instances of the defined source and target element class are assigned as source and target element of some relationship. Likewise, the *ref* function has to be restricted with respect to the type of the reference, and in case of a single-valued reference, it must assign only sequences of length zero or one[1].

The idea of the extensional transformation is to define the target model according to the above definition. That is, if the target model is a real graph with first-class relationships (e.g., a TGraph), the five components $(E, R, inc, type, value)$ have to be specified. If the target model is an object network with only references (e.g., an EMF model), the four components $(E, type, ref, value)$ have to be specified.

In [EH14; HE11], it has been shown that this can be done in a *compositional* way by specifying the *extension* of each metamodel constituent separately. These constituents are element classes, either relationship classes (including the incidence functions) or references, and attributes.

Let *ElementClass* and *RelationshipClass* be the sets of element and relationship classes defined by a metamodel, and let $subtypes^* : ElementClass \cup RelationshipClass \rightarrow \mathcal{P}(ElementClass) \cup \mathcal{P}(RelationshipClass)$ be a reflexive function assigning to each metamodel type the set containing the type itself and all its direct or indirect subtypes. Of course, for an element class it returns a set of element classes and for a relationship class, it returns a set of relationship classes.

Then, the extensions of the metamodel constituents in a model M are simple mathematical objects, namely sets and functions.

(1) There is a set $E_{ec} \subseteq E$ for every $ec \in ElementClass$ containing the direct instances of ec.
(2) There is a set $R_{rc} \subseteq R$ for every $rc \in RelationshipClass$ containing the direct instances of rc. Assuming that rc is defined with source element class sec and target element class tec, there is an incidence function

$$inc_{rc} : R_{rc} \rightarrow \bigcup_{sec^* \in subtypes^*(sec)} E_{sec^*} \times \bigcup_{tec^* \in subtypes^*(tec)} E_{tec^*}$$

assigning each relationship of type rc a source and a target element which is a direct or indirect instance of the declared source element class sec or target element class tec, respectively.

---

[1] In practice, the value of multi-valued references is a list of elements whereas the value of a single-valued references is either nil or an element and not an empty sequence or a sequence containing just one element. However, formalizing this distinction would require many additional definitions by cases without providing any benefit.

(3) For every reference r defined by the element class ec with target element class tec, there is a function

$$ref_r : \bigcup_{ec^* \in subtypes^*(ec)} E_{ec^*} \to \{\langle e_1, e_2, ... \rangle \mid e_i \in \bigcup_{tec^* \in subtypes^*(tec)} E_{tec^*}\}$$

which assigns to direct or indirect instances of element class ec the sequence of referenced elements. Those need to be direct or indirect instances of the target element class tec.

(4) For every attribute a defined by element or relationship class xc with value type $Domain_a \subset Value$, there is a function

$$value_a : \begin{cases} \bigcup_{xc^* \in subtypes^*(xc)} E_{xc^*} \to Domain_a & \text{if } a \text{ is an element class attribute} \\ \bigcup_{xc^* \in subtypes^*(xc)} R_{xc^*} \to Domain_a & \text{if } a \text{ is a relationship class attribute} \end{cases}$$

which assigns to direct or indirect instances of element or relationship class xc an attribute value complying with the declared type $Domain_a$ of attribute a.

Of course, (2) only applies to models with first-class edges, and (3) only to models with references.

Given these sets and functions, a corresponding model $M = (E, R, inc, type, value)$ or $M = (E, type, ref, value)$ is uniquely determined with

(i) $E = \bigcup_{ec \in ElementClass} E_{ec}$,

(ii) $R = \bigcup_{rc \in RelationshipClass} R_{rc}$,

(iii) $inc = \bigcup_{rc \in RelationshipClass} inc_{rc}$,

(iv) $type : E \cup R \to TypeId$ with (a) $\forall e \in E : type(e) = ec \iff e \in E_{ec}$ and (b) $\forall r \in R : type(r) = rc \iff r \in R_{rc}$,

(v) $ref : E \to (PropId \to \{\langle e_1, e_2, ... \rangle \mid e_i \in E\})$ with $\forall e \in E : ref(e)(r) = refed \iff ref_r(e) = refed$ for all references r, and finally

(vi) $value : E \cup R \to (PropId \to Value)$ with $\forall x \in E \cup R : value(x)(a) = v \iff value_a(x) = v$ for all attributes a.

Again, (ii), (iii), and (iv b) are relevant only for models with first-class relationships whereas (v) is only relevant for models with references.

27.2   Indirect Specification of Extensions

In the previous section, it has been shown that a model can be uniquely determined by defining the extensions of its metamodel's constituents and those are just simple mathematical objects, i.e., sets and functions. Therefore, one operation for each kind of metamodel constituent is needed and actually provided by the `funnyqt.extensional` namespace.

`create-elements!` defines the extension E_{ec} of an element class ec.

`create-relationships!` defines the extension R_{rc} of a relationship class rc together with the corresponding incidence function inc_{rc}.

`set-adjs!` defines the extension of a reference r, i.e., it defines the function ref_r.

`set-avals!` defines the extension of an attribute a, i.e., it defines the function $value_a$.

These operations are discussed in detail later in section 27.4.3 on page 290.

Because the extension of, e.g., an element class, is its set of direct instances, the extensions cannot be specified directly. Because the intention of `create-elements!` is to create elements of some given element class, the existence of these elements must not be a prerequisite. Instead, the extensional transformation approach uses a concept of *archetypes* and *images* in order to specify the extensions of element and relationship classes indirectly:

When defining the extension E_{ec} of an element class ec with `create-elements!`, a function returning a set of archetypes is provided and for each such archetype, one element of type ec is created in the target graph of the transformation. Likewise, when defining the extension of a relationship class rc with `create-relationships!`, a function returning a set of triples (a, s, t) is provided where a denotes an archetype for a new relationship and s and t denote the source and target element of the new relationship and thereby encode the inc_{rc} function. The newly created elements and relationships are called the images of their corresponding archetypes in this context.

In both cases, archetypes can be arbitrary objects (but not `nil`). In many typical transformation scenarios, the archetypes are elements which are queried from the source model or set of source models but this is no requirement. They can also be numbers, strings, collections, etc[2].

As an example, if the `create-elements!` operation was called with an element type X and an archetype set $\{1, 2, 3\}$, three new elements x_1, x_2, and x_3 of type X would be created in the target model. One is the image of the archetype 1, one is the image of the archetype 2, and the last one is the image of the archetype 3. If then the `create-relationships!` operation was called with the relationship type Y and the set of triples $\{("a", x_1, x_2), ("b", x_1, x_3)\}$, two new relationships y_1 and y_2 were created where one is the image of the archetype `"a"` (a string) and one is the image of the archetype `"b"`. The new relationship being the image of `"a"` starts at x_1 and ends at x_2, and the new relationship being the image of `"b"` starts at x_1, too, and ends at x_3.

27.3 Traceability

When defining the extensions of element and relationship classes using `create-elements!` and `create-relationships!`, traceability mappings are automatically instantiated. Concretely, when defining the extension of an element or relationship class xc, the two functions

---

[2]The only technical requirement is that they must be valid keys in hashed collections, i.e., their hash code must not change during the transformation.

$$img_{xc} : Object_{xc} \xrightarrow{\ 1:1, onto\ } E_{xc} \cup R_{xc}$$
$$arch_{xc} = img_{xc}^{-1}$$

are defined. Here, the domain $Object_{xc} \subset Object$ denotes the sets of archetypes which have actually been used as archetypes for the element or relationship class xc. The img functions assign to each archetype the corresponding image and the $arch$ functions are simply the inverse functions. They are trivially bijections because one image is created for each object in a set of archetypes, so there is a one-to-one correspondence out of construction.

The img_{xc} and $arch_{xc}$ functions allow for a bidirectional, unambiguous navigation between archetypes and images of an element or relationship class xc.

The incidence functions inc_{rc} for relationship classes, the reference functions ref_r, and the attribute functions $value_a$ all have to consider the generalization hierarchy of the element and relationship classes defined by the metamodel. For example, if an attribute a is defined for an element class ec, then the corresponding $value_a$ function assigns a value to each direct or indirect instance of ec because the attribute is inherited by all subclasses, too. In order to make use of the traceability functions also in such cases, two more traceability functions are defined.

Concretely, for an element or relationship class xc, the generalization-aware traceability functions $image_{xc}$ and $archetype_{xc}$ are defined:

$$image_{xc} : Object_{xc} \xrightarrow{\ 1:1, onto\ } \bigcup_{xc^* \in subtypes^*(xc)} E_{xc^*} \cup R_{xc^*}$$
$$image_{xc} = \bigcup_{xc^* \in subtypes^*(xc)} img_{xc^*}$$
$$archetype_{xc} = image_{xc}^{-1},$$

These traceability functions must also be bijections in order to guarantee bidirectional, unambiguous navigation between archetypes and images of an element or relationship class including all its subclasses. This implies that all archetype sets used for creating instances of classes in a complete generalization hierarchy have to be disjoint, i.e.,

$$\forall xc \in ElementClass \cup RelationshipClass :$$
$$\forall xc_1^*, xc_2^* \in subtypes^*(xc) : dom(img_{xc_1^*}) \cap dom(img_{xc_2^*}) = \emptyset.$$

This is a quite sharp constraint which is enforced by the implementation. But the extensional transformation API also provides some macros which allow to circumvent this restriction for parts of a transformation (see section 27.4.2 on page 288).

27.4 Extensional Transformation Constructs

In this section, the actual functions and macros provided by the `funnyqt.extensional` namespace are discussed and related with the formal definitions of the previous sections. These functions and macros can be categorized into three groups. First, there are functions for accessing the traceability information (section 27.4.1), then there are macros for controlling which traceability information is captured (section 27.4.2 on the following page), and lastly there are the actual transformation operations which define the target model in terms of the extensions of its metamodel's constituents (section 27.4.3 on page 290).

27.4.1 Traceability Resolution

The `image` function resolves an image from a given archetype `arch` in the trace mappings of some given metamodel class `cls` and its subclasses. If there's no image for the given archetype, it returns `nil`.

The `archetype` function is `image`'s inverse counterpart, that is, it looks up the archetype of some given image with respect to some target metamodel class and its subclasses. If there is no archetype, it returns `nil`[3].

Function: funnyqt.extensional/image
(image cls arch)
(image m cls arch)

Function: funnyqt.extensional/archetype
(archetype cls img)
(archetype m cls img)

`cls` may be given as an actual metamodel class, i.e., a JGraLab VertexClass, EdgeClass, or an EMF EClass, or it may be given as a symbol denoting the qualified or unique name of the metamodel class. In the latter case, the target model m has to be given in order to access the metamodel.

The `image` and `archetype` functions correspond to the *image* and *archetype* functions defined formally above, i.e., (image m 'SomeClass arch) is $image_{SomeClass}(arch)$.

The functions `image-map` and `archetyp-map` return the complete traceability maps from archetypes to images or from images to archetypes with respect to the given metamodel class and all its subclasses.

Function: funnyqt.extensional/image-map
(image-map cls)
(image-map m cls)
Function: funnyqt.extensional/archetype-map
(archetype-map cls)
(archetype-map m cls)

Again, `cls` may be given as actual metamodel class or as symbol denoting the class' qualified or unique name. In the latter case, the target model m whose metamodel defines the class must be provided.

The `image-map` and `archetype-map` functions also correspond exactly to the *image*

---

[3]This might happen when a transformation is applied to a model which already contains elements and relationships, or if elements or relationships were created without recording traceability information or discarding it (see the next paragraph).

and $archetype$ functions defined formally above, i.e., (image-map m 'SomeClass) is $image_{SomeClass}$.

The difference between image and image-map (and analogously archetype and archetype-map) is the following. Internally, FunnyQT only maintains the img_{xc} and $arch_{xc}$ functions which only map to or from direct instances of the element or relationship class xc. In contrast, the resolution functions image and image-map and their inverse counterparts do consider the inheritance hierarchy. Whereas image immediately returns when the image of the given archetype has been found, image-map constructs and returns a complete map from archetypes to images for the given class and all transitive subclasses. Thus, when an looking up a single image for an archetype, image is to be preferred. In contrast, when resolution of images of many archetypes is intended, retrieving the image-map and then looking up all images in that is preferred. Most importantly, because image-map returns a map, one can easily iterate over the keys (the archetypes), the values (the images), or the entries (tuples of archetypes with images).

There are some more shorthand resolution functions which are only bound in the context of some of the extensional transformation operations. These operations are going to be discussed in section 27.4.3 on page 290 where the shorthand resolution functions are introduced, too.

27.4.2 Traceability Capturing

The   actual   extensional   transformation   operations   create-elements!, create-relationships!, set-adjs!, and set-avals! rely on some internal traceability mapping data structures to be instantiated. This can be done using either the with-trace-mappings or the ensure-trace-mappings macro.

The former macro and the macro without-trace-recording introduced at the end of this subsection also allow for working around the restriction of disjointness of all archetypes used for creating elements of one generalization hierarchy (see section 27.3 on page 285). This is discussed at the end of this section.

The macro with-trace-mappings establishes new, empty traceability mappings and then executes its body which consists of calls to the extensional transformation operations[4].

Macro: funnyqt.extensional/with-trace-mappings
(with-trace-mappings & body)

Therefore, an extensional transformation usually has the following shape.

```
(defn example-transformation [source-model target-model]
  (with-trace-mappings
    ;; calls to the extensional transformation functions discussed in the
    ;; next section.
    ))
```

---

[4]It may also contain arbitrary other code.

A transformation is a plain Clojure function that receives a source and a target model[5]. The function establishes new traceability mappings which are required by the extensional transformation operations which are going to be discussed in section 27.4.3 on the following page. Calls to those are then performed in the with-trace-mappings' body and populate the internal traceability mapping data structures.

Similar to with-trace-mappings is the ensure-trace-mappings macro. If there are already traceability mappings available in the current dynamic scope (see section 6.5 on page 38), then it just executes body. That is, the operation calls in the body populate the traceability mappings of the surrounding scope. If there are no traceability mappings available, it is equivalent to with-trace-mappings.

Macro: funnyqt.extensional/ensure-trace-mappings
(ensure-trace-mappings & body)

This is useful when a larger transformation should be structured into several smaller transformations which may also be used separately.

```
(defn t-part-1 [in out]
  (ensure-trace-mappings ...))

(defn t-part-2 [in out]
  (ensure-trace-mappings ...))

(defn t-complete [in out]
  (with-trace-mappings
    (t-part-1 in out)
    (t-part-2 in out)))
```

The transformation functions t-part-1 and t-part-2 can be used separately but also be called from some other transformation like t-complete. In the latter case, the traceability mappings of the calling transformation are simply reused, i.e., the extensional transformation functions called in t-part-1 and t-part-2 add to the mappings of t-complete.

The macro without-trace-recording allows to execute its body without having the transformation operation calls contained in it add additional traceability mappings. However, the mappings of the surrounding scope can still be accessed using image and image-map and their inverse counterparts.

Macro: funnyqt.extensional/without-trace-recording
(without-trace-recording & body)

This macro allows to circumvent the restriction that all archetypes used for specifying the extensions of the metamodel classes in one generalization hierarchy have to be disjoint (see section 27.3 on page 285). But of course, resolving the elements created using the extensional transformation functions in the body using their archetypes is not possible, too. Their traceability mappings are simply discarded.

Another means to circumvent the restriction is to wrap the parts of a transformation which create elements with archetypes having already been used for

---

[5]In fact, there could be zero or many source models and one or many target models.

other elements with `with-trace-mappings`. In that case, resolving elements by their archetypes that have been created previously in this `with-trace-mappings` form is possible, however the traceability mappings of the surrounding scope are inaccessible.

27.4.3   Extensional Transformation Functions

As shown in section 27.1 on page 282 and section 27.2 on page 284, every model can be specified uniquely by four operations. There is one operation `create-elements!` for defining the extension of an element class, one operation `create-relationships!` for defining the extension of a relationship class including the corresponding incidence function, one operation `set-adjs!` for defining the extension of a reference, and one operation `set-avals!` for defining the extension of an attribute.

The `create-relationships!` operation is only supported for models with first-class relationships (e.g., TGraphs). The `set-adjs!` operation is only supported for models with references (e.g., EMF models). Some kinds of models support both. With TGraphs, edge classes may have role names which provide a reference-like view for visiting adjacent vertices which internally translates to traversal of incident edges, so `set-adjs!` is supported, too, and it implies creation of edges and thus is equivalent to a `create-relationships!` call. There might be future modeling frameworks which support both first-class relationships and references where the latter is not just a view on the former but a different concept. Here, both operations could be supported, and then there is no equivalence between them.

In the following paragraphs, the actual extensional transformation operations are discussed in detail.

Creating elements.   The `create-elements!` function creates new elements of the element class provided as argument `cls` in the model `m`. The `cls` may be given as an actual element class defined by `m`'s metamodel or as a symbol denoting the qualified or unique name of such an element class.

Function: `funnyqt.extensional/create-elements!`
`(create-elements! m cls archfn)`

The argument `archfn` is a function of zero parameters which will be evaluated internally and must result in a collection of arbitrary archetypes, i.e., arbitrary objects. This collection is taken as a set and one element of type `cls` is created in the model `m` for each of the set's objects. The return value of the function is the sequence of newly created elements, i.e., the images of the archetypes.

The traceability mappings from archetypes to images and the inverse mappings are implicitly captured and accessible in the following operation calls in terms of the traceability resolution functions `image`, `image-map`, `archetype`, and `archetype-map` that have been discussed in section 27.4.1 on page 287.

The `archfn` only needs to return an arbitrary collection of archetypes instead of a set of archetypes. This fact is only for convenience because almost all Clojure collection functions are based on the sequence abstraction. However, the collection must contain no duplicates in order to guarantee an unambiguous resolution from archetypes to images and vice versa. In case the collection contains some object more than once or in case it contains an object for which an image already exists with respect to the given `cls` or one of its super- or subclasses, an exception is thrown as shown by the following example.

```
;; Create 10 TargetClass elements for the archetypes 0 to 9.
(create-elements! m 'TargetClass (fn [] (range 10)))
;=> (#<TargetClass> ...)
;; Try creating two more elements for the archetypes 0 and 1.
(create-elements! m 'TargetClass (fn [] [0 1]))
; Exception: Bijectivity violation: the archetypes (0 1) are already contained
; in the domain of *img* for class TargetClass or a sub- or superclass thereof.
```

This restriction on disjointness of archetypes can be relaxed using the macros introduced in section 27.4.2 on page 288. If the second `create-elements!` call was wrapped in either `with-trace-mappings` or `without-trace-recording`, two more Target-Class elements would be created successfully. With `with-trace-mappings`, the trace-ability mappings would be added to new, empty traceability maps which were only accessible in this `with-trace-mappings`' scope. With `without-trace-recording`, the image and archetype mappings wouldn't be recorded altogether.

Creating relationships. The `create-relationships!` function creates new relationships of relationship class `cls` in the model `m`. Like with `create-elements!`, the class may be an actual relationship class or a symbol denoting its qualified or unique name. The function's return value is the sequence of newly created relationships.

Function: funnyqt.extensional/create-relationships!
```
(create-relationships! m cls archfn)
```

As shown in section 27.1 on page 282, the extension of a relationship class is its set of instances. Additionally, a type-specific incidence function assigning to each relationship its start and end element has to be defined. These two constituents are combined here. The given `archfn` must be a function of zero arguments which evaluates to a collection of triples of the form [arch start-el end-el] where arch is an arbitrary object used as archetype for the new relationship and start-el and end-el are the start and end element of the new edge.

The mappings from archetypes to images and vice versa are again captured implicitly and are accessible in following operation calls using the standard resolution functions introduced in section 27.4.1 on page 287.

In the context in which `archfn` is evaluated, the following two additional resolution functions are bound.

Function: funnyqt.extensional/source-image
```
(source-image source-arch)
```
Function: funnyqt.extensional/target-image
```
(target-image target-arch)
```

Both return the image of a given archetype or `nil` if there is none. Hereby, `source-image` performs the lookup with respect to the current relationship class' source element class and `target-image` considers the relationship class' target element class.

For example, if the metamodel defines a relationship class A2B starting at the element class A and ending at the element class B, then the call

```
(create-relationships! m 'A2B
  (fn []
    (for [x2y (relationships source-model 'X2Y)]
      [x2y (source-image (source x2y)) (target-image (target x2y))])))
```

creates one A2B relationship for each X2Y relationship in the source-model where the relationship's source and target elements are the images of the corresponding source and target vertices in the source-model. I.e., (source-image el) is a shorthand for (image m 'A el) and (target-image el) is a shorthand for (image m 'B el).

Setting attribute values.   The set-avals! function sets the value of the given attr defined for metamodel class cls for direct and indirect instances of that class in the model m. The attribute name attr is given as keyword and the class cls may again be an actual metamodel class or a symbol denoting its qualified or unique name.

Function: funnyqt.extensional/set-avals!
(set-avals! m cls attr valfn)

As defined in section 27.1 on page 282, the extension of an attribute $attr$ is a function $value_{attr}$ that assigns to elements having this attribute a corresponding value which conforms to the attribute's declared type. The provided valfn is a function of zero arguments which must return the attribute's extension, i.e., the return value is $value_{attr}$. Three different representations of the extension are supported.

1. The valfn may return a map of the form {el value, ...}.
2. It may also return a collection of [el value] tuples.
3. It may also return a function (fn [el] value) which receives an element el and returns the attribute value to be set for this element.

The former two cases allow to specify the attribute's extension partially, i.e., there may be instances of cls for which no entry in the map or tuple in the collection exists and thus no attribute value is set for these elements. In the third case, the function representing the attribute's extension is called for each direct or indirect instance of cls in the model m and the returned value is set.

Like with create-relationships!, some additional resolution functions are bound in the context where the valfn is called.

Function: funnyqt.extensional/element-image
(element-image arch)
Function: funnyqt.extensional/element-archetype
(element-archetype img)

The element-image function resolves a given archetype to its image with respect to the cls given at the set-avals! call, i.e., the element or relationship class the attribute attr is defined for. Thus, it is a shorthand for (image m cls arch). The element-archetype function is the inverse of element-image, i.e., it resolves archetypes from images.

Considering a transformation which has already created one Person element for each Contact element in the source model and using these contacts as archetypes for the persons, the following two set-avals! calls are equivalent and both simply copy over the name attribute values from contacts to persons.

```
;; representation 2: valfn returning a sequence of tuples
(set-avals! m 'Person :name
  (fn []
    (for [c (elements source-model 'Contact)]
      [(element-image c) (aval c :name)])))

;; representation 3: valfn returning a function
(set-avals! m 'Person :name
  (fn []
    (fn [p]
      (aval (element-archetype p) :name))))
```

As can be seen, when specifying the attribute's extension as a sequence of tuples (or a map) computed by an expression on the source model, the usage of element-image is convenient in order to resolve the target model persons. When specifying the attribute's extension with a function receiving a target person, then the usage of element-archetype is convenient.

Setting references. The set-adjs! function sets the elements referenced by the reference ref defined for element class cls for instances contained in model m. Again, ref is given as a keyword denoting the reference's name and cls may be given as actual element class or as a symbol denoting the qualified or unique name of the element class.

Function: funnyqt.extensional/set-adjs!
(set-adjs! m cls ref reffn)

The reference's extension is defined by the return value of reffn. By the formal definition in section 27.1 on page 282, the extension of a reference r is a function ref_r which assigns to each element for which this reference is defined the sequence of referenced elements. In case of a single-valued reference, this sequence must either be empty or contain just one element. However, this definition is this way only in order to treat single- and multi-valued references equally, i.e., to have one common codomain for all reference functions. Practically, the set-adjs! function diverges a bit from the formal definition and is more intuitive.

Concretely, the reffn must return one of three possible representations of the ref reference's extension:

1. It may return a map of the form {el refed, ...}.
2. It may also return a collection of [el refed] tuples.
3. It may also return a function (fn [el] refed) which receives an element el and returns the element or elements which should be referenced by el's reference ref.

Here, refed must be a single element or nil in case of a single-valued reference and it must be a sequence of elements in case of a multi-valued reference.

With the third representation, the returned function representing the reference's extension is called once for every direct or indirect instance of `cls` in the model `m` in order to compute and set the reference.

In the context where `reffn` is executed, the `element-image` and `element-archetype` resolution functions are bound as discussed for `set-avals!` above. In addition, two more resolution functions are bound.

Function: `funnyqt.extensional/target-image`
`(target-image arch)`
Function: `funnyqt.extensional/target-images`
`(target-images arches)`

The `target-image` function resolves a given archetype to its image with respect to the element class being the type of the reference, i.e., `(target-image arch)` is a shorthand for `(image m tcls arch)` where `tcls` denotes the target type of the reference `ref`. Likewise, `(target-images arches)` function is a shorthand for `(map target-image arches)`, i.e., it looks up the images of all archetypes in a given sequence `arches` of archetypes. This is convenient when setting multi-valued references.

Like its name suggests, `set-adjs!` sets the references of elements which implies that elements which have been referenced previously won't be referenced anymore after the call. For this reason, there's also a function `add-adjs!` with purely additive semantics.

Function: `funnyqt.extensional/add-adjs!`
`(add-adjs! m cls ref reffn)`

In contrast to `set-adjs!`, it adds the references defined by `reffn` to the elements of class `cls` while keeping the previously referenced elements. Of course, this function is only applicable to multi-valued references.

27.5   Example

In this section, the simple transformation problem which has already been solved using the rule-based out-place transformation DSL in section 26.2 on page 276 is solved again using a transformation specified with the extensional transformation API. The transformation assumes the helper functions `family`, `male?`, `parents`, and `wife` being defined as on page 278.

The complete transformation definition is given operation call by operation call below. As discussed previously, an extensional transformation is just a plain Clojure function. It receives a families model `fs` and a genealogy TGraph `g`. The fact that the target model is a TGraph is only important in so far that this modeling framework supports first-class edges which are created implicitly when setting references of vertices. Thus, this example can demonstrate the use of both `create-relationships!` and `set-adjs!`.

```
(defn families2genealogy
  "Transforms the family model `fs` to the genealogy `g`."
```

```
[fs g]
(with-trace-mappings
  ;; Body containing calls of the extensional transformation ops
  )
```

In the function's body, empty traceability mappings are established using the `with-trace-mappings` macro[6]. Inside its dynamic scope, calls to the extensional transformations are performed which create elements and relationships in the target model g and set their attributes.

In the following, all calls of the extensional transformation operations realizing the complete transformation are discussed one by one.

The first `create-elements!` call creates one Male element for each source model Member element for which the `male?` predicate returns true.

```
(create-elements! g 'Male
                  (fn []
                      (filter male? (elements fs 'Member))))
```

After this operation has been evaluated, the following traceability functions are defined and can be accessed using the resolution functions discussed in section 27.4.1 on page 287 or their shorthands introduced alongside the actual transformation operations in section 27.4.3 on page 290.

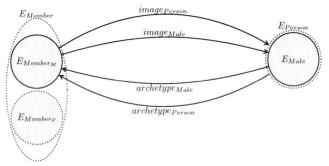

Circles with light gray background represent non-empty extensions. Dotted circle lines denote the extensions which have not yet been considered. Thus, in the source family model on the left, the extension of the Member class is divided into two partitions: the members who are male (notated as E_{Member_M}) and the members who are female (notated as E_{Member_F}), and there are no members which are outside these two partitions[7]. In the target genealogy on the right, the extension of the element class Male has been initialized by the operation call and a corresponding $image_{Male}$ traceability function came into being[8]. The extension of the abstract Person element

---

[6]`ensure-trace-mappings` could have been used as well.

[7]The extension of the Address element class is not shown for brevity.

[8]The inverse $archetype$ functions are always brought into life, too, so they are not mentioned in the text.

class equals the extension of the Male element class and thus also the corresponding $image_{Person}$ function equals $image_{Male}$.

The next `create-elements!` call creates one target model Female element for each source model member who is not male.

```
(create-elements! g 'Female
                  (fn []
                    (remove male? (elements fs 'Member))))
```

The updated traceability functions are shown below.

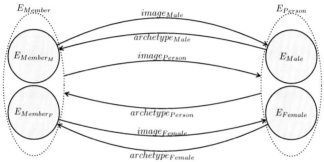

A new function $image_{Female}$ came into being which returns a new target model Female element for a given source model Member which has been recognized to be female. Furthermore, img_{Person} is now a total function assigning to every source model member a corresponding target model person.

The `set-avals!` call in the next listing then sets the fullName attribute value of any Person element which has been created in the target graph. Its value function iterates all mappings of the img_{Person} function, binding m to the member being the archetype of the person p. It returns a sequence of pairs where the first element is the person and the second element is the value to be set as full name, i.e., the concatenation of the archetype member's first name, a space, and then the member family's last name.

```
(set-avals! g 'Person :fullName
            (fn []
              (for [[m p] (image-map g 'Person)]
                [p (str (aval m :firstName) " "
                        (aval (family m) :lastName))])))
```

The next call creates HasChild edges using the `create-relationships!` function. The given archetype function returns a sequence of triples where the first element is the archetype for the new relationship and the second and third element are the source and target elements. A comprehension iterating over the source Member elements and the parents of each such member is used to compute the triples and the `source-image` and `target-image` functions are used to resolve the target model persons being the images of the source model members.

```
(create-relationships! g 'HasChild
                (fn []
                  (for [m (elements fs 'Member)
                        p (parents m)]
                    [[m p] (source-image m) (target-image p)])))
```

The `create-relationships!` call also instantiates traceability mappings from [mem p] to the new target model relationships in terms of the $img_{HasChild}$ function.

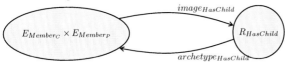

In this case, the traceability mappings are not between source and target model elements. The domain of $image_{HasChild}$ is a relation between two member elements, one in the role of a child ($\in E_{Member_C}$), the other in the role of a parent ($\in E_{Member_P}$). The codomain which equals the function's range is the set of HasChild relationships.

The next `set-adjs!` call sets the single-valued wife reference of instances of the target vertex class Male which implicitly creates HasSpouse relationships. Here, the reference function returns a function which receives a target graph Male vertex and returns its wife or `nil` if that male has no spouse. It does so by resolving the source model member corresponding to the given `male` vertex. From that, the wife is queried and translated back into the corresponding target graph Female vertex using the `target-image` function.

```
(set-adjs! g 'Male :wife
          (fn []
            (fn [male]
              (let [m (element-archetype male)]
                (target-image (wife m)))))))
```

As said, with TGraph models, using `set-adjs!` implies the creation of relationships. However, in contrast to `create-relationships!` no traceability mappings will be recorded.

The next `create-elements!` call creates one target model Address element per unique tuple of two plain string values. The former denotes the name and number of the street, the latter denotes the name of the town. Those values are taken from the corresponding attributes of the source model Family elements. So if there were multiple source model families whose street and town values are equal, only one unique target model address would be created[9].

---

[9]This is very similar to how input identities have been used with the rule-based out-place transformation DSL.

```
(create-elements! g 'Address
                (fn []
                  (for [f (elements fs 'Family)]
                    [(aval f :street) (aval f :town)]))))
```

This is reflected in the new traceability mappings. The domain of $image_{Address}$ is a binary relation of strings denoting street names ($Value_{Strings}$) and strings denoting town names ($Value_{String_T}$).

The next two set-avals! calls set the values of the new Address elements' street and town attributes. Here, the archetype-map function is used to compute the complete map assigning to every new target model Address element its corresponding archetypes. The archetypes are tuples of exactly the needed street and town names, so picking out the first or second element of each such tuple gives the value to be set.

```
(let [address-arch-map (archetype-map g 'Address)]
  (set-avals! g 'Address :street
              (fn []
                (fn [addr]
                  (first (address-arch-map addr)))))
  (set-avals! g 'Address :town
              (fn []
                (fn [addr]
                  (second (address-arch-map addr))))))
```

The final operation call of the transformation creates the LivesAt relationships connecting each person to the address where he or she is living at. The archetype function simply iterates over all source model members. The members themselves are used as archetypes for the new relationships. The relationships' source elements are the images of the given member with respect to the Person element class because the initial two operations of the transformation defined $image_{Person} : E_{Member} \xrightarrow{1:1,onto} E_{Person}$. The target address elements are retrieved by creating a tuple containing the street and town attribute values of the member m's family. By resolving these tuples with respect to the target element class Address, the actual address elements are retrieved.

```
(create-relationships! g 'LivesAt
                       (fn []
                         (for [m (elements fs 'Member)]
                           [m
                            (source-image m)
```

```
(let [f (family m)]
  (target-image [(aval f :street)
                 (aval f :town)])])])))
```

The complete transformation consists of 44 lines of code. Thus, it is almost twice as long as the very same transformation specified using the rule-based out-place transformation DSL (see section 26.2 on page 276). However, the completely isolated treatment of all metamodel constituents makes the extensional transformation approach suitable as the foundation for FunnyQT's co-evolution transformation API which allows to evolve a given model and its metamodel simultaneously at runtime. This API is discussed in part X starting on page 375.

Chapter 28

Related Work

In this chapter, several unidirectional out-place transformation approaches are briefly discussed, and similarities and differences with FunnyQT's rule-based out-place transformation DSL and its extensional transformation API are revealed.

ATL [Jou+08] is one of the first approaches implemented as responses to the OMG's Query/Views/Transformations RFP[1]. It provides means to produce one or many EMF target models from one or many EMF source models. A transformation consists of rules that define how elements of the source models are matched and how the models are navigated in order to create and initialize the elements of the target models.

ATL provides three kinds of rules: matched rules, lazy rules, and called rules. A matched rule specifies a source and a target pattern and for all matches of the source pattern elements in the target model are created according to the target pattern. The source pattern may contain only one pattern element which specifies the source model elements matched by the rule by stating the source metamodel type and an optional condition expressed in a variant of the OCL [OMG14b].

The target pattern may specify multiple elements to be created for each matched source element, however, the first one is called the rule's default target pattern element and plays a special role with respect to traceability. In the target pattern, there are also assignments to the attributes and references. Interestingly, the values being assigned to references are source model elements which will automatically be translated to corresponding target model elements.

ATL transformations are executed in two phases. In the matching phase, source elements are matched according to the source patterns of all matched rules and the target elements are created according to the target patterns of rules but not yet initialized, i.e., attributes and references are not set. Traceability mappings are established between a rule's single source element and its default target element. In the target model initialization phase, the assignments of attributes and references are executed. Since every source element considered by the transformation rules already has a corresponding target model element, assignments of source model

---

[1]http://www.omg.org/cgi-bin/doc?ad/2002-4-10 (last visited: 2015-10-07)

elements to references of target model elements actually assign the corresponding target elements.

Matched rules may also contain blocks of imperative code which is executed during the target model initialization phase. Here, also a special traceability operation can be called which gives access to non-default target elements created by some rule for some source element.

There's also an inheritance concept for matched rules where a rule may extend at most one other rule. This allows to align rules according to the specialization hierarchy of the source metamodel. The types of elements in the source and target pattern of the extending rule must be identical or more specific than in the extended rule. Furthermore, the same names must be used. This is similar to rule disjunction in FunnyQT's rule-based transformation DSL where a superclass rule sets common properties and then calls one of many disjunct rules corresponding to subclasses although with the latter, the dispatch is not necessarily based on typing.

ATL also offers a specialization-like concept called superimposition for transformations as a whole. A transformation may be superimposed on some other transformation in which case it overrides rules of the same name of the other transformation.

To some extend, top-level rules in FunnyQT's out-place transformation DSL are similar to ATL's matched rules. However, with FunnyQT rules always call other rules or functions in order to initialize references of target model elements, so it can be seen as less declarative than ATL's implicit approach on rule invocation and traceability.

As mentioned above, ATL also knows lazy rules. A lazy rule has to be called explicitly from the target patterns of other rules and creates elements as declared by its target pattern on each call. It may be declared as being unique in which case it executes its target pattern only once per given source element. Therefore, unique lazy rules are very similar to non-top-level rules in FunnyQT's out-place transformation DSL.

Lastly, ATL supports called rules which may have parameters, a target pattern, and an imperative code block but no source pattern. Those can only be called from within imperative code blocks of other rules.

ATL also supports a so-called refining mode which provides some in-place transformation capabilities. However, it is much less powerful than FunnyQT's in-place transformation DSL or the related in-place transformation approaches discussed in chapter 24 starting on page 249.

ATL has frequently been used as a testbed for further transformation research. For example, [JT10] discusses an extension to ATL for incremental model transformation and [Tis+11] proposes the lazy execution of model transformations. The incremental ATL transformation extension executes transformations as live transformations which run as a kind of demon in the background and observes changes to the source model in order to propagate them immediately to the target model. With lazy execution, target model elements are not created until they are accessed which allows having transformations which generate possibly infinite target models. However, both incremental and lazy ATL transformations handle only subsets of the ATL language and the latter required even a modified version of EMF. Therefore, both approaches exist only as proof-of-concepts and are not part of the distributed version of ATL.

An out-place transformation language which is both syntactically and semantically very similar to ATL is the *Epsilon Transformation Language* (*ETL*, [KPP08]) which is part of the Epsilon framework [Kol+15].

Like with ATL, rules have one source pattern element with an optional guard and one or many target pattern elements. Each rule may have a block of imperative code written in the Epsilon Object Language.

In contrast to ATL, resolution of target model elements from source elements is performed explicitly using a special *equivalents()* operation instead of implicitly.

Normal ETL rules correspond to matched rules in ATL or top-level rules in FunnyQT, i.e., for all source elements matching the source pattern of a rule, corresponding target elements are created automatically. Like ATL, ETL has lazy rules which are invoked only when needed in terms of the *equivalents()* operation mentioned above.

ETL also provides a rule specialization concept which in contrast to ATL allows for having rules which extend multiple other rules.

Amongst others, the QVT standard [OMG11b] specifies the *Operational Mappings* language (*QVTo*) which comprises an imperative extension to OCL [OMG14b] which allows to create, delete, and modify model elements in conjunction to a few transformation constructs. It is mainly intended for defining out-place transformations but not restricted to this use-case.

A QVTo transformation consists of a main operation which is the transformation's entry point and arbitrary many so-called mapping operations. A mapping operation is essentially an operation defined for some source metamodel class. There may be further parameters, one or many output elements may be declared either just as return type or as declarations of the form `var1:TargetType1, var2:TargetType2`, and an optional guard OCL expression.

Usually, the operation's body consists only of assignments to properties of the target elements. When the operation is called for an instance of the declared source metamodel class and possibly further arguments and the guard expression evaluates to true, then instances of the declared target types are created and their properties are set according to the body. In contrast to ATL and similar to FunnyQT, references of newly created elements are set to the values returned by calling other mapping operations instead of source model elements which then get resolved to target elements implicitly.

A mapping operation creates target elements each time it is called, even if it is called multiple times for the same source element. In order to resolve target elements for given source elements, there are several traceability functions which look up the target element or target elements that have been created by a given mapping operation for a given source element. However, this traceability information can only resolve elements which have been created prior to the call. To cope with this situation, there is also a concept of late resolution. Late resolutions are postponed until the end of the transformation where all target model elements have already been created. In contrast, FunnyQT's rule-based out-place transformation DSL uses the concept of rule invocation both for triggering the creation of target elements (the first call with a given sequence of arguments) as well as for resolving target elements (all following calls with the same arguments) which is a much simpler and more intuitive concept from a user's point of view.

QVTo provides three reuse mechanisms on the mapping operation level: mapping disjunction, mapping inheritance, and mapping merges. FunnyQT's concept of rule disjunction (see section 26.1.5 on page 273) is borrowed from the QVTo concept of mapping disjunction. Mapping inheritance is very similar to overriding of methods in object-oriented languages because mapping operations are essentially operations defined for source metamodel classes. However, the QVT specification is not very detailed in this respect[2]. With mapping merges, a mapping operation is able to express that a sequence of other operations are to be executed on its results after its completion.

Transformations can be reused as a whole, too. An operational transformation may call other transformations (not only other operational transformations), and an operational transformation may specialize another operational transformation. Again, the exact semantics of transformation inheritance are not specified in too much detail but it should be understood as a concept similar to specialization between classes in Java. Thus, an overriding semantics may be assumed where the operations of the extending transformation override the operations of the same name of the extended transformation.

With QVTo, a transformation may also define intermediate properties for source metamodel classes, and they may define completely new intermediate classes. Those only can be instantiated by mapping rules in order to hold intermediate data which can then be accessed from other operations. As soon as the transformation finishes, all intermediate classes, properties, and their values disappear.

Another interesting feature of QVTo are type extensions which allows to define new names for existing types with possible further constraints. For example, it is possible to define a type FullName as an alias for an OCL tuple with string-valued components for a first name and a last name. One can also define a custom type AbstractClass whose instances are all instances of the existing class Class whose abstract attribute has the value true. And one can define a type AorB as a kind of superclass of some existing types A and B.

At the current point in time, there is only one implementation of QVTo which is provided by the Eclipse project[3] and is able to transform EMF models. However, it does not implement all features specified by the standard.

Tefkat[4] [LS05] is a transformation approach which, like ATL, has been developed initially as a response to the QMG's Query/Views/Transformations RFP[1] on page 301.

Tefkat is a declarative, logic-based transformation language where traceability information is explicitly defined. I.e., each transformation defines custom tracking

---

[2]For example, the semantics of guards in the presence of inheritance is not specified, e.g., what happens when the guard of the specialized operation succeeds but the guard of the specializing operation does not, or the other way round.

[3]https://projects.eclipse.org/projects/modeling.mmt.qvt-oml (last visited: 2015-10-07)

[4]http://tefkat.sourceforge.net/ (last visited: 2015-10-07)

classes (a traceability metamodel) which are explicitly instantiated in a so-called tracking model during the transformation and link source element to target elements.

Transformations consist of rules where each rule consists of two constraints src and trg. The src constraint is used as a query on the transformation's source model and the tracking model. The trg constraint expresses a kind of postcondition for a rule which defines for elements satisfying the src constraints which corresponding elements have to exist in the target model and the tracking model. Thus, rules have a declarative forall-there-exists semantics.

Tefkat also allows to define stand-alone constraints on the source and tracking model called patterns which may then be used as part of the src constraints of multiple rules.

Rules may extend or supersede other rules. With the former, the extending rule applies to elements for which the src constraints of both the extending and the extended rule apply. With the latter, the superseding rule applies to all elements matching its own src constraint. In both cases, the extended/superseded rule applies to all elements which do not satisfy the extending/superseding rule's src constraint but which satisfy their own src constraint.

Tefkat also has reflective capabilities and supports an Any type which acts as a supertype of all metamodel types. This allows to define transformations spanning meta-levels. Everywhere a metamodel type is expected, there may also be an expression which evaluates to a type. This makes it easy to write a generic copy transformation. Here, a rule can simply accept elements of all types using the Any type and create target elements of the same type using the reflective capabilities.

There are various model transformation approaches which are realized as embedded DSLs in several different host languages.

RubyTL [CMT06] is a DSL for out-place model transformations embedded in the Ruby programming language[5].

A RubyTL transformation consists of rules where each rule declares a single source metamodel class and one or many target metamodel classes. For each instance of the source metamodel class, one instance of each target metamodel class will be created.

Optionally, a rule may contain a filter block[6] which is applied to all instances of the rule's source metamodel class. Only for those instances the block yields true, corresponding target elements are created.

Furthermore, a rule usually contains a mapping block which receives the source element and all target elements. Here, assignments of properties are performed. Like with ATL, source elements are assigned to target element instances where the resolution to appropriate target elements in terms of calling other rules is performed implicitly.

The core of RubyTL is intentionally very simple. Advanced concepts such as specialization between rules or complete transformations are not supported. However, RubyTL is extensible using a plugin system where plugins can change and extend

---

[5]https://www.ruby-lang.org (last visited: 2015-10-08)
[6]A block in Ruby defines a Proc object which is a kind of a lambda, i.e., an anonymous function.

most aspects of the language. For example, by default a RubyTL transformation's entry point is its first rule but there is a plugin which adds the ability to define top-level rules thus allowing to have transformations with multiple entry points.

Scala MTL [GWS12] is a rule-based out-place transformation language which is implemented as an embedded DSL in the multi-paradigm language[7] Scala[8]. The approach allows for transforming EMF models and is similar to RubyTL.

Rules are objects which are instantiated with one source metamodel class and one target metamodel class with the semantics that for each instance of the source metamodel class, a corresponding target metamodel class is to be created.

A rule may define a when function which is a predicate used for filtering the source elements. It also may contain a perform function which is called with each source element accepted by the rule and the corresponding newly created target element. Here, the properties of the target element are set. Like with ATL and RubyTL, the references of target model elements are set to source model elements which implies invoking a rule which is able to transform the given source elements to the expected target model elements. This feature could be implemented elegantly using Scala's implicit conversion facility.

Scala MTL requires that interfaces and classes have been generated for the source and target metamodels and models are being represented using those. But then it provides static type-safety without clutter because Scala's advanced type inference and implicit conversion features usually allow for omitting explicit type declarations at most places.

SIGMA [KCF14] is a model manipulation library for EMF models which is also implemented as a set of embedded DSLs in Scala. SIGMA provides DSLs for model manipulation, constraint checking, model-to-model transformations, and model-to-text transformations.

Its out-place transformation DSL is very similar in capabilities to the Scala MTL discussed above. With SIGMA, transformations are defined as classes whose methods are the rules. The first parameter of a rule denotes the source element, and the second to last element denote target elements which are to be created. Rules may have a guard expression restricting their applicability. In the body of a rule, properties of the newly created target elements are set. Like with ETL, a special operation srcElement.sTarget[TargetType] is used in order to resolve target elements of a given type for some given source element which might cause another rule to be called.

Like Scala MTL, SIGMA transformations require that code has been generated for the source and target metamodels but then transformations are statically type-safe.

NMF [HH14] is a modeling framework for the .NET platform implemented in C# which is, among others, equipped with an embedded DSL for realizing model-to-model transformations called *NTL*.

---

[7]Scala is both a functional and an object-oriented language.
[8]http://www.scala-lang.org/ (last visited: 2015-10-08)

However, here the term embedded DSL is a bit overstating. Transformations are defined as classes extending a predefined framework class. Transformation rules are also defined as classes extending a predefined framework class. The base class for rules has two type parameters representing the rule's single source and target element class. Those are fixed during specialization in order to define a concrete rule.

A concrete rule class then overrides the Transform() method of the base class. This method is called with the source and the target element and here the target element's attributes can be set.

In order to define for which source elements a rule is to be called and which other rules have to be called, dependencies can be specified by overriding the RegisterDependencies() method. The specifications in this method also contain assignments to references.

Given that transformations and rules are defined as classes, the normal C# inheritance concept can be used for specializing rules and whole transformations.

All in all, NTL transformations are provided as a solid C# API rather than an embedded DSL with a somewhat autonomic syntax. Nevertheless, the typical embedded DSL goals of being task-oriented while still retaining the host language's flexibility are mostly achieved although NTL requires transformation developers to write a lot of infrastructural code which has nothing to do with the actual transformation task.

The FunnyQT extensional transformation API which has been discussed in section 27.4 on page 287 can be seen as a direct successor of the transformation language *GReTL* [EH14; HE11] with some differences in details. GReTL is implemented as a Java API but also has a simple external DSL syntax.

Where GReTL was specific to the TGraph modeling framework JGraLab and followed the concept of creating the target metamodel of a transformation in conjunction with one conforming target model, FunnyQT's extensional transformation API works for any modeling framework but only supports operations on the instance level. FunnyQT's co-evolution API which will be discussed in part X starting on page 375 again builds on GReTL concepts in order to allow the specification of transformations that change a metamodel and a conforming model simultaneously.

GReTL had the same operations as FunnyQT's extensional transformation API with essentially the same archetype concept. Only some details have been changed. With GReTL, when creating edges, the archetypes of the start and end vertex had to be given. Likewise, when setting attributes the archetypes of the elements whose attributes were to be set had to be given. With FunnyQT, the actual start and end elements or the actual elements whose values are to be set are to be given. This allows for transformations which extend a given model in place where the elements don't have archetypes and is generally less confusing.

GReTL uses GReQL [EB10] for its querying part. Usually, extensional FunnyQT transformations obviously use FunnyQT's querying facilities. With both GReTL and FunnyQT, any other form of querying, e.g., querying a relational database using SQL, could be used, too.

Part VIII

On Relational Model Querying

Summary

This part is again dedicated to model querying. However, here the emphasis is on querying models relationally where a query declaratively defines relations between logic variables and the evaluation finds possible bindings of these variables which make the relations hold.

Chapter 29 starting on page 313 introduces into the topic of relational querying and then chapter 30 starting on page 323 describes FunnyQT's DSL for querying models relationally.

The approach is illustrated with a set of example queries in chapter 31 starting on page 331.

The part closes with chapter 32 starting on page 335 where related relational and logic-based approaches for program and model querying are discussed.

Chapter 29

Introduction

Until now, a model query has been considered to be a function. It receives a model and possibly additional arguments and returns a result. The arguments are the inputs to the query and the return value is the single output.

Relational model queries are quite different. A relational query declaratively defines relations that need to hold between a set of logical variables. Each such variable can either be fresh (not bound to a value) or ground (bound to a value). Evaluating a relational query means finding bindings for the fresh logical variables which fulfill the relations defined by the query. Thus, any variable of a relational query can be input (when it is ground) or output (when it is fresh) and a relational query may have zero or arbitrarily many results. As an example, the same relational program which is able to compute a sorted list from a given list can also be used to compute all permutations of a given sorted list. Therefore, it is frequently said that a relational program can be run "backwards," too.

Mathematically, a relation is a subset of the Cartesian product of the universes of its arguments, i.e., a relation is a set of tuples. For example, there might be a binary relation $parent \subseteq Person \times Person$ which relates persons in the role of a parent with persons in the role of a child. On top of this relation which might be manifested in a model with person elements and references or relationships for assigning children to parents, other relations can be defined using conjunction, disjunction, or quantification. For example, two persons a and b are siblings if they have at least one common parent.

$$sibling : Person \times Person$$
$$sibling = \{(a,b) \mid \exists c \in Person : (c,a) \in parent \land (c,b) \in parent\}$$

These concepts combined with unification form the core of relational model querying and relational programming in general.

With respect to *relational algebra* in database systems, the *siblings* relation can be seen as a *selection* of the Cartesian product *parent* × *parent* where the first and third attribute are equal followed by a *projection* on the second and fourth attribute.

Relational model querying is a nice feature on its own. All simple patterns with positive and negative application conditions or constraints which have been discussed in part V starting on page 181 can also be formulated as relations. On the one hand, the fact that any parameter of a relation may be used both as input and output allows for even more flexibility. On the other hand, patterns can be evaluated much faster in general and so are to be preferred if performance matters or the queried models are large. However, the utmost declarative nature of relations make them very suitable for defining bidirectional transformations, and in fact, the relational model querying API is the foundation of FunnyQT's bidirectional transformation DSL which is going to be discussed later in part IX starting on page 339.

FunnyQT's relational model querying DSL is not invented and implemented from scratch. Instead, it extends the Clojure *core.logic* library which provides relational programming capabilities on Clojure data structures with relations for querying models. An introduction to relational programming with *core.logic* is given in section 29.1. Thereafter, chapter 30 starting on page 323 introduces FunnyQT's extensions to *core.logic* which enable relational model querying. Chapter 31 starting on page 331 demonstrates relational querying by defining some example relations on models representing a genealogy.

Appendix A.6 on page 427 explains how the relational querying capabilities can be extended upon other modeling frameworks in addition to EMF and JGraLab.

29.1   Relational Programming with core.logic

The core.logic library is a Clojure port of *miniKanren*[1] [FBK05; Byr09] which embeds Prolog-style [II95] relational programming into the Lisp-dialect Scheme.

The beauty of miniKanren lays in its implementation which consists of less than 300 lines of functional Scheme code and yet suffices to solve about the same set of problems which a standard Prolog implementation tackles[2]. However, the design philosophies of Prolog and miniKanren are very different. Prolog's main goal is efficiency up to the point of sacrificing correctness[3] where solutions of a program are computed using a depth-first search thereby mutating data structures and undoing the changes while backtracking. In contrast, miniKanren's main goals are simplicity and purity of the implementation and extensibility. The complete implementation is free of mutation and side-effects.

One extension to miniKanren is *cKanren* [Alv+11] which supports constraint logic programming over trees ($CLP(Tree)$) and finite domains ($CLP(FD)$). The former allows for specifying inequalities, the latter allows for defining arithmetical constraints over integral values. Both extensions are supported by core.logic, too, and they are also useful for relational model querying.

---

[1]http://miniKanren.org
[2]In the meantime, the core concepts of miniKanren have been extracted into a minimal relational language named *μKanren* [HF13] consisting only of 40 lines of code.
[3]For example, Prolog implementations omit the *occurs check* on unification which forbids unifying a variable with a term containing that variable. This omission may lead to cyclic structures and non-termination.

Both core.logic and miniKanren *embed* relational programming inside their functional host languages Clojure and Scheme, i.e., there is a macro run* inside which code has to be placed that is evaluated according to relational semantics. A minimal example relational program is given in the following listing.

```
(run* [q]
  (== q true))
;=> (true)
```

Logic variables. The run* macro receives a vector declaring one or more logic variables. So in the example above, one logic variable q is declared. The logic variables declared by run* are *fresh* initially, i.e., they are not bound to any value. Variables which are bound to a variable are said to be *ground*.

Goals. After the logic variables vector, one or many *goals* are specified. A goal is an application of a *relational operator* or a *relation* to logic variables. The semantics of run* is to find all possible bindings of the declared logic variables which fulfill all specified goals. In logic terms, the task of a relational program is to find all *models* (in the logical sense), i.e., all *interpretations* of the logic variables fulfilling the goals specified by the program.

One says a goal *succeeds* if and only if there exists at least one possible binding of its logic variables satisfying the goal. Otherwise, i.e., if there is no such binding, the goal is said to *fail*.

Unification and equality. In the example above, there is only one goal (== q true). Here, the *equality operator* ==[4] tries to *unify* the logic variable q with the boolean literal true.

Unification of a fresh variable and a *term* (an actual datum or a ground variable) assigns the value to the variable. Unification of two fresh variables guarantees that whatever the values of the two variables will eventually be, they must be equal. And lastly, the unification of two terms succeeds if they are equal and fails otherwise.

In the example above, q is fresh, thus unifying it with true succeeds. This is also the only possible solution, so the list of solutions delivered by the program contains just the single solution true.

Note that a term may contain logic variables itself. For example, the goal (== q [a b c]) unifies q with a vector of length three where the actual elements are defined by three other logic variables. Such a unification works according to the rules above and there is one additional restriction: the unified variable must not be contained in the structure being unified with. If it is, the unification fails. So the goal (== q [q]) or a conjunction of goals (== q a) (== q [a]) will fail. This constraint is called the *occurs check* and essentially forbids self-referential structures and is required by a sound unification algorithm.

---

[4]Here, == is the equality operator clojure.core.logic/== and not the numeric comparison function clojure.core/==.

Relations.   Relations are introduced best by comparing them with functions. Whereas a function has separate input values (its arguments) and one single output value (its return value), a relation's arguments are logic variables which can act both as inputs (when they are ground) or as outputs (when they are fresh). Thus, when a relation is called (i.e., used as a goal) and all arguments are ground, it acts like a predicate. When it is called and at least some arguments are fresh, it emits all possible bindings of the fresh arguments which would make the relation hold.

Many Clojure functions have one or several relational counterparts. For example, there is the relation (conso o r l) provided by core.logic. conso is a ternary relation where o is some object, r is some list, and l is a list where o is the first element and r is the rest. Its functional Clojure counterparts are first, rest, and cons. (first l) returns the first element of the list l, (rest l) returns the rest of the list l, and (cons o r) returns a new list whose first element is o and the rest is r.

In the following program, conso is used to decompose a given list q into its first element o and its rest r.

```
(let [q (list 1 2 3 4)]
  (run* [o r]
    (conso o r q)))
;=> ([1 (2 3 4)])
```

Obviously, there is only one solution. But other programs might have an infinite number of solutions. For example, the following program queries for all lists q (and their rests r) which have the number 1 as first element.

```
(let [o 1]
  (run* [r q]
    (conso o r q)))
;=> ([_0 (1 . _0)])
```

Interestingly, the program still terminates immediately. The notation (1 . _0) represents a list where 1 is the first element and _0 is the rest. $\_n : n \in N$ is the print representation of a fresh logic variable, i.e., here the single result subsumes all possible lists with the first element being 1. One could substitute _0 with any list and get a correct answer.

As said, the core.logic library is a port of miniKanren which has been originally implemented in Scheme. Although most Scheme implementations have a namespace facility, the Scheme standard [Spe+10] doesn't require one. Therefore, the convention of suffixing relations with an "o" in order to disambiguate them from functions while still indicating a correspondence with some existing function came into being and it is generally followed in core.logic and the whole community around miniKanren[5].

Existential quantification.   The fresh macro receives a vector of symbols which are to be declared as new, fresh variables, and one or many goals. Its semantics is that there has to be at least one binding for the newly declared fresh variables

---

[5]The actual miniKanren publications use a superscript "o" for relations, e.g., *cons^o*, *rest^o*, and *append^o*.

which would make all the given goals succeed. Therefore, it acts like an existential qualification.

For example, the last program can be rewritten using fresh so that the rest of the list r is not reported in the answers. The goal is read as *there exists an r such that adding o to the head of r gives q.*

```
(let [o 1]
  (run* [q]
    (fresh [r]
      (conso o r q))))
;=> ((1 . _0))
```

Here, the result is a sequence of possible values for the logic variable q rather than a sequence of vectors, each containing a possible value of r and q.

Existential quantification is especially needed when defining custom relations which are going to be discussed below.

Defining custom relations. Custom relations can be defined as ordinary Clojure functions provided that they are defined completely using other relations or relational operators. The following example defines a relation cconso which is like conso but relates the first two elements f and s of a list with the rest r of the list l. The definition states that when adding s to the front of r, one gets a new list l1, and when adding f to that, one gets the final list l.

```
(defn cconso [f s r l]
  (fresh [l1]
    (conso s r l1)
    (conso f l1 l)))

(run* [q]
  (cconso 1 2 q (list 1 2 3 4 5)))
;=> ((3 4 5))
```

The query then asks for the list to which adding 2 and 1 in this order would result in the list (1 2 3 4 5).

Conjunction. The goals in a run* or a fresh are wrapped in an implicit conjunction, i.e., the solutions of a relational program must fulfill all the goals specified by it. However, when defining custom relations just as as sequence of goals, conjunctions have to be stated explicitly using all.

Disjunction. A disjunction can be specified using conde which consists of two or many clauses. Each clause is a vector of goals which are wrapped in an implicit conjunction.

The following relation `membero*`[6] succeeds if o is a member of the list l. The definition uses `conso` to decompose the list l into its first element f and its rest r. Now two cases are distinguished by `conde`. o is a member of l if l's first element f unifies with o, or if o is a member of the rest r of l.

```
(defn membero* [o l]
  (fresh [f r]
    (conso f r l)
    (conde
      [(== f o)]
      [(membero* o r)]])))

(run* [q]
  (fresh [a b c]
    (== q (list a b c))
    (membero* 1 q)
    (membero* 2 q)))
;=> ((1 2 _0) (1 _0 2) (2 1 _0) (_0 1 2) (2 _0 1) (_0 2 1))
```

The query then asks for all lists of length three which contain both 1 and 2. As can be seen, there are six answers because there are 3! permutations of elements in a list of length three. Every answer contains one fresh variable. Again, it could be substituted with any value and the answer would still be correct.

Note that the delivery of all possible solution also means that `conde` is not short-circuiting. If a clause succeeds, the other clauses are evaluated anyway and thus have a chance to deliver more answers. There is some anecdotal evidence that this fact also explains the "e" suffix of `conde`: *every clause may succeed*.

However, there are certain situations where not all possible solutions are needed or trying to retrieve them would lead to non-termination. Therefore, miniKanren and core.logic provide the additional disjunction operators `conda` (*soft cut*) and `condu` (*committed choice*). They have the same syntax as `conde` but treat the head (the first goal) of each clause specially. Concretely, the clauses are evaluated in order and if the head of a clause succeeds, then these disjunctions commit to this clause and ignore all other clauses. This corresponds to Prolog's cut operator !. The difference between `conda` and `condu` is that with the former, the head of the clause committed to may still succeed an unbounded number of times whereas it may succeed at most once with `condu`.

The following example demonstrates the differences in the behaviors between `conde`, `conda`, and `condu`.

```
(defn y-or-n [x]
  (conde
    [(== x :y)]
    [(== x :n)]))

(run* [x y]
  (conde
```

---

[6]`membero` is a built-in core.logic relation, thus an asterisk is used in order not to overwrite it in the defining namespace.

```
    [(y-or-n x) (== y 1)]    ;; delivers [:y 1] and [:n 1]
    [(== x :y)  (== y 2)]))  ;; delivers [:y 2]
;=> ([:y 2] [:y 1] [:n 1])

(run* [x y]
  (conda
    [(y-or-n x) (== y 1)]    ;; delivers [:y 1] and [:n 1]
    [(== x :y)  (== y 2)]))  ;; isn't evaluated
;=> ([:y 1] [:n 1])

(run* [x y]
  (condu
    [(y-or-n x) (== y 1)]    ;; delivers only [:y 1] (once-semantics)
    [(== x :y)  (== y 2)]))  ;; isn't evaluated
;=> ([:y 1])
```

Inequalities. As said in the introduction, core.logic supports constraint logic programming over tree terms (*CLP(Tree)*[7]). This feature adds just one additional relational operator != which can be used to express *inequalities*. A goal (!= a b) states that whatever the final values of a and b may be, they must not be equal.

The following relational program illustrates the features provided by CLP(Tree) by defining a relation dedupeo. It is a binary relation over two lists l and nl where nl is l with consecutive duplicates removed.

```
(defn dedupeo [l nl]
  (conde
    [(conde [(== l ())]              ;; (1)
            [(fresh [x]
               (== l (list x)))])
     (== nl l)]
    [(fresh [f s r rl]                ;; (2)
       (conso f r l)
       (conso s rl r)
       (conde
         [(== f s) (dedupeo r nl)]    ;; (2.1)
         [(!= f s) (fresh [acc]       ;; (2.2)
                     (dedupeo r acc)
                     (conso f acc nl))]))]))
```

Two main cases are to be distinguished. For an empty or one-element list l as in case (1), the deduped version nl simply equals the original list l.

For a list l starting with at least two elements f and s as in case (2), there are again two cases to be handled. If the first element f and the second element s are equal as in case (2.1), then deduping the rest r of the original list l, i.e., the second to last element, will yield the same result nl. That is, the first element may be ignored. If f and s are equal, then the deduped list nl is defined by deduping the rest r of the original list l and adding the first element f to its head.

---

[7]The name CLP(Tree) is slightly misleading. The "tree" refers to the fact that terms may be trees. Normal logic programming is already a restricted version of CLP(Tree) where the single constraint is equality.

Now, the new relation can be used to dedupe a given list which of course always yields exactly one result.

```
(run* [q]
  (dedupeo (list 1 2 2 3 3 3) q))
;=> ((1 2 3))
```

It can also be used to test if a given list is a deduped version of another given list.

```
(run* [q]
  (dedupeo (list 1 2 2 3 3 3) (list 1 2 3)))
;;=> (_0)   ;; yes
(run* [q]
  (dedupeo (list 1 2 2 3 3 3) (list 3 2 1)))
;=> ()      ;; no, obviously not
(run* [q]
  (dedupeo (list 1 2 2 3 3 3) (list 1 2 2 3)))
;=> ()      ;; no, nl isn't even deduped!
```

And lastly, it can be used to generate versions of a deduped list containing duplicates.

```
(run 10 [q]
  (dedupeo q (list 1 2 3)))
;=> ((1 2 3)
;    (1 2 3 3)
;    (1 1 2 3)
;    (1 2 2 3)
;    (1 2 3 3 3)
;    (1 1 2 3 3)
;    (1 1 1 2 3)
;    (1 2 2 3 3)
;    (1 1 2 2 3)
;    (1 2 2 2 3))
```

Of course, the number of such lists is unbounded. So here, we use the core.logic macro run which is similar to run* except that it receives an additional argument which acts as the maximum number of solutions to be computed.

Constraints over finite domains. The core.logic library also implements constraint logic programming over finite domains (*CLP(FD)*) which means that the domain of each logic variable may be restricted to a finite set.

In core.logic, this extension essentially allows to define simple arithmetic goals on integral numbers by restricting the domain of the involved logic variables to a certain finite subset of $\mathbb{Z}$.

The following example uses the finite domain constraints < and > and the - relation in order to define a relation (modo x y r) where x and y are positive integers and r is the remainder of x divided by y. In the example, the alias fd maps to the namespace clojure.core.logic.fd.

```
(defn modo [x y r]
  (conde
    [(== y 0)    fail]              ;; (1)
    [(== x y)    (== r 0)]          ;; (2)
    [(fd/< x y) (== r x)]           ;; (3)
    [(fd/> x y) (fresh [d]          ;; (4)
                  (fd/- x y d)
                  (modo d y r))]]))
```

Four cases are distinguished. If the divisor y is zero as in case (1), the relation fails[8]. If the dividend x and the divisor y are equal as in case (2), the remainder r is zero. If the dividend is smaller than the divisor as in case (3), the remainder equals the dividend. And lastly, if the dividend is larger than the divisor as in case (4), on obtains the very same remainder r when computing the remainder of the difference between x and y as dividend and y an divisor.

This relation can be used to compute the modulo of two given numbers.

```
(run* [q]
  (modo 15 6 q))
;=> (3)

(run* [q]
  (modo 271 13 3))
;=> ()  ;; no, the modulo is 11
```

The modo relation can also be used to compute numbers whose division would return a given rest, or even all triples of integers related by modo. However, in these cases CLP(FD) requires the fresh variables denoting integers to be restricted to some finite domain, i.e., some finite subset of $\mathbb{Z}$. This is done using the in and interval constructs of core.logic's CLP(FD) API.

```
(run* [x y]
  (fd/in x y (fd/interval 1 15))
  (modo x y 3))
;=> ([3 4] [7 4] [3 5] [3 6] [11 4] [8 5] [3 7] [3 8] [9 6] [3 9]
;     [3 10] [15 4] [10 7] [3 11] [13 5] [3 12] [11 8] [3 13]
;     [3 14] [12 9] [3 15] [13 10] [15 6] [14 11] [15 12])

(run 10 [x y r]
  (fd/in x y r (fd/interval 1 15))
  (modo x y r))
;=> ([1 2 1] [3 2 1] [2 3 2] [1 3 1] [4 3 1]
;     [1 4 1] [5 2 1] [3 4 3] [2 4 2] [5 3 2])
```

Negation as failure and universal quantification. The *negation as failure constraint* with signature (nafc rel & args) succeeds if and only if the goal defined by applying the relation rel to the given args fails. nafc is non-relational, i.e., the given args won't be unified with all combinations of objects for which rel does not hold.

---

[8] clojure.core.logic/fail is a goal which always fails.

Instead, other goals must ensure that at some point in time, all args are ground, and then the constraint will be checked.

The *universal quantifier* everyg is a pseudo-relation (or higher-order relation) with signature (everyg rel coll) which succeeds if and only if (rel el) succeeds for every element el contained in the collection coll.

In the following example, the relation answero unifies x with possible answers to a yes-or-no question. Like in real life, answers to such questions aren't as sharp as the asker would like to, i.e., possible answers may also be :maybe and :dont-know.

```
(defn answero [x]
  (conde
    [(== x :yes)]
    [(== x :no)]
    [(== x :maybe)]
    [(== x :dont-know)]))

(run* [q]
  (fresh [a b]
    (== q (list a b))
    (everyg answero q)
    (nafc membero :maybe q)
    (nafc membero :dont-know q)))
;=> ((:yes :yes) (:yes :no) (:no :yes) (:no :no))
```

The run* query then asks for all two-element lists q containing only definitive answers, i.e., answers which are not :maybe or :dont-know. It does so by asserting that :maybe and :dont-know must not be members of the list q.

Chapter 30

Defining Relational Model Queries

For providing relational model querying, FunnyQT simply defines some generic relations on models and model elements. These are discussed in section 30.1. Built upon these generic relations, more convenient metamodel-specific relational querying APIs can be generated. This feature is discussed in section 30.2 on page 328.

30.1 Generic Relations

The generic model querying relations discussed in this section are designed along the generic view of models which has been introduced in chapter 8 starting on page 83. In this view, a model is a container for elements and optionally relationships between the elements. Elements and possibly relationships are typed and attributed. Furthermore, elements may link to other elements in terms of named references which may either be single-valued or multi-valued.

FunnyQT's `funnyqt.relational` namespace provides one relation for each of these properties, i.e., there is one relation concerned with elements in a model, one relation concerned with relationships in a model, one relation concerned with typing, one relation concerned with attribution, and one relation concerned with references.

Elements. `elemento` is a relation where `el` is a model element. If `el` is fresh, it will be unified once with each element of model `m`. Thus, `elemento` corresponds to the generic protocol methods `funnyqt.generic/elements` (see section 12.2 on page 109) and `funnyqt.generic/element?` (see section 12.5 on page 113), but in contrast to the former, it is not concerned with typing.

Relation: `funnyqt.relational/elemento`
`(elemento m el)`

The model parameter m must always be ground, so elemento is not fully relational in the strict sense. If it were, it had to unify a fresh m with all possible models containing el which is obviously infeasible.

All other model relations discussed in the following also have the model as first argument. It would have been possible to define the relations without an explicit model parameter and instead having it implicitly defined using, e.g., a dynamically scoped var, however this would have restricted relational model queries to operate on just one model or at least a set of models without being able to control which elements belong to which models. Therefore, it is best to view the model argument as some technical detail and consider elemento as a fully relational unary relation.

As discussed in the introduction to core.logic, custom relations can be defined as plain functions provided that they only use existing relations for their definition. Since relations are Clojure functions, it is easily possible to define higher-order relations which receive other relations.

For example, there might be a relation constrained-elemento which restricts elemento with some other relation given as a parameter.

```
(defn constrained-elemento [m relation el]
  (all
    (elemento m el)
    (relation el)))
```

Again, the given relation is a technical parameter just like the model. If it were part of the relation and could be fresh, it would have to be unified with all possible relations which succeed for el.

Relationships. relationshipo is a relation where rel is a relationship, src is its source element and trg is its target elements. Therefore, it is the relational counterpart to the protocol methods funnyqt.generic/relationships (see section 12.2 on page 109), funnyqt.generic/relationship? (see section 12.5 on page 113), funnyqt.generic/source, and funnyqt.generic/target (see section 12.2 on page 111). Like with elemento, it is not concerned with typing.

Relation: funnyqt.relational/relationshipo
(relationshipo m rel src trg)

If relationshipo is used on a model m which has no first-class relationships, e.g., an EMF model, an exception is thrown.

Using relationshipo, questions about reachability in a graph can be easily answered. As an example, the following relation reachableo succeeds for each pair of model elements x and y where y is reachable from x by a path which traverses all relationships only in the direction dir which is either :forward or :backward.

```
(defn reachableo [m x y dir]
  (conde
    [(== dir :backward) (reachableo m y x :forward)]     ;; (1)
    [(== dir :forward) (fresh [r]                         ;; (2)
                         (conde
```

```
[(relationshipo m r x y)]          ;; (2.1)
[(fresh [i]
    (relationshipo m r x i)        ;; (2.2)
    (reachableo m i y dir))])])]))
```

In clause (1) dealing with :backward direction, the question is simply reversed. Clause (2) deals with the :forward direction, and here two cases can be distinguished. There might be an edge r which starts at x and ends at y (2.1), or there might be some intermediate model element i being the target element of edge r starting at x, and y is reachable from i.

This definition of reachableo is fully relational (except for the model parameter m). It unifies x and y once for each path with direction dir leading from x to y. For this reason, the graph m must be acyclic. Otherwise, the relation won't terminate because the number of paths is infinite.

If the relation were to be used on possibly cyclic graphs, the conde of clause (2) could be changed to conda in which case the search for indirect connections (2.2) would be skipped in presence of a direct connection (2.1).

Typing. typeo is a relation where el-or-rel is a model element or a relation and type is its type. If provided, type may be an arbitrary type specification (see concept 3 on page 109). However reversely, i.e., when type is fresh, it will only be unified with the simplest type specification matching the type of el-or-rel, namely a symbol denoting the fully qualified name of el-or-rel's metamodel class.

Relation: funnyqt.relational/typeo
(typeo m el-or-rel type)

typeo does not distinguish between elements and relationships, so a query like (typeo m x t) on a TGraph model unifies x with all vertices and edges and t with the corresponding type.

Attributes. avalo is a relation where el-or-rel is a model element or relationship, attr is an attribute name (a keyword) and val is the attr value of el-or-rel. Thus, it is the relational counterpart of the protocol method funnyqt.generic/aval (see section 12.3 on page 111).

Relation: funnyqt.relational/avalo
(avalo m el-or-rel attr val)

avalo is quite interesting as it allows some very unusual kinds of queries which would be complicated to formulate using the functional model querying API discussed in part IV starting on page 105. For example, the following query results in all tuples of an element or relationship in the model m together with an attribute name (a keyword) whose value equals "John Doe."

```
(run* [el-or-rel attr]
  (avalo m el-or-rel attr "John Doe"))
```

References. `adjo` is a relation where the model element `el` references the element `refed-el` using its `ref` reference (a keyword). As such, it is the relational counterpart of the functions `funnyqt.generic/adj` and `funnyqt.generic/adjs` (see section 12.4 on page 112).

Relation: `funnyqt.relational/adjo`
`(adjo m el ref refed-el)`

With `adjo`, `refed-el` is always an element. That is, if `ref` denotes a single-valued reference, `refed-el` will be unified with the element referenced by `el`. If the `ref` reference of `el` is unset, then `adjo` fails. If `ref` denotes a multi-valued reference, then for each `el`, `refed-el` will be unified once with each referenced object.

Like with `relationshipo`, reachability questions can be answered easily with `adjo`, too. The following `adj-reachableo` is a relation where the element `y` can be reached from the element `x` via a path following arbitrary references.

```
(defn adj-reachableo [m x y]
  (fresh [ref]
    (conda
     [(adjo m x ref y)]
     [(fresh [i]
        (adjo m x ref i)
        (adj-reachableo m i y))])))
```

In this example, `conda` has been used in order to guarantee termination in case of cycles in the model[1].

Declarativeness versus order of goals. Relational or logic programming is declarative, and with the exception of the non-relational disjunctions `conda` and `condu`, the order in which goals are states has no severe effect on the result of a relational program except that the order in which solutions are found may also change. However, the order of goals may have a tremendous impact on the performance.

In theory, every relation simply has to make the core.logic machinery aware of all the values its arguments may take. For example, a valid but inefficient implementation for `relationshipo` could simply emit all tuples of the form (r, src, trg) where r is some relationship, src is r's source element and trg is r's target element. The unification machinery would then filter all possible bindings to determine the solutions in the relational program where `relationshipo` is used as a goal. However, it is clearly inefficient when every `relationshipo` goal would always emit as many candidate bindings as there are relationships in the model.

Therefore, the actual implementations of the model querying relations use case differentiations in order to emit only a minimum number of candidate bindings or even no candidate bindings at all. Obviously, the differentiation is based on which subset of arguments is ground already. For example, if the logic variable `r` denoting the relationship in the goal `(relationshipo m r src trg)` is already ground, two cases need to be distinguished. If `r` is in fact a relationship, then `src` and `trg` are unified with `r`'s source and target element, i.e., there is only one candidate binding for the

---

[1]Two elements connected by a bidirectional reference form a cycle already.

remaining fresh variables. If r is not a relationship, then relationshipo immediately fails without emitting any candidate binding. In case src or trg are ground and valid model elements, only candidate bindings for the outgoing or incoming incident relationships need to be emitted. Again, those are usually much fewer than the number of relationships in the complete model. So as a rule of thumb one can say that the performance of evaluating a goal depends on the how many of its logic variables are ground already.

Because the order in which logic variables are grounded is defined by the order of goals, the order also has an effect on the efficiency of evaluating a relational query. For example, the following relational model query computes all tuples (a, b, c, u, v) where a, b, and c are elements of the metamodel classes A, B, and C respectively, u is a relationship starting at a and ending at b, and v is a relationship starting at b and ending at c.

```
(run* [a b c u v]
  (typeo m a 'A)
  (typeo m b 'B)
  (typeo m c 'C)
  (relationshipo m u a b)
  (relationshipo m v b c))
```

This query is written in the worst possible way. The three typeo goals emit all possible candidate bindings for a, b, and c where the candidates have the respective types A, B, and C. Then, the candidate bindings are filtered by the two relationshipo goals which also emit candidate bindings for u and v. In order to do so, the relationships incident to a or b, or b or c have to be iterated, respectively. So essentially, the query first computes the Cartesian product of all A elements with all B element and all C elements and then restricts the possible candidate bindings using the connection constraints.

The same query could be defined much more efficient as shown in the next listing.

```
;; Much faster version of the query in the previous listing
(run* [a b c u v]
  (typeo m a 'A)
  (relationshipo m u a b)
  (typeo m b 'B)
  (relationshipo m v b c)
  (typeo m c 'C))
```

Here, the first goal emits one candidate binding for the logic variable a for all A element in the model. Thus, a is already ground when the second goal, (relationshipo m u a b) is evaluated, and therefore only bindings for u and b with an existing a need to be computed by iterating the incident relationships of the already ground a. The third goal restricts the candidate bindings for b to those where b is an instance of the metamodel class B and then two further goals compute c and v. For all but the first goal, there is at least one ground argument which restricts the number of candidate bindings and the two last typeo goals don't need to compute any candidate bindings at all but only need to perform a fast type-check.

30.2 Metamodel-Specific Relations

The relations `elemento`, `relationshipo`, `typeo`, `avalo`, and `adjo` together with the relational operators provided by core.logic, especially `==` (equality), `fresh` (existential quantification), `all` (conjunction), `conde` (disjunction), `conda`, and `condu` (both nonrelational forms of disjunction) suffice for formulating the most important model queries. However, they are on a very low-level of abstraction.

The single macro `generate-metamodel-relations` relations discussed in this section generates a complete, relational API which is specific to one given metamodel and thus specialized to write relations on models conforming to this metamodel.

Macro: `funnyqt.generic/generate-metamodel-relations`
```
(generate-metamodel-relations mm-file)
(generate-metamodel-relations mm-file nssym)
(generate-metamodel-relations mm-file nssym alias)
(generate-metamodel-relations mm-file nssym alias prefix)
```

The macro receives a string `mm-file` denoting the file containing the metamodel, an optional namespace (as a symbol) in which to generate the relational API (default is the current namespace), an optional `alias` (as a symbol) for the namespace `nssym`, and an optional `prefix` which is to be prepended to the names of all generated relations.

The following relations are generated:

1. For every element class `ElementClass` defined by the metamodel, there are the following relations.
   `(ElementClass m el)` is a relation where `el` is a direct or indirect instance of ElementClass.
   `(ElementClass! m el)` is a relation where `el` is a direct instance of ElementClass.
   `(!ElementClass m el)` is a relation where `el` is not a direct or indirect instance of ElementClass.
   `(!ElementClass! m el)` is a relation where `el` is not a direct instance of ElementClass.
2. For every relationship class `RelationshipClass` defined by the metamodel, there are the following relations.
   `(RelationshipClass m rel s t)` is a relation where `rel` is a direct or indirect instance of RelationshipClass, and `s` and `t` are its source and target elements.
   `(RelationshipClass! m el s t)` is a relation where `rel` is a direct instance of RelationshipClass, and `s` and `t` are its source and target elements.
   `(!RelationshipClass m el s t)` is a relation where `rel` is not a direct or indirect instance of RelationshipClass, and `s` and `t` are its source and target elements.
   `(!RelationshipClass! m el s t)` is a relation where `rel` is not a direct instance of RelationshipClass, and `s` and `t` are its source and target elements.
3. For every attribute name `attr` defined for some element or relationship class, there is the following relation.
   `(attr m el-or-rel val)` is a relation where `el-or-rel`'s `attr` value is `val`.
4. For every reference name `role` defined for some element class, there is the following relation.
   `(->role m el refed-el)` is a relation where `el` references `refed-el` using its `role` reference.

These generated relations simply wrap the generic model querying relations discussed in the previous section. They are slightly less flexible due to the type, attribute, or reference name being fixed but they are more convenient and readable because the concepts used in a query are more outstanding.

30.3   Utilities

The core.logic relations and relational operators plus FunnyQT's model querying relations almost suffice for defining arbitrary relational queries on models. In this short section, three additional constructs are introduced which extend the capabilities for queries working on strings (e.g., string-valued attributes), for higher-order relations, and for more convenience.

The `stro` relation is the relational counterpart of Clojure's `str` function which concatenates strings. That is, `stro` is a relation where `xy` is the concatenation of the strings `x` and `y`. Likewise, the version of arity four is a relation where `xyz` is the concatenation of `x`, `y`, and `z`.

Relation: `funnyqt.relational/stro`
```
(stro x y xy)
(stro x y z xyz)
```

`stro` is not fully relational. The substrings `x` and `y` (and `z`) have to be ground or the concatenation `xy` (or `xyz`) has to be ground.

The `alwayso` relation receives arbitrary many `args` and always succeeds.

Relation: `funnyqt.relational/alwayso`
```
(alwayso & args)
```

It is useful for higher-order relations which receive other relations in order to use them as constraints restricting their own possible solutions. In such a case, `alwayso` acts as a constraint which accepts anything.

The `with-fresh` macro receives one or many `goals`. All logic variables used in these goals which are prefixed with a question mark are automatically declared as new, fresh variables. Additionally, all occurrences of the *don't care* logic variable `_` are replaced with distinct fresh logic variables.

Macro: `funnyqt.relational/with-fresh`
```
(with-fresh & goals)
```

The `with-fresh` macro is very convenient when defining relations which work on intermediate elements. For example, the following two relations `example1` and `example1*` are completely equivalent.

```
(defn example1 [in out]
  (with-fresh
    (goal1 _ in ?b _)
    (goal2 ?b ?c)
```

```
    (goal3 _ ?c out _)))

(defn example1* [in out]
  (fresh [dc1 ?b dc2 ?c dc3 dc4]
    (goal1 dc1 in ?b dc2)
    (goal2 ?b ?c)
    (goal3 dc3 ?c out dc4)))
```

The version using `with-fresh` is much easier to read because it makes the important variables outstanding whereas the variables which the developer doesn't care
about are faded out. It is also easier to write because there is no need to invent
names for the variables which aren't interesting anyhow.

Chapter 31

Example

To demonstrate relational model querying, the relations specified in the following are defined on TGraphs conforming to the schema shown in fig. 31.1.

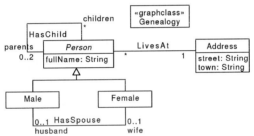

Figure 31.1: A simple genealogy metamodel

This is the simple genealogy metamodel which has already been used as target schema for the out-place transformation examples in section 26.2 on page 276 and section 27.5 on page 294.

Persons are either males or females which can be related to each other using two kinds of relationships. HasChild relationships assign the parents to a person in the role of a child and HasSpouse relationships connect a husband and a wife. Furthermore, the addresses of persons are modeled where any person lives at exactly one address but multiple persons may live at the same address.

For illustrating the relational queries which are going to be defined in the following, the example TGraph genealogy model shown in fig. 31.2 on the following page is used.

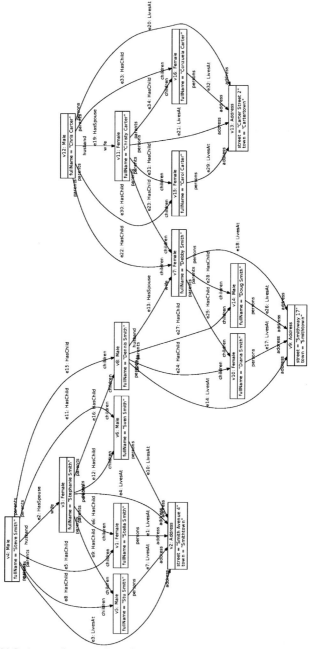

Figure 31.2: A genealogy graph conforming to the schema of fig. 31.1 on page 331

The example queries are defined using the metamodel-specific relational API generated by the `generate-metamodel-relations` which has been introduced in section 30.2 on page 328. The relations have been generated into some namespace which is accessed using the alias `gen` in the following.

The first relation `parento` succeeds when `parent` is a parent of `child`. The version of arity three just delegates to the generated `->children` relation. The version of arity five is more interesting. It accepts two more arguments `parent-c` and `child-c` which can be used to constrain the `parent` and the `child`, respectively. Those are non-relational arguments expecting two relations to be given, i.e., they must be ground.

```
(defn parento
  ([m parent child]
   (gen/->children m parent child))
  ([m parent-c child-c parent child]
   (all
    (parento m parent child)
    (parent-c m parent)
    (child-c m child))))
```

Using this second version, the typical roles in a family can be defined easily and concisely. For example, a father is a parent who happens to be male and a daughter is a child who happens to be female. In all cases, either a constraint on the parent or on the child is needed but never both. Since two constraint have to be given, `alwayso` is used as constraint on the element which does not need to be constrained.

```
(defn fathero [m father child]
  (parento m gen/Male alwayso father child))

(defn mothero [m mother child]
  (parento m gen/Female alwayso mother child))

(defn sono [m parent son]
  (parento m alwayso gen/Male parent son))

(defn daughtero [m parent daughter]
  (parento m alwayso gen/Female parent daughter))
```

Using these relations, one can easily query for all fathers with their daughters like so.

```
;; Alternative 1
(run* [f d]
  (fathero g f d)
  (daughtero g f d))
;=> ([#<v4: Male> #<v1: Female>]
;    [#<v8: Male> #<v10: Female>]
;    [#<v12: Male> #<v7: Female>]
;    [#<v12: Male> #<v15: Female>]
;    [#<v12: Male> #<v16: Female>])
```

```
;; Alternative 2
(run* [f d]
  (parento g gen/Male gen/Female f d))
;=> same result as above
```

Next, the considered family circle is extended to the grandparents. A grandparent of a grandchild is a parent of some intermediate ?parent who is in turn parent of grandchild. Again, a second version of arity five could have been added in analogy to parento to make is easy to define more relations for grandmothers, grandfathers, granddaughters, and grandsons.

```
(defn grandparento [m grandparent grandchild]
  (with-fresh
    (parento m grandparent ?parent)
    (parento m ?parent grandchild)))
```

Two persons are siblings when they have at least one common parent and are distinct.

```
(defn siblingo [m s1 s2]
  (with-fresh
    (parento m ?parent s1)
    (parento m ?parent s2)
    (!= s1 s2)))
```

And then an aunt is a female sibling of one of a nephew's parents.

```
(defn aunto [m aunt nephew]
  (with-fresh
    (gen/Female m aunt)
    (siblingo m ?parent aunt)
    (parento m ?parent nephew)))

(distinct
 (run* [aunt nephew]
   (aunto g aunt nephew)))
;=> ([#<v15: Female> #<v10: Female>] [#<v1: Female> #<v10: Female>]
;    [#<v16: Female> #<v10: Female>] [#<v15: Female> #<v14: Male>]
;    [#<v16: Female> #<v14: Male>] [#<v1: Female> #<v14: Male>])
```

The last relation going to be defined here is ancestoro. It is a relation where a is an ancestor of the predecessor p. Two cases are distinguished: a might be a parent of p, or a might be a parent of some intermediate child ?i who is an ancestor of p in turn.

```
(defn ancestoro [m a p]
  (conde
   [(parento m a p)]
   [(with-fresh
      (parento m a ?i)
      (ancestoro m ?i p))]))
```

Chapter 32

Related Work

In this chapter, several related logic-based program and model querying approaches are discussed.

Ekeko [RS14] is a tool for analyzing Java software which like FunnyQT's relational querying facility is provided as an API extending Clojure's core.logic library. With Ekeko, queries are specified directly on the abstract Java syntax graphs provided by JDT (Java Development Tools[1]). Additionally, inter-procedural control flow and data flow information computed by the Soot program analysis framework [Lam+11] can be accessed in queries.

Built on top of the logic-based querying API, there is also a functional graph manipulation layer which allows to define in-place transformations on Java syntax graphs, e.g., in order to implement refactoring operations.

Ekeko is tightly integrated with Eclipse. Query results can be visualized using the ZEST Eclipse Visualization Toolkit[2], Java elements contained in query results are highlighted in the Java editor, problem markers can be added to AST nodes based on query results which are then shown in the Eclipse Java editor and quick fix operations can be defined using the AST manipulation API which can then be applied for a given problem marker.

Ekeko is based on previous work on program querying in Eclipse of the same authors. The *SOUL* tool suite [Roo+11; Nog+11] already provided a very similar approach. It consists of the query language SOUL (*Smalltalk Open Unification Language*) which in combination with *CAVA* library supports querying Java programs using logic predicates over abstract JDT syntax graphs and it also supports querying by example where the query contains concrete Java code with placeholder variables. Lastly, *Barrista* integrates the Smalltalk parts of the tool suite with Eclipse and provides extension points for other Eclipse plugins which want to make use of the features provided by SOUL.

The problem with SOUL is the impedance mismatch between Smalltalk and Java

---

[1]http://www.eclipse.org/jdt (last visited: 2015-10-12)
[2]http://www.eclipse.org/gef/zest/ (last visited: 2015-10-12)

(Eclipse, JDT). All required communication and data access has to be implemented using foreign function interfaces in C and thus query results don't contain the actual JDT elements but only proxies which then need to resolved again. In contrast, Ekeko runs natively on the JVM and therefore can work on the native JDT elements and interact with Eclipse directly.

Similar to Ekeko and SOUL is the *JQuery* tool [Vol06] which provides Eclipse-integrated declarative querying on JDT syntax graphs. It is based on the TyRuBa[3] logic programming language.

Whereas Ekeko and SOUL allow for defining arbitrary complex queries, JQuery only provides predicates which allow for querying Java artifacts up to the signature level in a very concise and easy manner, i.e., query writers don't need to know the details of JDT syntax graphs. For example, the query `type(?T),re_name(?T,/Figure$/),method(?T,?M),returns(?M,?R)` searches for classes and interfaces ?T whose name ends in "Figure" which contain a method ?M whose return type is ?R.

The results of such queries are displayed in tree-view code browsers where the elements are linked to the actual source code. Therefore, JQuery can be seen as a sophisticated extension to the Eclipse Java search features.

EMF-Query [NJ15] is a relational querying approach for EMF models. Like Ekeko and FunnyQT's relational querying facility, it provides an API for defining queries based on Clojure's core.logic library. Essentially, this API consists of the relations (1) `eobject` which is almost identical to FunnyQT's `elemento` relation, (2) `eobject-eclass` which is similar to FunnyQT's `typeo` relation, and (3) `ehas` which is similar to FunnyQT's `avalo` and `adjo` relations, i.e., it is a relation where some eobject has some value set for some property.

In addition, there are the advanced relations `reachable` and `echild+`. `reachable` is a relation between two eobjects where the second can be reached from the first, and `echild+` which is a variant of `ehas` for references where the given reference may be traversed one or many times, i.e., (`echild+ eo :refName reo`) is the transitive closure of (`ehas eo :refName reo`). The evaluation of queries using the basic and advanced relations is implemented as an extension to Ekeko.

While queries can be defined using just core.logic and the EMF-Query relations, the authors argue that this is too complicated and inconvenient for most developers. Therefore, EMF-Query also allows to define queries visually using so-called model templates. A model template is essentially a pattern in the form of an object diagram. The types of the objects, the slots, and the links are determined by the queried model's metamodel. Into this metamodel, a generic query metamodel is woven in which allows for naming the objects and for notating links corresponding to the advanced relations `echild+` and `reachable`. From these visual query specifications, corresponding code using the relational querying API can be generated and evaluated.

So all in all, EMF-Query provides a slim relational querying API and support for defining simple patterns visually.

---

[3]http://tyruba.sourceforge.net/ (last visited: 2015-10-12)

Part IX

On Bidirectional Transformations

Summary

This part is concerned with bidirectional transformations and chapter 33 starting on page 341 introduces into the topic.

Thereafter, chapter 34 starting on page 345 introduces FunnyQT's embedded DSL for defining bidirectional transformations and chapter 35 starting on page 361 classifies the approach according to several properties which can be found in the bidirectional transformation literature.

FunnyQT's take on bidirectional transformations is then illustrated using a non-trivial example in chapter 36 starting on page 363.

A discussion of related approaches closes this part in chapter 37 starting on page 369.

Chapter 33

Introduction

Unidirectional out-place transformations which have been discussed in part VII starting on page 259 have clearly defined inputs and outputs. One model or a set of models is the source of the transformation and another model or set of models is the target of the transformation. The transformation itself describes how elements in the source models are translated to elements in the target models.

With model driven engineering, it is common that a model is developed further even though it might have been the source of a transformation already. Let the model b conforming to a metamodel B be the result of applying a transformation $t : A \to B$ to some initial model a conforming to metamodel A, i.e., $t(a) = b$. If the source model a of the transformation is changed to a', these changes might introduce an inconsistency with respect to the transformation t, i.e., $t(a') \neq b$. In such a case, one can recreate a new target model b' by applying the transformation again to a', i.e., $t(a') = b'$.

Instead of recomputing the target model anew, there are also some *incremental model transformation* approaches which update the original target model b in-place in order to have it reflect the changes performed to the source model [HLR06; JT10; Ber+15]. Most of these incremental approaches use *live* transformations (in contrast to *batch* transformations) where the transformation keeps running as a demon after the creation of the target model in order to observe changes applied to the source model and then propagates them immediately to the target model. However, FunnyQT's two out-place transformation approaches which have been discussed in part VII starting on page 259 only define batch transformations.

Another problematic scenario occurs when the target model b of a transformation t is changed afterwards to a model b'. Again, the models a and b' may have become inconsistent with respect to the transformation t, i.e., $t(a) \neq b'$. In such cases, it is often desirable to propagate the changes applied to the model b back to model a. However, this is infeasible if t is a unidirectional transformation.

Lastly, there is also the worst-case scenario in which both the source and target models of a transformation have been changed independently from each other in which case it is often desired to synchronize the models again, i.e., to propagate the changes performed in one model to the respective other model in either one direction only or both directions.

A bidirectional transformation $t : A \leftrightarrows B$ defined between models conforming to metamodels A and B is a transformation which can be executed in both directions. That is, a model a conforming to metamodel A can be transformed to a model b conforming to metamodel B (*forward transformation*), and likewise a model b conforming to metamodel B can be transformed to a model a conforming to metamodel A (*backward transformation*).

One important point here is that the transformation's specification is inherently agnostic to direction, i.e., one specification defines both forward and backward transformation instead of having to specify the directions separately. Whereas a unidirectional transformation rule may define how to create some target element for a given source element using complex queries and imperative code, a bidirectional transformation must be completely declarative. This is usually done by defining correspondences between elements in one model and elements in the other model.

For example, in a bidirectional transformation between a UML class diagram and a relational database schema, a rule might define a correspondence between a UML class and a database table where the class and the table have the same name. When executed in forward direction, this specification implies that one table has to be created for each class and the new table's name has to be set to the class' name. When executed in backward direction, the specification implies that one class has to be created for each table, and the new class' name has to be set to the table's name.

Most bidirectional transformation approaches provide more services to the user than just being able to perform batch forward and backward transformations. Concretely, they allow for *consistency checking* and *model synchronization*, too.

Consistency checking means to be able to test if two given models a and b are consistent with respect to the transformation specification, i.e., if for all elements in one model there exists a corresponding element in the respective other model.

Model synchronization is possibly the most important and challenging feature a bidirectional model transformation approach has to offer. It deals with the scenarios sketched above where two models are consistent with respect to a transformation's rules and then one of the models (or even both) is further changed. Depending on the changes, the models might not be consistent with respect to the transformation anymore and the task is to restore consistency by propagating the changes to the respective other model. Thus, model synchronization is even mode general than incremental model transformations, i.e., the latter is essentially the forward-only version of the former.

FunnyQT's take on bidirectional transformations which is introduced starting with the following chapter is based on the relational model querying API discussed in part VIII starting on page 311 and offers all three services mentioned above, i.e., forward and backward transformations, consistency checking, and model synchronization. Transformations define so-called transformation relations which relate elements in a left model with elements in a right model. Each transformation relation defines one conjunction of goals on the left model and one conjunction of goals on the right model and the two conjunctions of goals are related by shared logic variables usually denoting equality of attribute values of elements in both models.

A transformation is always executed in one direction and then the semantics of such a transformation relation is to ensure that for all solutions of the conjunction of goals on the respective source model, there exists at least one solution of the goals on the respective target model. In order to achieve this, new elements may be created in the target model or existing elements might be changed.

Chapter 34

Defining Bidirectional Transformations

In FunnyQT, bidirectional transformations consist of transformation relations (*t-relations* for short) which relate elements in a left model with elements in a right model by defining a `:left` and a `:right` clause. These clauses specify conjunctions of relational goals.

By sharing logic variables between the two clauses, equality of certain values can be specified. E.g., a t-relation might define that an element of type X in the left model corresponds to an element of type Y in the right model if and only if the name attribute of the X instance has the same value as the id attribute of the Y instance.

Bidirectional transformations are always executed in one direction and then either the left or the right model becomes the target model and the respective other model becomes the source model. The semantics of a t-relation is that it has to ensure that for all solutions of the source clause, there exists at least one solution of the target clause.

T-relations can have two different kinds of dependencies to other t-relations. On the one hand, there are *preconditions* (see section 34.5 on page 353) which allow to define that a t-relation only needs to hold under certain conditions. The most common condition is to define that a relation only needs to hold if some subset of the elements it relates have already been related by some other t-relation. On the other hand, there are *postconditions* (see section 34.7 on page 355) which allow to define that whenever the current t-relation is ensured, the specified other t-relations also need to be ensured[1].

In addition to the normal *enforcement* mode, bidirectional transformations can also be run in a directed *checkonly* mode (see section 34.4 on page 349). In this mode, the chosen target model will not be modified but only the traceability information

---

[1] FunnyQT's bidirectional transformation DSL is intentionally very similar to the QVT Relations [OMG11b] language and borrows the term postcondition with its described meaning from it. This meaning differs from the meaning in program specification where the postcondition relates the inputs of a function/method and the state of the object or system before the execution to its outputs and the state of the object or system after the execution.

will be computed. I.e., for each t-relation, there is a map from elements satisfying the conjunction of goals on the source model to corresponding elements satisfying the conjunction of goals on the target model. Additionally, the elements satisfying the conjunction of goals on the source model but have no existing correspondence in the target model are also reported.

For supporting reusability, there are inheritance concepts available for both t-relations (see section 34.8 on page 356) and for complete bidirectional transformations (see section 34.9 on page 357).

Lastly, transformations may also define local relations (in the sense of plain core.logic relations) which can then be used by other relations or t-relations (see section 34.10 on page 359).

34.1   Transformation Definitions

A bidirectional FunnyQT transformation is defined using the `deftransformation` macro.

Macro: `funnyqt.bidi/deftransformation`
```
(deftransformation name [left right & args] & t-relations)
(deftransformation name [left right & args] extends-clause & t-relations)
```

It receives the `name` of the transformation to be defined, a vector of arguments, an optional `extends-clause` for transformation inheritance (see section 34.9 on page 357), and one or many `t-relations`. The vector of arguments always starts with the formal parameter for the left model and the formal parameter for the right model. Arbitrarily many additional parameters may follow.

For example, a hypothetical transformation between class diagram and database schema models could be defined like shown below[2].

```
(deftransformation class-diagram2database-schema [cd db]
  ;; t-relation definitions
  )
```

This defines a new bidirectional transformation `class-diagram2database-schema` between a class diagram model `cd` and a database schema model `db`. The class diagram is the left model and the database schema is the right model.

A bidirectional transformation definition expands into a plain Clojure function at compile-time. This function has the arguments as declared by the transformation definition and one additional parameter is appended which determines the transformation's direction and mode (see section 34.4 on page 349).

The effects of a bidirectional transformation, i.e., the modification of the respective target model in order to make it consistent with the source model, happens as a side-effect. The return value of the transformation is a map of traceability information (see section 34.3 on the next page).

---

[2]A complete version of this bidirectional transformation is discussed in chapter 36 starting on page 363.

34.2 Transformation Relations

A transformation relation has a name (a symbol), one :left, and one :right clause. Both clauses are conjunctions of goals where the goals are formulated using the relational model querying API which has previously been discussed in chapter 30 starting on page 323. They could use the generic relations typeo, elemento, relationshipo, avalo, and adjo but it is advisable to use the generated, metamodel-specific relational querying APIs (see section 30.2 on page 328).

All logic variables used in the clauses must be prefixed with a question mark and they don't need to be declared using fresh because the goals are wrapped in an implicit with-fresh (see page 329).

A t-relation may be defined as a *top-level t-relation* by annotating the t-relation name with ^:top metadata. Such top-level t-relations are automatically ensured in their declaration order. All other t-relations must be invoked explicitly using postconditions (see section 34.7 on page 355).

A simple top-level t-relation is given in the following listing. It assumes that metamodel-specific relational APIs have been generated for the class diagram and database schema metamodels and that these namespaces have been required using the namespace aliases cd and db, respectively.

```
(^:top class2table
 :left  [(cd/Class cd ?class)
         (cd/name  cd ?class ?name)]
 :right [(db/Table db ?table)
         (db/name  db ?table ?name)])
```

This t-relation defines that a class in the class diagram model corresponds to a table in the database schema model given that the class and the table have the same name.

The semantics of this t-relation when the transformation is executed in the direction of the database schema model is that for every class in the class diagram, there must exist at least one table in the database schema model which has the same name as the class.

The semantics of the t-relation when the transformation is executed in the direction of the class diagram model is that for every table in the database schema model, there must exist at least one class in the class diagram which has the same name as the table.

The exact semantics of the respective target clause, i.e., how the existence of the elements in the target clause is ensured by creating new elements or changing existing elements, is discussed in detail in section 34.4 on page 349.

34.3 Traceability

Whenever a t-relation relates elements and values from the left model with elements and values from the right model, this relationship is saved as traceability information.

Concretely, every t-relation's traceability information is saved as a set of maps where the maps assign to the names of the logic variables used in the t-relation (represented as keywords) their final ground values. In the following, this set of logic variable bindings providing a t-relation's traceability information is called the *t-relation's bindings*.

For example, assuming that the t-relation `class2table` defined above has been invoked in order to ensure that there are corresponding database tables for classes A and B in the class diagram model, its t-relation bindings would look like given in the next listing:

```
#{;; Binding for the class A and the corresponding table A
  {:?class #<Class>,   ;; defined by the :left clause
   :?table #<Table>,   ;; defined by the :right clause
   :?name "A"},        ;; defined by both :left and :right clauses
  ;; Binding for the class B and the corresponding table B
  {:?class #<Class>,   ;; defined by the :left clause
   :?table #<Table>,   ;; defined by the :right clause
   :?name "B"}}        ;; defined by both :left and :right clauses
```

Then, the traceability information of a complete bidirectional transformation is a map from t-relation names (keywords) to t-relation bindings, e.g.:

```
{:class2table     #{...}, ;; as shown above
 :attribute2column #{...},
 ...}
```

The t-relation bindings being sets of logic variable assignments are actually relations in the mathematical sense and the FunnyQT implementation ensures that they can also be used as relations in the core.logic sense. This means that `(class2table :?class ?c :?table ?t)` is a valid goal which can be used inside the `:left` or `:right` clauses of t-relations. The goal succeeds for every combination of a class `?c` and a table `?t` which have previously been related by `class2table`[3], i.e., the keywords `:?class` and `:?table` refer to the logic variables of the same name in the t-relation `class2table`.

Technically, t-relations are not relations in the strict core.logic sense. They are local functions which query the respective source model and adapt the respective target model. That they can still be used as relational goals is a convenience feature provided by the `deftransformation` macro. It replaces any goal of the form above, i.e., a goal where the relation is a t-relation defined by the transformation, with a `relateo` goal. For example, the `class2table` goal will be replaced with `(relateo :class2table :?class ?c :?table ?t)`.

Relation: `funnyqt.bidi/relateo`
`(relateo t-relation & bindings)`

`relateo` is a relation where the given `t-relation` (a keyword) defines the given `bindings`. It is not fully relational, i.e., the `t-relation` must be ground and also all

---

[3]Such traceability goals are not specific to any of the two models. Therefore, they should actually be defined in a `:when` clause defining a precondition (see section 34.5 on page 353).

keywords referring to logic variables of t-relation must be ground[4].

As mentioned above in section 34.1 on page 346, the return value of executing a bidirectional transformation is its complete traceability information. This is represented as a map again with two entries.

```
{:related {:class2table      #{...},
           :attribute2column #{...},
           ...},
 :unrelated {:class2table      #{...},
             :attribute2column #{...}}}}
```

The value of the entry with the key :related is the map assigning to t-relation names the corresponding t-relation bindings as discussed above. The value of the entry with the key :unrelated has the same structure, i.e., it is also a map where t-relation names get assigned a set of bindings. However, those sets contain only the bindings for the logic variables in the respective source clause and precondition (see section 34.5 on page 353) which could not be related to target model elements by the t-relation. Usually, a bidirectional transformation enforces the existence of corresponding elements defined by a t-relation's target clause. Thus, the value of the :unrelated entry is usually the empty map. However, transformations can also be run in a *checkonly* mode where the target model won't be modified. This is discussed in section 34.4.

34.4 Transformation Direction and Modes

As already mentioned, a bidirectional transformation is always executed in one direction and then either the :left clauses become the source clauses and the :right clause become the target clauses, or it is the opposite way round.

In addition to the direction, every bidirectional transformation can be run in two modes. First, there is the *enforcement mode* where the respective target model will be adapted in order to ensure that for each binding of the logic variables in a t-relation's source clause (and precondition), there exists at least one binding for the logic variables in the respective target clause. The exact enforcement algorithm will be discussed below. Secondly, there is the *checkonly mode* where the target model will not be modified. This mode is useful to test if two existing models are consistent with each other with respect to the transformation's t-relations. In this mode, the value of the entry with key :unrelated in the transformation's traceability map will be populated as discussed in the previous section.

Section 34.1 on page 346 already mentioned that each bidirectional transformation has one last formal parameter which is not declared by the transformation definition and defines the transformation's direction and mode for the current call. Thus, the complete signature of the example class-diagram2database-schema transformation is (class-diagram2database-schema left right dir). The dir argument may take the following values:

---

[4]relateo could be defined so that it is fully relational but there is no need for that because it already suffices for its intended use-case, i.e., accessing existing bindings of previously executed t-relations.

`:right` Enforcement mode in the direction of the right model, i.e., a forward transformation.

`:left` Enforcement mode in the direction of the left model, i.e., a backward transformation.

`:right-checkonly` Checkonly mode in the direction of the right model, i.e., a forward
consistency check.

`:left-checkonly` Checkonly mode in the direction of the left model, i.e., a backward
consistency check.

To illustrate how these modes and directions can be used, consider there is an
existing class diagram model `cd` and an existing database schema model `db`. Possibly,
one has been created from the other by some transformation but thereafter they
have been developed further individually. The task is to synchronize them again,
i.e., to make them consistent with each other with respect to the transformation's
t-relations. There are multiple ways to do so.

After executing (`class-diagram2database-schema cd db :right`), the models are *for-
ward-consistent*, i.e., all class diagram elements considered by the transformation's
t-relations have corresponding elements in the database schema model. However,
there might be database schema elements in the right model which have no counterparts in the left class diagram model.

There are two options to restore full consistency. Obviously, one can simply run
the transformation in the other direction in order to ensure *backward consistency*,
too, i.e., (`class-diagram2database-schema cd db :left`). This is probably the best solution in scenarios where the changes applied to each of the two models are equally
important. In case the database schema model has no important changes, one could
also use the traceability information[5] returned by (`class-diagram2database-schema
cd db :left-checkonly`) in order to delete those elements from the database schema
model `db` which have no counterpart in the class diagram model `cd`.

In case the class diagram model's changes are not important to us, we would
have started with a backward transformation followed by a forward consistency
check in order to figure out the elements that need to be deleted in the class diagram
model.

In the following, it is discussed how a t-relation's target clause is enforced. For
illustration purposes, the t-relation in the following listing is used and it is assumed
that the transformation is run in the direction of the right model. Additionally, the
logic variables denoting attribute values, i.e., `?name`, `?cname`, and `?ctype` are assumed
to be bound by the `:left` clause or a precondition (see section 34.5 on page 353).

```
(example-t-relation
 :left  [...]
 :right [(db/Table   db ?table)
         (db/name     db ?table ?name)
         (db/->cols db ?table ?col)
         (db/Column db ?col)
         (db/name     db ?col     ?cname)
         (db/type     db ?col     ?ctype)])
```

---

[5]Especially the value of the `:unrelated` key.

The task of enforcement is to ensure that for all unique logic variable bindings of the `:left` clause, a corresponding logic variable binding for the remaining fresh variables in the `:right` clause exists. That is, for each unique binding of the `:left` clause, there has to exist some table whose name is `?name`. Furthermore, the table must have some column `?col` whose name is `?cname` and whose type is `?ctype`.

When using the usual metamodel-specific model relations discussed in section 30.2 on page 328, the implementation enforces target clauses by only four means:

(1) new elements and relationships may be created,
(2) elements may be added to multi-valued references,
(3) attribute values may be set in case they are currently unset, and
(4) single-valued references may be set in case they are currently unset.

All these adaptations are completely additive. Attribute values and single-valued references which are already set are never changed. Likewise, if an element is already contained by some other element, it will never be assigned to a different container. And most importantly, FunnyQT will never delete elements.

So with respect to the example, if the model `db` already contains a table with the required name and already contains a column of the required name and type, then those are simply taken and no modification is performed. Otherwise, modifications in the categories (1)-(4) are performed in order to make the t-relation hold.

Concretely, if there exists a table with the required name but the table does not contain a column of the required name and type, then a new column will be created and assigned to the table.

If there is no table with the required name, then it will be created. The required column will be created, too, even though it is possible that the model already contains a column with the required name and type. The reason is that (`db/->cols db ?table ?col`) only considers columns that are already contained by `?table` because this variable is already ground. If that is not the intended behavior, then the goal (`db/Column db ?col`) could be added before the `db/->cols` goal. In this case, all columns in the complete model would be considered. Because FunnyQT won't assign elements to a different container, valid bindings for `?col` would be restricted to columns which are not contained by any table already[6].

Relations changing attribute values and single-valued references. As discussed above, by default FunnyQT's bidirectional transformation implementation performs only additive changes in order to enforce the target clauses of t-relations. New elements and relationships may be created, elements may be added to multi-valued references, and attribute values and single-valued references may be set in case they are currently unset. And most importantly, elements and relationships will never be deleted.

The benefit of this approach is that it is impossible to lose any information. The source model won't be changed anyway and the above rules guarantee that nothing will be deleted or overwritten in the target model.

---

[6]However, columns without a containing table can be considered as errors in the model, thus one would typically not cater for such situations in a transformation.

However, this approach has also a downside in that it may create duplicate elements which are almost equal to existing elements in the target model. Consider a t-relation which relates attributes of some class which have a name and a type to columns in a table which also have a name and a type. If this t-relation is enforced in the direction of the database schema model, the following situation might occur. For a given attribute, there already exists a corresponding column of the same name. However, the attribute's and the column's type don't match. Therefore, FunnyQT creates a new column with the required name and type and assigns it to the table corresponding to the given class. As a result, the table now has two columns of the very same name, only their types are different.

Even worse, such element creations can cascade. Consider two models with one root element and a very deep containment hierarchy each and a transformation which essentially has one t-relation for the elements of every layer in the hierarchy. If the two root elements cannot be related because of some minor mismatch in some attribute value, a new one will be created. And because FunnyQT will never change the container of some element, this means that also all contents of the new root element will have to be created anew, transitively. The result is that the final target model contains two root elements whose complete transitive contents could be completely equal. Essentially, the target model has been created anew from scratch.

So clearly, these purely additive change semantics are not suitable for practical purposes. In order to cope with such situations, the metamodel-specific relational querying APIs that can be generated by FunnyQT and which were discussed in section 30.2 on page 328 define some more relations than have been discussed there. In addition to the relations which have been discussed already, the following starred relations are generated:

1. For every attribute name `attr` defined for some element or relationship class, there is the following relation.
   `(attr* m el-or-rel val)` is a relation where `el-or-rel`'s `attr` value is `val`.
2. For every reference name `role` which is defined as a single-valued reference for at least one element class, there is the following relation.
   `(->role* m el refed-el)` is a relation where `el` references `refed-el` using its `role` reference.

When using these relations as goals in relational queries or the source clause of bidirectional transformations, they are completely equivalent to their unstarred counterparts. But when they are used as goals in the target clause of a bidirectional transformation, they allow that the attribute value or single-valued reference they refer to may be changed even if it is already set. Thus, they allow for overwriting existing attribute values and single-valued references.

Typically, most if not all elements can be uniquely identified by only a subset of their attributes and references. For example, a class in a class diagram is uniquely determined by its qualified name and an attribute is uniquely determined by its containing class and its name. Likewise, in a database schema, all tables have unique names and every column is uniquely determined by its containing table and its name. The data type of a column is of no importance for identification purposes. Therefore, the example t-relation discussed above could be changed to the following one.

```
(example-t-relation
 :left  [...]
 :right [(db/Table   db ?table)
         (db/name    db ?table ?name)
         (db/->cols  db ?table ?col)
         (db/Column  db ?col)
         (db/name    db ?col    ?cname)
         (db/type*   db ?col    ?ctype)]) ;; the type may be changed
```

The semantics of this variant when being enforced in the direction of the right
database schema model is equivalent to the previous version except for one case: if
there is an existing table ?table having the required ?name and containing an existing
column ?col with the required ?cname but a type different from ?ctype, then the
currently set type may be overridden with the value of ?ctype.

In general, it is advisable to use the unstarred model relations for all attributes
and references which define or contribute to the identity of elements or relationships
of a given metamodel class. For all other attributes and single-valued references,
the starred relations are usually a better fit in practice.

34.5 Preconditions

In addition to a :left and a :right clause, a t-relation may have a :when clause which
defines a kind of *precondition*. Like the :left and :right clauses, the :when clause is
a conjunction of goals.

The :left and :right clauses have different semantics depending on the direction
in which the transformation is executed. I.e., when transforming in the direction
of the right model, the :left clause is the source clause and used only as a query
whereas the :right clause is the target clause and enforced which implies querying
the right model and possibly creating new elements in it and changing existing
elements. When transforming in the direction of the left model, the roles are
reversed.

In contrast, :when clauses are always used for querying only and their goals are
never enforced. Above it has been said that a t-relation ensures that for all possibly
bindings of the logic variables in its source clause, there exists at least one binding
of the logic variables in its target clause. This statement is still correct but the
source clause of a t-relation is not only either its :left or its :right clause. Instead
the actual source clause of a t-relation is the conjunction of the goals in the :left
clause and the :when clause when transforming in the right direction, or it is the
conjunction of the goals in the :right clause and the :when clause when transforming
in the left direction.

Precondition clauses are especially suited for goals which translate attribute
values between the two models and for restricting the applicability of t-relations in
terms of asserting that certain traceability relationships have to exist.

For example, consider the following top-level t-relation attribute2column which, as its name suggests, relates attributes of classes to columns of tables.

```
(^:top attribute2column
 :left  [(cd/Class     cd ?cls)
         (cd/->attrs   cd ?cls ?attr)
         (cd/Attribute cd ?attr)
         (cd/name      cd ?attr ?aname)]
 :right [(db/Table  db ?table)
         (db/->cols db ?table ?col)
         (db/Column db ?col)
         (db/name   db ?col ?cname)]
 :when  [(stro "c_" ?aname ?cname)
         (class2table :?class ?cls :?table ?table)])
```

In this t-relation, the names of the attributes and the corresponding columns are not defined to be equal. Instead, the columns are prefixed with the string `"c_"`, e.g., if there is some attribute with name `"description"`, then the corresponding column must have the name `"c_description"`. This is specified by the goal (`stro "c_"` `?aname ?cname`)[7] in the precondition. In addition, the precondition also defines that the class `?cls` containing the attribute and the table `?table` containing the column have already been related by the t-relation `class2table`.

34.6   Target Clauses

Every t-relation may define one `:target` clause which is a vector of goals just like the `:left`, `:right`, and `:when` clauses.

As mentioned in the last section, the goals defined in the `:when` clause of a t-relation are appended to the respective source clause when executing the transformation, i.e., they are appended to either the `:left` clause when transforming in the right direction, and they are appended to the `:right` clause when transforming into the left direction.

Technically, the `:target` clause is the inverse of the `:when` clause. Its goals are appended to the respective target clause, i.e., they are appended to the `:left` clause when transforming in the left direction, and they are appended to the `:right` clause when transforming in the right direction.

The use-case of the target clause is handling non-bijective mappings. For example with respect to the running example, class diagrams have one unique type for strings whereas database systems usually have multiple string types, i.e., they have types for strings of a fixed length (CHAR(N)), strings of a variable length with a given maximum length (VARCHAR(N)), and truly variable-length strings (TEXT). Thus, when transforming a string attribute to a column, there is a choice to make for the column's type. A sensible default would be to use the largest type, i.e., TEXT. However, when synchronizing in the same direction and there is already a column, its type should be allowed to be any one of the three possibilities without imposing a change of the model.

---

[7]The `stro` relation for concatenating strings has been discussed on page 329.

This hypothetical situation with non-bijective correspondences in both direction is handled by the complete transformation example which is going to be discussed in chapter 36 starting on page 363.

34.7 Postconditions

Every t-relation may also have a *postcondition* which is specified by a `:where` clause. In contrast to the other clauses, the postcondition is not a conjunction of relational goals but a vector containing arbitrary Clojure code which has access to all variables bound by the other clauses. This code is executed once for every logic variable binding established by the t-relation's `:left`, `:right`, and `:when` clauses.

The main intention of the postcondition is to define the control flow between the individual t-relations in terms of an implication. If there exists a binding between the current t-relation's source and target clause, then also bindings for the t-relations called in the `:where` clause have to exist. Speaking in terms of the example: if a class and a table could be related, then their attributes and columns must also be related.

As already mentioned in footnote [1] on page 345, the term postcondition for the `:where` clause is borrowed from QVT Relational and doesn't really fit too well. It's actually more of a post-processing instruction rather than a condition. If the current t-relation holds, then the other t-relations called from the `:where` clause also need to be enforced and therefore will eventually hold, too.

Usually, there are only few top-level t-relations and they invoke other t-relations from their `:where` clauses. Those may in turn invoke further t-relations from their postconditions. Like with rule-based unidirectional out-place transformations (see chapter 26 starting on page 265), the t-relations in a transformation and their call dependencies are usually aligned according to the containment hierarchy of the transformed models.

The following t-relations give an example. Instead of defining `attribute2column` as a top-level t-relation and then testing in a precondition if the containing class and table have already been related by `class2table`, the latter can call the former from a `:where` clause. Additionally, the `:where` clause prints the related class and table.

```
(^:top class2table
 :left  [(cd/Class cd ?class)
         (cd/name   cd ?class ?name)]
 :right [(db/Table db ?table)
         (db/name   db ?table ?name)]
 :where [(println "Related" ?class "with" ?table)
         (attribute2column :?cls ?class :?table ?table)])

(attribute2column
 :left  [(cd/->attrs   cd ?cls ?attr)
         (cd/Attribute cd ?attr)
         (cd/name      cd ?attr ?aname)]
 :right [(db/->cols db ?table ?col)
         (db/Column db ?col)
```

```
     (db/name    db ?col ?cname)]
:when  [(stro "c_" ?aname ?cname)]])
```

In this example, `attribute2column` is called once for every pair of a class being related with a table by `class2table`. The related elements are passed as arguments, so `?cls` and `?table` in `attribute2column` are ground already when it starts executing. Note that the invocations of `attribute2column` do not happen immediately when a new binding has been established by `class2table` but they are deferred until `class2table` has been completely enforced. Thus, `attribute2column` may assume that all classes already have a corresponding table when transforming in the right direction, or that all tables have a corresponding class when transforming in the left direction.

As mentioned above, top-level t-relations are executed in their declaration order. Therefore, top-level t-relations with `:when` clauses restricting elements to those which have already been related by other t-relations like in the example of the previous section suffice for many transformation tasks. However, postconditions allow for a more explicit control flow definition and they usually also perform better. The `attribute2column` version on page 354 has to do a global search in the complete model and then restrict the candidates according to the previously established t-relation bindings of `class2table`. The effort for the latter is linear in the number of bindings established by `class2table`. In contrast, the version presented in this section is called once for every t-relation binding of `class2table` but since the class and the table are already provided as arguments, only a local search has to be performed.

34.8   Transformation Relation Inheritance

The FunnyQT bidirectional transformation DSL provides a concept of *t-relation inheritance* which allows to factor out common parts of multiple t-relations.

Let's assume that the class diagram metamodel defines some abstract Classifier element class and Class and Interface are two concrete subclasses. Both classes and interfaces should be related to tables by the transformation[8] and the relation is again determined by equality of the name. This is what the abstract `classifier2table` t-relation in the following listing defines.

```
(^:abstract classifier2table
 :left   [(cd/Classifier cd ?classifier)
          (cd/name        cd ?classifier ?name)]
 :right  [(db/Table db ?table)
          (db/name  db ?name)])

(class2table
 :extends [(classifier2table :?classifier ?class)]
 :left    [(cd/Class cd ?class)]
 :right   [(class-tableo ?table)])

(interface2table
```

---

[8]This is obviously a contrived example. Objects are always instances of some class, so there is no need for having tables for interfaces in an object-relational mapping scenario.

```
:extends [(classifier2table :?classifier ?iface)]
:left    [(cd/Interface cd ?iface)]
:right   [(iface-tableo ?table)]])
```

The two t-relations `class2table` and `interface2table` extend the abstract t-relation `classifier2table` which means that their `:left`, `:right`, `:when`, and `:where` clauses are the union of the extended t-relation's clauses and their own clauses.

Like with pattern inheritance which has been discussed in section 18.1.17 on page 211, the extending t-relations may define renamings for the logic variables of the extended pattern. E.g., the logic variable `?classifier` in the `classifier2table` t-relation is named `?class` in `class2table` and `?iface` in `interface2table`.

Thus, `class2table` inherits that a left classifier corresponds to a right table with the same name. It further restricts the left classifier to be a class and it restricts the right table to be a table corresponding to a class. The `class-tableo` relation isn't specified further here but it is assumed that it succeeds if and only if the given table corresponds to a class when the transformation is executed in the direction of the left model.

A t-relation may extend multiple other t-relations and extension works transitively. There mustn't be cycles in a inheritance hierarchy. Metadata annotations such as `^:top` and `^:abstract` are not propagated from extended to extending t-relations.

When a t-relation is annotated with the `^:abstract` metadata annotation, this defines that the single purpose of this t-relation is to be extended by other t-relations. For abstract t-relations, no code is generated, i.e., they disappear during macro-expansion with the result that they cannot be used as goals nor can they be called from postconditions.

In contrast, non-abstract t-relations can still be extended by other t-relations but they can also be used as goals or called from postconditions. Note that t-relation inheritance has no effect on the traceability information: the t-relation bindings of an extended t-relation do not contain the union of all extending t-relations' bindings.

34.9 Transformation Inheritance

As already mentioned in section 34.1 on page 346, the first form after a bidirectional transformation definition's argument vector may be an `:extends` clause. The value of the `:extends` clause is either a symbol denoting the name of the bidirectional transformation to be extended or a vector of symbols in case multiple other transformations are to be extended as illustrated in the next listing.

```
(deftransformation class-diagram2database-schema-1 [cd db]
  :extends class-diagram2database-schema-base
  ;; t-relation definitions
  )

(deftransformation class-diagram2database-schema-2 [cd db]
  :extends [class-diagram2database-schema-base
            class-diagram2database-schema-helpers]
```

```
;; t-relation definitions
)
```

The extending transformation consists of the union of all t-relations it inherits from the extended transformations plus its own t-relations. Inherited top-level t-relations are top-level t-relations also in the extending transformation.

If the extending transformation defines a t-relation whose name equals the name of an inherited t-relation, the former overrides the latter. If multiple extended transformations define a t-relation of the same name, the version of the last extended transformation is effective[9] unless it is overridden again by a t-relation of the extending transformation.

When a t-relation in an extending transformation overrides some inherited t-relation, it should use the same logic variable names in its `:left` and `:right` clauses and its precondition. This is because the names of the logic variables are referred to by t-relation bindings, by traceability goals in preconditions, and by t-relation calls in postconditions.

The extending transformation's arguments must be compatible with the extended transformations' arguments because it inherits t-relations which use these arguments. Compatibility of arguments is defined in the following sense:

1. The first and second argument denoting the left and right model may have different names in the extending and all extended transformations. The names defined for the extending transformation are the effective ones.
2. For all additional arguments holds:
   a) The extending transformation must have the union of all additional arguments of all extended transformations and it may declare further arguments.
   b) If there is an argument of a given name which occurs as argument of multiple transformations (no matter if the extending or some extended transformation), then this argument must have the same meaning in all transformations.
   c) The order of arguments is not important.

Of course, if the extending transformation overrides all inherited t-relations where some additional argument is used, then it may choose a different name for this argument or omit it completely in case it is not used by the overriding t-relations.

As discussed above, t-relation overriding and having many different transformation arguments next to the parameters for the left and the right model can introduce additional complexity. Therefore, it is advisable to use transformation inheritance in a civilized manner, i.e., to extend some given transformation but not to change it fundamentally. For example, there might be some simple transformation which only considers subsets of the involved two metamodels which could then be extended by a transformation which adds further t-relations for transforming elements which haven't been considered by the original transformation.

---

[9]This situation should generally be avoided or at least be well-documented.

34.10 Plain Relations

Lastly, a bidirectional transformation may also define plain relations, i.e., locally bound relations in the sense of relational model querying (see part VIII starting on page 311). Those are defined using the syntax of `letfn` and can then be used as helpers in the `:left`, `:right`, and `:when` clauses of t-relations.

For example, the goal (`stro "c_" ?aname ?cname`) in `attribute2column` above could be factored out into its own helper relation in order to give it a meaningful name as shown in the next listing.

```
(attribute-name2column-name [an cn]
  (stro "c_" an cn))

(attribute2column
 :left  [(cd/->attrs   cd ?cls ?attr)
         (cd/Attribute cd ?attr)
         (cd/name       cd ?attr ?aname)]
 :right [(db/->cols db ?table ?col)
         (db/Column db ?col)
         (db/name    db ?col ?cname)]
 :when  [(attribute-name2column-name ?aname ?cname)])
```

In contrast to t-relations, the logic variables of plain helper relations don't need to be prefixed with a question mark.

The difference between a plain relation defined locally inside a transformation and a relation defined globally in some namespace (like `stro`, `cd/->attrs`, etc.) is that the former are also subject to transformation inheritance, i.e., an extending transformation could override `attribute-name2column-name` in order to define a different correspondence between attribute and column names. A second difference is that plain relations defined inside a transformation may use traceability goals in the form of (`t-rel :?a ?u :?b ?v`) whereas relations defined elsewhere have no access to the transformation's t-relations and thus would need to use (`relateo :t-rel :?a ?u :?b ?v`) (see page 348).

Chapter 35

Characteristics

The literature (e.g., Stevens in [Ste10]), distinguishes several properties such as *determinism, correctness, hippocraticness,* and *undoability* that bidirectional transformations may have. In the following, it is discussed which of those apply to bidirectional transformations with FunnyQT.

FunnyQT bidirectional transformations are always *deterministic*. Running a transformation in either direction on the same two models will always result in the same effects in the respective target model in whose direction the transformation is executed, and the same traceability information is returned.

Correctness is defined in the following sense. Let $T \subseteq M \times N$ be a relation between models conforming to the metamodels M and N, and $T(m,n)$ holds if and only if m and n are consistent. Such a consistency relation encodes two directional transformations $\overrightarrow{T} : M \times N \longrightarrow N$ and $\overleftarrow{T} : M \times N \longrightarrow M$. T is said to be correct if and only if $\forall m \in M \; \forall n \in N : T(m, \overrightarrow{T}(m,n)) \wedge T(\overleftarrow{T}(m,n),n)$ holds. Informally speaking, the definition says that after applying either $\overrightarrow{T}$ or $\overleftarrow{T}$, the two models are consistent with respect to T.

It is questionable if conforming to this definition is preferable in practice as it implies the deletion of those elements in the respective target model which have no correspondence in the respective source model. Consider the situation of two consistent models that are then extended in parallel. If FunnyQT transformations were correct according to the above definition, synchronization between the models would be impossible because $\overrightarrow{T}(m,n)$ is required to delete the elements in the right model n which have no counterpart in the left model m, and $\overleftarrow{T}(m,n)$ is required to delete the elements in the left model m which have no counterpart in the right model n.

For example, let $m = \{1,2,3\}$ and $n = \{a,b,d\}$ with T defining that the integers in m are the indices in the Latin alphabet of the characters in n. Then for a correct transformation, $\overrightarrow{T}(m,n)$ must modify n to $\{a,b,c\}$ in order to be consistent with m. However, the additional information d which has been contained in n has irreversibly been deleted[1].

FunnyQT has made the design decision of never deleting elements. The result is that $\overrightarrow{T}(m,n)$ only restores forward consistency, i.e., everything in m has a corresponding counterpart in n but not the other way round. Analogously, $\overleftarrow{T}(m,n)$ restores only backward consistency, i.e., everything in n has a corresponding counterpart in m but not the other way round. Thus, $\overrightarrow{T}(m,n) = \{a,b,c,d\}$ and $\overleftarrow{T}(m,n) = \{1,2,3,4\}$.

Since FunnyQT transformations return the complete traceability mappings, it is easy to delete elements with no correspondence after the transformation has finished so that the composition of the transformation in one direction followed by the cleanup is correct according the correctness definition above. The other way to regain full consistency is to apply either $\overleftarrow{T}(m, \overrightarrow{T}(m,n))$ or $\overrightarrow{T}(\overleftarrow{T}(m,n),n)$.

Hippocraticness means that if two models are already consistent according to the relation implied by the transformation, transforming in either direction won't modify the models. Bidirectional FunnyQT transformations are *hippocratic*.

The last property is *undoability*. Let $T(m,n)$, i.e., the models m and n are consistent. Now, the model m is modified to m'. T is undoable if and only if $\overrightarrow{T}(m, \overrightarrow{T}(m',n)) = n$ and analogously for $\overleftarrow{T}$ with a modified version n' of n.

For practical reasons, undoability is too strong as a general requirement. But note that with transformations being correct according the definition discussed above, $\overrightarrow{T}$ might delete information which is irreversibly lost at least in non-bijective scenarios. In contrast, because FunnyQT transformations won't delete elements, the result of $\overrightarrow{T}(m, \overrightarrow{T}(m',n))$ is a model which at least contains n but which might also contain additional elements with no corresponding elements in m. So one can argue that FunnyQT due to its slightly relaxed notion of correctness enables undoability.

---

[1]In case $\overrightarrow{T}$ and $\overleftarrow{T}$ created new models instead of modifying the respective target model, the information would not be lost. But still there is no way to integrate the information from the old version of the target model into the new model in terms of $\overrightarrow{T}$ or $\overleftarrow{T}$.

Chapter 36

Example

In this chapter, a complete bidirectional transformation between a simple version of UML class diagrams and relational database schemas is discussed in order to illustrate how the features provided by FunnyQT's bidirectional transformation DSL are to be used in practice.

The class diagram metamodel is shown in fig. 36.1, and the database schema metamodel is shown in fig. 36.2 on the next page. Both metamodels are simplified in order to keep the solution compact but they are still substantial enough to keep the problem interesting.

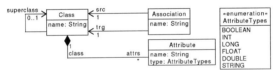

Figure 36.1: A simple class diagram metamodel

The class diagram considers classes which have a name. The name is assumed to be unique, e.g., it could be the qualified name of a class. Every class may have attributes which in turn have a name and a type. It is assumed that the names of all attributes are unique with respect to the containing class. The attribute types are modeled as an enumeration.

In addition to classes, a class diagram consists of associations. Like with classes, association names are assumed to be unique in the complete model. Every association starts and ends at some class.

Lastly, every class may have at most one superclass with the usual generalization semantics. I.e., the set of attributes of a class is the union of its own attributes and the attributes inherited from the superclass. Likewise, if an association is declared to start or end at instances of some class, then it may also start or end at subclass instances.

The database schema metamodel is even much simpler. A database schema consists of tables which have a name. Again, the names is assumed to be unique in

363

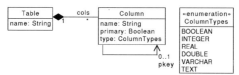

Figure 36.2: A simple database schema metamodel

the whole model. Tables consist of columns where each column has a name which is unique with respect to the containing table, a type which is again modeled using an enumeration, and a flag primary which is to be set to true for columns denoting the primary key for a table in case there is any.

A column may refer to the primary key column of another table using the pkey reference, i.e., a column where this reference is set denotes a foreign key constraint.

Before discussing the actual implementation of the transformation between class diagrams and database schemas, the correspondences between the elements in the models is first described informally.

(1) A class corresponds to a table where the class and the table have the same name and the table has a primary key column named ID of type integer.

(2) An attribute of a class corresponds to a column in a table in case the class and the table are already related and the attribute and the column have the same name. The type of attributes and columns may be changed in enforcement mode. One complication here is that there is no bijective mapping between the attribute and column types. There are BOOLEAN and DOUBLE in both type worlds and FLOAT corresponds to REAL. However, the class diagram STRING type corresponds to both database types VARCHAR and TEXT. And the other way round, the database type INTEGER corresponds to both class diagram types INT and LONG.
The transformation should handle these ambiguities in the following way:

   (a) When setting an attribute's or column's type initially, the transformation should use the most general type, i.e., LONG and TEXT.

   (b) When encountering attributes and columns where the type is already set, the value must not be modified in case it is a valid choice. E.g., when transforming a string attribute to a column and a column of the attribute's name already exists, its type may be either TEXT or VARCHAR. Only if its type is something else, the attribute value should be changed.

(3) A generalization between two classes corresponds to a foreign key constraint between the corresponding tables' primary key columns. This means that the primary key ID column of a table corresponding to a subclass has a foreign key constraint to the primary key column of the table corresponding to its superclass.

(4) An association between two classes in the class diagram model corresponds to a table of the same name in the database schema. This table has two columns SRC and TRG which have foreign key constraints referencing the primary key columns of the tables corresponding to the association's source and target classes, respectively.

In the following, the complete implementation of the bidirectional transformation between class diagrams and relational database schemas is discussed. It is assumed that relational querying APIs have been generated for the two metamodels and the resulting namespaces are assumed to be accessible via the namespace aliases cd and db, respectively.

As every bidirectional FunnyQT transformation, it is defined using the macro deftransformation (see section 34.1 on page 346) as shown in the following listing.

```
(deftransformation class-diagram2database-schema [l r]
  ;; all following t-relations and relations are contained here
  )
```

The transformation's name is class-diagram2database-schema, and it only receives the two mandatory model arguments. The left model l denotes the class diagram model and the right model r denotes the database schema model.

All plain relations and t-relations discussed in the following are placed inside the transformation's body as indicated by the comment.

Before introducing the first t-relation, a very simple helper relation enum-const is defined. It is a relation where m is a model, const is a symbol denoting the qualified name of an enumeration constant in m's metamodel and val is the runtime representation of this enumeration constant.

```
(enum-const [m const val]
  (== (funnyqt.generic/enum-constant m const) val))
```

As can be seen, this relation simply calls the generic enum-constant function and asserts that its return value equals val. Therefore, both m and const have to be ground when using this relation as a goal, i.e., it is not fully relational. However, it is intended to be used only as a simple helper to retrieve a specific enumeration constant and for this purpose it suffices.

The first actual t-relation is class2table which implements the informal rule (1) and is shown in the next listing. This t-relation is a top-level t-relation which means that it will be applied automatically to all possible and unique logic variable bindings of the respective source clause, i.e., the :left clause when transforming into the direction of the database schema model, and the :right clause when transforming into the direction of the class diagram model.

```
(^:top class2table
 :left  [(cd/Class l ?cls)
         (cd/name l ?cls ?name)]
 :right [(db/Table    r ?table)
         (db/name      r ?table ?name)
         (db/->cols    r ?table ?col)
         (db/name      r ?col "ID")
         (db/primary*  r ?col true)
         (enum-const   r 'ColumnTypes.INTEGER ?ctype)
         (db/type*     r ?col ?ctype)]
 :where [(generalization2foreign-key :?subcls ?cls :?subcol ?col)
         (attribute2column :?cls ?cls :?table ?table :?pkey-col-name "ID")])
```

The t-relation expresses that a class `?cls` in the left model having some `?name` corresponds to a table `?table` of the same name in the right model. Furthermore, the table must have a primary key column named ID of type INTEGER. The usage of the relations `db/primary*` and `db/type*` allows modifications of the attributes of the same name when enforcing the `:right` clause. Thus, when transforming into the direction of the database schema, if `?table` already has an ID column, it will be set as primary column and its type will be set to INTEGER.

The postcondition then defines that if a class and a table could be related by `class2table`, then `generalization2foreign-key` and `attribute2column` must also hold for the given arguments.

The next listing shows the `generalization2foreign-key` t-relation which implements the informal rule (3). A generalization indicated by the existence of a superclass reference between a `?subcls` and a `?superclass` corresponds to a foreign key constraint where a `?subcol` refers to some `?supercol`.

```
(generalization2foreign-key
 :left  [(cd/->superclass l ?subcls ?supercls)]
 :right [(db/->pkey r ?subcol ?supercol)]
 :when  [(class2table :?cls ?supercls :?col ?supercol)
         (class2table :?cls ?subcls   :?col ?subcol)])
```

The two traceability goals in the precondition define that `?subcol` is the primary key column of the table corresponding to `?subcls` and `?supercol` is the primary key column of the table corresponding to `?supercls`.

The next listing shows the plain relation `cd-type2db-type` which relates a class diagram type `cdt` to a database type `dbt`.

```
(cd-type2db-type [cdt dbt]
  (conda
   [(all (enum-const l 'AttributeTypes.BOOLEAN cdt)
         (enum-const r 'ColumnTypes.BOOLEAN dbt))]
   [(all (enum-const l 'AttributeTypes.LONG cdt)
         (enum-const r 'ColumnTypes.INTEGER dbt))]
   [(all (enum-const l 'AttributeTypes.INT cdt)
         (enum-const r 'ColumnTypes.INTEGER dbt))]
   [(all (enum-const l 'AttributeTypes.FLOAT cdt)
         (enum-const r 'ColumnTypes.REAL dbt))]
   [(all (enum-const l 'AttributeTypes.DOUBLE cdt)
         (enum-const r 'ColumnTypes.DOUBLE dbt))]
   [(all (enum-const l 'AttributeTypes.STRING cdt)
         (enum-const r 'ColumnTypes.TEXT dbt))]
   [(all (enum-const l 'AttributeTypes.STRING cdt)
         (enum-const r 'ColumnTypes.VARCHAR dbt))]))
```

The relation uses `conda` to define a disjunction. As discussed in section 29.1 on page 314, `conda` commits to the first clause whose head succeeds. All clauses in the above relation have just one conjunctive goal. The effect of using `conda` is that at most one clause can succeed and the order is significant. Thus, the attribute type LONG is preferred over INT if cdt is fresh and the database column type TEXT is preferred over VARCHAR if dbt is fresh.

The attribute2column t-relation shown in the next listing relates an attribute ?attr having some ?name to some column ?col of the same name and also relates the types. This t-relation implements the informal rule (2).

```
(attribute2column
 :left   [(cd/->attrs l ?cls ?attr)
          (cd/name    l ?attr ?name)
          (cd/type*   l ?attr ?atype)]
 :right  [(db/->cols r ?table ?col)
          (db/name   r ?col ?name)
          (db/type*  r ?col ?ctype)]
 :when   [(ccl/!= ?name ?pkey-col-name)]
 :target [(cd-type2db-type ?atype ?ctype)])
```

This t-relation is called from the :where clause of class2table so the containing class ?cls and its corresponding ?table are already ground. The call also binds the ?pkey-col-name variable to "ID" and the :when clause forbids equality between that variable and ?name. The reason is that when transforming in the direction of the class diagram, the synthetic primary key ID columns should not be transformed to attributes.

Lastly, the relation between an attribute type ?atype and a corresponding column type ?ctype is established by the cd-type2db-type goal in the :target clause.

In order to implement the semantics discussed in the beginning of this chapter, it is utmost important that this goal is located in the :target clause. This ensures that when this goal is evaluated, both ?atype and ?ctype are ground in the case where there exists a target attribute or column of the right name already. Therefore, there is at most one disjunctive clause in cd-type2db-type's conda which may succeed. For example, when trying to relate a string attribute to some existing VARCHAR column of the same name, the last conda clause is the only possible choice and this choice imposes no change of the column's type.

If the goal was in the :when clause instead, then either ?atype or ?ctype would still be fresh. A fresh variable can be unified with anything, so in case of the ambiguous type mappings, always the first clause succeeding for the respective source type would be chosen, and thus the target type would always be set to the most general type, i.e., TEXT or LONG. That is, in the scenario sketched in the previous paragraph, the VARCHAR column would be changed to TEXT.

Lastly, if the goal was the last goal in either the :left or the :right clause, then the ambiguities were solved as intended only when transforming into one direction whereas they would be solved by overriding with the most general type in the other direction.

Thus, the semantics of a t-relation with respect to handling ambiguities are deterministic and can be changed by placing the goal handling them in one of the four different clauses (:left, :right, :when, or :target).

The final t-relation of the transformation is `association2table` which implements the informal rule (4). An association `?assoc` in the class diagram with a given `?name` corresponds to a table `?table` in the database schema of the same name. Additionally, the table must have SRC and TRG columns for which there are foreign key constraints referencing the primary key columns of the tables corresponding to the association's source and target class.

```
(^:top association2table
 :left  [(cd/Association l ?assoc)
          (cd/name          l ?assoc ?name)
          (cd/->src*        l ?assoc ?src)
          (cd/->trg*        l ?assoc ?trg)]
 :right [(db/Table    r ?table)
          (db/name     r ?table ?name)
          (db/->cols   r ?table ?src-col)
          (db/name     r ?src-col "SRC")
          (db/type*    r ?src-col ?src-pkey-type)
          (db/->pkey*  r ?src-col ?src-pkey)
          (db/->cols   r ?table ?trg-col)
          (db/name     r ?trg-col "TRG")
          (db/type*    r ?trg-col ?trg-pkey-type)
          (db/->pkey*  r ?trg-col ?trg-pkey)]
 :when  [(class2table :?cls ?src :?col ?src-pkey :?ctype ?src-pkey-type)
          (class2table :?cls ?trg :?col ?trg-pkey :?ctype ?trg-pkey-type)])
```

Obviously, foreign key columns must have the same type as the primary key columns they refer to. Therefore, the precondition queries the correspondence between the association's source and target classes and the corresponding primary key columns and their types of the corresponding tables.

Chapter 37

Related Work

In this chapter, several bidirectional transformation approaches are discussed. Thereby, commonalities and differences with FunnyQT's bidirectional transformation DSL are highlighted.

FunnyQT's bidirectional transformation API is intentionally designed to be similar to the *QVT Relations* language (*QVTr*, [OMG11b]).

A QVTr transformation is decomposed into relations, each relating elements in two or more domains where each domain matches elements in one of the involved models. In contrast to FunnyQT, a QVTr transformation might have more than two involved models and for execution, exactly one of those has to be selected as target model. Then the enforcement semantics are that for each valid binding of the source domains of a relation, there has to exist a binding of the target domains of the relation.

Like with FunnyQT, QVTr transformations can be run in an enforcement mode or in a checkonly mode. In addition, domains in a relation can be marked as checkonly in which case they have checkonly semantics also when the transformation is enforced into the direction of the model corresponding to this domain.

There has to be at least one top-level relation that is executed automatically and a QVTr relation may enforce other relations in terms of a where clause.

Similar to FunnyQT, when clauses can be used specify that a relation only needs to hold for elements that are already related by other relations.

There are some notable differences between QVTr and FunnyQT's bidirectional transformation facility, though. QVTr transformations delete target elements that correspond to no source domain (according to the correctness definition discussed in chapter 35 starting on page 361) whereas FunnyQT transformations intentionally do not. But because FunnyQT transformations return the complete traceability information, the deletion of elements with no correspondence may be implemented as an additional step if required.

Furthermore, QVTr and FunnyQT have different concepts for specifying which element properties may be overridden. In QVTr, there is the concept of *keys* which allows to specify which subset of properties of a metamodel class should be used to uniquely identify instances of that class. Whenever a QVTr relation doesn't find a valid target element and a new one is going to be created, it is first checked if there is one where at least the key properties match. If there is, this element is modified in order to make it match instead of creating a completely new element. FunnyQT provides separate starred relations for attributes and single-valued references which are allowed to modify their value and which may be used in t-relations. Thus, FunnyQT provides a more fine-granular (t-relation specific) means for allowing property modifications than the transformation-global key concept of QVTr.

There are currently three implementations of QVTr. *ModelMorf*[1] is a proprietary and standard-compliant QVTr implementation developed by Tata Consultancy Services (TCS). A trial version consisting only of a command line tool can be obtained for free which is able to transform XMI [OMG14c] models and the full version also transforms models of the proprietary TCS MasterCraft framework[2]. It is unclear if the tool is further developed. Its latest release is more than six years old.

The second implementation is *mediniQVT*[3]. It is able to transform EMF models and provides an Eclipse-integrated editor and debugger. However, mediniQVT is not fully compliant with the QVT standard and the project seems to be discontinued. At least no release has been made since the last release candidate for version 1.7.0 appeared in 2011.

The third QVTr implementation is *Eclipse QVTd (QVT Declarative)*[4] which had its initial appearance in Eclipse Mars, released on June 24th, 2015. However, this is only a preliminary release intended for experimenters according to the release notes.

The *Janus Transformation Language* (*JTL* [Cic+10]) is similar to FunnyQT bidirectional transformations in that it also uses logic programming, namely *answer set programming* [GL88], and exploits the DLV constraint solver [Leo+06] for finding solutions. JTL uses the concrete syntax of QVTr.

Whereas FunnyQT works on the native model representations (EMF or JGraLab) directly, JTL transformations translate the EMF models into an intermediate representation which is then used by the constraint solver and its results are eventually re-translated back into their original EMF model representation.

The crucial benefit of JTL is that it allows for finding alternative solutions in non-bijective bidirectional transformations scenarios. If there are multiple target models that are consistent with the source model with respect to the transformation relations, JTL is able to enumerate all of them. In contrast, bidirectional non-bijective FunnyQT transformations always have an implied preferred target model where alternative target models are only tolerated but would not be created when transforming in the direction of an empty target model.

Also, if a target model is manually changed in a way that it cannot be derived by a forward transformation from the source model, JTL utilizes traceability information

---

[1]`http://www.tcs-trddc.com/trddc_website/ModelMorf/ModelMorf.htm` (last visited: 2015-10-15)
[2]`http://www.tcs.com/mastercraft/Pages/default.aspx` (last visited: 2015-10-15)
[3]`http://projects.ikv.de/qvt/` (last visited: 2015-10-15)
[4]`https://projects.eclipse.org/projects/modeling.mmt.qvtd` (last visited: 2015-10-15)

to propagate back the changes from the modified target model by inferring the closest approximation of an ideal source model.

Echo[5] [MC13] also provides a bidirectional transformation language re-using the concrete syntax of QVTr. Like JTL, Echo exploits an external tool, namely the *Alloy*[6] [Jac06] model finder.

Echo transformations work according to the principle of least change meaning that the target model is modified with the minimum sequence of graph edit operations required in order to bring it into a consistent state with respect to the source model. The possible operations are creation or deletion of an element, and setting an attribute value or reference.

This differs from the original QVTr semantics especially in the case of relations between two elements where there is no key constraint defined for the target element class. If there is no target element, the QVTr semantics require a new element to be created. With the principle of least change, the most similar element which has no corresponding partner in the source model is modified instead, i.e., attribute values and references are overridden. These are obviously fewer changes because when creating new elements, the attributes and references need to be set, too, and possibly elements with no counterparts need to be deleted which implies that information not considered by the transformation might get lost.

By default, any edit operation has the cost 1 but Echo also allows for defining custom costs for certain edit operations on a per-metamodel basis. Furthermore, it is possible to define which edit operations are allowed at all.

Whereas the approaches discussed so far are based on a relational, logic-based calculus, *Triple Graph Grammars* (*TGG* [Sch94]) provide a graph transformation based approach to bidirectional transformations.

A TGG consists of rules. Like with graph grammars (GG), each rule consists of a left-hand side and a right-hand side. There are two major differences with respect to GG rules, though. (1) Whereas a GG rule describes how a single graph evolves, a TGG rule describes how a triple consisting of a left graph, a right graph, and a correspondence graph which connects elements of the left and right graphs evolves. (2) TGG rules are monotonic, i.e., they cannot specify deletion or modification of existing elements.

The correspondence graph can be seen as an explicit traceability model. Its nodes reference the elements in the left graph and the right graph which are in correspondence with respect to the transformation already.

With TGGs, there are special rules called axioms which have an empty LHS and usually their RHS specifies the creation of the top-level elements in the left and right graph connected by a new node referencing both in the correspondence graph.

So what the rules of a TGG transformation describe is how to build up a left and a right graph simultaneously so that at all times, both graph are consistent with each other. The axioms can be seen as the start symbols of the grammar: when applied

---

[5] http://haslab.github.io/echo/ (last visited: 2015-10-15)
[6] http://alloy.mit.edu/alloy/ (last visited: 2015-10-15)

to two empty graphs, they create some initial elements with correspondence links in between which make the LHS of other TGG rules applicable.

From any TGG transformation, a forward and a backward transformation can be derived automatically which can then be applied to two existing graphs. Those can be used for populating an empty right or left graph, or for synchronizing changes in one graph into the respective other graph. They can also be used for testing if two given graphs are already consistent in which case the transformation only tries to build up the correspondence graph between the given left and right graph. If this is possible, the graphs are consistent with respect to the TGG rules, otherwise they are not.

The article [Leb+14] gives a good overview of three current TGG implementations: *MoTE*[7] [GHL14], the *TGG Interpreter*[8] [GK10], and *eMoflon*[9] [LAS14].

---

[7]https://www.hpi.uni-potsdam.de/giese/public/mdelab/mdelab-projects/
mote-a-tgg-based-model-transformation-engine/ (last visited: 2015-10-16)
[8]http://www-old.cs.uni-paderborn.de/en/research-group/software-engineering/research/
projects/tgg-interpreter.html (last visited: 2015-10-16)
[9]http://www.emoflon.org (last visited: 2015-10-16)

Part X

On Co-Evolution Transformations

Summary

The topic of this part are transformations for co-evolution of metamodels and models where chapter 38 starting on page 377 gives an introduction.

FunnyQT's co-evolution API which allows to evolve a metamodel and one conforming model simultaneously is explained in section 39.1 on page 381.

Chapter 40 starting on page 393 illustrates the use of this API with an example.

Lastly, chapter 41 starting on page 397 concludes this part with a discussion of related work.

Chapter 38

Introduction

As every software artifact, metamodels are subject to evolution. New classes, attributes, or references may be introduced, and existing classes, attributes, or references may be renamed, deleted, or their properties like the type of an attribute or reference may be changed.

The problem with metamodel evolution is that many changes applied to a metamodel during evolution make existing models non-conforming to the new metamodel. I.e., a model conforming to version 1.0 of some metamodel might not be a valid instance of version 1.1 of the same metamodel, thus it needs to be adapted.

The research field *co-evolution* or *coupled evolution* of metamodels and models is concerned with developing techniques and tools for evolving metamodels and updating conforming models accordingly[1].

In the related work chapter 41 starting on page 397, several current co-evolution approaches are discussed. What they all have in common is the idea of co-evolution as a two-step process. First, the metamodel is evolved and then the model instances are co-adapted.

FunnyQT's take on co-evolution of models and metamodels pursues an idea which is quite different from these approaches. Instead of considering co-evolution as a two step process where the metamodel adaptation is followed by some co-adaptation of the models, the transformation API which is going to be described in the next chapter provides operations which change the metamodel of a loaded model in-place while keeping the model compliant at the same time. The metamodel evolution and the co-adaptation happen simultaneously at runtime.

The operations provided by FunnyQT's co-evolution API perform small, atomic changes to the metamodel and many imply a predefined semantics on the instance level or can be parametrized in order to let the user define the intended semantics.

This approach will be described in detail in chapter 39 starting on page 379 and then exemplified in chapter 40 starting on page 393.

---

[1]Co-evolution is actually an old topic which has been investigated much earlier in the context of database systems. For example, [MS90] discusses the topic in the context of relational database systems and [Ban+87] in the context of object-oriented databases. A broad overview of works in the database context is given in [Rod92].

Chapter 39

Defining Co-Evolution Transformations

The FunnyQT co-evolution API provides a set of functions that allow the user to change the metamodel of an already loaded model in-place while keeping the instance conforming to its metamodel at all times. I.e., the model and its metamodel are changed simultaneously and before and after each operation call, the model is a valid instance of its metamodel.

The provided operations define atomic changes on the metamodel, e.g., creating a new element class, or deleting some attribute. Some operations on the metamodel have an impact on the model, e.g., deleting some class implies the deletion of all its instances, while other operations such as renaming some class or attribute have no impact on the model at least in the sense that no elements are created or deleted or attribute values are changed. Of course, even renaming a class has some kind of impact, e.g., before the renaming (elements m 'OldName) returned the lazy sequence of OldName elements and after the renaming it throws an exception because OldName doesn't denote an element class in the metamodel anymore.

In contrast to all querying and transformation services provided by FunnyQT, the co-evolution API is not generic but specific to TGraph models. The reason is that the co-evolution API requires a much deeper integration between the FunnyQT operations and the respective metamodel and model APIs which heavily depends on how models and metamodels are represented at runtime. Especially, many metamodel changes require certain low-level fix-up actions to be applied to the elements in the model which need to adapt things which are not accessible via the public modeling framework API. Since the TGraph modeling framework JGraLab (see section 7.1 on page 69) is under our control, these required low-level manipulation constructs could be added. Patching EMF similarly has no chance of ever getting accepted upstream.

For example, in JGraLab the attribute values of a TGraph vertex or edge are represented as an array of type Object which is sorted lexicographically according to the names of the attributes of the corresponding vertex or edge class. Thus, when renaming an attribute, the arrays holding the attribute values of all direct or indirect

379

instances of classes for which this attribute is declared need to be re-sorted. With a another model representation, a completely different model fix-up action could be needed for the same change to the metamodel and this can hardly be abstracted into a generic interface.

Another reason which makes TGraphs suitable for this kind of co-evolution transformations is that every TGraph has its own, private copy of the schema (metamodel). Of course there may be many graphs of the same schema but technically their schemas are equal but not identical. Thus, the co-evolution operations only change the private schema of the TGraph under transformation and simultaneously co-adapt the graph itself, i.e., the schema changes are isolated and leave other graphs conforming to the same schema which might be loaded unaffected. In contrast, Ecore metamodels may be shared by multiple instance models. In this situation, changing the metamodel would affect all instances loaded at the current point in time and some of them might not be accessible by the transformation and thus become invalid.

In addition to being restricted to TGraphs, co-evolution operations can only be applied to TGraphs which use the generic graph representation, i.e., they are not applicable if the graph is represented by objects being instances of the interfaces and implementation classes which can optionally be generated for the graph's schema[1]. The reason is that otherwise schema adaptations would require changing Java classes with life instances at runtime which is infeasible.

As mentioned above, FunnyQT's co-evolution API provides operations performing atomic changes to the graph's schema. Because this API is specific to JGraLab anyway, its operations are named according to the TGraph terminology. Concretely, the API provides the following operations.

`create-abstract-vertex-class!` creates an abstract vertex class.

`create-vertex-class!` creates a concrete vertex class and allows to create new instances at the same time.

`create-abstract-edge-class!` creates an abstract edge class.

`create-edge-class!` creates a concrete edge class and allows to create new instances at the same time.

`set-incidence-class-props!` sets the properties (multiplicities, role names) of the incidence classes of an edge class.

`set-abstract!` sets the abstractness property of a vertex or edge class.

`create-attribute!` creates a new attribute at some existing attributed element class and allows to set the values of instances at the same time.

`create-enum-domain!` creates a new enumeration domain.

`create-record-domain!` creates a new record domain.

`create-specialization!` creates a new specialization relationship between two vertex classes or edge classes, respectively.

`rename-attributed-element-class!` renames an attributed element class.

`rename-attribute!` renames an attribute.

`rename-domain!` renames a custom enumeration or record domain.

`delete-graph-element-class!` deletes a vertex or edge class and deletes all its instances.

`delete-attribute!` deletes an attribute.

---

[1]By default, `funnyqt.tg/load-graph` loads graphs using this generic representation.

`delete-specialization!` deletes a specialization relationship between two vertex or
   edge classes.
`delete-domain!` deletes a custom enumeration or record domain.

These co-evolution operations are discussed in detail in section 39.2 on page 383.

All these operations ensure that after each operation call (1) the schema is valid,
i.e., it still conforms to the grUML metaschema, and (2) the graph is valid, i.e., it
still conforms to the evolved schema. Therefore, some operations have very strict
preconditions and calling them when those are not met will result in an exception.
For example, a concrete vertex or edge class cannot be set abstract in case there
are still direct instances of that class in the graph. The exact preconditions of each
operation are listed in section 39.2 when discussing the co-evolution operations one
by one.

A full list of all constraints with respect of conformance of a schema to the grUML
metaschema on the one hand and conformance of a graph to a schema on the other
hand is given in the next section.

39.1 Conformance of Schemas and Graphs

Conformance of a schema to the grUML metaschema. A TGraph schema is
valid, i.e., it conforms to the grUML metaschema, if and only if the constraints given
below hold. Every constraint is preceded with an identifier which will be used for
referencing these constraints later in section 39.2.

C-one-gc There must be exactly one graph class which must be located in the
   default package of the schema, i.e., its qualified name must equal its simple
   name.
C-unique-qnames The qualified names of all named elements (i.e., the graph class,
   all vertex and edge classes, all packages, and all domains) must be unique,
   e.g., it is not valid to have a vertex class with some qualified name and have an
   edge class with the same qualified name.
C-unique-props All property names defined for a class must be unique also with
   respect to specialization. This means that a vertex or edge class must not
   declare an attribute of a name which it already owns or inherits from some
   direct or indirect superclass[2]. For vertex classes, this constraint is widened
   to cover also the role names defined by its own or inherited far-end incidence
   classes. Likewise, it is also forbidden to inherit two different properties of the
   same name but it is valid to inherit the same property via different paths.
C-naming All qualified names and property names must conform to the Java naming
   conventions. This means class names have the form pkg.ClassName, package
   names have the form pkg.sub_pkg, property names have the form propertyName,
   and enumeration constants have the form ENUM_CONSTANT.
C-aggregation-kind At most one incidence class of an edge class may have an
   aggregation kind different from NONE. Informally, this means that in a part-of

---

[2]Note that this constraint is more strict than in Java where a subclass may define a field of a name
which it already inherits. Here, the two fields would be independent, the subclass field would *hide*
the superclass field, and the latter could still be accessed with `super.fieldName`. But even in Java this is
arguably a bad design.

relationships either A contains B or B contains A but not both.

C-multiplicities For every incidence class, the minimum multiplicity must be zero or positive and the maximum multiplicity must be greater than or equal to the minimum multiplicity.

C-acyclic-specialization Specializations between vertex classes on the one hand and edge classes on the other hand must be acyclic.

C-ec-specialization-vc An edge class may specialize another edge class only if its source and target vertex classes are equal to or subclasses of the source and target vertex classes of the specialized edge class, respectively.

C-ec-specialization-ak With edge class specialization, the aggregation kinds of the incidence classes of the sub-edge classes must equal the aggregation kinds of the super-edge classes' incidence classes, i.e., if an edge class defines a plain relationship, then its subclasses must not define aggregation or composition semantics or vice versa.

C-ec-specialization-multies With edge class specialization, the multiplicities of the incidence classes of the subclasses must be equal to or more restrictive than the ones defined for the superclass' incidence classes. I.e., both the lower bounds and the upper bounds defined for a subclass must be less than or equal to the bounds defined for the superclass.

This list does not contain the structural constraints which are already implied by the class diagram defining the grUML language (see section 7.1 on page 69). E.g., the grUML class diagram already defines that every attribute must be contained by exactly one attributed element class and must reference exactly one domain defining the attribute's type. These constraints must also be preserved by the co-evolution operations, of course. But they can be preserved constructively in terms of API design, e.g., the `create-attribute!` operation requires that the new attribute's containing attribute element class and its domain are given as arguments.

Conformance of a graph to its schema. A TGraph is valid, i.e., it conforms to its schema, if and only if it satisfies its structural properties and also all further constraints which may optionally be defined using GReQL.

The implementation in JGraLab enforces all structural constraints with the exception of multiplicities. For example, it is not possible to create an edge between two vertices if the source and target vertices are no direct or indirect instances of the corresponding edge class' source and target vertex class. Likewise, it is impossible to assign a value to some attribute if the value doesn't match the attribute's domain. When trying to do so, exceptions are thrown[3].

In contrast, multiplicities and further constraints specified using GReQL are not enforced but can only be checked on demand. In fact, some of them cannot be enforced strictly because they are necessarily invalidated at least at some points in time. For example, constraints such as non-zero minimum multiplicities or attributes which must not be null but have no default value will always be invalidated temporary when elements are created.

The same notion of conformance is also ensured by FunnyQT's co-evolution

---

[3]If Java interfaces and implementation classes are generated for a schema, then these constraints are ensured statically.

operations. After every operation call, the TGraph under transformations is a valid instance of its evolved schema except that the number of edges incident to some vertex might not be allowed by the multiplicities defined in the schema. Likewise, further constraints specified using GReQL might not hold anymore[4].

39.2 Co-Evolution Operations

In this section, the actual co-evolution operations are introduced one by one. Their semantics on the instance-level is based on the extensional transformation API which has been discussed in chapter 27 starting on page 281, i.e., when creating a new vertex class, new vertices of that class may be created simultaneously, when creating a new edge class, new edges of that class may be created simultaneously, and when creating a new attribute, its value may be set for instances of the new attribute's class. For these purposes, the co-evolution operations accept optional archetype and value function and simply delegate to the extensional transformation operations `create-elements!`, `create-relationships!`, and `set-values!` after the adaptation of the schema has been performed.

For every co-evolution operation discussed in the following, its preconditions are listed. Hereby, the constraints the preconditions ensure are referenced using their identifiers defined in section 39.1 on page 381.

The co-evolution operation `create-abstract-vertex-class!` receives the graph g under transformation and creates a new abstract vertex class with the qualified name qname in its schema.

Function: `funnyqt.coevo.tg/create-abstract-vertex-class!`
`(create-abstract-vertex-class! g qname)`

The following preconditions need to be satisfied.

Preconditions:
- qname must be a valid qualified name (*C-naming*).
- g's schema must not contain a named element with qualified name qname already (*C-unique-qnames*).

The `create-abstract-vertex-class!` operation has no effect on the instance level.

The co-evolution operation `create-vertex-class!` creates a new concrete vertex class with the qualified name qname in the schema of the graph g. Optionally, an archetype function archfn may be provided in case new instances should be created immediately. If an archfn is provided, the effect is equivalent to performing a call to `funnyqt.extensional/create-elements!` (see page 290) after creating the new vertex class.

Function: `funnyqt.coevo.tg/create-vertex-class!`
`(create-vertex-class! g qname)`
`(create-vertex-class! g qname archfn)`

---

[4]In fact, GReQL constraints might even become invalid in case they include type or attribute names which are renamed or deleted by a co-evolution operation call.

The preconditions are the same as for `create-abstract-vertex-class!`.

The operation's effect on the instance level is solely determined by `archfn`, i.e., one new vertex being an instance of the newly created vertex class is created for every unique object in the sequence of archetypes returned by `archfn`. In this case, traceability mappings are established as per `create-elements!` which implies that if an `archfn` is given, the `create-vertex-class!` call must be located in the dynamic scope of one of the traceability mapping initializing macros which have been discussed in section 27.4.2 on page 288. This applies to all other creational co-evolution operations so it won't be restated in the following.

The co-evolution operation `create-abstract-edge-class!` creates a new abstract edge class with the qualified name `qname` in the schema of the graph `g` which starts at the vertex class `from` and ends at the vertex class `to`. These two vertex classes may be given by their qualified names or as actual VertexClass objects.

Function: funnyqt.coevo.tg/create-abstract-edge-class!
```
(create-abstract-edge-class! g qname from to)
(create-abstract-edge-class! g qname from to props)
```

Optionally, a map `props` may be given in order to define the properties of the two incidence classes implied by the new edge class. This map has the following form. The listing shows the default values which are used for missing entries in the map or if the map is omitted.

```
{:from-multis [0, Integer/MAX_VALUE]
 :from-role   " "
 :from-kind   AggregationKind/NONE
 :to-multis   [0, Integer/MAX_VALUE]
 :to-role     " "
 :to-kind     AggregationKind/NONE}
```

I.e., the `props` map can be used to define the multiplicities (default: `0..*`), the role name (default: no role name), and the aggregation kind (default: `NONE`) of the source and target incidence classes.

Preconditions:
- `qname` must be a valid qualified name (*C-naming*).
- `g`'s schema must not contain a named element with qualified name `qname` already (*C-unique-qnames*).
- The incidence class properties must be valid, i.e., the role names must be strings or keywords conforming to the Java naming conventions for fields (*C-naming*), the maximum multiplicity must be equal to or greater than the minimum multiplicity which in turn must be zero or positive (*C-multiplicities*), and lastly, at most one incidence class may have an aggregation kind different from `NONE` (*C-aggregation-kind*).

The `create-abstract-edge-class!` operation has no effect on the instance level.

The co-evolution operation `create-edge-class!` creates a new concrete edge class with qualified name `qname` starting at vertex class `from` and ending at vertex class to in the schema of the graph g. Again, the vertex classes may be given by their qualified names or as actual VertexClass objects.

Function: `funnyqt.coevo.tg/create-edge-class!`
```
(create-edge-class! g qname from to)
(create-edge-class! g qname from to props-or-archfn)
(create-edge-class! g qname from to props archfn)
```

Two optional parameters are accepted: a `props` map for defining the properties of the incidence classes of the new edge class, and an archetype function `archfn` which allows to create new instances of the new edge class. Providing an `archfn` has the same effect as performing a call to the extensional transformation function `funnyqt.extensional/create-relationships!` (see page 291) after the call to the co-evolution operation.

The `create-edge-class!` co-evolution operation has the same preconditions as `create-abstract-edge-class!`.

The operation's effect on the instance level is solely determined by `archfn`, i.e., it has to return a sequence of triples `[arch src trg]` where `arch` denotes an archetype for a new edge, and `src` and `trg` denote its source and target vertex. For each unique archetype, a new edge being an instance of the newly created edge class is created.

The co-evolution operation `set-incidence-class-props!` allows to change the properties of the incidence classes of the edge class `ec` which may be given by its qualified name or as actual EdgeClass object. The argument `props` is an incidence class properties map with the same format as the argument of the same name in `create-abstract-edge-class!` and `create-edge-class!`.

Function: `funnyqt.coevo.tg/set-incidence-class-props!`
```
(set-incidence-class-props! g ec props)
```

The same preconditions about the validity of the provided incidence class properties as for `create-abstract-edge-class!` and `create-edge-class!` have to be satisfied. In contrast to these two operations, properties which have not been specified stay unchanged instead of setting them to the default values.

This operation has no effect on the instance level.

The co-evolution operation `set-abstract!` sets the abstractness property of the given graph element class `gec` to `val` which must be a boolean. The graph element class may be given by its qualified name or as actual VertexClass or EdgeClass object.

Function: `funnyqt.coevo.tg/set-abstract!`
```
(set-abstract! g gec val)
```

Preconditions:
  • If `gec` is currently a concrete graph element class and `val` is `true`, then `gec` must have no direct instances.

Thus, making an abstract class concrete is always possible but the inverse is forbidden in case there are direct instances.

The `set-abstract!` operation has no effect on the instance level.

The co-evolution operation `create-attribute!` creates a new attribute of name `attr` with the given `domain` at the attributed element class `aec`. The attributed element class and the domain may be given by their qualified names or as actual GraphClass, VertexClass, EdgeClass, or Domain object, respectively.

Function: `funnyqt.coevo.tg/create-attribute!`
```
(create-attribute! g aec attr domain)
(create-attribute! g aec attr domain default-or-valfn)
(create-attribute! g aec attr domain default valfn)
```

Two optional arguments are accepted: firstly, a `default` value may be specified, and secondly, a value function `valfn` may be given in order to set the value of the new attribute for existing instances of the attributed element class. The effect of providing a `valfn` is the same as performing a call to the extensional transformation function `funnyqt.extensional/set-avals!` (see page 292) after the call to the co-evolution operation.

> Preconditions:
> - `attr` must be a valid attribute name (*C-naming*).
> - In the complete inheritance hierarchy of `aec`, there must not exist a property with name `attr` already (*C-unique-props*).
> - The `default` value must be an instance of `domain`.

The effects on the instance level are solely determined by the optionally given `valfn`.

The co-evolution operation `create-enum-domain!` creates a new enumeration domain with qualified name `qname` and the given `literals` in the schema of graph g. The `literals` are given as a collection of symbols, e.g., (`create-enum-domain` g 'Modifier (list 'PRIVATE 'PUBLIC ...)).

Function: `funnyqt.coevo.tg/create-enum-domain!`
```
(create-enum-domain! g qname literals)
```

The following preconditions need to be satisfied.

> Preconditions:
> - `qname` must be a valid qualified name (*C-naming*).
> - All `literals` must be valid enumeration literal names, i.e., all-capitals with numbers and underscores (*C-naming*).
> - g's schema must not contain a named element with qualified name `qname` already (C-unique-qnames).

The `create-enum-domain!` operation has no effect on the instance level.

The co-evolution operation `create-record-domain!` creates a new record domain with qualified name `qname` in the schema of the graph g. `comp-doms` is a map defining the record domain's components using entries consisting of the name of the component and its domain, e.g., (`create-record-domain!` g 'SourcePosition {:file 'String, :line 'Integer}).

Function: `funnyqt.coevo.tg/create-record-domain!`
```
(create-record-domain! g qname comp-doms)
```

The following preconditions need to be satisfied.

Preconditions:
- `qname` must be a valid qualified name (*C-naming*).
- All component names defined by `comp-doms` must be valid, i.e., they must conform to the Java naming conventions for fields (*C-naming*).
- `g`'s schema must not contain a named element with qualified name `qname` already (C-unique-qnames).

The `create-record-domain!` operation has no effect on the instance level.

The co-evolution operation `create-specialization!` creates a new specialization between the given `super` class and the given `sub` class which may be either vertex classes, edge classes, or the qualified names of two vertex or edge classes, respectively.

Function: `funnyqt.coevo.tg/create-specialization!`
`(create-specialization! g super sub)`

The following preconditions must hold.

Preconditions:
- The new specialization must not add a cycle to the specialization hierarchy (*C-acyclic-specialization*).
- The subclass `sub` or any of its subclasses must not own a property of the same name as `super` or any of its superclasses (*C-unique-props*).
- In case `super` and `sub` are edge classes, the following additional preconditions must be satisfied.
    - The source and target vertex class of `sub` must be identical or subclasses of the source and target vertex class of `super` (*C-ec-specialization-vc*).
    - `sub` must specify the same aggregation semantics as `super` (*C-ec-specialization-ak*).
    - The multiplicities of `sub`'s incidence classes must be in conformance with *C-ec-specialization-multies*, i.e., both lower and upper bound must be equal or lower than the corresponding multiplicity of `super`'s incidence classes.
- The traceability archetype and image mappings for `super` and `sub` must be disjoint.

The last precondition ensures that navigation between archetypes and images stays possible even though the inheritance hierarchy is modified.

The operation has no effect on the instance level.

The co-evolution operation `rename-attributed-element-class!` renames the given attributed element class `aec` to the new qualified name `new-qname` in the schema of graph `g`. The attributed element class may be specified using its current qualified name or as actual GraphClass, VertexClass, or EdgeClass object.

Function: `funnyqt.coevo.tg/rename-attributed-element-class!`
`(rename-attributed-element-class! g aec new-qname)`

This operation can also be used to move a graph element class from one package to another package, e.g., (`rename-attributed-element-class! g 'pgk_one.C 'pkg_two.C`).

The following preconditions must be satisfied.

Preconditions:
- `new-qname` must be a valid qualified (*C-naming*).
- In case the graph class is renamed, `new-qname` must have no package part (*C-one-gc*).
- No named element with qualified name `new-qname` must exist already (*C-unique-qnames*).

The operation has no effect on the instance level.

The co-evolution operation `rename-attribute!` renames the attribute `oldname` defined for the attributed element class `aec` to `newname`. The attribute element class may be given by its qualified name or as actual GraphClass, VertexClass, or EdgeClass object.

Function: `funnyqt.coevo.tg/rename-attribute!`
(`rename-attribute! g aec oldname newname`)

The following preconditions have to hold.

Preconditions:
- `newname` is a valid attribute name (*C-naming*).
- In the complete inheritance hierarchy of `aec` there exists no property with name `newname` already (*C-unique-props*).

The operation has no effect on the instance level.

The `rename-domain!` operation renames the given `domain` to `new-qname`. The standard domains like Integer or List cannot be renamed. Again, the domain may be given by its qualified name or as actual Domain object.

Function: `funnyqt.coevo.tg/rename-domain!`
(`rename-domain! g domain new-qname`)

The following preconditions need to be satisfied.

Preconditions:
- `domain` must be a custom enumeration or record domain.
- `new-qname` is a valid qualified name (*C-naming*).
- The schema doesn't contain a named element with qualified name `new-name` already (*C-unique-qnames*).

The operation has no effect on the instance level.

The co-evolution operation `delete-graph-element-class!` deletes the graph element class `gec` from the schema of graph `g`. All subclasses of `gec` are deleted, too, and likewise all direct and indirect instances of `gec` are deleted from the graph `g`.

Function: `funnyqt.coevo.tg/delete-graph-element-class!`
`(delete-graph-element-class! g gec)`

In addition, all archetype and image mappings which have been recorded with respect to `gec` and its subclasses are deleted.

Preconditions:
- If `gec` is a vertex class, there must be no edge classes connected to itself or any of its subclasses.

The co-evolution operation `delete-attribute!` deletes the attribute `attr` defined for the attributed element class `aec` in the schema of graph `g`. Like always, the attributed element class may be specified by its qualified name or as actual GraphClass, VertexClass, or EdgeClass object.

Function: `funnyqt.coevo.tg/delete-attribute!`
`(delete-attribute! g aec attr)`

The operation has no preconditions. The effect on the instance level is that afterwards no `attr` attribute can be accessed anymore for `aec` instances and the corresponding values are erased.

The co-evolution operation `delete-specialization!` deletes a specialization between two vertex or edge classes `super` and `sub`.

Function: `funnyqt.coevo.tg/delete-specialization!`
`(delete-specialization! g super sub)`

The following precondition has to be met.

Preconditions:
- When deleting a specialization between two vertex classes `super` and `sub`, there must not be edge classes incident to `super` and `sub` which are specialized themselves because this would invalidate *C-ec-specialization-vc*.

The operation has no effects on the instance level except that properties originally inherited from `super` to `sub` cannot be accessed anymore.

The co-evolution operation `delete-domain!` deletes the given `domain` from the schema of the graph `g`. The domain must be an enumeration or record domain, i.e., the standard domains like Integer or List cannot be deleted. The domain may be specified by its qualified name or as actual Domain object.

Function: `funnyqt.coevo.tg/delete-domain!`
`(delete-domain! g domain)`

The following precondition needs to hold.

Preconditions:
- The schema must not contain an attribute of the given `domain`.

The operation has no effect on the instance level.

Those were the actual co-evolution operations which operate on the schema and possibly the instance level and implement one single, atomic co-evolution change each. There are three more functions defined in the `funnyqt.coevo.tg` namespace, namely `pull-up-attribute!`, `downtype!` and `empty-graph` which are useful in many co-evolution scenarios.

The `pull-up-attribute!` operation receives a graph g, a graph element class `super`, and an attribute name `attr` (a keyword), and then performs the well-known *pull up attribute* refactoring operation. Concretely, it deletes the `attr` attribute from all direct subclasses of `super` and creates it for `super` itself.

Function: `funnyqt.coevo.tg/pull-up-attribute!`
`(pull-up-attribute! g super attr)`

This refactoring operation has the following precondition.

> Preconditions:
> - All subclasses of `super` must declare an attribute of name `attr`.
> - The domains of all subclass `attr` attributes must be equal.
> - The default values (if any) of all subclass `attr` attributes must be equal.

The `attr` values of subclass instances stay the same as they were before. If `super` is concrete and has direct instances, those will have `attr`'s default value afterwards.

The `downtype!` function works only on the instance level. It receives the graph under transformation g, a graph element class `super`, one of its subclasses `sub`, and a `predicate`. It then "downtypes" all direct `super` instances for which `predicate` holds to `sub` instances. The graph element classes `super` and `sub` may be given by their qualified names or as actual VertexClass or EdgeClass objects.

Function: `funnyqt.coevo.tg/downtype!`
`(downtype! g super sub predicate)`

Concretely, for every direct `super` instance for which `predicate` holds, a new `sub` instance is created and all attribute values are copied over. If `super` and `sub` denote vertex classes, then also all edges incident to the `super` vertices are relinked to the corresponding new `sub` vertices. Thereafter, the original `super` instances are deleted.

If there have been image and archetype traceability mappings for the original `super` instances, those are adapted to point to/from the new `sub` instances afterwards.

The `downtype!` function allows to conveniently handle the instance-adaptation of the frequently re-occurring metamodel evolution scenario where a formerly concrete class is subclassed and then made abstract. This scenario also occurs in the example in chapter chapter 40 starting on page 393.

The `empty-graph` function receives a qualified schema name `sqname` and a graph class name `gcname` and returns an empty graph conforming to a minimal schema which contains nothing but a graph class of the given name.

Function: `funnyqt.coevo.tg/empty-graph`
`(empty-graph sqname gcname)`

This function is useful when a transformation should create a completely new target schema simultaneously with a conforming graph instead of evolving an existing schema and graph. This allows for defining transformations is the style of the GReTL transformation language [EH14; HE11].

Chapter 40

Example

In this chapter, an example co-evolution transformation is illustrated. Figure 40.1 shows a very simple component metamodel[1].

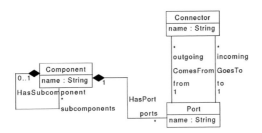

Figure 40.1: A simple component schema

A component has a name and may contain sub-components and ports. Ports can be connected to each other using connectors.

This metamodel has some weaknesses which should be fixed in a new version. (1) All three element classes declare a name attribute instead of abstracting that away. (2) The metamodel allows for connectors that start and end at the same port but connectors should always connect two different ports. (3) Each port should act as either input or output but the metamodel allows for ports which act as both.

The first weakness is only a minor design flaw without negative consequences. However, the second and third weakness allow model instances which are actually wrong and could easily be excluded statically by a more restrictive metamodel. Therefore, the metamodel should be evolved accordingly so that it equals the one in fig. 40.2 on the following page.

Here, the name attribute has been extracted into a new abstract NamedElement

---

[1]The metamodels used here are variants of the ones found in [Ros+14].

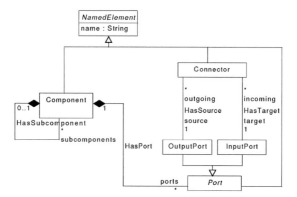

Figure 40.2: The evolved component schema

element class which is specialized by the other element classes fixing issue (1) from above. Furthermore, the element class Port has been made abstract and is specialized by two new element classes OutputPort and InputPort fixing problem (3). Because connectors now always start at an output-port and end at an input-port, problem (2) is fixed, too. In addition, the ComesFrom and GoesTo relationship classes have been renamed to HasSource and HasTarget, respectively, and the role names have been changed, too.

The transformation evolve-component-schema is a plain function and performs this co-evolution to some given graph g and its schema. Its complete definition is given in listing 2 on the next page.

First, it tests if the graph can be handled by the transformation as indicated by comment (1). It checks if the graph contains ports which are not connected at all or have both incoming and outgoing connectors. For the former, there is no way to decide if the port is meant to model an input or an output port, and the latter ports are not representable in the evolved metamodel where each port is either an input or an output port. Therefore, some user intervention would be needed here before the transformation can be applied.

Of course, in a concrete scenario there might be other possibilities to handle these situations. For example, there might be a convention for the names of ports which could be used to decide if an unconnected port is intended to model an input or an output port. Likewise, for ports with incoming and outgoing connectors, the connectors which are wrong according to the port's name could be deleted.

The first actual co-evolution operation calls follow the comment with number (2). A new, abstract vertex class NamedElement is created in the schema of the graph g using create-abstract-vertex-class!. Then the already existing vertex classes Component, Port, and Connector are made subclasses of the new NamedElement class

```
(defn evolve-component-schema [g]
  ;; (1) Check preconditions
  (when-not (forall? #(xor (seq (adjs % :incoming))
                           (seq (adjs % :outgoing)))
                     (vseq g 'Port))
    (error "There're ports which are not connected or both input and output!"))

  ;; (2) NamedElement specialization
  (create-abstract-vertex-class! g 'NamedElement)
  (create-specialization! g 'NamedElement 'Component)
  (create-specialization! g 'NamedElement 'Port)
  (create-specialization! g 'NamedElement 'Connector)
  (pull-up-attribute! g 'NamedElement :name)

  ;; (3) Port specialization
  (create-vertex-class! g 'InputPort)
  (create-vertex-class! g 'OutputPort)
  (create-specialization! g 'Port 'InputPort)
  (create-specialization! g 'Port 'OutputPort)
  (downtype! g 'Port 'InputPort  #(seq (adjs % :incoming)))
  (downtype! g 'Port 'OutputPort #(seq (adjs % :outgoing))))
  (set-abstract! g 'Port true)

  ;; (4) EdgeClass & role renaming
  (rename-attributed-element-class! g 'ComesFrom 'HasSource)
  (rename-attributed-element-class! g 'GoesTo    'HasTarget)
  (set-incidence-class-props! g 'HasSource {:to-role :source})
  (set-incidence-class-props! g 'HasTarget {:to-role :target}))
```

Listing 2: A co-evolution transformation from the schema version shown in fig. 40.1 on page 393 to the schema version shown in fig. 40.2 on page 394

by calling create-specialization! three times. Finally, the name attribute is pulled up into NamedElement from all three subclasses. These changes affect only the schema but have no effects on the graph g.

The next four co-evolution operation calls following the comment with number (3) create two new vertex classes InputPort and OutputPort as specialization of the existing Port class. Then, two downtype! calls replace the existing Port vertices of the graph with instances of the subclasses InputPort and OutputPort. The predicate #(seq (adjs % :incoming)) at the first call defines that a port is an input port if there are incoming connectors. Likewise, the predicate at the second call defines that a port is an output port if there are outgoing connectors. Because of the precondition (1), there cannot be any direct Port instances left after the two calls and therefore it is possible to set the vertex class to be abstract.

The final changes of the co-evolution follow the comment with number (4). The edge classes ComesFrom and GoesTo are renamed to HasSource and HasTarget, respectively, and similarly the role names of the two edge classes at the side of the Port vertex class are changed to source and target. These changes have again no effect on the instance level.

Note that the transformation did not establish image and archetype traceability mappings using either `with-trace-mappings` or `ensure-trace-mappings` (see section 27.4.2 on page 288). The reason is that those are only required in case the `create-vertex-class!` and `create-edge-class!` operations are called with an archetype function in order to create new instances of the newly created vertex or edge class, or in case the extensional transformation operations `create-elements!` or `create-relationships!` are used directly. The transformation in listing 2 did create new instances, namely new input and output ports, but it did so using the `downtype!` operation. This operation does not require traceability mappings but if they were in place, it would modify them in order to transfer the original archetypes of the superclass (i.e., Port) instances to the newly created subclass (i.e., InputPort or OutputPort) instances.

Chapter 41

Related Work

All existing co-evolution approaches with the exception of FunnyQT realize co-evolution in a two-step manner. First, the metamodel is evolved and then the instances of the old metamodel version are co-adapted in order to conform to the new metamodel version. Frequently, the actual metamodel evolution is not in the scope of the tool but it is only concerned with the co-adaptation step.

Of course, any co-adaptation can be specified as an out-place transformation from metamodel version MM_1 to metamodel version MM_2. However, with reasonable large metamodels and frequent releases of new metamodel versions, the effort needed for implementing co-adaptation transformations manually becomes much too high.

In [Wac07], different relations between two versions MM_1 and MM_2 of a metamodel are considered according to *semantics-preservation* and *instance-preservation* properties. A metamodel transformation t with $t(MM_1) = MM_2$ is strictly semantics-preserving if the extensions, i.e., the sets of possible instances, of MM_1 and MM_2 are equal. A metamodel evolution where common properties of several subclasses are extracted into a new, abstract superclass would fall into this category. Co-evolution in such scenarios doesn't require any co-adaptation. Models conforming to MM_1 conform to MM_2 and the reverse is also true.

More interesting in the context of co-evolution are instance-preserving metamodel adaptations. A metamodel transformation t with $t(MM_1) = MM_2$ is strictly instance-preserving if the extension of MM_1 is equal to or a subset of MM_2, i.e., every instance of MM_1 is an instance of MM_2 but the reverse may not hold. So again, an instance-preserving metamodel adaptation requires no co-adaptation to be performed on the models but only in one single direction. Adding new classes or adding non-mandatory attributes and references fall into this category.

In most co-evolution scenarios, the metamodel adaptation is not strictly instance-preserving and certainly not semantics-preserving but less strict preservation properties apply. For many cases, a co-adaptation transformation can be generated automatically, and for others, it can be generated semi-automatically. For example, when a class is deleted from a metamodel, a co-adaptation transformation can simply delete the instances. When a new mandatory attribute is introduced instead, some default value or function computing an appropriate value is needed. Based on these insights, several co-evolution tools have been developed.

In [Bor07], an algorithm coined *conservative copying* for model transformations is described. This algorithm copies over the instances of unchanged metamodel classes from the source model conforming to the old metamodel version to the target model conforming to the new metamodel version.

This algorithm is implemented in *Epsilon Flock* [Kol+15; Ros+10; Ros+14]. Using it, the transformation writer has to define migration rules only for the source metamodel classes whose instances require co-adaptation and all other elements are handled automatically. This greatly reduces the size of the transformation specification because usually the changes between two metamodel versions affect only a small and localized fraction of classes.

A similar but visual approach is provided by the *Model Change Language* (*MCL*, [Nar+09]). MCL is a domain-specific modeling language. The base and the evolved metamodel are loaded in a visual editor where the user defines which old metamodel elements correspond to which evolved metamodel elements and specifies the translation rules.

For example, if some port class has been made abstract and specialized by two new classes input-port and output-port, then the old port class corresponds to both new subclasses and some predicate has to be stated in order to define which old port is to be transformed into an input-port and which is to be transformed into an output-port. For elements for which no explicit correspondence is defined, the tool uses a conservative copying algorithm.

Other approaches and tools utilize metamodel differencing in order to perform co-adaptation. For example, the approach discussed in [Gar+09] computes the differences between a current and an evolved metamodel version and then automatically generates a higher-order transformation for the co-adaptation by using a set of heuristics.

Edapt[1] is a tool for co-evolving Ecore metamodels and conforming EMF models. It incorporates the facilities originating from the COPE Workbench [Her10; Her11]. The tool is a visual Ecore editor providing so-called *coupled operations*. These operations specify adaptations on the metamodel (e.g., create opposite reference, make class abstract, extract superclass), and they also define a certain semantics on instance models. The user is supposed to evolve the metamodel using these operations whose application is recorded in a history. Using this history, co-adaptation transformations from any version to any other version can be generated and then applied to model instances.

All approaches cited above perform the co-adaptation step in terms of an out-place transformation between the old version and the new version of the metamodel.

---

[1]https://www.eclipse.org/edapt/ (last visited: 2015-09-04)

In [Mey+11], a step-wise co-evolution approach based on in-place transformations is suggested.

The overall metamodel delta is computed by differencing and then decomposed into a sequence of sub-deltas, each one describing some well-known, frequently occurring change. For each such sub-delta, there is a default co-adaptation transformation which a user may select, edit, or replace with a completely new one. The interesting point here is that these co-adaptation transformations are in-place transformation rules which are executed on a merged metamodel $MM_{i-1,i}$. This metamodel has the property that every model conforming to MM_{i-1} or MM_i also conforms to $MM_{i-1,i}$. This merged metamodel is generated from metamodel version MM_{i-1} and the delta to version MM_i.

The authors argue that this step-wise, in-place approach provides crucial benefits. Firstly, in-place transformation rules don't touch unaffected elements thus external references to such elements stay valid. And secondly, the step-wise approach reduces accidental complexity because in each step, the scope is narrowed down to the elements affected by the change. Changes which are introduced by a delta from version i to $i + 1$ or a later version are not visible in the merged metamodel $MM_{i-1,i}$.

This is a little bit similar to FunnyQT's co-evolution approach. With that, every invocation of a co-evolution operations performs a small, atomic evolution step which changes one single metamodel constituent and immediately adapts the corresponding model.

Although it is no co-evolution approach, the *GReTL* [EH14; HE11] transformation language can be seen as a direct predecessor of FunnyQT's co-evolution API.

GReTL is specific to the TGraph modeling framework JGraLab and is implemented as a Java API where a simple external DSL is provided, too. GReTL transformations are able to create a new target schema including one conforming target graph. Such transformations are also possible with FunnyQT's co-evolution API by having a transformation which starts with an empty schema and changes that (and the single conforming graph) to the desired evolved schema.

The archetype concept used by FunnyQT's extensional transformation and co-evolution APIs also stems from GReTL although it is implemented with several differences in details in FunnyQT. These details have already been discussed in chapter 28 starting on page 301.

Part XI

Finale

Summary

Many of the FunnyQT services discussed in this thesis have been evaluated by participating in all editions of the Transformation Tool Contest since 2013. Chapter 42 starting on page 405 summarizes the cases which have been solved and the parts of FunnyQT which have been used in doing so. The solutions scored very well and the awards which have been won are also mentioned.

Thereafter, a conclusion is given in chapter 43 starting on page 415 which closes the thesis with a summary of FunnyQT's contributions and an outlook on possible future directions.

Chapter 42

Evaluation

Due to the short FunnyQT project period and the large amount of work that had to fit into it, there has not been enough time left for an evaluation in a strictly scientific sense. Instead, FunnyQT has been extensively tested by participating in the last three editions of the *Transformation Tool Contest* (*TTC*). The aims of the TTC are given on its homepage[1].

> The aim of this event is to evaluate and compare the expressiveness, the usability and the performance of transformation tools for structured data along a number of selected challenging case studies. That is, we want to learn about the pros and cons of each tool considering different applications. A deeper understanding of the relative merits of different tool features will help to further improve the existing tools, to indicate open problems, and to integrate and standardize transformation tools.

As quoted above, people can submit case studies related to model querying and transformations. In each edition, the two or three most interesting and challenging case studies are selected and then users and developers of querying and transformation tools may submit solutions. These solutions are discussed and reviewed in an open review phase where solution submitters score the other solutions submitted for the same case. During the workshop, the solutions are presented to a wider audience[2] which also has a chance to give scores to the solutions. Based on the results of the open review phase and the audience scores, overall scores are computed and awards are assigned to solutions. Usually, for every case there is an overall winner award and there might be additional awards for certain evaluation criteria which the case authors considered as most important for the case.

In the TTC editions from 2013 to 2015, eight case studies have been selected and all of them could be solved appropriately using FunnyQT. Three of these eight solutions were awarded with the overall winner award for the respective case and five additional awards in categories such as correctness or performance have been

---

[1]http://www.transformation-tool-contest.eu (last visited: 2015-12-30)

[2]Since the TTC is part of the STAF conference series which also hosts the ICMT and ICGT conferences, the audience usually consists of experts in model-driven technologies.

won making FunnyQT the most successful competitor in the whole history of the TTC. This gives strong evidence that FunnyQT's comprehensiveness makes it applicable to a very broad set of different model querying and transformation tasks.

One benefit of this kind of evaluation was that there was actually one evaluation per year. Thus, FunnyQT received early feedback in its very initial, prototypical version in the year 2013, then again in an improved version in 2014, and lastly in the almost complete version in 2015. The feedback and critics received at the TTC have been a major driving force in the further development of FunnyQT which eventually led to the current version which is extensively documented in this thesis.

In the remainder of this part, the different TTC case studies and their FunnyQT solutions are briefly described. For each solution, the FunnyQT features which have been utilized for solving the case are mentioned and the full case and solution descriptions in the TTC proceedings are referenced.

42.1 The TTC 2013 Flowgraphs Case

Analysis and transformations in compiler construction were the topic of the TTC'13 flowgraphs case [Hor13d]. From abstract syntax graphs of Java programs, control flow and data flow graphs had to be generated.

In order to reduce the effort for solution developers, the Java programs to be considered contained only one single class with a single method but no restrictions were made with respect to control structures. Programs used for validating the solutions contained deeply nested loops and the jump statements `break` and `continue` including jumps to loop labels had to be handled, too.

The Java programs to be analyzed were given as JaMoPP [Hei+09] models representing the abstract syntax graphs of the programs. The first actual task required the solution developers to implement an out-place transformation which takes such a very detailed and syntax-near JaMoPP model and generates a structure graph representing the same program with a much simpler and more manageable metamodel.

The second task, stated as an in-place transformation problem, required to analyze the structure graph according to the Java language semantics and to enrich it with control flow edges, i.e., for every statement the possible successor statements had to be computed and linked to the predecessor.

In the third task, an intra-procedural data flow analysis had to be performed. For this purpose, the out-place transformation from task 1 had to be extended so that it creates variable and parameter objects which are connected to the statements that read from or write to them. Then, the control flow graph with the enriched information about variable uses had to be analyzed in order to create data flow edges to come to a *program dependence graph* [FOW87].

The FunnyQT solution [Hor13c] to the flowgraphs case realized task 1 with an early, prototypical version of the rule-base out-place transformation DSL whose current version is discussed in chapter 26 starting on page 265. The transformation also utilized polymorphic functions (see section 15.2 on page 154).

The second and third task were tackled algorithmically using the EMF-specific model management and querying API which has been introduced in chapter 14 starting on page 137 and plain Clojure programming.

The FunnyQT solution won the *best efficiency award* and it has been by far the *most concise solution*[3].

42.2 The TTC 2013 Class Diagram Restructuring Case

The class diagram restructuring case [LR13] dealt with performing in-place refactoring operations [Fow99] to UML class diagrams.

The first refactoring to be implemented was *pull up attributes*. When the model contains a class with several subclasses which all declare an attribute of the same name and type, then the attribute should be pulled up into the superclass and deleted from the subclasses.

The second refactoring to be implemented was *extract superclass*. When the model contains a class with several subclasses where a subset of the subclasses declares an attribute of the same name and type, this attribute should be pulled up into a new abstract superclass. In case there are multiple attributes that could be pulled up, those with the largest subset of declaring subclasses should be preferred.

The third refactoring task was very similar to the second refactoring task but here classes which are on top of the specialization hierarchy had to be considered. If there are multiple top-level classes declaring some attribute of the same name and type, the attribute had to be pulled up into a new abstract superclass.

The FunnyQT solution to the class diagram restructuring case [Hor13a] solves all three tasks in an improved way which has not been required by the case description. Instead of pulling up one attribute at a time, the solution always pulls up the maximal set of attributes which are duplicated in a maximum set of classes. The case has been solved algorithmically using only FunnyQT's model management and querying API (see part IV starting on page 105).

The solution won the *best overall solution award* for this case.

42.3 The TTC 2013 Petri-Nets to Statechart Case

The TTC Petri-nets to statecharts case [GR13] dealt with transforming flat Petri-net models to hierarchical statechart models. The overall transformation which had to be implemented works in two phases.

The *initialization* phase executes a simple out-place transformation which creates one state in the target statechart model for any place in the source Petri-net. Likewise, transitions between places are translated to hyper-edges between states.

---

[3]Most concise in terms of usual metrics such as number of lines of code or number of statements.

The job of the *reduction* phase is to build up the hierarchy in the statechart model resulting from the initialization phase. Here, two in-place transformation rules had to be implemented which query and change both the source Petri-net model and the target statechart model. One rule is responsible for creating compound AND states, the other one is responsible for creating compound OR states. Both match a certain structure in the Petri-net and then delete parts of this structure while creating the respective compound state in the statechart. Thus, the transformation is input-destructive, and the transformation is guaranteed to terminate with a Petri-net model which only consists of one single place left.

The FunnyQT solution [Hor13b] implemented the initialization transformation using an early version of its rule-based outplace transformation DLS (see chapter 26 starting on page 265). The reduction rules have been implemented algorithmically using only FunnyQT's model management and querying API which has been introduced in part IV starting on page 105.

The FunnyQT solution has won the *best overall solution award* and the *best efficiency award*.

42.4 The TTC 2014 Movie Database Case

The TTC movie database case [HKT14] was mainly intended as a pattern matching performance evaluation case. The models to be considered contained the information from the *International Movie Database*[4] (*IMDb*), i.e., movies with their participating actors, directors, and user ratings.

The first task dealt with generating synthetical test models for verification purposes.

The second task dealt with finding couples of two actors who acted together in at least three movies. For those, new couple elements linking the actors had to be created.

For the third task, the newly created couple elements had to be enriched with the average rating of the common movies.

The first extension task requested that two top-15 lists had to be generated. One list had to be sorted according to the average rating of common movies, the other list had to be sorted according to the number of common movies.

The second extension task extended task 2. Instead of finding and creating couples of two actors, cliques of size 3, 4, and 5 had to be found and manifested in the model. The task encouraged solution developers to implement this task as a higher-order transformation which receives the clique size as a parameter and then generates an appropriate transformation rule.

The third extension task extended task 3 for cliques instead of couples.

The FunnyQT solution [Hor14b] to the movie database case implemented all core and extension tasks. The generation of test models has been realized using only

---

[4]http://www.imdb.com/ (last visited: 2015-09-28)

the model management and querying API discussed in part IV starting on page 105. The tasks 2 and 3, and the extension tasks 2 and 3 have been solved by providing a Clojure macro which generates a suitable FunnyQT in-place transformation rule (see part VI starting on page 221) for a given number of actors, i.e., when given the number 2, the macro generates an in-place transformation rule identifying and manifesting couples. The top-15 lists required by task 3 and extension task 3 have again been solved using FunnyQT's model querying API, polymorphic functions, and general Clojure programming.

The FunnyQT solution was ranked third of all nine submitted solutions and it has been the only solution with a full correctness and completeness score.

42.5 The TTC 2014 FIXML to Java, C#, and C++ Case

The TTC FIXML case [LMT14] dealt with transforming XML files conforming to the FIXML schema[5] to appropriate classes in several object-oriented languages which could then be used to represent the data encoded in the files. The core task required to target Java, and extension tasks for C# and C++ have been stated. Additionally, it has been encouraged to think about how the transformation could be extended in order to target a non-object-oriented language such as C.

The transformation had to be structured into three separate tasks. In the first task, a given FIXML document had to be transformed into a model conforming to a simple XML metamodel.

The second task required a transformation which takes an XML model and creates a model conforming to a metamodel suitable for the targeted object-oriented language.

In the third task, a model-to-text transformation had to be written which takes a model resulting from task 2 and generates program text in the targeted programming language.

As an extension task, it has been encouraged to guess appropriate data types for the fields of the generated classes by inspecting the values of the corresponding XML attributes in the FIXML documents.

The FunnyQT solution [Hor14a] to the FIXML case solves all core and extension tasks. The conversion from XML documents to XML models has been realized by using FunnyQT's XML processing API which has been discussed in section 15.4 on page 159. Task 2 has been implemented using FunnyQT's rule-based out-place transformation DSL (see chapter 26 starting on page 265). This transformation targets a generic metamodel which is suitable for all object-oriented languages and it also implements the heuristics for guessing appropriate data types for the fields of classes. The model-to-text transformation is implemented using FunnyQT's model querying API (see part IV starting on page 105) and polymorphic functions

---

[5]http://fixwiki.org/fixwiki/FIXwiki (last visited: 2015-09-28)

(see section 15.2 on page 154) in combination with the Clojure templating library *Stencil*[6].

The FunnyQT solution is able to target the languages Java, C#, C++, and C. For the former three, appropriate classes with fields are generated. With C as the target language, structs are generated instead. For C++, the solution also generates the appropriate destructors for the generated classes, and for C, additional functions for freeing pointers to the generated structs are created. For C++ and C, the generated code is also split into header and implementation files which are properly guarded using `#ifndef`-ed `#include` preprocessor statements. All generated files for all four target languages compile without warnings when using the standard compilers for those languages.

The FunnyQT solution has won the *most accurate solution award* and scored in the second place in the overall evaluation for this case.

42.6   The TTC 2015 Model Execution Case

The TTC model execution case [MW15] required solution developers to implement the execution semantics of the UML activity diagram language in terms of an in-place transformation. The execution semantics are defined using a token game where the currently executed activity nodes have tokens which are then offered on outgoing control flow edges. In general, an activity node can start its execution as soon as there are tokens offered on all control flow edges leading to this node. Specific activity node types such as fork nodes, join nodes, decision nodes, or opaque actions have more complex execution semantics.

The case could be solved in different variations with increased complexity starting with simple control flows to complex control flow including the evaluation of expressions.

The FunnyQT solution to the model execution case [Hor15c] implements the most ambitious variant realizing the complete UML activity diagram execution semantics with the exception of object flows which have not been considered by the case.

The case has been solved algorithmically using FunnyQT's model management and querying API and an activity diagram specific API which has been generated from the metamodel (see section 14.8 on page 144). To implement different execution semantics depending on the type of activity nodes, polymorphic functions have been used which were introduced in section 15.2 on page 154. The solution is an almost literal translation of the informal specification of the execution semantics given in the case description. For every step in the execution, there is exactly one function performing this step.

The FunnyQT solution has won the *most correct solution award* for this case, and in fact, it has been the only solution with a full correctness score.

---

[6]`https://github.com/davidsantiago/stencil` (last visited: 2015-09-28)

42.7   The TTC 2015 Java Refactoring Case

The TTC Java refactoring case [KPL15] dealt with refactoring Java programs. The solutions had to be structured into three steps.

In the first step, solutions should utilize some arbitrary Java parser such as JaMoPP[7] or MoDisco[8] in order to parse the given Java source code and generate a model representation from it. Then, an out-place transformation had to be defined which transforms this tool-specific representation to a model of a predefined program graph metamodel.

In the second step, the actual refactorings had to be applied to the program graph model. The refactorings to be considered where *pull up method, create superclass,* and *extract superclass* (extension). Additionally, a second extension task suggested to implement a means for proposing refactorings to the user.

The third step of the transformation dealt with propagating the changes performed in the program graph model back to the Java source code where unchanged parts must not be modified. Because the program graph model did not contain all the details of the original Java source code, this task is dependent on the transformation from step 1, i.e., the changes in the program graph had to be propagated into the original JaMoPP or MoDisco model, and then this one had to be serialized again.

An extensive test framework was provided which calls the transformations of the different steps on several test files and validates the results.

The FunnyQT solution to the Java refactoring case [Hor15b] uses JaMoPP to parse the Java source code and generated a model representation from it. The transformation to a program graph model has been realized using the rule-based out-place transformation DSL from chapter 26 starting on page 265.

The actual refactoring operations are implemented using in-place transformation rules (see part VI starting on page 221) which heavily utilize FunnyQT's pattern inheritance feature. The solution implements the more general *pull up member* refactoring instead of only being able to pull up methods. The extension task of proposing possible refactorings to the user has been solved using the `interactive-rule` combinator (see section 22.1.1 on page 234).

The third step of the transformation is encoded already in the refactoring rules of step 2. The refactoring rules receive an additional parameter which is a map from program graph elements to corresponding JaMoPP model elements. This map is built from the traceability information of the JaMoPP to program graph transformation in step 1. Whenever a refactoring rule is applied, it immediately performs the changes on the program graph model and then returns a closure which will perform the corresponding changes in the original JaMoPP model. These closures are eventually executed by the test framework. Thus, the only thing that remains to be done is saving the JaMoPP models which automatically serializes the changed parts to the corresponding Java files.

The FunnyQT solution has won the *overall winner award* for the Java refactoring

---

[7]http://www.jamopp.org/index.php/JaMoPP (last visited: 2015-09-28)
[8]https://eclipse.org/MoDisco/ (last visited: 2015-09-28)

case.

42.8   The TTC 2015 Train Benchmark Case

The TTC train benchmark case [Szá+15] dealt with incremental model validation. The models to be considered represented railway networks with routes, switches, sensors, segments, and semaphores. A valid model must respect several constraints of increasing complexity such as the length of a segment must be greater than zero, every switch must be connected to a sensor, or all sensors that are associated with a switch that belongs to a route must also be associated directly with the same route. Solutions had to discover invalidations of these constraints and fix them appropriately.

The case had a special focus on incrementality because the idea was that users define such models using a visual editor and should always have an up-to-date list of invalid parts in their model. Performing an edit operation could create a new invalidation or fix one or many existing problems and therefore it would be desirable if the list of invalid elements could be updated without having to search the complete model again. Thus, the transformation task was custom-tailored to incremental pattern matching approaches such as EMF-IncQuery [Ujh+15].

An extensive testing framework has been provided which calls the solutions, measures the execution time and validates the results for different model sizes. The execution was structured into two phases. In the first phase, the solutions had to compute all invalidations in the complete model. The second phase consisted of ten repair and re-check cycles in which either a fixed number or 10% of all invalid elements were repaired. For an incremental pattern matching approach, the re-check phase is obviously not needed because the matches of a pattern are up-to-date at all times, however non-incremental approaches need to re-evaluate the patterns in each cycle.

The FunnyQT solution to the train benchmark case [Hor15d] uses the in-place transformation DSL which has been introduced in part VI starting on page 221 for identifying and fixing elements invalidating the constraints defined by the case description. Especially its rule application modifier as-test (see section 22.2 on page 235) has been a very convenient utility here since it allowed to define the queries and corresponding fixes as in-place transformation rules while still allowing to compute the sequence of invalid elements first and to defer the execution of the repair actions to a later point in time.

The solution ranked first in the reviewer scores which considered correctness, conciseness, and readability and therefore won the *overall quality award* for this case. With respect to performance, the FunnyQT solution was reasonably fast given that it is no incremental pattern matching approach.

42.9 TTC Summary

Table 42.1 summarizes the eight TTC cases for which FunnyQT solutions have been implemented. For every case, the kinds of tasks that had to be solved are summarized together with the FunnyQT services which were employed for solving them[9]. Lastly, also the awards that have been won are listed, too.

TTC Case	Tasks	Used Services	Awards
Flowgraphs '13	out-place transf., control- and data-flow analysis	`funnyqt.emf,` `funnyqt.generic*,` `funnyqt.model2model*,` `funnyqt.polyfns,` `funnyqt.query`	best efficiency
CD Restr. '13	refactoring (in-place transf.)	`funnyqt.emf,` `funnyqt.generic*,` `funnyqt.query`	best overall solution
PN2SC '13	out-place transf., in-place transf.	`funnyqt.emf,` `funnyqt.generic*,` `funnyqt.model2model*,` `funnyqt.query`	best overall solution, best efficiency
MovieDB '14	model generation, in-place transf., querying	`funnyqt.emf,` `funnyqt.generic,` `funnyqt.in-place,` `funnyqt.polyfns,` `funnyqt.query`	3rd overall winner
FIXML '14	XML-to-model, out-place, model-to-text	`funnyqt.emf,` `funnyqt.generic,` `funnyqt.model2model,` `funnyqt.polyfns,` `funnyqt.tg,` `funnyqt.xmltg`	most accurate solution, 2nd overall winner
Model Exec. '15	model interpretation/execution	`funnyqt.emf,` `funnyqt.polyfns,` `funnyqt.query`	most correct solution
Java Refact. '15	out-place, refactoring (in-place transf.), change propagation	`funnyqt.emf,` `funnyqt.generic,` `funnyqt.in-place,` `funnyqt.model2model,` `funnyqt.pmatch,` `funnyqt.query`	overall winner
Train Bench. '15	incremental pattern matching, in-place transf.	`funnyqt.emf,` `funnyqt.in-place`	overall quality

Table 42.1: Summary of the FunnyQT TTC solutions

---

[9]Some namespaces are marked with an asterisk meaning that at the time of the case, the namespace had a different name and/or provided its service in a very preliminary shape compared with the current version.

Chapter 43

Conclusion

This final chapter of the thesis first summarizes the realized querying and transformation approach in section 43.1 and highlights its contributions. Lastly, an outlook is given in section 43.2 on page 418.

43.1 Summary and Contributions

This thesis described the model querying and transformation approach FunnyQT.

Part I gave an *introduction into the context* of this thesis and motivated why the current state of the art querying and transformation approaches do not suffice by pointing out their tender spots. Based on these weaknesses, *requirements* have been derived, and a *solution concept* has been sketched. This concept envisioned a *comprehensive model querying and transformation approach* which is generic and can handle models of *different modeling frameworks*, is *embedded in a functional language*, and provides its services in the form of *APIs and embedded DSLs*. As host language, the functional JVM-based Lisp-dialect *Clojure* has been chosen.

Part II was concerned with the foundations required to use FunnyQT. Since queries and transformations are essentially just Clojure programs, quite some space has been devoted to introduce the most important concepts of the language which are useful also in the querying or transformation context. Furthermore, the modeling frameworks *EMF* and *JGraLab* have been described and compared briefly.

Part III mainly discussed FunnyQT's *protocol-based approach on genericity* which provides a duck-typed view on models of different kinds. EMF and JGraLab models are supported by default and support for further modeling frameworks can be added without touching FunnyQT's internals. This part also introduced the *terminology and conventions* which are used both in this thesis and FunnyQT itself. Lastly, the overall architecture has been depicted.

Part IV then introduced FunnyQT's *model management API* which provides the basis onto which all other querying and transformation services are built. In combination with Clojure's standard language features, this API can be used for scripting queries and transformations, or for writing algorithms on models and their elements. The same part also introduced some powerful *querying constructs* such as *regular path expressions* and several auxiliary services including *model visualization, persistence of model-related data, XML processing*, and *polymorphic functions* which can be seen as methods that are dynamically attached to metamodel classes.

Part V was devoted to *pattern matching* where FunnyQT provides very sophisticated capabilities. Patterns are defined using a concise and convenient embedded DSL and compile to normal Clojure functions which receive at least a model and return the lazy sequence of the pattern's matches. Patterns may also be declared to be evaluated eagerly and then the pattern matching process is automatically parallelized on multi-core systems for improved efficiency. The embedded DSL supports the definition of patterns with arbitrary constraints, positive and negative application conditions (and a generalization thereof), patterns with alternatives, and patterns with nested subpatterns which are matched in the context of a match of the surrounding pattern. For reusability, there is also a concept of pattern inheritance.

Part VI then turned towards the topic of *in-place transformations*. FunnyQT allows the definition of such transformations in terms of rules which use pattern matching in order to find one match of the pattern and then apply arbitrary actions to it. Alternatively, rules with for-all semantics can be specified, too, where the actions are applied to all matches of the rule's pattern. In the latter case, the pattern matching process is again parallelized automatically. In-place transformation rules can be composed to new rules with certain semantics, e.g., as-long-as-possible-application or non-deterministic choice, using higher-order rule combinator functions. Furthermore, rules can be applied as patterns where they just return their pattern's matches, and they can be applied as tests where they return a thunk encapsulating the rule's actions in case their pattern has a match. This allows to test a rule's applicability while omitting or deferring the rule's actions. Finally, FunnyQT supports a highly customizable state space analysis framework. Essentially, there is a higher-order function for generating the state space which is parametrized with transformation rules, a function for comparing states, and several different kinds of constraints to be tested on the states or the state space itself.

Part VII was dedicated to *out-place transformations* which populate target models from given source models and usually realize unidirectional language translations. Here, FunnyQT provides two different approaches. First, there is an embedded DSL where transformations are defined in terms of mapping rules which translate one or many given source elements to one or many target elements. Such rules usually define one-to-one mappings between a rule's input and output. FunnyQT's concept of input identities allows for defining different notions of equality on a per-rule basis and permits to specify many-to-one mappings, too. For reusability, inheritance between transformations is supported. Secondly, there is an operational approach for defining out-place transformations where the target graph of the transformation is defined in terms of the extensions of its metamodel's constituents.

Part VIII then discussed *relational, logic-based model querying*. With FunnyQT's embedded relational model querying DSL, queries declaratively define relations between logic variables. Each variable can either be fresh (unbound) or ground (bound) and the evaluation of a query finds all possible variable bindings which make all relations hold.

Part IX was concerned with *bidirectional transformations*. With FunnyQT's embedded bidirectional transformation DSL, a transformation consists of relations which relate elements in a left model with elements in a right model. Such transformations can be used as a pair of unidirectional transformations, i.e., they can produce a right model for a given left model and vice versa. But more importantly, they can be used in a checkonly mode to test if two given models are consistent with respect to the transformation, and if not, they can be used for synchronizing the models in order to regain consistency again.

Part X then introduced the last service provided by FunnyQT: *co-evolution transformations*. In contrast to existing approaches, FunnyQT does not consider co-evolution as a two-step process where first the metamodel is evolved and then the instance models are co-adapted, i.e., migrated to the new metamodel version. Instead, FunnyQT provides an operational co-evolution API which evolves a given model's metamodel at runtime and simultaneously adapts the model to keep it conforming.

The goals underlying the design of FunnyQT which have been outlined in chapter 3 have been achieved. There is no doubt that FunnyQT is a very comprehensive approach providing a diverse set of powerful and expressive query and transformation concepts. As the evaluation in chapter 42 has shown, all transformation cases of the last three editions of the TTC could be easily solved using it. But still it is a very light-weight, maintainable, and extensible approach consisting of only about 12.000 well-documented lines of code.

With the single exception of its co-evolution API, it is also completely generic and extensible for adding support for modeling frameworks other than EMF and JGraLab.

The embedding in the functional language Clojure allows for excellent reusability and flexibility. Queries, patterns, rules, and complete transformations are essentially just functions which can be passed around and composed to new functions and they can be parametrized with other queries and transformations themselves. They are not isolated but can interact with and make use of any other software components and libraries available on the JVM.

The embedding in Clojure also enhances usability in that no dedicated editing environment is required for conveniently defining queries and transformations. Any editor or IDE with Clojure support, from Emacs and Vim to IntelliJ IDEA, NetBeans, and Eclipse, is a good FunnyQT editing environment providing the usual features such as syntax highlighting and auto-completion. Most importantly, all the mentioned tools provide support for interactive development where changes are instantly deployed to a running JVM and can immediately be tested and refined further.

43.2   Outlook

At the time of this writing, FunnyQT[1] is complete and all its services are well-tested
and working as described in this thesis. But that, of course, doesn't mean that
there's no more room for improvements. In this section, some suggestions on future
directions and extensions are given.

First of all, one future direction could be *adding support for model representations
other than those of JGraLab and EMF*. Given that *Big Data* is one of the major trends
in computer science, modern graph databases which promise the efficient handling
of distributed graphs of unlimited sizes are prime candidates in this respect. A
suitable choice could be the Java-based *Neo4J*[2]. Its graph model is simple and just
consists of nodes and binary and directed relationships between nodes. Both nodes
and relationships may be attributed. The nodes are labeled with possibly multiple
labels per node and the relationships are typed where the type is essentially just a
string. In contrast to modeling frameworks like EMF and JGraLab, Neo4J graphs
have no metamodel but attributes, node labels, and relationship types come into
being dynamically.

Another interesting extension to FunnyQT would be to add support for *incremental pattern matching* as provided by EMF-IncQuery [Ujh+15]. With incremental
pattern matching, a special data structure based on RETE networks [For82] is
created for patterns where every node in the network represents a part of some
pattern. The top nodes represent just elements of some type, intermediate nodes
represent connection constraints, nodes further down represent subpatterns, and
the bottom nodes represent the complete patterns defined by the user. The nodes in
the network cache all matches of the subpattern or pattern they represent and the
modeling framework's notification facilities are used to propagate changes applied
to the model through the network in order to update the caches. With incremental
pattern matching, the complete sets of matches of all patterns are available at all
times. The downside is that the caches induce a high memory overhead.

Incremental pattern matching also gives rise to *reactive transformations* as
supported by VIATRA [Ber+15] which builds upon EMF-IncQuery. Here, the nodes
representing the patterns in the RETE network emit events themselves when their
caches are updated, e.g., a new match came into being or an existing match has
been modified in such a way that it is no match any longer. Applications built
around models can register for receiving these events and then react appropriately,
e.g., initiate a transformation. This capability would be very useful especially with
models@run.time where a system's execution is monitored, validated, and possibly
adapted based on models which are managed at runtime.

Another possibility for future work is to add support for *incremental execution
of FunnyQT's rule-based out-place transformations*. Such transformations keep
running after all source model elements have been transformed to target model
elements and then observe changes applied to the source model and immediately
propagate them to the target models. For purely additive changes, this should be
rather easy to implement. However, the consequences of deletion and property
changes of source model elements are much more severe and might cause massive

---

[1] http://funnyqt.org
[2] http://neo4j.com/ (last visited: 2015-10-31)

changes on the target models.

The state of the art in bidirectional model transformations is a step ahead of FunnyQT's implementation. With the latter, transformations are completely deterministic. Given two models and the transformation specification, one can derive how the respective target model will look alike after executing the transformation in either direction. Non-bijective transformations can be defined but they always encode a preference order among the possible solutions. Advanced bidirectional transformation implementations such as JTL [Cic+10] allow for *enumerating all possible solutions* or even query the user to let him decide among a given set of alternatives. Another advanced language is Echo [MC13] which is able to guarantee that consistency is restored with the least amount of changes. Implementing such features is most likely not feasible with FunnyQT's current implementation which accesses the models directly in their native representation as it would entail speculatively trying out possible solutions, assessing them, and possibly undoing them. But both JTL and Echo don't work on the native model representations either but instead convert the models to some logical representation used by different constraint solvers. A similar approach can be envisioned for FunnyQT, too.

FunnyQT's co-evolution API allows for solving typical coupled evolution scenarios where models conforming to a metamodel version i are to be updated to a metamodel version j. However, since the evolution of the metamodel and one conforming model happen simultaneously at runtime, they are not limited to this scenario. Again, the context of *models@run.time* could be a good opportunity for *evaluating this capability* in a novel context. Consider a system where parts of its behavior is executed by interpreting some model which is managed at runtime. The interpreter could be realized using FunnyQT's polymorphic functions which also support modification at runtime. Thus, in this scenario co-evolution transformations could be used to evolve the model's metamodel at runtime and thereby adapting both the model and also the model interpreter.

So to conclude, FunnyQT as it is today provides a solid and practically usable foundation. Most of its services have been evaluated with great success in the course of the Transformation Tool Contest. Some other services, especially its relational querying API, its bidirectional transformation DSL, and its co-evolution API are well-tested internally but are still waiting for actual real-world cases to be solved using them.

I really hope others share my excitement for FunnyQT and I'd love to see it used out there in the wild. This thesis comes to its end now but FunnyQT is and will stay freely available[3] for everyone interested in playing with it at http://funnyqt.org.

---

[3]Free as in freedom as well as in free beer.

Part XII

Appendix

Appendix A

Extensibility

A.1 Extending Regular Path Expressions

In order to add support for regular path expressions which have been discussed in section 15.1 on page 147 for models of modeling frameworks other than JGraLab and EMF, two protocols need to be extended.

The ISimpleRegularPathExpression protocol must be extended upon that framework's interface or class whose instances represent model elements. By default, it is extended upon JGraLab's Vertex interface, EMF's EObject interface, and upon java.util.Collection. When one of its methods is called with a collection of model elements, the implementation simply calls itself for each element in the collection combining the results of each call.

Likewise, in order to support traversal to neighboring nodes in terms of role names by using keywords, the IAdjacenciesInternal procotol discussed on page 112 has to be extended upon the modeling framework's element representation interface or class.

All regular path operators are purely generic with the exception of the regular path restriction funnyqt.query/p-restr. In order to support it for model representations other than JGraLab's TGraphs or EMF, the ITypeMatcher protocol discussed on page 110 has to be extended upon that representation's model element class.

A.2 Extending Polymorphic Functions

In order to make the FunnyQT polymorphic function facility (see section 15.2 on page 154) work with model representations other than JGraLab and EMF, the following four protocols have to be extended upon that model representation's classes.

IQualifiedName for getting the qualified name of a metamodel class (see page 108)

423

IMMDirectSuperclasses for getting the direct superclasses of a metamodel class (see page 118)

IMMElementClasses for getting the sequence of classes contained in a metamodel (see page 117)

IMMClass for getting the metamodel class of a model element (see page 117)

A.3 Extending the Pattern Matching Facilities

The FunnyQT pattern matching facilities which has been discussed in part V starting on page 181 can be extended in two ways to support model representations other than JGraLab and EMF. The obvious choice is to extend the relevant protocols needed by the generic pattern matching variant. This possibility is discussed in appendix A.3.1. It is also possible to provide custom framework-specific pattern matching capabilities that can be enabled by the pattern option :pattern-expansion-context. The latter option is explained in appendix A.3.2.

A.3.1 Extending the Generic Pattern Matching Facility

The generic pattern matching variant relies on the following four protocols being extended upon the relevant model representation's interfaces or classes.

ITypeMatcher for testing if a model element is instance of a given type using the has-type? function (see concept 3 on page 110 for the ITypeMatcher protocol and section 12.5 on page 113 for the has-type? function)

IElements for retrieving all model elements of a given type (see section 12.2 on page 109)

IAdjacenciesInternal for retrieving the adjacent model elements given a role name with edge symbols of the form -<:role>-> (see section 12.4 on page 112)

INeighbors for retrieving all adjacent model elements with edge symbols without role, i.e., --> (see section 12.7 on page 115)

A.3.2 Providing Framework-Specific Pattern Matching Facilities

In order to provide a framework-specific pattern matching variant, a function has to be provided which transforms a pattern graph to a binding form suitable for a sequence comprehension. Such a function must take as arguments the argument vector of the pattern to be defined, and its pattern graph. Then, this function can be added to the hash-map valued var pattern-graph-transform-function-map.

Var: funnyqt.pmatch/pattern-graph-transform-function-map

The value of this var is a map from keywords denoting pattern matching variants to transformer functions from pattern graph to sequence comprehension binding forms. Its default value is given below.

```
{:generic pg-to-for+-bindings-generic
 :tg      pg-to-for+-bindings-tg
 :emf     pg-to-for+-bindings-emf}
```

Clearly, providing such a transformer function is a non-trivial task. However, because the generic and EMF versions are very similar, they have been abstracted into a common base function named pg-to-for+-bindings-only-refs.

Function: funnyqt.generic/pg-to-for+-bindings-only-refs
(pg-to-for+-bindings-only-refs argvec pg elements-fn adjs-fn neighbors-fn)

The base transformer function receives the pattern's argument vector, its pattern graph, and three functions. The elements-fn has to be a function for retrieving all elements of a given type from a model, adjs-fn has to be a function that given an element and a role name returns the elements in that role, and neighbors-fn is a function returning all elements referenced by a given element.

The generic and EMF-specific transformer functions simply call this base function with different parametrizations.

```
(defn pg-to-for+-bindings-generic [argvec pg]
  (pg-to-for+-bindings-only-refs argvec pg
    `funnyqt.generic/elements
    `funnyqt.generic/adjs
    `funnyqt.generic/neighbors))

(defn pg-to-for+-bindings-emf [argvec pg]
  (pg-to-for+-bindings-only-refs argvec pg
    `funnyqt.emf/eallcontents
    `eget-1  ;; A small wrapper around `eget-raw`
    `funnyqt.emf/erefs))
```

This base function can be used to provide a framework-specific pattern matching variant with the same feature set as the generic and EMF variants. That is, the variant is not aware of possible first-class edges, i.e., only nodes can be matched and only role name navigation is possible.

The sequence comprehension form emitted by the base transformer function still contains calls to the has-type? function, thus the ITypeMatcher protocol (see concept 3 on page 110) needs to be extended upon the relevant interfaces or classes.

In order to provide a framework-specific variant that supports first-class edges, there is no special implementation support provided, i.e., a transformer function from pattern graph to sequence comprehension binding form has to be written from scratch. Having a look at the JGraLab version pg-to-for+-bindings-tg is highly recommended.

A.4 Extending the Rule-Based Out-Place Transformation DSL

In order to extend the out-place transformation capabilities provided by the FunnyQT namespace `funnyqt.model2model` which has been discussed in chapter 26 starting on page 265 to models of other kinds than JGraLab and EMF, the following protocols declared in the namespace `funnyqt.generic` have to be extended upon the types of the new model representation.

`ITypeMatcher` for constraining the rules' input elements by the optionally given type specifications in the rules' `:from` clauses.

`IElements` for the transformation being able to iterate the elements in the input models annotated with `^:in` or `^:inout` metadata in case top-level rules are used as the transformation's entry points.

`ICreateElement` for creating new elements in the output models as defined by the rules' `:to` clauses.

`IAttributeValueAccess` for setting attribute values.

`IModifyAdjacencies` for setting references.

A.5 Extending the Extensional Out-Place Transformation API

In order to extend the transformation capabilities provided by the FunnyQT namespace `funnyqt.extensional` which has been depicted in chapter 27 starting on page 281 to models of other kinds than JGraLab and EMF, the following protocols declared in the namespace `funnyqt.generic` have to be extended upon the appropriate types of the new model representation.

`ICreateElement` for creating elements in the target model using `create-elements!`.

`ICreateRelationship` for creating relationships in the target model using the function `create-relationships!`.

`IAttributeValueAccess` for setting the attributes of target model elements using `set-avals!`.

`IModifyAdjacencies` for setting the references of target model elements using the `set-adjs!` and `add-adjs!` functions.

`IElements` for iterating the target model elements when attribute or reference extensions are specified as functions receiving an element and returning a value.

`IRelationships` for iterating the target model relationships when the extension of an attribute defined for a relationship class are specified as functions receiving a relationship and returning a value.

`IMMClass` for retrieving metamodel class by its qualified or unique name.

`IMMAllSubclasses` for querying the subclasses of a given metamodel class when resolving images from archetypes and vice versa using the `image` and `archetype` functions or their variants.

`IMMDirectSuperclasses` for querying the superclasses of a given metamodel class.

`IMMRelationshipClassSourceTarget` for querying the source and target element classes of a relationship class when instances are created using `create-relationships!`.

A.6 Extending the Relational Querying API

In order to extend the transformation capabilities provided by the FunnyQT namespace `funnyqt.extensional` which has been introduced in part VIII starting on page 311 to models of other kinds than JGraLab and EMF, the following protocols declared in the namespace `funnyqt.generic` have to be extended upon the appropriate types of the new model representation.

`IElements` for iterating all elements in a model.
`IElement` for testing if some object is an element.
`IRelationships` for iterating all relationships in a model.
`IRelationship` for testing if some object is a relationship.
`IIncidentRelationships` for iterating incident relationships of some element.
`IAttributeValueAccess` getting the attribute value of an element or relationship.
`IAdjacenciesInternal` for getting the elements referenced by some element.
`IQualifiedName` for accessing the qualified name of metamodel classes.
`IMMClass` for retrieving the metamodel class of some element or relationship.
`IMMElementClass` for testing if some object is an element class.
`IMMRelationshipClass` for testing if some object is a relationship class.
`IMMAttributes` for getting the attributes defined for some metamodel class.
`IMMReferences` for getting the references defined for some metamodel element class.
`IMMDirectSuperclasses` for querying the superclasses of a given metamodel class.

A.7 Extending the Bidirectional Transformation DSL

In order to extend the applicability of FunnyQT's bidirectional transformation DSL which has been introduced in part IX starting on page 339 to models of frameworks other than EMF or JGraLab, all the protocols required for relational querying have to be satisfied (see appendix A.6).

In addition, the following protocols must be extended:

`IMMSuperclass` for testing generalization relationships.
`IUnset` for testing if an attribute or reference is unset.
`IMMMultiValuedProperty` for testing if a reference is multi-valued.
`IModifyAdjacencies` for setting and adding to references.
`ICreateElement` for creating elements.
`ICreateRelationship` for creating relationships.
`IContainer` for accessing the container of an element.

Bibliography

[ABE09]   Faisal Alkhateeb, Jean-François Baget, and Jérôme Euzenat. "Extending
           SPARQL with regular expression patterns (for querying RDF)". In: *J.
           Web Sem.* 7.2 (2009), pp. 57–73. DOI: 10.1016/j.websem.2009.02.002.

[Alv+11]   Claire E. Alvis et al. "cKanren: miniKanren with Constraints". In: *Work-
           shop on Scheme and Functional Programming'11, Portland, Oregon.*
           Oct. 2011.

[Are+10]   Thorsten Arendt et al. "Henshin: Advanced Concepts and Tools for
           In-Place EMF Model Transformations". English. In: *Model Driven En-
           gineering Languages and Systems.* Ed. by DorinaC. Petriu, Nicolas
           Rouquette, and Øystein Haugen. Vol. 6394. Lecture Notes in Computer
           Science. Springer Berlin Heidelberg, 2010, pp. 121–135. ISBN: 978-
           3-642-16144-5. DOI: 10.1007/978-3-642-16145-2_9.

[Ban+87]   Jay Banerjee et al. "Semantics and Implementation of Schema Evolu-
           tion in Object-oriented Databases". In: *Proceedings of the 1987 ACM
           SIGMOD International Conference on Management of Data.* SIGMOD
           '87. San Francisco, California, USA: ACM, 1987, pp. 311–322. ISBN:
           0-89791-236-5. DOI: 10.1145/38713.38748.

[BCW12]   Marco Brambilla, Jordi Cabot, and Manuel Wimmer. *Model-Driven
           Software Engineering in Practice.* Synthesis Lectures on Software
           Engineering. Morgan & Claypool Publishers, 2012. DOI: 10.2200/
           S00441ED1V01Y201208SWE001. URL: http://dx.doi.org/10.2200/
           S00441ED1V01Y201208SWE001.

[BE11]   Daniel Bildhauer and Jürgen Ebert. "DHHTGraphs - Modeling beyond
           plain graphs". In: *Workshops Proceedings of the 27th International Con-
           ference on Data Engineering, ICDE 2011, April 11-16, 2011, Hannover,
           Germany.* Ed. by Serge Abiteboul et al. IEEE, 2011, pp. 100–105. ISBN:
           978-1-4244-9194-0. DOI: 10.1109/ICDEW.2011.5767620.

[Ber+15]   Gábor Bergmann et al. "Viatra 3: A Reactive Model Transformation Plat-
           form". In: *Theory and Practice of Model Transformations - 8th Interna-
           tional Conference, ICMT 2015, Held as Part of STAF 2015, L'Aquila, Italy,
           July 20-21, 2015. Proceedings.* Ed. by Dimitris S. Kolovos and Manuel
           Wimmer. Vol. 9152. Lecture Notes in Computer Science. Springer, 2015,
           pp. 101–110. ISBN: 978-3-319-21154-1. DOI: 10.1007/978-3-319-
           21155-8_8.

[BET12]   Enrico Biermann, Claudia Ermel, and Gabriele Taentzer. "Formal foun-
            dation of consistent EMF model transformations by algebraic graph
            transformation". English. In: *Software & Systems Modeling* 11.2 (2012),
            pp. 227–250. ISSN: 1619-1366. DOI: 10.1007/s10270-011-0199-7.

[Bil12]   Daniel Bildhauer. "Verteilte Hierarchische Hyper-TGraphen. Definition
            und Implementation eines ausdrucksstarken Graphenkonzepts". Dis-
            sertation. University Koblenz-Landau, 2012. ISBN: 978-3-8325-3157-7.

[BOM15]   Juan Boubeta-Puig, Guadalupe Ortiz, and Inmaculada Medina-Bulo.
            "ModeL4CEP: Graphical domain-specific modeling languages for CEP
            domains and event patterns". In: *Expert Syst. Appl.* 42.21 (2015),
            pp. 8095–8110. DOI: 10.1016/j.eswa.2015.06.045. URL: http://
            dx.doi.org/10.1016/j.eswa.2015.06.045.

[Bor07]   Boris Gruschko, Dimitrios S. Kolovos, Richard F. Paige. "Towards Syn-
            chronizing Models with Evolving Metamodels". In: *Proceedings of the
            International Workshop on Model-Driven Software Evolution held with
            the ECSMR*. 2007.

[Bru+14]   Hugo Brunelière et al. "MoDisco: A model driven reverse engineer-
            ing framework". In: *Information & Software Technology* 56.8 (2014),
            pp. 1012–1032. DOI: 10.1016/j.infsof.2014.04.007. URL: http:
            //dx.doi.org/10.1016/j.infsof.2014.04.007.

[Búr+15]   Márton Búr et al. "Local Search-Based Pattern Matching Features in
            EMF-IncQuery". In: *Graph Transformation - 8th International Confer-
            ence, ICGT 2015, Held as Part of STAF 2015, L'Aquila, Italy, July 21-23,
            2015. Proceedings*. Ed. by Francesco Parisi-Presicce and Bernhard
            Westfechtel. Vol. 9151. Lecture Notes in Computer Science. Springer,
            2015, pp. 275–282. ISBN: 978-3-319-21144-2. DOI: 10.1007/978-3-
            319-21145-9_18. URL: http://dx.doi.org/10.1007/978-3-319-21145-
            9_18.

[Byr09]   William E. Byrd. "Relational Programming in miniKanren: Techniques,
            Applications, and Implementations". PhD thesis. Indiana University,
            Sept. 2009.

[Cic+10]   Antonio Cicchetti et al. "JTL: A Bidirectional and Change Propagat-
            ing Transformation Language". In: *Software Language Engineering
            - Third International Conference, SLE 2010, Eindhoven, The Nether-
            lands, October 12-13, 2010, Revised Selected Papers*. Ed. by Brian A.
            Malloy, Steffen Staab, and Mark van den Brand. Vol. 6563. Lecture
            Notes in Computer Science. Springer, 2010, pp. 183–202. ISBN: 978-
            3-642-19439-9. DOI: 10.1007/978-3-642-19440-5_11. URL: http:
            //dx.doi.org/10.1007/978-3-642-19440-5_11.

[CMT06]   Jesús Sánchez Cuadrado, Jesús García Molina, and Marcos Menárguez
            Tortosa. "RubyTL: A Practical, Extensible Transformation Language".
            In: *Model Driven Architecture - Foundations and Applications, Second
            European Conference, ECMDA-FA 2006*. Ed. by Arend Rensink and
            Jos Warmer. Vol. 4066. LNCS. Springer, 2006, pp. 158–172. ISBN: 3-
            540-35909-5.

[Cor+97]   Andrea Corradini et al. "Algebraic Approaches to Graph Transformation - Part I: Basic Concepts and Double Pushout Approach". In: *Handbook of Graph Grammars and Computing by Graph Transformations, Volume 1: Foundations*. Ed. by Grzegorz Rozenberg. World Scientific, 1997, pp. 163–246. ISBN: 9810228848.

[Der14]   Mahdi Derakhshanmanesh. "A Realization Concept for Model-Integrating Software Components". PhD thesis. Faculty of Computer Science, University of Koblenz-Landau, 2014.

[EB10]   Jürgen Ebert and Daniel Bildhauer. "Reverse Engineering Using Graph Queries". In: *Graph Transformations and Model-Driven Engineering - Essays Dedicated to Manfred Nagl on the Occasion of his 65th Birthday*. Ed. by Gregor Engels et al. Vol. 5765. Lecture Notes in Computer Science. Springer, 2010, pp. 335–362. ISBN: 978-3-642-17321-9. DOI: 10.1007/978-3-642-17322-6_15.

[Ebe+02]   Jürgen Ebert et al. "GUPRO — Generic Understanding of Programs — An Overview". In: *Electronic Notes in Theoretical Computer Science* 72.2 (2002). GraBaTs 2002, Graph-Based Tools (First International Conference on Graph Transformation), pp. 47–56. ISSN: 1571-0661. DOI: 10.1016/S1571-0661(05)80528-6. URL: http://www.sciencedirect.com/science/article/pii/S1571066105805286.

[EH14]   Jürgen Ebert and Tassilo Horn. "GReTL: an extensible, operational, graph-based transformation language". In: *Software and System Modeling* 13.1 (2014), pp. 301–321. DOI: 10.1007/s10270-012-0250-3.

[Ehr+97]   Hartmut Ehrig et al. "Algebraic Approaches to Graph Transformation - Part II: Single Pushout Approach and Comparison with Double Pushout Approach". In: *Handbook of Graph Grammars and Computing by Graph Transformations, Volume 1: Foundations*. Ed. by Grzegorz Rozenberg. World Scientific, 1997, pp. 247–312. ISBN: 9810228848.

[Eic+14]   Christoph Eickhoff et al. "The SDMLib Solution to the MovieDB Case for TTC2014". In: *Proceedings of the 7th Transformation Tool Contest part of the Software Technologies: Applications and Foundations (STAF 2014) federation of conferences, York, United Kingdom, July 25, 2014*. Ed. by Louis M. Rose, Christian Krause, and Tassilo Horn. Vol. 1305. CEUR Workshop Proceedings. CEUR-WS.org, 2014, pp. 145–149. URL: http://ceur-ws.org/Vol-1305/paper6.pdf.

[Erw01]   Martin Erwig. "Inductive Graphs and Functional Graph Algorithms". In: *Journal of Functional Programming* 11.5 (Sept. 2001), pp. 467–492. ISSN: 0956-7968. DOI: 10.1017/S0956796801004075.

[ERW08]   J. Ebert, V. Riediger, and A. Winter. "Graph Technology in Reverse Engineering, The TGraph Approach". In: *10th Workshop Software Reengineering (WSR 2008)*. Ed. by Rainer Gimnich et al. Vol. 126. GI Lecture Notes in Informatics. GI, 2008, pp. 67–81. ISBN: 978-3-88579-220-8.

[Erw97]   Martin Erwig. "Fully Persistent Graphs - Which One to Choose?" In: *9th International Workshop on Implementation of Functional Languages*. 1997, pp. 123–140. URL: http://web.engr.oregonstate.edu/~erwig/papers/PersistentGraphs_IFL97.pdf (visited on 01/19/2015).

[FBK05] Daniel P. Friedman, William E. Byrd, and Oleg Kiselyov. *The Reasoned Schemer*. Cambridge, MA: MIT Press, 2005. ISBN: 0262562146.

[FHR11] Andreas Fuhr, Tassilo Horn, and Volker Riediger. "An Integrated Tool Suite for Model-Driven Software Migration towards Service-Oriented Architectures". In: *Softwaretechnik-Trends* 31.2 (2011). URL: http://pi.informatik.uni-siegen.de/stt/31_2/01_Fachgruppenberichte/sre/04-fuhr.pdf.

[For82] Charles Forgy. "Rete: A Fast Algorithm for the Many Patterns/Many Objects Match Problem". In: *Artif. Intell.* 19.1 (1982), pp. 17–37. DOI: 10.1016/0004-3702(82)90020-0. URL: http://dx.doi.org/10.1016/0004-3702(82)90020-0.

[Fow11] Martin Fowler. *Domain-Specific Languages*. The Addison-Wesley signature series. Addison-Wesley, 2011. ISBN: 978-0-321-71294-3. URL: http://vig.pearsoned.com/store/product/1,1207,store-12521_isbn-0321712943,00.html.

[FOW87] Jeanne Ferrante, Karl J. Ottenstein, and Joe D. Warren. "The Program Dependence Graph and Its Use in Optimization". In: *ACM Trans. Program. Lang. Syst.* 9.3 (1987), pp. 319–349. DOI: 10.1145/24039.24041. URL: http://doi.acm.org/10.1145/24039.24041.

[Fow99] Martin Fowler. *Refactoring: Improving the Design of Existing Code*. Boston, MA, USA: Addison-Wesley Longman Publishing Co., Inc., 1999. ISBN: 0-201-48567-2.

[Gam+95] Erich Gamma et al. *Design Patterns: Elements of Reusable Object-oriented Software*. Boston, MA, USA: Addison-Wesley Longman Publishing Co., Inc., 1995. ISBN: 0-201-63361-2.

[Gar+09] Kelly Garcés et al. "Managing Model Adaptation by Precise Detection of Metamodel Changes". In: *Model Driven Architecture - Foundations and Applications, 5th European Conference, ECMDA-FA 2009, Enschede, The Netherlands, June 23-26, 2009. Proceedings*. Ed. by Richard F. Paige, Alan Hartman, and Arend Rensink. Vol. 5562. Lecture Notes in Computer Science. Springer, 2009, pp. 34–49. ISBN: 978-3-642-02673-7. DOI: 10.1007/978-3-642-02674-4_4.

[Gei08] Rubino Geiß. "Graphersetzung mit Anwendungen im Übersetzerbau". PhD thesis. Fakultät für Informatik, Nov. 2008. URL: http://www.info.uni-karlsruhe.de/papers/diss_geiss.pdf (visited on 01/19/2015).

[Gha+12] Amir Hossein Ghamarian et al. "Modelling and analysis using GROOVE". In: *STTT* 14.1 (2012), pp. 15–40. DOI: 10.1007/s10009-011-0186-x.

[GHL14] Holger Giese, Stephan Hildebrandt, and Leen Lambers. "Bridging the gap between formal semantics and implementation of triple graph grammars - Ensuring conformance of relational model transformation specifications and implementations". In: *Software and System Modeling* 13.1 (2014), pp. 273–299. DOI: 10.1007/s10270-012-0247-y. URL: http://dx.doi.org/10.1007/s10270-012-0247-y.

[GK10]   Joel Greenyer and Ekkart Kindler. "Comparing relational model trans-
           formation technologies: implementing Query/View/Transformation with
           Triple Graph Grammars". In: *Software and System Modeling* 9.1 (2010),
           pp. 21–46. DOI: 10.1007/s10270-009-0121-8. URL: http://dx.doi.
           org/10.1007/s10270-009-0121-8.

[GL88]   Michael Gelfond and Vladimir Lifschitz. "The Stable Model Semantics
           for Logic Programming". In: *Logic Programming, Proceedings of the
           Fifth International Conference and Symposium, Seattle, Washington,
           August 15-19, 1988 (2 Volumes).* Ed. by Robert A. Kowalski and Kenneth
           A. Bowen. MIT Press, 1988, pp. 1070–1080. ISBN: 0-262-61056-6.

[GR13]   Pieter Van Gorp and Louis M. Rose. "The Petri-Nets to Statecharts
           Transformation Case". In: *Proceedings Sixth Transformation Tool Con-
           test, TTC 2013, Budapest, Hungary, 19-20 June, 2013.* Ed. by Pieter Van
           Gorp, Louis M. Rose, and Christian Krause. Vol. 135. EPTCS. 2013,
           pp. 16–31. DOI: 10.4204/EPTCS.135.3. URL: http://dx.doi.org/10.
           4204/EPTCS.135.3.

[GRK13]   Pieter Van Gorp, Louis M. Rose, and Christian Krause, eds. *Proceedings
           Sixth Transformation Tool Contest, TTC 2013, Budapest, Hungary, 19-20
           June, 2013.* Vol. 135. EPTCS. 2013.

[GWS12]   Lars George, Arif Wider, and Markus Scheidgen. "Type-Safe Model
           Transformation Languages as Internal DSLs in Scala". In: *Theory and
           Practice of Model Transformations - 5th International Conference, ICMT
           2012.* Ed. by Zhenjiang Hu and Juan de Lara. Vol. 7307. LNCS. Springer,
           2012, pp. 160–175. ISBN: 978-3-642-30475-0.

[HE11]   Tassilo Horn and Jürgen Ebert. "The GReTL Transformation Language".
           In: *Theory and Practice of Model Transformations - 4th International
           Conference, ICMT 2011, Zurich, Switzerland, June 27-28, 2011. Pro-
           ceedings.* Ed. by Jordi Cabot and Eelco Visser. Vol. 6707. Lecture
           Notes in Computer Science. Springer, 2011, pp. 183–197. ISBN: 978-
           3-642-21731-9. DOI: 10.1007/978-3-642-21732-6_13.

[Hei+09]   Florian Heidenreich et al. "Closing the Gap between Modelling and
           Java". In: *Software Language Engineering, Second International Confer-
           ence, SLE 2009, Denver, CO, USA, October 5-6, 2009, Revised Selected
           Papers.* Ed. by Mark van den Brand, Dragan Gasevic, and Jeff Gray.
           Vol. 5969. Lecture Notes in Computer Science. Springer, 2009, pp. 374–
           383. ISBN: 978-3-642-12106-7. DOI: 10.1007/978-3-642-12107-4_25.
           URL: http://dx.doi.org/10.1007/978-3-642-12107-4_25.

[Her10]   Markus Herrmannsdoerfer. "COPE - A Workbench for the Coupled
           Evolution of Metamodels and Models". In: *Software Language Engi-
           neering - Third International Conference, SLE 2010, Eindhoven, The
           Netherlands, October 12-13, 2010, Revised Selected Papers.* Ed. by
           Brian A. Malloy, Steffen Staab, and Mark van den Brand. Vol. 6563. Lec-
           ture Notes in Computer Science. Springer, 2010, pp. 286–295. ISBN:
           978-3-642-19439-9. DOI: 10.1007/978-3-642-19440-5_18.

[Her11]   Markus Herrmannsdörfer. "Evolutionary Metamodeling". Dissertation.
           München: Technische Universität München, 2011.

[HF13]   Jason Hemann and Daniel P. Friedman. "μKanren: A Minimal Func-
              tional Core for Relational Programming". In: *Scheme and Functional
              Programming Workshop 2013*. Nov. 2013.

[HH14]   Georg Hinkel and Lucia Happe. "Using Component Frameworks for
              Model Transformations by an Internal DSL". In: *Proceedings of the 1st
              International Workshop on Model-Driven Engineering for Component-
              Based Software Systems co-located with MODELS 2014*. Ed. by Federico
              Ciccozzi, Massimo Tivoli, and Jan Carlson. Vol. 1281. CEUR Workshop
              Proceedings. CEUR-WS.org, 2014, pp. 6–15.

[HH15]   Georg Hinkel and Lucia Happe. "An NMF solution to the Train Bench-
              mark Case at the TTC 2015". In: *Proceedings of the 8th Transformation
              Tool Contest part of the Software Technologies: Applications and Foun-
              dations (STAF 2015) federation of conferences, L'Aquila, Italy, July 24,
              2015*. Ed. by Louis M. Rose, Filip Krikava, and Tassilo Horn. Vol. to
              appear. CEUR Workshop Proceedings. CEUR-WS.org, 2015.

[HKT02]   Reiko Heckel, Jochen Malte Küster, and Gabriele Taentzer. "Conflu-
              ence of Typed Attributed Graph Transformation Systems". In: *Graph
              Transformation, First International Conference, ICGT 2002, Barcelona,
              Spain, October 7-12, 2002, Proceedings*. Ed. by Andrea Corradini et al.
              Vol. 2505. Lecture Notes in Computer Science. Springer, 2002, pp. 161–
              176. ISBN: 3-540-44310-X. DOI: 10.1007/3-540-45832-8_14. URL:
              http://dx.doi.org/10.1007/3-540-45832-8_14.

[HKT14]   Tassilo Horn, Christian Krause, and Matthias Tichy. "The TTC 2014
              Movie Database Case". In: *Proceedings of the 7th Transformation Tool
              Contest part of the Software Technologies: Applications and Founda-
              tions (STAF 2014) federation of conferences, York, United Kingdom,
              July 25, 2014*. Ed. by Louis M. Rose, Christian Krause, and Tassilo Horn.
              Vol. 1305. CEUR Workshop Proceedings. CEUR-WS.org, 2014, pp. 93–
              97. URL: http://ceur-ws.org/Vol-1305/paper2.pdf.

[HLM06]   Reiko Heckel, Georgios Lajios, and Sebastian Menge. "Stochastic Graph
              Transformation Systems". In: *Fundam. Inform.* 74.1 (2006), pp. 63–84.
              URL: http://content.iospress.com/articles/fundamenta-informaticae/
              fi74-1-04.

[HLR06]   David Hearnden, Michael Lawley, and Kerry Raymond. "Incremental
              Model Transformation for the Evolution of Model-Driven Systems".
              In: *Model Driven Engineering Languages and Systems, 9th Interna-
              tional Conference, MoDELS 2006, Genova, Italy, October 1-6, 2006,
              Proceedings*. Ed. by Oscar Nierstrasz et al. Vol. 4199. Lecture Notes in
              Computer Science. Springer, 2006, pp. 321–335. ISBN: 3-540-45772-0.
              DOI: 10.1007/11880240_23.

[Hor13a]   Tassilo Horn. "Solving the Class Diagram Restructuring Transformation
              Case with FunnyQT". In: *Proceedings Sixth Transformation Tool Con-
              test, TTC 2013, Budapest, Hungary, 19-20 June, 2013*. Ed. by Pieter Van
              Gorp, Louis M. Rose, and Christian Krause. Vol. 135. EPTCS. 2013,
              pp. 75–82. DOI: 10.4204/EPTCS.135.9. URL: http://dx.doi.org/10.
              4204/EPTCS.135.9.

[Hor13b]   Tassilo Horn. "Solving the Petri-Nets to Statecharts Transformation Case with FunnyQT". In: *Proceedings Sixth Transformation Tool Contest, TTC 2013, Budapest, Hungary, 19-20 June, 2013*. Ed. by Pieter Van Gorp, Louis M. Rose, and Christian Krause. Vol. 135. EPTCS. 2013, pp. 88–94. DOI: 10.4204/EPTCS.135.11. URL: http://dx.doi.org/10.4204/EPTCS.135.11.

[Hor13c]   Tassilo Horn. "Solving the TTC 2013 Flowgraphs Case with FunnyQT". In: *Proceedings Sixth Transformation Tool Contest, TTC 2013, Budapest, Hungary, 19-20 June, 2013*. Ed. by Pieter Van Gorp, Louis M. Rose, and Christian Krause. Vol. 135. EPTCS. 2013, pp. 57–68. DOI: 10.4204/EPTCS.135.7. URL: http://dx.doi.org/10.4204/EPTCS.135.7.

[Hor13d]   Tassilo Horn. "The TTC 2013 Flowgraphs Case". In: *Proceedings Sixth Transformation Tool Contest, TTC 2013, Budapest, Hungary, 19-20 June, 2013*. Ed. by Pieter Van Gorp, Louis M. Rose, and Christian Krause. Vol. 135. EPTCS. 2013, pp. 3–7. DOI: 10.4204/EPTCS.135.1. URL: http://dx.doi.org/10.4204/EPTCS.135.1.

[Hor14a]   Tassilo Horn. "Solving the TTC FIXML Case with FunnyQT". In: *Proceedings of the 7th Transformation Tool Contest part of the Software Technologies: Applications and Foundations (STAF 2014) federation of conferences, York, United Kingdom, July 25, 2014*. Ed. by Louis M. Rose, Christian Krause, and Tassilo Horn. Vol. 1305. CEUR Workshop Proceedings. CEUR-WS.org, 2014, pp. 7–21. URL: http://ceur-ws.org/Vol-1305/paper3.pdf.

[Hor14b]   Tassilo Horn. "Solving the TTC Movie Database Case with FunnyQT". In: *Proceedings of the 7th Transformation Tool Contest part of the Software Technologies: Applications and Foundations (STAF 2014) federation of conferences, York, United Kingdom, July 25, 2014*. Ed. by Louis M. Rose, Christian Krause, and Tassilo Horn. Vol. 1305. CEUR Workshop Proceedings. CEUR-WS.org, 2014, pp. 139–144. URL: http://ceur-ws.org/Vol-1305/paper4.pdf.

[Hor15a]   Tassilo Horn. "Graph Pattern Matching as an Embedded Clojure DSL". In: *Graph Transformation - 8th International Conference, ICGT 2015, Held as Part of STAF 2015, L'Aquila, Italy, July 21-23, 2015. Proceedings*. Ed. by Francesco Parisi-Presicce and Bernhard Westfechtel. Vol. 9151. Lecture Notes in Computer Science. Springer, 2015, pp. 189–204. ISBN: 978-3-319-21144-2. DOI: 10.1007/978-3-319-21145-9_12. URL: http://dx.doi.org/10.1007/978-3-319-21145-9_12.

[Hor15b]   Tassilo Horn. "Solving the TTC Java Refactoring Case with FunnyQT". In: *Proceedings of the 8th Transformation Tool Contest part of the Software Technologies: Applications and Foundations (STAF 2015) federation of conferences, L'Aquila, Italy, July 24, 2015*. Ed. by Louis M. Rose, Filip Krikava, and Tassilo Horn. Vol. to appear. CEUR Workshop Proceedings. CEUR-WS.org, 2015.

[Hor15c]   Tassilo Horn. "Solving the TTC Model Execution Case with FunnyQT". In: *Proceedings of the 8th Transformation Tool Contest part of the Software Technologies: Applications and Foundations (STAF 2015) federation of conferences, L'Aquila, Italy, July 24, 2015*. Ed. by Louis M. Rose, Filip

Krikava, and Tassilo Horn. Vol. to appear. CEUR Workshop Proceedings. CEUR-WS.org, 2015.

[Hor15d]   Tassilo Horn. "Solving the TTC Train Benchmark Case with FunnyQT". In: *Proceedings of the 8th Transformation Tool Contest part of the Software Technologies: Applications and Foundations (STAF 2015) federation of conferences, L'Aquila, Italy, July 24, 2015.* Ed. by Louis M. Rose, Filip Krikava, and Tassilo Horn. Vol. to appear. CEUR Workshop Proceedings. CEUR-WS.org, 2015.

[IC96]   American National Standards Institute and Information Technology Industry Council. *American National Standard for information technology: programming language — Common LISP: ANSI X3.226-1994.* 1430 Broadway, New York, NY 10018, USA: American National Standards Institute, 1996, various.

[II95]   ISO and IEC. *ISO/IEC 13211-1:1995: Information technology – Programming languages – Prolog – Part 1: General core.* 1995. URL: http://www.iso.org/iso/catalogue_detail.htm?csnumber=21413.

[ISO01]   ISO/IEC. *ISO/IEC 9126. Software engineering – Product quality.* ISO/IEC, 2001.

[Jac06]   Daniel Jackson. *Software Abstractions - Logic, Language, and Analysis.* MIT Press, 2006. ISBN: 978-0-262-10114-1. URL: http://mitpress.mit.edu/catalog/item/default.asp?ttype=2&tid=10928.

[JBG15]   Edgar Jakumeit, Jakob Blomer, and Rubino Geiß. *The GrGen.NET User Manual.* July 29, 2015. URL: http://www.info.uni-karlsruhe.de/software/grgen/GrGenNET-Manual.pdf (visited on 10/05/2015).

[JBK10]   Edgar Jakumeit, Sebastian Buchwald, and Moritz Kroll. "GrGen.NET - The expressive, convenient and fast graph rewrite system". In: *STTT* 12.3-4 (2010), pp. 263–271.

[Jou+08]   Frédéric Jouault et al. "ATL: A model transformation tool". In: *Sci. Comput. Program.* 72.1-2 (2008), pp. 31–39. DOI: 10.1016/j.scico.2007.08.002.

[JT10]   Frédéric Jouault and Massimo Tisi. "Towards Incremental Execution of ATL Transformations". In: *Theory and Practice of Model Transformations, Third International Conference, ICMT 2010, Malaga, Spain, June 28-July 2, 2010. Proceedings.* Ed. by Laurence Tratt and Martin Gogolla. Vol. 6142. Lecture Notes in Computer Science. Springer, 2010, pp. 123–137. ISBN: 978-3-642-13687-0. DOI: 10.1007/978-3-642-13688-7_9.

[KAL14]   Gábor Kövesdán, Márk Asztalos, and László Lengyel. "Modeling Cloud Messaging with a Domain-Specific Modeling Language". In: *Proceedings of the 2nd International Workshop on Model-Driven Engineering on and for the Cloud co-located with the 17th International Conference on Model Driven Engineering Languages and Systems, CloudMDE@MoD-ELS 2014, Valencia, Spain, September 30, 2014.* Ed. by Richard F. Paige et al. Vol. 1242. CEUR Workshop Proceedings. CEUR-WS.org, 2014, pp. 26–35. URL: http://ceur-ws.org/Vol-1242/paper2.pdf.

[KCF14]   Filip Krikava, Philippe Collet, and Robert B. France. "SIGMA: Scala Internal Domain-Specific Languages for Model Manipulations". In: *Model-Driven Engineering Languages and Systems - 17th International Conference, MODELS 2014, Valencia, Spain, September 28 - October 3, 2014. Proceedings*. Ed. by Jürgen Dingel et al. Vol. 8767. Lecture Notes in Computer Science. Springer, 2014, pp. 569–585. ISBN: 978-3-319-11652-5. DOI: 10.1007/978-3-319-11653-2_35. URL: http://dx.doi.org/10.1007/978-3-319-11653-2_35.

[Ken02]   Stuart Kent. "Model Driven Engineering". In: *Integrated Formal Methods, Third International Conference, IFM 2002, Turku, Finland, May 15-18, 2002, Proceedings*. Ed. by Michael J. Butler, Luigia Petre, and Kaisa Sere. Vol. 2335. Lecture Notes in Computer Science. Springer, 2002, pp. 286–298. ISBN: 3-540-43703-7. DOI: 10.1007/3-540-47884-1_16. URL: http://dx.doi.org/10.1007/3-540-47884-1_16.

[KG12]   Christian Krause and Holger Giese. "Probabilistic Graph Transformation Systems". In: *Graph Transformations - 6th International Conference, ICGT 2012, Bremen, Germany, September 24-29, 2012. Proceedings*. Ed. by Hartmut Ehrig et al. Vol. 7562. Lecture Notes in Computer Science. Springer, 2012, pp. 311–325. ISBN: 978-3-642-33653-9. DOI: 10.1007/978-3-642-33654-6_21. URL: http://dx.doi.org/10.1007/978-3-642-33654-6_21.

[Kic+01] Gregor Kiczales et al. "An Overview of AspectJ". In: *Proceedings of the 15th European Conference on Object-Oriented Programming*. ECOOP '01. London, UK, UK: Springer, 2001, pp. 327–353. ISBN: 3-540-42206-4. URL: http://dl.acm.org/citation.cfm?id=646158.680006 (visited on 01/19/2015).

[Kic96]   Gregor Kiczales. "Aspect-oriented Programming". In: *ACM Computing Surveys* 28.4es (Dec. 1996). ISSN: 0360-0300. DOI: 10.1145/242224.242420.

[KN02]   G. Klyne and C. Newman. *Date and Time on the Internet: Timestamps*. RFC 3339 (Proposed Standard). Internet Engineering Task Force, July 2002. URL: http://www.ietf.org/rfc/rfc3339.txt.

[Kol+15] Dimitris Kolovos et al. *The Epsilon Book*. July 27, 2015. URL: http://www.eclipse.org/epsilon/doc/book/ (visited on 09/22/2015).

[KPL15]   Géza Kulcsár, Sven Peldszus, and Malte Lochau. "Case Study: Object-oriented Refactoring of Java Programs using Graph Transformation". In: *Proceedings of the 8th Transformation Tool Contest part of the Software Technologies: Applications and Foundations (STAF 2015) federation of conferences, L'Aquila, Italy, July 24, 2015*. Ed. by Louis M. Rose, Filip Krikava, and Tassilo Horn. Vol. to appear. CEUR Workshop Proceedings. CEUR-WS.org, 2015.

[KPP08]   Dimitrios S. Kolovos, Richard F. Paige, and Fiona Polack. "The Epsilon Transformation Language". In: *Theory and Practice of Model Transformations, First International Conference, ICMT 2008, Zürich, Switzerland, July 1-2, 2008, Proceedings*. Ed. by Antonio Vallecillo, Jeff Gray, and Alfonso Pierantonio. Vol. 5063. Lecture Notes in Computer Science. Springer, 2008, pp. 46–60. ISBN: 978-3-540-69926-2. DOI: 10.1007/978-

3-540-69927-9_4. URL: http://dx.doi.org/10.1007/978-3-540-69927-9_4.

[Lam+11]   Patrick Lam et al. "The Soot framework for Java program analysis: a retrospective". In: *Cetus Users and Compiler Infastructure Workshop (CETUS 2011)*. Oct. 2011. URL: http://tubiblio.ulb.tu-darmstadt.de/59322/.

[Lar03]   Juan de Lara. "Meta-Modelling and Graph Transformation for the Simulation of Systems". In: *Bulletin of the EATCS* 81 (2003), pp. 180–194.

[LAS14]   Erhan Leblebici, Anthony Anjorin, and Andy Schürr. "Developing eMoflon with eMoflon". In: *Theory and Practice of Model Transformations - 7th International Conference, ICMT 2014, Held as Part of STAF 2014, York, UK, July 21-22, 2014. Proceedings*. Ed. by Davide Di Ruscio and Dániel Varró. Vol. 8568. Lecture Notes in Computer Science. Springer, 2014, pp. 138–145. ISBN: 978-3-319-08788-7. DOI: 10.1007/978-3-319-08789-4_10. URL: http://dx.doi.org/10.1007/978-3-319-08789-4_10.

[Leb+14]   Erhan Leblebici et al. "A Comparison of Incremental Triple Graph Grammar Tools". In: *ECEASST* 67 (2014). URL: http://journal.ub.tu-berlin.de/eceasst/article/view/939.

[Leo+06]   Nicola Leone et al. "The DLV system for knowledge representation and reasoning". In: *ACM Trans. Comput. Log.* 7.3 (2006), pp. 499–562. DOI: 10.1145/1149114.1149117. URL: http://doi.acm.org/10.1145/1149114.1149117.

[LMS05]   P. Leach, M. Mealling, and R. Salz. *A Universally Unique IDentifier (UUID) URN Namespace*. RFC 4122 (Proposed Standard). Internet Engineering Task Force, July 2005. URL: http://www.ietf.org/rfc/rfc4122.txt.

[LMT14]   Kevin Lano, Krikor Maroukian, and Sobhan Yassipour Tehrani. "Case study: FIXML to Java, C# and C++". In: *Proceedings of the 7th Transformation Tool Contest part of the Software Technologies: Applications and Foundations (STAF 2014) federation of conferences, York, United Kingdom, July 25, 2014*. Ed. by Louis M. Rose, Christian Krause, and Tassilo Horn. Vol. 1305. CEUR Workshop Proceedings. CEUR-WS.org, 2014, pp. 2–6. URL: http://ceur-ws.org/Vol-1305/preface.pdf.

[LR13]   Kevin Lano and Shekoufeh Kolahdouz Rahimi. "Case study: Class diagram restructuring". In: *Proceedings Sixth Transformation Tool Contest, TTC 2013, Budapest, Hungary, 19-20 June, 2013*. Ed. by Pieter Van Gorp, Louis M. Rose, and Christian Krause. Vol. 135. EPTCS. 2013, pp. 8–15. DOI: 10.4204/EPTCS.135.2. URL: http://dx.doi.org/10.4204/EPTCS.135.2.

[LS05]   Michael Lawley and Jim Steel. "Practical Declarative Model Transformation with Tefkat". In: *Satellite Events at the MoDELS 2005 Conference, MoDELS 2005 International Workshops, Doctoral Symposium, Educators Symposium, Montego Bay, Jamaica, October 2-7, 2005, Revised Selected Papers*. Ed. by Jean-Michel Bruel. Vol. 3844. Lecture Notes in Computer Science. Springer, 2005, pp. 139–150. ISBN: 3-540-31780-5.

DOI: 10.1007/11663430_15. URL: http://dx.doi.org/10.1007/
11663430_15.

[Mar08]   Luc Maranget. "Compiling Pattern Matching to good Decision Trees". In:
           ML. Ed. by Eijiro Sumii. ACM, 2008, pp. 35–46. ISBN: 978-1-60558-062-3.

[May14]   Tanja Mayerhofer. "Defining Executable Modeling Languages with
           fUML". PhD thesis. Institute of Software Technology and Interactive
           Systems, TU Vienna, 2014. URL: http://publik.tuwien.ac.at/files/
           PubDat_233990.pdf (visited on 10/29/2015).

[MC13]   Nuno Macedo and Alcino Cunha. "Implementing QVT-R Bidirectional
           Model Transformations Using Alloy". In: Fundamental Approaches to
           Software Engineering - 16th International Conference, FASE 2013,
           Held as Part of the European Joint Conferences on Theory and Practice
           of Software, ETAPS 2013, Rome, Italy, March 16-24, 2013. Proceed-
           ings. Ed. by Vittorio Cortellessa and Dániel Varró. Vol. 7793. Lecture
           Notes in Computer Science. Springer, 2013, pp. 297–311. ISBN: 978-
           3-642-37056-4. DOI: 10.1007/978-3-642-37057-1_22. URL: http:
           //dx.doi.org/10.1007/978-3-642-37057-1_22.

[Mey+11]   Bart Meyers et al. "A Generic In-Place Transformation-Based Approach
           to Structured Model Co-Evolution". In: ECEASST 42 (2011). URL: http:
           //journal.ub.tu-berlin.de/eceasst/article/view/608.

[MFJ05]   Pierre-Alain Muller, Franck Fleurey, and Jean-Marc Jézéquel. "Weaving
           Executability into Object-Oriented Meta-languages". In: Model Driven
           Engineering Languages and Systems, 8th International Conference,
           MoDELS 2005, Montego Bay, Jamaica, October 2-7, 2005, Proceedings.
           Ed. by Lionel C. Briand and Clay Williams. Vol. 3713. Lecture Notes in
           Computer Science. Springer, 2005, pp. 264–278. ISBN: 3-540-29010-9.
           DOI: 10.1007/11557432_19.

[MS90]   Edwin McKenzie and Richard Snodgrass. "Schema Evolution and the
           Relational Algebra". In: Information Systems 15.2 (1990), pp. 207–232.
           ISSN: 0306-4379. DOI: 10.1016/0306-4379(90)90036-0.

[MSB11]   Brian A. Malloy, Steffen Staab, and Mark van den Brand, eds. Software
           Language Engineering - Third International Conference, SLE 2010,
           Eindhoven, The Netherlands, October 12-13, 2010, Revised Selected
           Papers. Vol. 6563. Lecture Notes in Computer Science. Springer, 2011.
           ISBN: 978-3-642-19439-9. DOI: 10.1007/978-3-642-19440-5.

[MW15]   Tanja Mayerhofer and Manuel Wimmer. "The TTC 2015 Model Execution
           Case". In: Proceedings of the 8th Transformation Tool Contest part of
           the Software Technologies: Applications and Foundations (STAF 2015)
           federation of conferences, L'Aquila, Italy, July 24, 2015. Ed. by Louis M.
           Rose, Filip Krikava, and Tassilo Horn. Vol. to appear. CEUR Workshop
           Proceedings. CEUR-WS.org, 2015.

[Nar+09]   Anantha Narayanan et al. "Automatic Domain Model Migration to Man-
           age Metamodel Evolution". In: Model Driven Engineering Languages
           and Systems, 12th International Conference, MODELS 2009, Denver,
           CO, USA, October 4-9, 2009. Proceedings. Ed. by Andy Schürr and
           Bran Selic. Vol. 5795. Lecture Notes in Computer Science. Springer,

2009, pp. 706–711. ISBN: 978-3-642-04424-3. DOI: 10.1007/978-3-642-04425-0_57.

[NJ15] Carlos Noguera and Viviane Jonckers. "Model Querying with Query Models". In: 14th International Conference on Generative Programming: Concepts & Experience (GPCE'15). (Pittsburgh, Pennsylvania, United States, Oct. 26, 2015). 2015. URL: http://2015.gpce.org/event/gpce2015-model-querying-with-query-models (visited on 10/09/2015).

[Nog+11] Carlos Noguera et al. "Program querying with a SOUL: The BARISTA tool suite". In: IEEE 27th International Conference on Software Maintenance, ICSM 2011, Williamsburg, VA, USA, September 25-30, 2011. IEEE Computer Society, 2011, pp. 582–585. ISBN: 978-1-4577-0663-9. DOI: 10.1109/ICSM.2011.6080835. URL: http://dx.doi.org/10.1109/ICSM.2011.6080835.

[Oka98] Chris Okasaki. Purely Functional Data Structures. New York, NY, USA: Cambridge University Press, 1998. ISBN: 0-521-63124-6.

[OMG11a] OMG. Business Process Model and Notation (BPMN), Version 2.0. Jan. 2011. URL: http://www.omg.org/spec/BPMN/2.0/ (visited on 10/29/2015).

[OMG11b] OMG. Meta Object Facility (MOF) 2.0 Query/View/Transformation Specification, Version 1.1. Object Management Group. 2011. URL: http://www.omg.org/spec/QVT/1.1/ (visited on 01/19/2015).

[OMG13] OMG. Semantics Of A Foundational Subset For Executable UML Models (FUML), Version 1.1. Aug. 2013. URL: http://www.omg.org/spec/FUML/1.1/ (visited on 10/29/2015).

[OMG14a] OMG. Model Driven Architecture (MDA), MDA Guide rev. 2.0. June 2014. URL: http://www.omg.org/cgi-bin/doc?ormsc/14-06-01 (visited on 10/29/2015).

[OMG14b] OMG. Object Constraint Language (OCL), Version 2.4. Feb. 2014. URL: http://www.omg.org/spec/OCL/2.4/ (visited on 09/22/2015).

[OMG14c] OMG. XML Metadata Interchange (XMI), Version 2.4.2. Apr. 2014. URL: http://www.omg.org/spec/XMI/2.4.2/ (visited on 05/28/2015).

[OMG15a] OMG. Meta Object Facility (MOF), Version 2.5. Object Management Group, June 2015. URL: http://www.omg.org/spec/MOF/2.5/ (visited on 09/23/2015).

[OMG15b] OMG. OMG Systems Modeling Language (OMG SysML), Version 1.4. June 2015. URL: http://www.omg.org/spec/SysML/1.4/ (visited on 10/29/2015).

[OMG15c] OMG. Unified Modeling Language (UML), Version 2.5. June 2015. URL: http://www.omg.org/spec/UML/2.5/ (visited on 09/23/2015).

[PR10] Paolo Pialorsi and Marco Russo. Programming Microsoft LINQ in Microsoft .NET Framework 4. 1st. Microsoft Press, 2010. ISBN: 9780735640573.

[PW15]   Francesco Parisi-Presicce and Bernhard Westfechtel, eds. *Graph Trans-*
          formation - 8th International Conference, ICGT 2015, Held as Part of
          STAF 2015, L'Aquila, Italy, July 21-23, 2015. Proceedings. Vol. 9151. Lec-
          ture Notes in Computer Science. Springer, 2015. ISBN: 978-3-319-21144-2.
          DOI: 10.1007/978-3-319-21145-9. URL: http://dx.doi.org/10.1007/
          978-3-319-21145-9.

[RKH14]   Louis M. Rose, Christian Krause, and Tassilo Horn, eds. *Proceedings of*
          the 7th Transformation Tool Contest part of the Software Technologies:
          Applications and Foundations (STAF 2014) federation of conferences,
          York, United Kingdom, July 25, 2014. Vol. 1305. CEUR Workshop Pro-
          ceedings. CEUR-WS.org, 2014. URL: http://ceur-ws.org/Vol-1305.

[RKH15]   Louis M. Rose, Filip Krikava, and Tassilo Horn, eds. *Proceedings of*
          the 8th Transformation Tool Contest part of the Software Technologies:
          Applications and Foundations (STAF 2015) federation of conferences,
          L'Aquila, Italy, July 24, 2015. Vol. to appear. CEUR Workshop Proceed-
          ings. CEUR-WS.org, 2015.

[Rod92]   John F. Roddick. "Schema Evolution in Database Systems: An Annotated
          Bibliography". In: *SIGMOD Rec.* 21.4 (Dec. 1992), pp. 35–40. ISSN:
          0163-5808. DOI: 10.1145/141818.141826.

[Roo+11] Coen De Roover et al. "The SOUL tool suite for querying programs
          in symbiosis with Eclipse". In: *Proceedings of the 9th International*
          Conference on Principles and Practice of Programming in Java, PPPJ
          2011, Kongens Lyngby, Denmark, August 24-26, 2011. Ed. by Christian
          W. Probst and Christian Wimmer. ACM, 2011, pp. 71–80. ISBN: 978-
          1-4503-0935-6. DOI: 10.1145/2093157.2093168. URL: http://doi.acm.
          org/10.1145/2093157.2093168.

[Ros+10] Louis M. Rose et al. "Model Migration with Epsilon Flock". In: *Theory*
          and Practice of Model Transformations, Third International Conference,
          ICMT 2010, Malaga, Spain, June 28-July 2, 2010. Proceedings. Ed. by
          Laurence Tratt and Martin Gogolla. Vol. 6142. Lecture Notes in Com-
          puter Science. Springer, 2010, pp. 184–198. ISBN: 978-3-642-13687-0.
          DOI: 10.1007/978-3-642-13688-7_13.

[Ros+14] Louis M. Rose et al. "Epsilon Flock: a model migration language". In:
          Software and System Modeling 13.2 (2014), pp. 735–755. DOI: 10.1007/
          s10270-012-0296-2.

[Roz97]   Grzegorz Rozenberg, ed. *Handbook of Graph Grammars and Computing*
          by Graph Transformations, Volume 1: Foundations. World Scientific,
          1997. ISBN: 9810228848.

[RS14]   Coen De Roover and Reinout Stevens. "Building development tools
          interactively using the EKEKO meta-programming library". In: *2014*
          Software Evolution Week - IEEE Conference on Software Maintenance,
          Reengineering, and Reverse Engineering, CSMR-WCRE 2014, Antwerp,
          Belgium, February 3-6, 2014. Ed. by Serge Demeyer, Dave Binkley,
          and Filippo Ricca. IEEE Computer Society, 2014, pp. 429–433. ISBN:
          978-1-4799-3752-3. DOI: 10.1109/CSMR-WCRE.2014.6747211. URL:
          http://dx.doi.org/10.1109/CSMR-WCRE.2014.6747211.

[Sch06]   Douglas C. Schmidt. "Guest Editor's Introduction: Model-Driven Engi-
            neering". In: *IEEE Computer* 39.2 (2006), pp. 25–31. DOI: 10.1109/
            MC.2006.58. URL: http://doi.ieeecomputersociety.org/10.1109/MC.
            2006.58.

[Sch94]   Andy Schürr. "Specification of Graph Translators with Triple Graph
            Grammars". In: *Graph-Theoretic Concepts in Computer Science, 20th In-
            ternational Workshop, WG '94, Herrsching, Germany, June 16-18, 1994,
            Proceedings*. Ed. by Ernst W. Mayr, Gunther Schmidt, and Gottfried
            Tinhofer. Vol. 903. Lecture Notes in Computer Science. Springer, 1994,
            pp. 151–163. ISBN: 3-540-59071-4. DOI: 10.1007/3-540-59071-4_45.
            URL: http://dx.doi.org/10.1007/3-540-59071-4_45.

[Spe+10]   Michael Sperber et al. *Revised [6] Report on the Algorithmic Language
            Scheme*. 1st. New York, NY, USA: Cambridge University Press, 2010.
            ISBN: 0521193990.

[Ste+09]   David Steinberg et al. *EMF: Eclipse Modeling Framework 2.0*. 2nd.
            Addison-Wesley Professional, 2009. ISBN: 0321331885.

[Ste10]   Perdita Stevens. "Bidirectional model transformations in QVT: semantic
            issues and open questions". In: *Software and System Modeling* 9.1
            (2010), pp. 7–20. DOI: 10.1007/s10270-008-0109-9. URL: http://dx.
            doi.org/10.1007/s10270-008-0109-9.

[Szá+15]   Gábor Szárnyas et al. "The TTC 2015 Train Benchmark Case for Incre-
            mental Model Validation". In: *Proceedings of the 8th Transformation
            Tool Contest part of the Software Technologies: Applications and Foun-
            dations (STAF 2015) federation of conferences, L'Aquila, Italy, July 24,
            2015*. Ed. by Louis M. Rose, Filip Krikava, and Tassilo Horn. Vol. to
            appear. CEUR Workshop Proceedings. CEUR-WS.org, 2015.

[Tae03]   Gabriele Taentzer. "AGG: A Graph Transformation Environment for
            Modeling and Validation of Software". In: *Applications of Graph Trans-
            formations with Industrial Relevance, Second International Workshop,
            AGTIVE 2003, Charlottesville, VA, USA, September 27 - October 1, 2003,
            Revised Selected and Invited Papers*. Ed. by John L. Pfaltz, Manfred
            Nagl, and Boris Böhlen. Vol. 3062. Lecture Notes in Computer Science.
            Springer, 2003, pp. 446–453. ISBN: 3-540-22120-4. DOI: 10.1007/978-
            3-540-25959-6_35. URL: http://dx.doi.org/10.1007/978-3-540-
            25959-6_35.

[TFW14]   Muhammad Umer Tariq, Jacques Florence, and Marilyn Wolf. "Design
            Specification of Cyber-Physical Systems: Towards a Domain-Specific
            Modeling Language based on Simulink, Eclipse Modeling Framework,
            and Giotto". In: *Proceedings of the 7th International Workshop on
            Model-based Architecting and Construction of Embedded Systems co-
            located with ACM/IEEE 17th International Conference on Model Driven
            Engineering Languages and Systems (MoDELS 2014), Valencia, Spain,
            September 30th, 2014*. Ed. by Florian Noyrit, Susanne Graf, and Iulia
            Dragomir. Vol. 1250. CEUR Workshop Proceedings. CEUR-WS.org, 2014,
            pp. 6–15. URL: http://ceur-ws.org/Vol-1250/paper2.pdf.

[TG10]   Laurence Tratt and Martin Gogolla, eds. *Theory and Practice of Model Transformations, Third International Conference, ICMT 2010, Malaga, Spain, June 28-July 2, 2010. Proceedings*. Vol. 6142. Lecture Notes in Computer Science. Springer, 2010. ISBN: 978-3-642-13687-0. DOI: 10.1007/978-3-642-13688-7.

[Tis+11]   Massimo Tisi et al. "Lazy Execution of Model-to-Model Transformations". In: *Model Driven Engineering Languages and Systems, 14th International Conference, MODELS 2011, Wellington, New Zealand, October 16-21, 2011. Proceedings*. Ed. by Jon Whittle, Tony Clark, and Thomas Kühne. Vol. 6981. Lecture Notes in Computer Science. Springer, 2011, pp. 32–46. ISBN: 978-3-642-24484-1. DOI: 10.1007/978-3-642-24485-8_4. URL: http://dx.doi.org/10.1007/978-3-642-24485-8_4.

[Ujh+15]   Zoltán Ujhelyi et al. "EMF-IncQuery: An integrated development environment for live model queries". In: *Science of Computer Programming* 98 (2015), pp. 80–99. DOI: 10.1016/j.scico.2014.01.004. URL: http://dx.doi.org/10.1016/j.scico.2014.01.004.

[Vol06]   Kris De Volder. "JQuery: A Generic Code Browser with a Declarative Configuration Language". In: *Practical Aspects of Declarative Languages, 8th International Symposium, PADL 2006, Charleston, SC, USA, January 9-10, 2006, Proceedings*. Ed. by Pascal Van Hentenryck. Vol. 3819. Lecture Notes in Computer Science. Springer, 2006, pp. 88–102. ISBN: 3-540-30947-0. DOI: 10.1007/11603023_7. URL: http://dx.doi.org/10.1007/11603023_7.

[VSV05]   Gergely Varró, Andy Schürr, and Dániel Varró. "Benchmarking for Graph Transformation". In: *2005 IEEE Symposium on Visual Languages and Human-Centric Computing (VL/HCC 2005), 21-24 September 2005, Dallas, TX, USA*. IEEE Computer Society, 2005, pp. 79–88. ISBN: 0-7695-2443-5. DOI: 10.1109/VLHCC.2005.23.

[W3C08]   W3C. *SPARQL Query Language for RDF*. World Wide Web Consortium (W3C), Jan. 2008. URL: http://www.w3.org/TR/rdf-sparql-query/ (visited on 10/14/2015).

[W3C10]   W3C. *XML Path Language (XPath) 2.0 (Second Edition)*. World Wide Web Consortium (W3C), Dec. 2010. URL: http://www.w3.org/TR/xpath20/ (visited on 10/14/2015).

[Wac07]   Guido Wachsmuth. "Metamodel Adaptation and Model Co-adaptation". In: *ECOOP 2007 - Object-Oriented Programming, 21st European Conference, Berlin, Germany, July 30 - August 3, 2007, Proceedings*. Ed. by Erik Ernst. Vol. 4609. Lecture Notes in Computer Science. Springer, 2007, pp. 600–624. ISBN: 978-3-540-73588-5. DOI: 10.1007/978-3-540-73589-2_28.

[Wag14]   Christian Wagner. *Model-Driven Software Migration: A Methodology - Reengineering, Recovery and Modernization of Legacy Systems*. Springer, 2014. ISBN: 978-3-658-05269-0. DOI: 10.1007/978-3-658-05270-6. URL: http://dx.doi.org/10.1007/978-3-658-05270-6.

[ZR11]   Eduardo Zambon and Arend Rensink. "Using Graph Transformations and Graph Abstractions for Software Verification". In: *ECEASST* 38 (2011). URL: http://journal.ub.tu-berlin.de/eceasst/article/view/560.

Index

Tassilo Horn

polyglot programmer & diplomate computer scientist

Jahnstraße 7
56179 Vallendar
+49 151 21530579
tsdh80@gmail.com

CAREER

SHD Einzelhandelssoftware GmbH & Co. KG, Andernach
Senior Software Developer

November 2015 - today

University Koblenz-Landau, Koblenz
Research Associate / PhD student

June 2008 - October 2015

Dissertation title: "A Functional, Comprehensive, Extensible Multi-Platform Querying and Transformation Approach"

University Koblenz-Landau, Koblenz
Student Assistant

2004 - 2007

Support for lectures and labs, e.g., "Programming", "Software Technology I", "Java course for mathematicians"

SCHOOL & STUDY

University Koblenz-Landau, Koblenz
Diploma, Grade: 1.0 (with excellence)

October 2001 - May 2008

Study of Computer Science
Major: Software Engineering
Minor: Math
Degree: Diploma

Peter-Paul-Cahensly-Schule, Limburg/Lahn
Abitur, Grade: 1.9

1997 - 2000

Majors: Math and Technology

PROJECTS

FunnyQT — *http://funnyqt.org*

Implementation of my dissertation studies
A comprehensive Clojure library for model querying and model transformation provided as a set of embedded DSLs

SOAMIG — *http://www.soamig.de*

Migration of legacy software into service-oriented architectures

ReDSeeDS — *http://smog.iem.pw.edu.pl/redseeds*

Requirements-Driven Software Development System

SKILLS

Functional programming
Clojure, Haskell

Object-oriented programming
Java, Common Lisp/CLOS, C#, C++

Logic programming
miniKanren, Prolog

Other languages
JavaScript, C, Ruby, Python, Scheme, Go, Emacs Lisp, Bash, ZSH

Modeling
UML, OCL, Ecore/EMF

Version control
Git, Mercurial, Bazaar, Subversion

Build Tools
Leiningen, Boot, Ant, Maven, Make

MEMBERSHIPS

Free Software Foundation
The GNU Project

LANGUAGES

German, native
English, fluent
French, basics

CONFERENCE TALKS & PUBLICATIONS

Horn, Tassilo (2015): *Graph Pattern Matching as an Embedded Clojure DSL*. In: Graph Transformation - 8th International Conference, ICGT 2015.

Ebert, Jürgen; Horn, Tassilo (2014): *GReTL: an extensible, operational, graph-based transformation language*. In: Software and System Modeling.

Horn, Tassilo (2013): *Model Querying with FunnyQT - (Extended Abstract)*. In: Theory and Practice of Model Transformations - 6th International Conference, ICMT 2013,. Springer.

Fuhr, Andreas; Horn, Tassilo; Riediger, Volker; Winter, Andreas (2013): *Model-driven software migration into service-oriented architectures*. In: Computer Science - Research and Development.

Fuhr, Andreas; Winter, Andreas; Erdmenger, Uwe; Horn, Tassilo; Kaiser, Uwe; Riediger, Volker; Teppe, Werner (2012): *Model-Driven Software Migration: Process Model, Tool Support and Application*. In: Migrating Legacy Applications: Challenges in Service Oriented Architecture and Cloud Computing Environments.

Horn, Tassilo; Ebert, Jürgen (2011): *The GReTL Transformation Language*. In: Theory and Practice of Model Transformations - 4th International Conference, ICMT 2011. Springer.

Erdmenger, Uwe; Fuhr, Andreas; Herget, Axel; Horn, Tassilo; Kaiser, Uwe; Riediger, Volker; Teppe, Werner; Theurer, Marianne; Uhlig, Denis; Winter, Andreas; Zillmann, Christian; Zimmermann, Yvonne (2011): *The SOAMIG Process Model in Industrial Applications*. In: Proceedings of the 15th European Conference on Software Maintenance and Reengineering, CSMR 2011.

Fuhr, Andreas; Riediger, Volker; Horn, Tassilo (2011): *An Integrated Tool Suite for Model-Driven Software Migration towards Service-Oriented Architectures*. In: Softwaretechnik-Trends.

Fuhr, Andreas; Horn, Tassilo; Riediger, Volker (2011): *Using Dynamic Analysis and Clustering for Implementing Services by Reusing Legacy Code*. In: Proceedings of the 18th Working Conference on Reverse Engineering (WCRE).

Fuhr, Andreas; Gimnich, Rainer; Horn, Tassilo; Winter, Andreas (2009): *Extending SOMA for Model-Driven Software Migration into SOA*. In: Softwaretechnik-Trends.

Horn, Tassilo; Fuhr, Andreas; Winter, Andreas (2009): *Towards Applying Model-Transformations and -Queries for SOA-Migration*. In: MDD, SOA, and IT-Management, MSI 2009.

Horn, Tassilo (2008): *Ein Referenzschema für die Sprachen der IEC 61131*. Institut für Softwaretechnik, Universität Koblenz-Landau. Nr. 13/2008. Arbeitsbericht aus dem Fachbereich Informatik.

TRANSFORMATION TOOL CONTEST

Horn, Tassilo (2015): *Solving the TTC Train Benchmark Case with FunnyQT*. Overall quality award.

Horn, Tassilo (2015): *Solving the TTC Model Execution Case with FunnyQT*. Most correct solution award.

Horn, Tassilo (2015): *Solving the TTC Java Refactoring Case with FunnyQT*. Overall winner award.

Horn, Tassilo (2014): *Solving the TTC Movie Database Case with FunnyQT*. 3rd overall winner award.

Horn, Tassilo (2014): *Solving the TTC FIXML Case with FunnyQT*. 2nd overall winner award & most accurate solution award.

Horn, Tassilo (2013): *Solving the Petri-Nets to Statecharts Transformation Case with FunnyQT*. Overall winner award & best efficiency award.

Horn, Tassilo (2013): *Solving the Class Diagram Restructuring Transformation Case with FunnyQT*. Overall winner award.

Horn, Tassilo (2013): *Solving the TTC 2013 Flowgraphs Case with FunnyQT*. Best performance award.

Horn, Tassilo (2011): *Solving the TTC 2011 Compiler Optimization Case with GReTL*. Best original solution award.

Horn, Tassilo (2011): *Solving the TTC 2011 Reengineering Case with GReTL*. Overall winner award.